West Africa and Islam

*A Study of Religious
Development from the
8th to the 20th Century*

by Peter B. Clarke

Edward Arnold

© Peter B. Clarke 1982

First published 1982 by
Edward Arnold (Publishers) Ltd
41 Bedford Square, London WC1B 3DQ
Reprinted 1984

British Library Cataloguing in Publication Data

ISBN 0 7131 8029 3

To My Family — Nuclear and Extended

Typeset in Singapore by Colset Pte Ltd.
Printed in Great Britain by Thomson Litho Ltd, East Kilbride, Scotland

Contents.

Maps and plates.

Acknowledgements.

I wish to thank all those who made this book possible. Many people in West Africa helped me with their advice and the information they so willingly provided. I cannot list them all here but I would like to mention Yusuf Abdulkarim, Saidu Musa Sudi Dalil and Hamidu Sale from Bauchi, Professor M. El-Garh, Alhaji D.O.S. Noibi, Dr M.O.A. Abdul and Dr I.A. Ogunbiyi from the Department of Arabic and Islamic Studies, University of Ibadan, Nigeria. I would also like to thank all my former colleagues and students of the History Department at Ibadan.

In Senegal I received interesting and helpful comments from Cheikh Tidjane Sy, Director of the Ecole Nationale D'Economie Appliquée, from Cheikh Touré, editor of Etudes Islamiques, from Khadime M'Backé, a research scholar at the Institut Fondamental d'Afrique Noir (I.F.A.N.), and from many others, and to all of them I am extremely grateful.

My sincere thanks go to Dr H.J. Fisher of the School of Oriental and African Studies, University of London, who over the years has given me his advice, help and critical comments whenever these were requested. He has also generously allowed me to see the typescript of his and Dr Conrad's research on the Almoravids which will soon be published. Dr Fisher also read and provided valuable comments on two chapters of this book. Mr Samir Haykal of the Oriental Institute, Oxford, deserves special mention for reading the first chapter and special credit for trying so hard, like Dr Ogunbiyi, to teach me Arabic. Dr H.T. Norris of the School of Oriental and African Studies, London, also read several chapters and provided me with useful criticisms, comments and advice. I am also grateful to Dr Norris for supplying me with the very interesting photograph on page 129. Dr M. Hiskett, also of S.O.A.S, read and made constructive and helpful criticisms of one chapter of the book. Other chapters were read and commented on by Mr Mahmud T. Minna, Dr D. Cruise O'Brien, S.O.A.S, Dr D.M. Last of University College, London, and Dr P. McKenzie of the University of Leicester. To them also go my sincere thanks. None of these people, of course, is to be blamed for any error of fact or interpretation, all of which are entirely my own.

I thank my parents and family, nuclear and extended, for their continuous help and encouragement. My wife, Kathy, typed this manuscript and offered comments and observations on the content of the book. To her I am extremely grateful. My son, Andrew, also played his part. Although he never agreed to forego entirely his play or story at bedtime he would nevertheless agree to wait patiently until the relevant sentence or paragraph had been completed.

The Publishers wish to thank the following for their permission to reproduce copyright photographs:

Hoa-Qui: plates II, VIII, IX & X;

Dr H.T. Norris, The School of Oriental and African Studies: plates III & VI;

Zomo Publicity: plates IV, XI & XII;

Mr Bernard Fagg: plate V;

Alan Hutchinson Library: plate VII.

Thanks are also due to J.D. Fage and Maureen Verity for the maps reproduced in this book which are taken from *An Atlas of African History*, 2nd edition (Edward Arnold, 1978).

The cover design is based on a fine example of West African calligraphy and illumination employing the traditional sub-Saharan Maghribi script with letter pointing and full vocalisation. It was the work of a Nigerian illuminator, probably in the late 19th century. Reproduced by courtesy of the British Library (Or. 74.d.23).

Introduction.

Islam in West Africa is not peripheral to or a mere appendage of the Muslim world. Today, either a substantial minority or in some cases the overwhelming majority of the inhabitants of a number of West African states — Mauretania, Senegal, Gambia, Guinea (Conakry), Niger, Mali, Sierra Leone, Nigeria, Guinea Bissau, the Ivory Coast, Upper Volta and Liberia — are Muslims. There are also Muslim communities in the other West African states: Ghana, where they form about 13 per cent of the population and in both Togo and the People's Republic of Benin where they make up an estimated 10 per cent of the inhabitants.

In this book I attempt to trace the "making" of this West African Muslim community over a period of some twelve hundred years, beginning with West Africa's first contacts with Islam in the 8th century and concluding with a study of the contemporary situation. During its long history in West Africa, Islam has occupied different positions and taken up different attitudes towards the surrounding society. The pace of expansion has also varied from one period to another, from being relatively slow in the first eleven hundred years and then becoming much quicker in the 19th and 20th centuries.

From being the religion of a small minority of expatriate business people from North Africa, who tended to live apart and thereby preserved their Islamic identity, Islam spread first among the ruling classes, merchants and town dwellers before being carried to the rural areas. The main agents of this diffusion were at first Muslim traders and missionaries. The trader was often, of course, a missionary as well, and the missionary a trader. Then, as we shall see, the Muslim brotherhoods and various other agencies assisted in drawing West Africans to Islam.

At different periods in the history of Islam in West Africa Muslims have, as I have already mentioned, tended to adopt different attitudes towards the wider society and have adopted different approaches on the question of how best to build the ideal Islamic society. Some have adopted at one time or another what I have described as a "pluralistic" response to society, maintaining, on doctrinal grounds or because circumstances dictated this response, that it was perfectly possible for different cultures and political and social systems to co-exist side by side. Others adopted the accommodationist response, again partly because this was dictated by circumstances, which led to their involvement and incorporation into the wider society at all levels. Then there were those who rejected pluralism and accommodation and sought by militant means to build the ideal Islamic society. With regard to the methods used to spread Islam Muslims in West Africa over the centuries have preferred the 'quietist', pacific approach, an approach that, although it has involved on occasion considerable compromise, has nevertheless been very effective.

After several years lecturing on West African history at the University of Ibadan, Nigeria, and after giving a series of lectures on Islam in West Africa at King's College, University of London, I decided to write this book. Since J.S. Trimingham wrote his in some ways pioneering *Studies of Islam in West Africa* a great deal of further research on Islam in West Africa, both in terms of geographical region and historical period, has been done. I have also been researching into various aspects of the history of Islam in West Africa for several years now. I decided, therefore, after putting together my own research material, to take the advice of the Muslim scholar, al-Biruni (973-1050 A.D.) and 'gather the traditions from those who have reported them, to correct them as much as possible and to leave the rest as it is. . . .' The result is *West Africa and Islam*.

I hope it will be of use to students at university level and to those studying for their Higher School Certificate, and also to the teacher and the interested, general reader.

Peter Clarke
Oxford
1981.

1

West Africa's first contacts with Islam.

West Africa made its first contacts with Islam in the 8th century. Since then Muslims in West Africa have been involved in building an Islamic community modelled on that established in Arabia between 610 and 632 A.D. by the Prophet Muhammad. Some knowledge, therefore, of the early Islamic community and of its founder, Prophet Muhammad, is essential for an understanding of the historical development of Islam in West Africa. I will begin, then, with a brief historical outline of the life and achievements of Prophet Muhammad before moving on to discuss the expansion of Islam to North Africa, and from there across the Sahara to West Africa.

Prophet Muhammad and the early Muslim community: an introduction.

Prophet Muhammad was born around 570 A.D. in Mecca in Arabia.[1] His father Abdullah died before his birth, and his mother Aminah died when he was six years old. It fell, therefore, first to his grandfather, Abd al-Muttalib, and then to his uncle, Abu Talib, to take care of Muhammad. In addition to working as a shepherd for his uncle Muhammad also joined him in the caravan trade from Mecca to Syria. Mecca at this time was an important centre of the caravan trade between southern Arabia and Syria and the Mediterranean countries to the north and west. Commodities such as spices, incense and silk arrived in Mecca from Ethiopia, India and elsewhere, and were carried overland from there to Egypt, Syria, Turkey and Greece.

Later, Muhammad's uncle, Abu Talib, arranged for him to become an agent for a commercial firm in Mecca owned by a widow named Khadija. At the age of 25 Muhammad, apparently a man of average height with a strong head of hair and a thick beard, married Khadija who was then 40. During the 25 years he was married to Khadija, Muhammad could have lived in style and comfort, without any cares or worries. He was, however, a thinker and reformer and began to consider ways and means of regenerating Meccan society, which he believed had been in part corrupted by the materialism of the wealthy and influential merchants of the city.

On Mount Hira, near Mecca, Muhammad thought about the situation in his own city, about the purpose of life, about what gives life its value and meaning, and about man's relationship to God. The people of Mecca did acknowledge the existence of a Supreme Being, Allah. Moreover, from the existence of Jews and Christians in their midst they were aware of religions which emphasised belief in a Supreme Being. The Meccans, however, were in the main polytheists, and their city, in addition to being an important commercial centre, was also a place of pilgrimage. People from all over Arabia travelled there to worship at the Ka'ba, which in pre-Islamic times was regarded as a holy place. Muhammad later re-incorporated it into Islam, making it the point towards which all Muslims must turn when at prayer. Moreover, Muslims, when performing the pilgrimage (*hajj*), process around the Ka'ba which stands in the centre of the courtyard of the mosque in Mecca. I say Muhammad re-incorporated the Ka'ba into Islam since, according to an Islamic tradition, Abraham, recognised by Muslims as a prophet, was one of several holy men who restored it when it was in need of repair.

Muhammad and the Qur'an.

While meditating on Mount Hira, Muhammad believed he received visions of the Angel Gabriel which convinced him that he was "the messenger of God". In fact from c. 610 A.D. until his death in 632, Muhammad was, he believed, the recipient of revelations from God which, as God's messenger, he had the duty to pass on to mankind. These revelations, the majority coming to Prophet Muhammad between 610 and 622, that is before he emigrated to Medina from Mecca, and the rest coming while he was in Medina, make up the Qur'an.

Muslims regard the Qur'an as the Word or Speech of God.[2] It is not Muhammad's word. It is God's most complete and final Word to man.

Prophets such as Moses, David and Jesus, Muslims acknowledge, spoke God's Words, but God's last Words, his final and most complete revelation to man, came through Muhammad. In this sense Muhammad is the seal of the prophets, and the Qur'an the revelation to end all revelation. The revised and authentic version of Muhammad's revelations from God was completed about 20 years after his death.

It is interesting to note how a great deal of the message Muhammad received from God bore directly on the situation in Mecca described above. For instance, there is the passage which obviously attacks the attitude to wealth prevalent, as Muhammad saw it, among some of the wealthy and influential Meccan merchants. The passage reads:

> "Woe to every slanderer, scoffer,
> Who gathers wealth and counts it,
> Thinking wealth will make him immortal".[3]

Muhammad was not against private enterprise or the acquisition of wealth. He was not a socialist in the Marxist sense. He did, however, oppose the attitude of those who placed their faith and confidence in riches instead of in Allah, their Creator.

Other themes in the Qur'an concern God's goodness and power, and the Day of Judgment. These themes underline the point that wealth cannot give a person ultimate security or release him from his duties and obligations to God and his fellow men. One passage in the Qur'an known as "The Opening"

(Al-Fatiha) contains, according to many Muslim scholars, all the essentials of the Islamic faith. Part of it reads:

> "In the name of Allah the Compassionate, the Merciful. Praise be to Allah, the Lord of the Universe . . . the Ruler on the Day of Judgment. You alone do we worship and from You alone do we seek help . . ."

The emphasis here is on the oneness of God, on the fact that God establishes the criteria of success and failure, and on man's duty to submit himself to God.

Opposition to Muhammad in Mecca and the emigration (hijra) to Yathrib (Medina), 622.

Opposition to Muhammad came in particular from the merchants of Mecca, and this was not surprising, since a good deal of the Prophet's teaching consisted of an attack on their attitudes to life and their criteria of success and failure. Abu Jahl, a merchant of the clan of Makhzum, was one of Muhammad's fiercest opponents. Some Meccans, however, did respond positively to the revelation "recited" by Muhammad. 'Abu Bakr, for example, a small businessman who succeeded Muhammad as leader of the Islamic community in 632, became one of the Prophet's first companions. There was also al-Argam, a rich young merchant from the clan of Makhzum. Al-Argam's house in fact became Muhammad's headquarters in Mecca.

   In addition to the opposition from the merchants who felt that the Prophet was a threat to their economic and political power, Muhammad experienced other setbacks. In 619 A.D., for example, his wife and loyal supporter, Khadija, died, and so too did his uncle and protector, Abu Talib, leader of the clan to which Muhammad belonged. The new clan leader, Abu Lahab, decided to reverse 'Abu Talib's policy towards Muhammad by withdrawing protection from him. In these circumstances Muhammad felt it was impossible to preach and teach, and having been offered support and protection by a number of leading citizens from Yathrib, later called Medina, to the north of Mecca, he planned to emigrate there. In July, 622, therefore, most of Muhammad's followers began the emigration to Medina, a tense and divided city inhabited by Arabs, Jews and Christians. In September, 622, Muhammad, 'Abu Bakr and Ali, one of Abu Talib's children whom Muhammad had looked after for several years, emigrated from Mecca to Medina. This planned withdrawal or emigration from Mecca to Medina, known as the *hijra*, marks the beginning of the Islamic calendar. The *hijra*, as we shall see in later chapters, was used as a model for future Muslim reformers in West Africa. On being opposed by rulers and others on account of their teaching and preaching, reformers like Usuman dan Fodio in the 19th century in Hausaland, withdrew or emigrated from the territory of the opposition and planned their return to that territory for purposes of reforming it, by military means if necessary (see Chapter 5). In this they believed they were following the practice of Muhammad when he emigrated from Mecca to Medina with the intention of one day returning to Mecca to have his teaching accepted there.

The formation of the Islamic community (umma) in Medina and the return to Mecca.

In Medina Muhammad gave the Islamic community (*umma*) a constitution known as the Constitution of Medina. Moreover, the Prophet was accepted as leader of this community, which was in effect a political and religious community founded on the Prophet's teaching. This new community gradually took on a distinctive form. The members recited regularly the *Shahada* or confession of divine unity and of Muhammad's prophethood: "There is no god but Allah and Muhammad is his prophet". In addition, they began to perform the five daily prayers (*salat*) facing Mecca, to observe the fast for one month during the year (*Ramadan*), and to give alms (*zakat*) from their earnings. Later they were to make the pilgrimage to Mecca (*hajj*). These activities make up what are known as the Five Pillars of Islam.

The community followed its own sacred law, the Shari'a or sacred law of Islam, revealed by God to Muhammad. This law was elaborated upon and codified by Islamic legal experts after Muhammad's death. The principal sources of the Shari'a are the Qur'an, the Sunna, that is the way or example of Muhammad, and the Hadith, the sayings of the Prophet handed down by his closest companions, those who knew his mind well enough to be able to say what he thought of a certain action or what advice and guidance he gave in certain situations.

Another practice which the Islamic community adopted in Medina was that of "striving in the path of Allah". This effort or striving is known as *jihad* and can be performed in a number of different ways. There is, for instance, jihad of the heart or the striving to purify the soul of evil thought and desires. Then there is jihad of the tongue, which consists in commanding people to do what is right and in forbidding them to do what is wrong or evil. Jihad of the hand consists in administering Islamic disciplinary measures. Jihad of the sword consists in striving in open warfare either to defend or to reform Islam or to convert to Islam unbelievers or enemies of the faith. This last mentioned type of jihad is a collective duty, an obligation for the community as a whole, and the obligation is fulfilled when a sufficient number of persons perform it.

Islam divides the world into two spheres: the land of Islam (*dar al-Islam*), and the land of war (*dar al-harb*), where non-Muslims reside.

The Islamic community in Medina engaged in a number of military encounters with its opponents, particularly its opponents in Mecca and the Jewish community in Medina. Muhammad wanted the Jews in Medina to recognise him as a prophet along the same lines as they recognised the prophets of the Old Testament. He did not intend, it would appear, to force them to abandon their own beliefs and religious practices. Many Jews, however, refused to accept Muhammad as a prophet and the Qur'an as the word of God. This refusal created tension between the Islamic and Jewish communities in Medina which led to a break between them in 624 A.D. Prior to this date the Muslims had prayed facing Jerusalem, but from 624 onwards they were ordered by Muhammad to turn towards Mecca while at prayer. As the years passed tension mounted between the two communities, leading eventually to conflict in which some Jews were expelled from Medina and others wiped out. Islam of course does not demand that Jews, or for that matter Christians, become Muslims. As people with Holy Books/Scriptures containing revelations from God, they are allowed to maintain and practice their faith, though they must pay the Muslim authorities a poll tax in return for the guarantee of protection and the preservation of their rights under their own personal law. Jews and Christians living in an Islamic state are known as *dhimmis*, those protected by Muslim law.

Most of the Islamic community's conflicts in the very early years, however, were with the Meccans. One of the more notable military encounters was the battle of Badr in 624 which resulted in a victory for Muhammad against the Meccans led by 'Abu Sufyan. In 625, however, at Uhud, Abu Sufyan defeated the Islamic community. Just before the start of this battle some Muslims withdrew their support from Muhammad and they became known as the "Hypocrites". In 627, in the battle of the Ditch (Khandaq), Muhammad successfully defended Medina against a Meccan army twice the size of his own. The following year Muhammad and the Meccans signed the Treaty of Hudaybiyah (March 628 A.D.) which called for a cessation of hostilities for a period of 10 years. However, in January 630 the Prophet, maintaining that the Meccans had violated the Treaty, set off from Medina with a force of 10,000 strong and with very little bloodshed he achieved his greatest triumph — the conquest of Mecca.

A general amnesty was granted to all Muhammad's opponents in Mecca, idols at the Ka'ba and other shrines were removed, and the offices and privileges of the wealthy merchants were abolished. After spending some 20 days in the city Muhammad left. He returned there again at the head of the pilgrimage to Mecca (hajj) in 632 A.D. This pilgrimage of 632, known as the "farewell pilgrimage", established the hajj as a uniquely Muslim rite.

Muhammad died in June 632 A.D., in the same year as he made the farewell pilgrimage. At his death the Islamic community was composed of the tribes in and around Mecca and Medina in western Arabia, of others in central Arabia, and others in the south-east and south-west of the peninsula, and of a few scattered tribes on the borders of Iraq and Syria. The great age of Islamic expansion was still to come in the hundred or so years after the Prophet's death.

The rightly guided Caliphs.

Under Muhammad's successors, the Caliphs, the Islamic community founded by the Prophet was transformed into a vast empire. This transformation was accomplished by peaceful means, by the preaching and teaching of Muslim missionaries, and by jihad of the sword.

Muhammad's first four successors, 'Abu Bakr, Caliph from 632 to 634, 'Umar (634 – 644), 'Uthman (644 – 656) and Ali (656 – 661), are regarded as the four rightly guided Caliphs, and the period in which they ruled the Islamic community as the "Golden Age" of Islam. These first Caliphs were all companions of Muhammad and elected to the office of Caliph. Though they do not enjoy the same status and authority in Muslim eyes as the Prophet, since they are not regarded as prophets nor as continuing Muhammad's prophetic role, they are nevertheless considered on account of their close association with him to have had a unique opportunity of understanding the mind and will of the founder of Islam.

'Abu Bakr (632–634 A.D.), although he was preoccupied for a time with putting down the revolts known as the Wars of Apostasy, completed the subjection of Arabia and entered Palestine. During 'Umar's term of office as Caliph (634–644 A.D.) and during that of his successor Uthman (644–656 A.D.), Islam expanded rapidly. During the Caliphate of Ali, however, this rapid expansion slowed down on account of a civil war within the Muslim community. I will now look briefly at the Caliphate of Ali (656–661 A.D.) before returning to the expansion of Islam to North and West Africa, since a number of developments which occurred during Ali's Caliphate had an important bearing on the early history of Islam in West Africa.

The Caliphate of Ali, 656–661 A.D.

The civil strife during Ali's time as Caliph was the result in part of personal rivalry between himself and Mu'awiya, the Muslim governor of Damascus in Syria and founder of the Umayyad dynasty. There were other factors, too, of a more ideological nature. For instance, among the troops under Ali's command there were those who believed that Ali, cousin of the Prophet, was infallible, while others held no such opinion of him. Indeed some believed Ali was actually living in sin and error because, among other things, he was prepared to submit issues to a court of arbitration rather than rely exclusively on the Qur'an.[4]

It was from these two groups, the ones who believed Ali was infallible and could do no wrong, and those who believed that he was failing to govern as they believed a Muslim ruler should, that two major Islamic sects emerged. These are known as the Shi'ites (*Shi'a* means party and the Shi'ites are the party of Ali) and the Kharijites or "seceders", from the Arabic *Kharaju*, to go out or secede. The Kharajites, therefore, are those who seceded from Ali.

The orthodox Muslims, the Sunnis, emphasise that what the Muslim community as a whole agrees upon over time is the guarantee of what is right. Of course the community will be assisted in preserving Islamic truth by religious experts. The Shi'ites, on the other hand, see the Imam as the leader of the Muslim community and regard him rather than the community as a whole as the guarantee and guardian of Islamic truth. The Imams are the sure guides. The Sunni Muslims give no such role to the Imam. For them, the Imam or Caliph is the Prophet's successor whose duty it is to keep intact the heritage of the Prophet. He is elected for this task by the people. The Shi'ites, however, see the Imams as descendants by blood of the Prophet himself. Ali, whom the Shi'ites claim as their first Imam, was the Prophet's cousin and had the same grandfather as Muhammad. Moreover, the Shi'ites hold that Muhammad's light and guidance is passed on to each Imam who has the responsibility for passing on his message to each successive age. Therefore to dispute with or to deny the Imam is to deny the message of the Prophet.[5]

The Kharijites held views of the Imam and Caliph which were opposed to those of the Shi'ites. Some Kharijites, moreover, adhered very strictly to the belief that if a Muslim committed a grave fault he or she should be automatically excluded from the Islamic community and should be condemned to death. Their slogan was "No judgment but God's". Anyone guilty of polytheism (*shirk*), that is associating in worship or anywhere else human things with Allah, or of usury, or of desertion on the battlefield, could no longer be considered a member of the Islamic community. They regarded such people as "the People of Hell" and themselves as "the People of Paradise". The People of Hell, since they were no longer members of the Islamic community, could be raided, pillaged, enslaved and even, as I have said, put to death. The Kharijites, furthermore, lived in camps close to commercial centres or along trade routes and they regarded all those living around who did not join or migrate to their community, in other words, make the hijra to the camps, as sinners and unbelievers and outside the dar al-Islam. They also held that no Kharijite could marry a non-Muslim.[6]

Many of these beliefs and practices are unacceptable to Sunni Muslims. Sunni Muslims do not, for instance, accept that grave sin committed by a Muslim excludes irrevocably the one who commits it from the Muslim community. The basic Muslim creed is that God is one and Muhammad is his Prophet. Anyone who rejects this creed cannot be considered a Muslim. In addition, loyalty to Islam is expressed by acceptance of the norms of Islamic life and by loyalty to the Islamic community. Moreover, Sunni Muslims believe that every individual is responsible for his or her own sins and that no one individual or group carries as it were the sins of another.

Sunni Muslims do not believe that Jews and Christians should be forced to become Muslims. They are, as we have seen, people with scriptures from God, although Muslims believe that these holy books are purified from error, completed and superseded by the Qur'an, God's final revelation. In addition, orthodox Islam has certain clearly defined rules regarding slavery. It is certainly not the case, for example, as the Kharijites believed, that anyone who commits a grave sin or who is outside the Islamic community can be automatically enslaved or pillaged and put to death.

Shi'ite and Kharijite groups were to be found in North Africa at the time when Islam was beginning to spread from there into West Africa. In fact the majority of the first Muslims to have contacts with West Africa were members of branches of the Kharijite movement. They belonged, as we shall see, to the Ibadiyya and Sufriyya sects, which, however, endorsed less extreme opinions than the main body of the Kharijite movement.

The expansion of Islam to North Africa.

'Abu Bakr, first Caliph (632—634) and successor to Prophet Muhammad, completed, as we have seen, the task of bringing Arabia under Islamic rule and pushed forward into Palestine. 'Umar, his successor and Caliph from 634 to 644, advanced as far as Damascus in Syria, winning a decisive victory over the Roman armies at the battle of Yarmuk in 636 A.D. This victory opened the way for the Islamic advance east to Mesopotamia, and west to Asia Minor.

By 642−3 Iran (Persia) to the east had been overrun, and to the west Alexandria in Egypt was occupied. From Egypt the Muslim forces marched on into the one time Greek and then Roman North African province of Cyrenaica, reaching as far as Tripoli before their progress was held up by Berber resistance.

With the occupation of the important sea port and dockyards of Alexandria in 642 A.D., Islam had the potential for becoming a formidable force at sea. The process began of building up a great naval and military base at Kairouan, a city in Ifriqiya (Tunisia and part of modern eastern Algeria) founded in the 675 by 'Uqba b. Nafi. Kairouan, as well as being an important naval and military base, also became an important centre of Islamic learning and missionary activity, and as we shall see its missionary and intellectual influence was felt in the western Sahara (see Chapter 2, p. 14).

The naval and military base at Kairouan enabled the Arab advance westward across North Africa, halted by Berber resistance, to be renewed. North West Africa came under Muslim control in the first decade of the 8th century. From North Africa the Muslim forces crossed the straits of Gibraltar and occupied large tracts of Spain, where divisions among the Christians facilitated the conquest. Then from Spain they advanced northwards into France taking Toulouse in 721 A.D. The advance into France, however, was finally checked at the battle of Poitiers in 732 and by 752 the Muslim forces had withdrawn south of the Pyrenees into Spain. Meanwhile the Muslim armies had overrun Kabul in Afghanistan in 664 A.D., opening up the way into Central Asia, Pakistan and India, and Pakistan was occupied in 712 A.D.

West Africa's first contacts with Islam.

According to a number of accounts West Africa's first contacts with Islam were made in the 7th century. These accounts state that the great Arab conqueror 'Uqba b. Nafi led his forces from their base in Kairouan into southern Morocco, and from there into the western Sahara and Sudan. There are other traditions, moreover, which speak of an expedition led by 'Uqba b. Nafi in 670 A.D., which penetrated into the Fezzan (in central Libya) almost as far as the northern border of the present day Republic of Niger.[7]

These accounts and traditions, however, which suggest that Islam was brought to West Africa by 'Uqba b. Nafi in the 7th century, are no longer accepted as accurate by many historians.[8] It is more likely that West Africa's first contacts with Islam were made in the 8th century. During the first half of the 8th century Islam began to work its way across the trans-Saharan trade routes from North to West Africa. Not long after the Arab conquerors had overrun North Africa, the Umayyad rulers there began organising military expeditions and slave raids into the southern regions of Morocco and as far south as the boundaries of Ancient Ghana.

One such slave raiding expedition seems to have been organised between 734 and 740 A.D. by the then Governor of Ifriqiyya, Ubayd Allah b. Al-Habib, and placed under the joint command of his son, Ismail, and General Habib b. Abi 'Ubayda. This expedition not only returned to North Africa

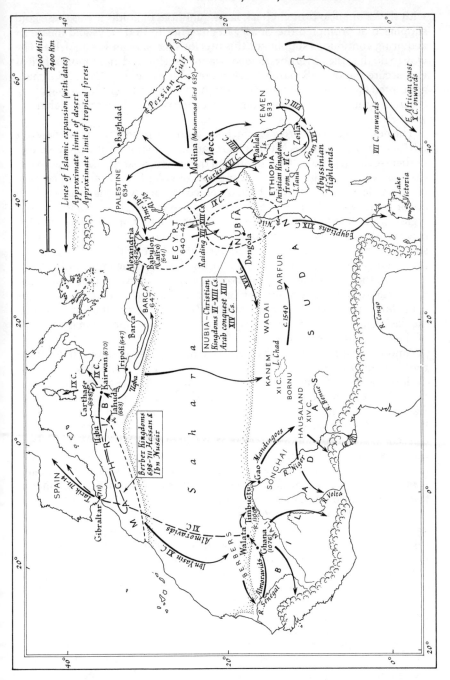

I Penetration of Islam

with slaves but also brought back large quantities of gold.[9] It was these gold supplies that prompted the Umayyad governor to find ways and means of acquiring continuous supplies of this precious metal from West Africa. The way to do this, the governor decided, was to develop and make more efficient and secure the trans-Saharan trade routes. To this effect Abd al-Rahman, appointed Governor of Ifriqiyya in 745 A.D., ordered wells to be dug along the trade routes leading from southern Morocco across the western Sahara to West Africa.

The next stage in the process which led to the early contacts between West Africa and Islam came as Muslim merchants, the majority of whom were of Berber stock, stepped up their interest in trade with West Africa, attracted by the prospect of obtaining plentiful supplies of gold. Prior to the 8th century North African merchants had been involved in trade with the peoples of the Sahara and with West Africans from Ancient Ghana and Kanem-Borno regions. The main interest of the North Africans at that time was in obtaining slaves and foodstuffs in return for cloth, salt and horses. The sale of horses, it should be noted, seems to have had very little to do with the emergence of these and other states in West Africa during the first millennium A.D.[10]

Drawn then principally by the prospects of obtaining commercial quantities of gold, a precious commodity in the Muslim world where it was used as a medium of exchange, North African Muslim merchants came in ever increasing numbers to settle in the commercial centres along or at the termini of the trans-Saharan trade routes.

Among the main commercial centres which sprang up along these trade routes from the 8th century onwards were Tahert, Sijilmasa, Wargla, Tadmakka and Awdaghost. Tahert (in modern Algeria) an important and flourishing commercial centre, was established in the 770s and was linked to Gao in West Africa by a trans-Saharan trade route which passed through Wargla and Tadmakka. Sijilmasa in Morocco, another important commercial centre, was also founded in the second half of the 8th century. For several centuries one of the main trans-Saharan trade routes passed through Sijilmasa and continued on southwards to Awdaghost in the western Sahara and from there on to Ancient Ghana. Much further east another trans-Saharan trade route linked the Kanem-Borno region with Cyrenaica in North Africa.

During the 8th century, therefore, the situation developed in which the Sanhaja of the western Sahara, who provided guidance and protection to the Muslim traders crossing the Sahara, came increasingly under the influence of Islam. It is probable that by the 10th century some of their leaders had themselves become Muslims. Moreover, West African merchants were also in contact with both the Sanhaja and the Muslim merchants from North Africa. By the late 9th and early 10th century some of the latter had begun to establish Muslim quarters in the capitals of the West African states of Gao, Ancient Ghana and Takrur.

A point worth noting here is that the majority of the North African Muslim merchants who became increasingly involved in trade with West Africa from the middle years of the 8th century were not only of Berber stock but they were also unorthodox Muslims. According to one Arabic scholar al-Zuhri, who wrote in the first half of the 12th century, "they adopted a school which

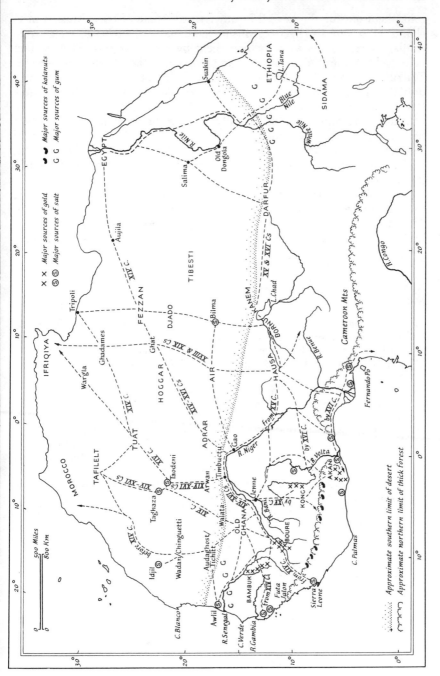

II Trade routes

took them outside the law".[11] In other words some of these Muslim merchants, who were also in effect Muslim missionaries, held beliefs which were similar in certain respects to those held by the Kharijites. They in fact belonged to either the Sufrite or Ibadite branch of the Kharijite movement. The ruler and most of the business people in Tahert, for example, were Ibadis until the Fatimids overran the town in 909. Awdaghost and Zawila also had a large number of Ibadis while in Sijilmasa a sizeable proportion of the Muslims were Sufrites. Consequently, among the Sanhaja in the western Sahara, part of which today is covered by the Islamic Republic of Mauretania, and elsewhere in West Africa early Islam was unorthodox. This was a situation which the Almoravid movement was determined to rectify (see Chapter 2).

The realisation, then, that West Africa was a "land of gold" made it the focus of greater attention in North Africa, attracting increasing numbers of Muslim traders to the commercial centres of the Sahara and West Africa itself. It was in this way that West Africa made its first contacts with Islam.

Notes.

1   Muhammad is said to have been born in the Year of the Elephant, the year in which the Abyssinian Viceroy of the Yemen marched as far as Mecca with a large army which included an elephant. This was probably sometime between 568–570 A.D. See W. Montgomery-Watt, *Muhammad, Prophet and Statesman* (Oxford, 1961), p. 7.
2   Among those who asserted that the Qur'an was "created" were the Mu'tazilites, a rationalist, theological movement in early Islam.
3   Qur'an, Sura 104 v. 1 *ff.*
4   On the opposition to Caliph Uthman and the dispute over his successor as Caliph, see C. Brockleman, *History of the Islamic Peoples* (New York, 1960), pp. 63 *ff.*
5   On Shi'ism, see W. Montgomery-Watt, *What is Islam?* (London, 1979), Chapter 7.
6   *Ibid.*, on the Kharijites. On the Ibadites and their activities in relation to Islam in West Africa, see T. Lewicki, *Etudes Ibadites Nord Africaines: I* (Warsaw, 1955).
7   See N. Levtzion, "Abd Allah b. Yasin and the Almoravids", in J.R. Willis, ed, *Studies in West African Islamic History*, Vol. I (London, 1979), p. 2.
8   *Ibid.*, p. 82.
9   See A.A. Batran, "The Kunta, Sidi al-Mukhtar al-Kunti, and the Office of Shaykh al-Tariq al-Qadiriyya" in J.R. Willis, *op. cit.*, p. 115.
10   R. Law, *The Horse in West African History* (Cambridge, England, 1980), pp. 176 *ff.*
11   Al-Zuhri in J. Cuoq, *Recueil des Sources Arabes* (Paris, 1975), p. 121.

2

The impact of the Almoravid movement on the development of Islam in West Africa in the 11th century.

The emergence of the Almoravid movement.

The Almoravid movement was launched among the Sanhaja in the Sahara by 'Abdullah b. Yasin in the first half of the 11th century. The founder of this movement was a Muslim reformer who aimed at purifying the Islam of the Sanhaja, described in Chapter 1 as being unorthodox, and at establishing in the Sahara and beyond an Islamic community modelled on that created by Prophet Muhammad and his immediate successors. In order to achieve these aims 'Abdullah b. Yasin made use of the classical Islamic doctrine of jihad of the sword or holy war[1] (see Chapter 1, p. 4). The term Almoravid has the meaning by extension of "holy war" and the Almoravid movement can therefore be described as the movement of those who engaged in holy war.[2] Whether in fact the founder and his successors as leaders of the movement and their followers were inspired and motivated solely by the desire to reform, defend and advance Islam is something that is discussed later in this chapter.

The first signs of an attempt to reform Islam in the Sahara appeared with the election at the beginning of the 11th century of 'Abdullah Muhammad b. Tifat, more commonly known by the name Tareshna al-Lamtuna, as chief of the Lamtuna branch of the Sanhaja. The Lamtuna at the time occupied the central region of what is today the West African Islamic Republic of Mauretania. According to the Arabic scholar al-Bakri, who included a short history of the Almoravid movement in his "Book of Journeys and Kingdoms", completed in 1068 A.D, Tareshna al-Lamtuna was a man of ability and worth, "a man of faith who performed the pilgrimage (hajj) and waged a holy war (jihad)".[3] Tareshna was, it appears, killed in a battle against Sudanese (black people) in the region of Adrar in central Mauretania in the western Sahara.

If Tareshna al-Lamtuna was responsible for initiating the process of Islamic reform among the Sanhaja and for restoring to the Sanhaja some of the unity and cohesion which they had lost, it was Yahya b. Ibrahim, with the help of a number of Sanhaja chiefs and scholars, who paved the way for the entry into the Sahara of 'Abdullah b. Yasin and thereby played an important role in the foundation of the Almoravid movement.

Yahya b. Ibrahim was chief of the Juddala branch of the Sanhaja who inhabited a stretch of land west of the Lamtuna along the Atlantic coast.

Moreover, they controlled the important salt mine of Awlil in southern Mauretania close to the Senegal river. Al-Bakri states that caravans of salt left Awlil for all the neighbouring countries.[4] Salt was in fact valued so highly that it could be exchanged in some places for the equivalent weight in gold.

Yahya b. Ibrahim was interested in unity and sought for ways and means of strengthening the political ties between the different branches of the Sanhaja. He may well have decided that adoption by the Sanhaja of orthodox Islam would help to provide greater unity and cohesion by giving the Sanhaja a common ideology and thereby enabling them to present a united front against their enemies. On the other hand Yahya b. Ibrahim was a devout and sincere Muslim and was, no doubt, anxious to see established in the Sahara an Islamic community which conformed to the standards laid down by Prophet Muhammad.

In the year 1035/36 A.D. Yahya b. Ibrahim, accompanied by a number of Sanhaja chiefs and an expert in Islamic law (*fiqh*), Jawhar b. Sakkum, set off on the pilgrimage to Mecca. On their return journey, the pilgrims stopped off at Kairouan, a centre, as I have already mentioned, of orthodox Islamic learning and missionary activity in Ifriqiya (Tunisia and part of eastern Algeria). A combative, militant spirit existed among some of the Muslim scholars in Kairouan. These scholars were determined not only to teach a pure, orthodox form of Islam, but also to ensure that orthodox Islam prevailed everywhere. Moreover, a number of their pupils had either established or joined Islamic centres in North Africa and elsewhere which were noted for their orthodoxy, asceticism and missionary zeal.

While in Kairouan Yahya b. Ibrahim asked a prominent scholar and teacher, Abu 'Imran al-Fasi, to send one of his students to the Sahara to instruct the Sanhaja in orthodox Islamic beliefs and practice. Abu 'Imran al-Fasi was unable at that moment to send one of his students but advised Yahya to contact one of his former pupils, Muhammad Wajjaj b. Zalwi. After completing his studies in Kairouan Wajjaj b. Zalwi went on to establish an Islamic centre in southern Morocco and from there spread the orthodox Islamic teaching and the approach to Islamic reform which he had learned in Kairouan.

Wajjaj b. Zalwi chose 'Abdullah b. Yasin, a Sanhaja on his mother's side, to accompany Yahya and his companions to the Sahara. On his way to the Sahara the reformer passed through areas under the influence of the heretical Islamic sect, the Barghawata, while other areas were occupied by Shi'ites and others by Kharajites and Jews. Moreover, in the Sahara 'Abdullah b. Yasin not only saw for himself the religious laxity and negligence of the Sanhaja but also the strong influence which the Ibadite brand of Islam had over them. All of this presumably made him think seriously about the necessity of a jihad of the sword to revive orthodox Islam in the Sahara and beyond.

The course of the Almoravid movement until the death of 'Abdullah b. Yasin in 1059 A.D.

Shortly after his arrival in the Sahara in 1039/40 'Abdullah b. Yasin began to gather a following from among the Juddala branch of the Sanhaja. At first about 60 men assembled around him to study and as al-Bakri put it "to obey him in everything".[5] Soon, as their numbers increased, the movement began raiding the Lamtuna to the east, taking possession of all the booty they could lay their hands on. From the outset 'Abdullah b. Yasin presented himself as a hard taskmaster. Among other things he refused to eat the meat or drink the milk provided by the Sanhaja on the grounds that their goods were unlawfully acquired and therefore impure.

'Abdullah's somewhat uncompromising attitude, his harshness and his authoritarianism and in the eyes of some, such as Jawhar b. Sakkum, his superficial knowledge of Islamic law, probably contributed to bringing about the first major crisis in the movement. This crisis occurred around the time of the death of Yahya b. Ibrahim who had been a firm supporter of 'Abdullah b. Yasin. It is not clear exactly what happened. Al-Bakri's account of the crisis is in essence as follows. The Juddala followers of 'Abdullah b. Yasin discerned a number of contradictions in their leader's statements on Islamic law and Jawhar b. Sakkum, supported by two noblemen, revolted against him and, among other things, refused to obey his orders, stripped him of the office of treasurer, demolished his house, allowed all his goods to be pillaged and expelled him.[6] Another account states that an incident occurred involving 'Abdullah b. Yasin and al-Jawhar b. Sakkum and others over 'Abdullah's strict enforcement of the penalties prescribed by Islamic sacred law (Shari'a) for certain offences.[7] This account of the crisis is not specific about the penalties imposed but it is known from al-Bakri that 'Abdullah ordered that those found guilty of fornication were to be given 100 lashes, the liar and those who drank wine 80 lashes, those absent from public prayer 20 lashes, and those who raised their voice in the mosque were to be punished at the discretion of whoever was in charge at the time the event occurred. Even those who joined the movement and repented of their previous faults committed during their youth were punished.

It would appear then that some of the Juddala resented 'Abdullah's strict and what they saw as his arbitrary interpretation of Islamic law. Moreover, the flames of resentment were probably fuelled when it came to the question of choosing Yahya b. Ibrahim's successor. However, whatever the reasons for the crisis within the movement, 'Abdullah left the Juddala. He perhaps saw his departure as a form of emigration (hijra) in line with the action of Prophet Muhammad who emigrated from Mecca to Medina in 622 A.D. in the teeth of opposition from the Meccan merchants. And as Prophet Muhammad had it in mind to return and reform Mecca at a later date, 'Abdullah also may well have intended to return and reform the Juddala Sanhaja.

According to another account, however, 'Abdullah wanted to leave the Juddala and go and work in the Sudan where, and this is the interesting point, "Islam had already begun to shine forth".[8] However, after contacting his former teacher Wajjaj al-Zalwi for advice and guidance, 'Abdullah returned to his missionary work among the Sanhaja and this time settled among the Lamtuna. With Yahya b. 'Umar in command of his troops, 'Abdullah b. Yasin, the Amir al-Muslimin (Commander of the Muslims), set about punishing his opponents and reforming Islam throughout the Sahara. Although he had his opponents and enemies 'Abdullah b. Yasin also had his loyal supporters. Al-Bakri wrote that his followers "demonstrated in combat an unbelievable boldness and courage preferring death to flight. They never draw back."[9] The same writer also tells us that 'Abdullah's followers regarded him as a saint and expected him to perform miracles. Al-Bakri recounts the story that during one expedition 'Abdullah's companions complained of thirst whereupon their leader said to them, "Let us hope God will bring to an end our suffering". Then after about an hour 'Abdullah told his followers to dig a hole, which they did, and they immediately found water not far below the surface.[10]

'Abdullah b. Yasin's zeal and the dedication and fearlessness of his troops enabled him to conquer and subdue a number of the peoples and the commercial centres in and beyond the confines of the Sahara. In 1054 he overran Sijilmasa, but shortly afterwards there was a revolt and this commercial centre had to be conquered again in 1056. His troops also took Awdaghost in 1054 and in this conquest displayed considerable harshness and brutality. Al-Bakri describes the conquest of Awdaghost in this way: "The Almoravids took the town, violated the women and regarded the fruit of their pillage as lawful booty. . .".[11] According to al-Bakri the Almoravids justified their harshness and brutality on the grounds that the people of Awdaghost had recognised no other authority than that of the non-Muslim king of Ancient Ghana.[12]

In addition to the revolt in Sijilmasa in 1054 A.D. there were revolts elsewhere against 'Abdullah b. Yasin's authority. In 1056 A.D., for instance, the Juddala rebelled, massacring many of the Almoravid troops, including their army commander Yahya b. Umar. 'Abdullah b. Yasin was himself killed in 1059 while fighting in southern Morocco against the heretical Muslim sect, the Barghawata. His inspiration and influence, however, lived on after his death. By the time al-Bakri was writing in 1067—8 his tomb had become a place of frequent pilgrimage and the mosque there was always full.[13]

At this point it is worth discussing briefly the nature of 'Abdullah b. Yasin's appeal to his followers. Was he a charismatic figure? From al-Bakri's portrait of the man, which is in fact a fairly critical one, 'Abdullah b. Yasin had tremendous appeal. This does not by itself, however, enable one to classify him as a charismatic leader although I believe he was. Charisma in the strict sense of the term is not a personality trait nor is it principally a quality possessed by an individual. It is a special form of "social" relationship existing between a leader and his followers. It is a relationship based on a claim made by the leader and accepted by his followers who also make claims on his behalf, that his authority has some form of supernatural backing or support.[14] From the accounts given by al-Bakri of the way in which 'Abdullah b. Yasin's troops obeyed his commands in battle, and attributed to him the power of working miracles, something 'Abdullah encouraged, it seems clear that a charismatic relationship existed between the leader of the Almoravid movement and his followers.

The Almoravid movement under Abu Bakr b. 'Umar (1059—87) and Ancient Ghana.

Abu Bakr b. 'Umar took over from 'Abdullah b. Yasin as leader of the Almoravid movement and under his leadership (1059—87) the movement divided into a southern and northern wing. Though Abu Bakr remained overall leader of the movement, he was for all practical purposes in control of the southern wing only, while his cousin, Yusuf b. Tashfin, had charge of the northern wing. Yusuf b. Tashfin and his successors went on to establish the Almoravid empire in north-west Africa and Spain, while Abu Bakr concentrated his attentions on the Sahara and the Sudan. It is the activities and impact of the southern wing of the movement in the western Sahara and West Africa that are the main concern here, since they are directly relevant to an understanding of the development of Islam in West Africa.

There is some debate among historians concerning the activities of Abu Bakr in the Sahara and the impact of the Almoravid movement between 1059—1087 A.D. on the growth of Islam in West Africa. According to some accounts he fought and expelled the Sudanese from the western Sahara, while other accounts indicate that he cultivated strong links with a number of West African kingdoms like Takrur in northern Senegal. Perhaps such alliances were necessary, for if al-Bakri's account of the Almoravid movement in 1067—8 A.D. is correct then the movement was by that time showing signs of decline. Al-Bakri wrote that "the Amir of the Almoravids is today, that is in 460 A.H.(1067—8 A.D.), Abu Bakr b. 'Umar. But their authority is fragile and infirm'.[15]

A number of historians have concentrated their attention on the conflict between the Almoravids and the Sudanese in the period 1059—87 thereby pushing into the background the question of alliances. Moreover, they have seemingly overlooked al-Bakri's point that the Almoravid movement was in the process of decline by 1067—8 A.D, and have presented it as a powerful force capable of conquering all before it, including the capital of Ancient Ghana in 1076—7 A.D. Boahen, for example, writes that the Almoravid forces "first wrested Awdaghost from Ghana in 1054 and then attacked and captured the Ghana capital itself some twenty-two years later (i.e. 1076)".[16] Moreover, these historians not only assert that the Almoravids conquered Ancient Ghana's capital, but that they also converted many of its inhabitants to Islam. On this point Levtzion is quite definite, stating that "the islamisation of the kingdom (Ancient Ghana) was one important result of the Almoravid conquest".[17] Trimingham takes a similar view of events claiming that the conquest of Ghana's capital by the Almoravids "led to the political triumph of Islam throughout the Sahil region between the Senegal and Niger (rivers)". Trimingham continues, "The Soninke of Ghana were compelled to adopt Islam and they not only did so *en masse* but began to spread it amongst the many peoples over whom they still ruled."[18]

The view that the Almoravids, led by Abu Bakr, overran the capital of Ancient Ghana and converted its ruler and many of its citizens to Islam has been challenged. So too has the idea that relations between the Almoravids and West African states were characterised essentially by hostility and conflict. Two of the principal opponents of the view that the Almoravids conquered Ancient Ghana and converted its rulers to Islam are the historians H.J. Fisher and D. Conrad.[19] They also form part of that group of historians who believe that too much emphasis has been placed by historians in the past on the element of conflict and not enough on that of alliance and interdependence when analysing Almoravid-West African relations.[20] Before treating of this second issue, I want to examine briefly what Fisher and Conrad have to say about the conquest of Ancient Ghana theory.

The conclusion reached by Fisher and Conrad, after examining numerous written sources and oral traditions relating to Ancient Ghana, is that they have discovered no unmistakeable evidence which points clearly to an Almoravid conquest of Ancient Ghana. There is no space here to look at all the sources examined by Fisher and Conrad so I will confine myself to a brief look at two of the written sources.

The first written source comes from a book on geography written by the Arabic scholar al-Zuhri who died either in 1154 or 1161 A.D. He probably finished his book in about the year 1133 A.D. The following short extract from al-Zuhri's book is important because it is one of the principal "early" sources which historians have used to support the view that the Almoravids conquered Ancient Ghana and converted its rulers and people to Islam. The two important sentences in al-Zuhri's passage on Ancient Ghana are:

> "The people of the town (Ghana) were hardened unbelievers until 469 A.H. (1076/77 A.D.) when Yahya b. Abi Bakr, Amir of the Masufa *came forth*. They (the people of Ghana) were converted to Islam during the time of the Lamtuna (Almoravids)."[21]

Does this passage suggest that the Almoravids conquered the capital of Ancient Ghana and converted its inhabitants to Islam? Does it suggest, further, that the leader of this alleged conquest was Abu Bakr b. 'Umar, head of the Almoravid movement, who at the time had confined his leadership to the southern wing of the movement? It could, I suppose, be argued that the verb *came forth* means *attacked*. Fisher and Conrad maintain that the Arabic verb from which it is derived, that is *khuruj*, is only rarely used to mean conquest. It can mean expedition, but a number of scholars give it the meanings of *emerge*, *appear* or *come forth*, or *go forth*, none of which necessarily implies conquest.[22]

Secondly, who was Yahya b. Abi Bakr? There is no evidence to suggest that he was the same person as Abu Bakr b. 'Umar who is credited with the alleged conquest. This passage, then, which historians have used as one of the foundation stones for their theory that Ancient Ghana was conquered by the Almoravids led by Abu Bakr b. 'Umar does not, according to Fisher and Conrad, support this conquest theory. Moreover, the Arabic scholar al-Idrisi, who was a contemporary of al-Zuhri and wrote in 1154 his "Book of Roger", which contains a good deal of information about Ancient Ghana, does not mention that the Almoravids converted the rulers and people of Ancient Ghana to Islam by conquest and force, although he does say that the king was a Muslim.[23]

There is, however, one clear reference in the Arabic sources to a conquest of Ancient Ghana by the Almoravids. The Arabic scholar al-Maqrizi (1364–1442) who wrote a book on Africa excluding Egypt, states that the king of Ghana was the greatest of kings but that Ghana was conquered first by the Almoravids, the people of the veil, and then by the Soso, before being ruled by the people of Mali.[24]

The well-known Arabic historian, Ibn Khaldun (1332–1406), also implies in his book *The Muqaddimah*, which forms part of his *Universal History* (*Kitab al-Ibar*) written between 1375 and 1382, that the Almoravids conquered Ancient Ghana and converted many of the people there to Islam. He wrote, for example, "Later the authority of Ancient Ghana waned and its power declined whilst that of the veiled people (the name given to the Almoravids by Arabic writers on account of the fact that the former wore the *litham* or veil) their neighbours on the north next to the land of the Berbers, increased. The latter (the Almoravids) overcame the Sudanese . . . and converted many of them to Islam. As a result the authority of Ghana dwindled away and they were overcome by the Soso, their Sudanese neighbours, who subdued and crushed them completely."[25]

It would seem then, on the surface, that these two written sources refer to an Almoravid conquest of Ancient Ghana and the conversion of many of that kingdom's inhabitants to Islam. Moreover, on the basis of these two texts it would appear that the view held by Fisher and Conrad that there is no unmistakeable evidence for such a conquest or for the conversion of the rulers and many of their subjects to Islam as a result of such a conquest, is inaccurate.

Fisher and Conrad, however, do not regard the statements made by al-Maqrizi and Ibn Khaldun as either conclusive evidence of a conquest of Ancient Ghana by the Almoravids, or as evidence as to when or how the rulers of Ancient Ghana became Muslims. One of their arguments is that the statements of al-Maqrizi and Ibn Khaldun appear very late in the day, in fact several hundred years after the alleged conquest and conversion. Why, Fisher and Conrad ask, did other Arabic scholars, who wrote much earlier than these two and knew a considerable amount about West Africa, fail to provide clear and accurate information about an Almoravid conquest of Ancient Ghana and the conversion to Islam of many of its people? The Arabic scholar al-Zuhri, for example, who, as we have seen, wrote about Ancient Ghana in the first half of the 12th century, does not refer explicitly to an Almoravid conquest leading to the conversion of its inhabitants. Al-Zuhri does, however, suggest that rather than conquering Ancient Ghana the Almoravids worked in alliance with that kingdom in order to put down revolts and possibly to spread and reform Islam in Silla and Tadmakka. He states: "The People of Ghana demanded, in order to triumph over them (the people of Silla and Tadmakka), the assistance of the Murabitun (the Almoravids).[26]

In addition to al-Zuhri, other Arabic geographers, writing long before al-Maqrizi and Ibn Khaldun, do not mention an Almoravid conquest of Ancient Ghana nor do they say how or when the rulers of Ancient Ghana became Muslims.

Does the fact, then, that only a few of the many Arabic scholars who wrote about Ancient Ghana refer to an Almoravid conquest of Ancient Ghana and the conversion of many of its inhabitants to Islam as a result of this invasion, mean that it is extremely unlikely that any such conquest and conversion took place? Further, does the fact that the statements of al-Maqrizi and Ibn Khaldun were made several hundred years after the event mean that they are unreliable as evidence?

These are not of course easy questions to answer and in order to answer them one needs to know something about the methods used by these Arabic geographers when writing their books. Later in this chapter I will offer some comments on the methods used by scholars such as al-Bakri and al-Umari and others (see p. 25). Here I want to summarise Fisher's and Conrad's answers.

These scholars maintain that the explicit reference to the Almoravid conquest of Ancient Ghana found in the writing of al-Maqrizi, and the vague, much less precise statement in Ibn Khaldun do not provide adequate proof on their own that either such a conquest took place or that the rulers and people of Ancient Ghana were converted to Islam as the result of such a conquest. Moreover, they say that al-Maqrizi may have obtained his information from Ibn Khaldun whose knowledge about Ancient Ghana was confused.[27] Furthermore, in their opinion, the oral sources do not support the theory of an Almoravid conquest of Ancient Ghana.[28] There is also evidence which indicates that Ancient Ghana was a strong power, perhaps even stronger than the Almoravids, and on occasion an ally of the Almoravids, around the time or soon after it was supposed to have been conquered by Almoravid forces.

Almoravid relations with Ancient Ghana and other West African states.

The relationship between the Almoravids and West African states were at times marked by hostility, but in general it is probably more accurate to suggest that they were characterised more by interdependence and alliances born of mutual interests. We know that Labe, the ruler of Takrur in Senegal, assisted the Almoravid commander, Yahya b. 'Umar, in the attempt to suppress the rebellion by the Juddala branch of the Sanhaja in 1056 A.D.[29] Moreover, as I have already mentioned, several years after the kings of Ancient Ghana had converted to Islam the Almoravids and Ancient Ghana forged an alliance and together "converted" Tadmakka and Silla to Islam.

Therefore, although conflict did take place between the Almoravids and the Sudanese, this should not be allowed to overshadow the fact that there was also considerable political, military and economic co-operation between the two groups. Moreover, if warfare had been the norm it would surely have badly disrupted the trans-Saharan trade, but there is no evidence that this actually happened. In fact the reverse seems to have been the case, for as one historian states: "Far from disrupting the trans-Saharan trade the Almoravids . . . raised the gold trade to a new peak".[30] This situation must be attributed in part at least to the existence of strong economic and trading links between the Almoravids and West African states such as Takrur and Ancient Ghana.

It seems that in these alliances and partnerships between the Almoravids and West African states neither side completely dominated or dictated terms to the other, at least until after the death of Abu Bakr, the leader of the

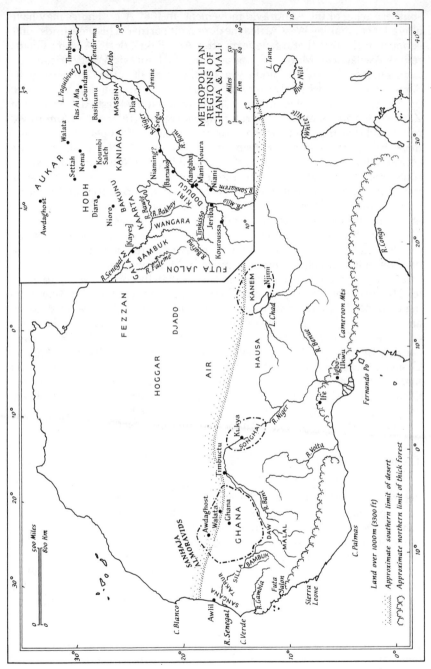

III The Sudan in the 11th century

southern wing of the Almoravid movement, in 1087 A.D. Things may have altered then, making West Africa the dominant partner. This view finds some support in the fact that a few years after Abu Bakr's death Ancient Ghana retook Awdaghost. Moreover, one account of Almoravid-West African relations suggests that by the middle years of the first half of the 12th century the Almoravids were definitely the weaker partner. The account is that provided by the Arabic geographer al-Yaqut. Writing about the West African state of Zafunu, al-Yaqut stated that its ruler was more powerful than the Almoravid rulers and that the latter for that reason "recognise his superiority . . . and have recourse to him for help where important affairs of state are concerned".[31] Al-Yaqut is probably describing the situation that existed sometime in the first half of the 12th century. Ancient Ghana remained a strong power throughout most of the 11th and 12th centuries and right up until the middle of the 13th century, something which seems to indicate that at no time was it a puppet state of the Almoravid movement.

It seems, therefore, that in the past too much emphasis has been placed on the element of conflict in Almoravid-West African relations and not enough on economic and military interdependence. Moreover, this type of relationship, characterised more by interdependence than by conflict, seems to me to lend further support to Fisher and Conrad's opinion that there is no convincing evidence of a written or oral nature pointing to an Almoravid invasion and conquest of Ghana which resulted directly in the conversion of the rulers of Ancient Ghana to Islam. Finally, therefore, if Fisher and Conrad are correct, then the traditional view of the development of Islam in Ancient Ghana, at least insofar as the conversion of the ruler of Ancient Ghana and many of his subjects is concerned, needs to be revised. The kings of Ancient Ghana and some of their subjects may well have been converted to Islam around this time, but this conversion may have been due more to internal circumstances rather than to an Almoravid invasion (see Chapter 3, p. 37).

The motives behind the Almoravid movement and its impact on Islam in West Africa in the 11th century.

Before giving an assessment of the impact of the Almoravid movement on the development of Islam in West Africa, I want to examine briefly the motives behind the movement, a question I raised on the first page of this chapter. Some of the points raised here will be relevant when we come to discuss the jihads in the 17th, 18th and 19th centuries.

Not everyone accepts that the Almoravid movement was motivated solely by the desire to revive and advance orthodox Islam. Friedrich Engels, for example, a friend and co-worker of Karl Marx, regarded the Almoravid movement as a clash between the impoverished, morally upright, nomadic Berbers of the Sahara, and the wealthy, morally lax Muslim merchants of the towns. The primary aim of the Sanhaja nomads, envious of the wealth of the merchants, was, according to Engels, to punish the merchants for their moral laxity by appropriating their wealth. Engels, moreover, regarded all medieval, Islamic holy wars in the same light, maintaining that "All these movements are clothed in religion but they have their source in economic causes".[32] Engels is not the only one to adopt this view; it is a view of *jihad* of the sword shared by a number of other writers.[33]

Other scholars take a somewhat different view from that of Engels and Marx concerning the causes and motives behind religious movements such as the Almoravid movement. Some historians and sociologists, following Max Weber, the German sociologist, maintain that religious ideals, interests and beliefs as well as material interests do play an important role in the emergence of a religious movement. Weber wrote: "However incisive the social influences, economically and politically determined, may have been upon a religious ethic in a particular case, it receives its stamp primarily from religious sources and first of all from the content of its annunciation and promise."[34]

Certainly insofar as the Almoravid movement is concerned both religious ideals and interests were present alongside material concerns. 'Abdullah b. Yasin, Yahya b. Ibrahim, Wajjaj b. Zalwi and many other participants in the Almoravid movement carried out their work and fought to revive, defend and spread orthodox Islam. Furthermore, in support of this view there is the point made by one historian that the military tactics and strategy used by the Almoravids were not necessarily the most suitable for winning battles, but were employed because they were the ones prescribed by Prophet Muhammad and laid down in the Qur'an.[35] Moreover, 'Abdullah b. Yasin's followers, as we have already heard from al-Bakri, were so inspired by their faith that they preferred to die rather than flee from their enemies. This attitude seems to have had something to do with Qur'anic teaching which prohibits flight from the battlefield except on certain conditions. One may flee, for example, in order to take up a better tactical position or if the Muslim army is out-numbered by more than two to one, or when the military leadership is convinced that defeat is inevitable.[36]

Among other interests which may have contributed to the emergence of the Almoravid movement was possibly the desire and need of the Sanhaja for more pastureland, for tighter control over the trans-Saharan trade, for greater cohesion and unity and some no doubt saw it as an opportunity to obtain booty and gain access to the "good life". A Muslim, of course, might justifiably argue that in principle the attempt to separate political from religious and other interests behind the movement serves no purpose. All life, whether political, commercial, religious, economic or social is for the Muslim regulated by Islamic sacred law (the *Shari'a*), and is therefore sacred and/or religious. Islam is seen, in fact, as a divine blueprint of the social order. This does not mean, of course, that people can do what they want on behalf of Islam. Whatever they do ought to conform to the Shari'a.

The Almoravid movement's character changed over time and in particular after the death of 'Abdullah b. Yasin. The charismatic relationship that existed between 'Abdullah and his followers began to disappear, or in the words of the sociologist became "routinised". The action, dynamism, spontaneity and personal belief of the followers in their leader's claims to have a supernatural basis for his authority, factors that characterised the movement during 'Abdullah b. Yasin's period of leadership, became much less important after his death.

In the northern wing of the movement, for instance, under Yusuf b. Tashfin, it was not so much faith or charisma but rather financial rewards that inspired the troops. Moreover, the northern wing of the movement under Yusuf b. Tashfin lost its Islamic revivalist character, for instead of being composed entirely of Sanhaja, many of whom were motivated by religious zeal, it became a multi-ethnic entity made up of Christians and Traditional Religionists as well as Muslims, with financial reward rather than religious ideals being the main inspiration.

The question of the motives and the purpose of holy wars will, as I have said, come up again in Chapters 4 and 5, but I will now conclude with some comments on the Almoravid contribution to the development of Islam in West Africa in the 11th century.

The Almoravids helped to stamp out a number of unorthodox Muslim beliefs and practices in the western Sahara, beliefs and practices introduced by Ibadite and Sufrite traders and missionaries. They did not, however, rid the western Sahara or West Africa of all Ibadite and Sufrite influences. Ibadis continued to live in both regions. Ibn Battuta, the Arabic scholar, noted in 1352 that one town in Mali was inhabited by black traders called "Wanjarata" and that with them are a certain number of white men who belong to the sect known as the Ibadis".[37] Moreover, in the sphere of architecture Ibadite influence persisted. The West African Fulani-built mosques are a case in point. These mosques were in general, contrary to the recommended Islamic practice, built without a "minbar". A minbar is a pulpit in a mosque and is believed to have been introduced by Prophet Muhammad. The reason for this absence of the minbar in Fulani mosques is due, according to one authority, to the persistence in West Africa of Ibadite influence.[38]

In terms of the attempt to revive Islamic orthodoxy among the Sanhaja the Almoravids enjoyed only a limited success. The Sanhaja retained a number of traditional un-Islamic customs such as the matrilineal system whereby succession to office, goods and property are controlled and inherited by the female's relations and children. Ibn Battuta, in his account of his travels across the Sahara to Mali in 1352, gave a description of the matrilineal system among the Massufa Sanhaja in Walata. He wrote: "No-one (in Walata) claims descent from his father, but on the contrary from his mother's brother. A person's heirs are his sister's sons, not his own. This is a thing which I have seen nowhere in the world except among the Indians of Malabar. But those (the people of Malabar) are heathens; these people, the Sanhaja, are Muslims, punctilious in observing the hours of prayer, studying books of law and memorising the Qur'an."[39]

The main contributions made by the Almoravids to Islam in the western Sahara and West Africa came in the fields of learning and missionary activity. But here too, the achievements, although not insignificant, were limited. 'Abdullah b. Yasin, a capable but not a distinguished scholar, and scholars such as Imam al-Hadrami, deepened the interest of many of the Sanhaja in Islamic theology, law, and the Arabic language and literature, interests first aroused by the merchant-missionaries from North Africa. There is, however, a debate among scholars, as we shall see in Chapter 3, as to whether future generations of Muslim scholars and reformers in the western Sahara, the

Senegambia and other parts of West Africa continued to be inspired and motivated by the ideals and teachings of the Almoravid movement.

Comment on the sources and methods of the medieval Arabic scholars.

Some of the following comments on the "historical" methods used by the "medieval" Arabic scholars are made with special reference to the issue already discussed of the supposed Almoravid conquest of Ancient Ghana and the conversion of its ruler to Islam. They are also applicable to other issues and indeed to analyses by historians both in medieval and in more recent times. Furthermore, it is worth remembering in the light of what follows that history, sociology and comparative religion did not exist as academic disciplines using "scientific" methods of enquiry until about 150 years ago. Of course "history" books were written before then, but very often the theory and the methods used in the writing of these books were in certain important respects different from those of today. Modern scientific methods and theory do not necessarily, of course, always produce more incisive and perceptive comment on the human condition than, for example, that provided by Ibn Khaldun in his *Kitab al-Ibar* (Universal History) written in the 14th century. They do, however, insist that the historian critically analyse and cross check his sources. This is something that does not appear to have been of very great importance for historians in general in the past, including Ibn Khaldun and other "medieval" Arabic scholars.

Some of the Arabic authors I have mentioned obtained their information on West Africa from merchants and other informants who had been in contact with the region. These writers then took the information provided and incorporated it into their works without critically checking it against other sources. And occasionally they would record two conflicting views and comment very honestly, "God knows", the implication being that they had no idea which one was correct.[40]

There was also a great deal of uncritical borrowing and repetition. Al-Bakri, for example, provided an account of the history of the Almoravid movement from its origin until 1067/8 A.D. Other writers, including Ibn Khaldun, copied this account. Again, many Arabic authors based their account of Mansa Musa's pilgrimage (see Chapter 3, p. 43) on the account provided by al-Umari (c. 1301–1349). This uncritical repetition and borrowing not only indicates a lack of concern with checking the information but also a certain disregard for the context in which events took place. This approach meant that information, whether accurate or not, could be passed on from one generation to the next unchecked.

Other points, too, are worth noting. These Arabic scholars, like their contemporaries in other parts of the world, sought through the medium of history to edify and even entertain people. Ibn Battuta's account of his travels through West Africa, for example, contains a great deal of edifying material and numerous anecdotes. Moral, philosophical, cultural and religious beliefs, therefore, were allowed to have a bearing on the information writers like Ibn Battuta and Ibn Khaldun and others were presenting to the reading public. Moreover, some of them were prepared, either because they were asked to do so or because it was an important part of their task, to link the people they were writing about with their world, their culture, their religion and civilisation. It seems, for example, that when a ruler became a Muslim he was provided with a genealogy and place of origin which either the new convert or the Arabic scholar regarded as appropriate for a Muslim. The Muslim ruler of Ancient Ghana, for example, was presented by Ibn Sa'id as belonging to the family of Prophet Muhammad through Ali, Caliph from 656 to 661 A.D. and cousin of Prophet Muhammad.

It hardly needs saying that the approach, attitudes and perspectives found in the writings of the Arabic scholars have appeared in the works of historians and political and social scientists from other parts of the world who have written about Africa in the 19th and 20th centuries.

Notes.

1   For an in-depth analysis of the classical doctrine of jihad, see R. Peters, *Islam and Colonialism* (The Hague, 1979), pp. 9–36.

2   For a full examination of the meaning of the term "Almoravid" see P.F de Moraes Farias, "The Almoravids: Some questions concerning the character of the Movement during its period of closest contact with the Sudan", *B.I.F.A.N.* Ser B, 3–4 (1967), p. 813 *et passim*. In this article the author suggests that the term Almoravid is derived from *ribat*, a fortified frontier post or fortified community. R. Peters, *op. cit.*, states that a special way of fulfilling one's jihad duty is called *ribat* after Qur'an Sura 8 v. 60. Peters adds that the word *ribat* came to mean, in law: remaining at the frontiers of Islamic territory with the intention of defending it. And he adds that the word *ribat* can be regarded as virtually synonymous with the term *jihad*, see R. Peters, *op. cit.*, p. 11. This would seem to indicate quite clearly that the Almoravid movement was first and foremost a jihad.

3   See V. Monteil's translation of al-Bakri's "Book of Journeys and Kingdoms" (Kitab al-masalik wa'l-mamalik) in *B.I.F.A.N.* Ser B, XXX (1968), p. 59.

4   *Ibid.*, p. 66.

5   *Ibid.*, p. 60.

6   *Ibid.*, p. 60.

7   H.T. Norris, "New Evidence on the life of 'Abdullah b. Yasin and the Origins of the Almoravid Movement", *Journal of African History* XII (1971), p. 256.

8   J.L. Triaud, *Islam et Sociétés Soudanaises au Moyen-Age* (Paris, 1973), p. 34.

9   Al-Bakri (V. Monteil's translation), p. 61.

10 *Ibid.*, p. 63.

11 *Ibid.*, pp. 62–3.

12 *Ibid.*, p. 63.

13 *Ibid.*, p. 63.

14 Max Weber, *The Theory of Social and Economic Organisation*, edited by Talcott Parsons (New York, 1964), p. 359.

15 Al-Bakri (V. Monteil's translation), p. 64.

16 Adu Boahen, *Topics in West African History* (London, 1966), p. 11.

17 N. Levtzion, *Ancient Ghana and Mali* (Reprint, London, 1980), p. 45.

18 J.S. Trimingham, *A History of Islam in West Africa* (Oxford, 1962), pp. 29–30.

19 Dr H.J. Fisher kindly allowed me to read the unpublished typescript of the article, "The Almoravid Conquest of Ghana in 1067" by David Conrad and Humphrey Fisher. Part I of the article is "The External Arabic Sources" and Part II, "The Oral Sources". A third section is planned and will deal with the historical theory and

method of the Arabic scholars from the 11th to the 17th centuries who wrote about West Africa.

20 P.F. de Moraes Farias, *op. cit.*, p. 798 *et passim*.
21 Al-Zuhri in J. Cuoq, *op. cit.*, p. 119, translated from the French by the author.
22 D. Conrad and H.J. Fisher, *op. cit.*, Part I, pp. 11–12.
23 Al-Idrisi in J. Cuoq, *op. cit.*, p. 133.
24 Al-Maqrizi in J. Cuoq, *op. cit.*, p. 388.
25 Ibn Khaldun in J. Cuoq, *op. cit.*, p. 343.
26 Al-Zuhri in J. Cuoq, *op. cit.*, p. 120.
27 Conrad and Fisher, *op. cit.*, p. 23 *ff*.
28 Ibid., Part II. The Oral Sources.
29 Al-Bakri (V. Monteil's translation), p. 62.
30 N. Levtzion, *op. cit.*, p. 129.
31 T. Lewicki, "Un Etat Soudanais Médiéval inconnu: le Royaume de Zafunu", *Cahiers d'Etudes Africaines* XI (1971), p. 523.
32 L.S. Feuer, *Marx and Engels* (Glasgow, 1969), p. 210.
33 See, for example, Maxime Rodinson's *Islam and Capitalism*, translated from the French by B. Pearce (London, 1974).
34 M. Weber, "Major Features of World Religions" in R. Robertson, *Sociology of Religion* (Penguin, England, 1969), p. 22.
35 P.F. de Moraes Farias, *op. cit.*, pp. 812–3, states that the Almoravids used the military technique of closed formation, a technique used by Prophet Muhammad. This technique, according to Moraes Farias, although not in the circumstances the most suitable or effective, was employed because it was the holiest technique, "the very original and sacred pattern of the jihad, the most consistent with the Qur'anic words".
36 R. Peters, *op. cit.*, pp. 24–5.
37 Hamdun and King, *Ibn Battuta in Black Africa* (London, 1975), p. 32.
38 J.Schacht, "Sur la diffusion des formes d'architecture religieuse musulmane à travers le Sahara", *Travaux de l'Institut des Recherches Sahariennes* XI (1953), pp. 11 *ff*.
39 Hamdun and King, *op. cit.*, p. 28.
40 See for example Ahmad ibn Fartuwa, "The Kanem Wars" in H.A.R. Palmer, *Sudanese Memoirs* (Lagos, 1928), Vol. 1, p. 56.

3

c. 1000–1600: the religion of court and commerce.

During the period 1000–1600 the majority of the people in West Africa who converted to Islam came from the ranks of the ruling élite, from the merchant class and from among the inhabitants of the towns. Islam, on the other hand, made little impact on the way of life and beliefs of the farmers, fishermen and the people in the rural areas in general.

The principal agents of the spread of Islam in West Africa in this period were Muslim merchants who also performed the role of Muslim missionary, and Muslim scholars and religious specialists who acted as religious, political and moral guides, judges, doctors and diviners.

Islam in the south-western Sahara (Shinqit/Mauretania).

Shinqit, the name given by the inhabitants to a part of the western Sahara most of which is today covered by the Islamic Republic of Mauretania, had no fixed, stable political boundaries during the period under review. There was, however, a certain cultural unity in this region, bounded in the north by the Saharan wilderness known as Hamada, and the Saqiya al-Hamra, the "red river valley", which came to enjoy a reputation for spirituality, mysticism and learning. In the west the Atlantic Ocean formed the boundary while the Senegal River marked the southern limit of the territory and the Niger River acted as a natural boundary in the east.

It must be emphasised that these boundaries were not the result of political deliberation and decision making, nor were they fixed and impenetrable barriers. People in the western Sahara saw themselves in a very general way as being culturally part of this whole region. Today the political boundaries have been, or are in the process of being, fixed. Part of the territory, the former Spanish province of the western Sahara, is being fought over by Morocco and the Polisario Front,[1] while another large section, most of Shinqit, is now the Islamic Republic of Mauretania. The Moors, of mixed Berber and Arab stock, make up the majority of the inhabitants of Mauretania, numbering some 6–700,000. In addition to the Moors there are about 80,000 Tokolor, whose ancestors founded the medieval kingdom of Takrur, and some 40,000 Soninke, descendants of the founders of Ancient Ghana, and about 2,000 Bambara from the region of Segu and Kaarta.

In Chapters 1 and 2 I outlined the beginnings and development of Islam in the western Sahara up to the end of the 11th century A.D. And, in Chapter 2,

I stated that there is some difference of opinion among scholars about the nature and extent of the impact of the Almoravid movement on this region. Some scholars have put forward the view that the Almoravids introduced literacy in Arabic, authorship in Arabic and the Maliki school of Islamic law into the western Sahara and by extension into West Africa as a whole.² Others are of the opinion that the first "durable" conversions to Islam in West Africa were due to Almoravid influence. With regard to the last point we have already seen that Islam was established in a number of centres of West Africa prior to the emergence of the Almoravid movement (see Chapter 2, p. 13).

Concerning the introduction of literacy in Arabic and Arabic authorship there were in all likelihood Muslim communities in existence with people literate in Arabic in Awdaghost, Koumbi-Saleh, Gao, Takrur and elsewhere in West Africa before the rise of the Almoravids. The contribution of the Almoravids in this sphere, therefore, lay not in beginning a tradition of literacy in Arabic but rather in developing that tradition. The Almoravids took a keen interest in Arabic poetry, in Islamic legal texts, in Islamic theological works, all written in Arabic, and in Arabic grammar and syntax.

Furthermore, groups or cells, zawaya, devoted to a stricter observance of Islamic law, the Shari'a, and to Islamic learning which included the study of Arabic syntax and grammar, were organised by 'Abdullah b. Yasin, founder of the Almoravid movement and by the well-known Almoravid scholar and missionary al-Hadrami, who was for a time the *qadi* (judge) in Azuqi, the main settlement of a branch of the Lamtuna Sanhaja. This tradition of learning spread among the Sanhaja and gave rise to communities of scholars who became renowned for among other things their knowledge of Islamic law. The Midlish from the province of Adrar were one such group, and another was the Lamtuna Tajakant of Tiniqi also in Adrar. The members of these scholastic communities (*zawaya*) which were composed of male and female students, became famous as experts on Maliki law. They in fact learned by heart the legal text, Muwatta. This, a two volume work, was the first compendium of Islamic law to be written, and the author was the Medinan scholar Malik b. Anas (d. 796), founder of the Maliki school of jurisprudence, the one followed by the majority of Muslims in West Africa.

Among other important developments during the period, which contributed to the bringing about of profound political, social and religious changes in the western Sahara and beyond its frontiers was the arrival in the region of Arab groups from southern Morocco. Another was the emergence of the Kunta as a religious, intellectual and economic force in the region and elsewhere in West Africa.

Arab migration to the western Sahara.

It is difficult to state when exactly Arab clans from southern Morocco began to emigrate to the western Sahara. It seems that by the 15th century the Banu Hassan, groups of Arab clans claiming a common descent and already established in Morocco by the 14th century, began moving south into the western Sahara. These Arab groups carried arms and were noted for their skills as warriors. Moreover, they enjoyed a number of privileges, including the right to levy a fee (*gharama*) on their tributaries in return for protection against armed attack. They also enjoyed the privilege of using the camps of their tributaries when they were travelling. This relationship at times led to tension and conflict between protector and protected.

By the end of the 16th century the Arabs occupied a dominant position in the western Sahara as the military and ruling class. Alongside this class, although one should not make too precise and clear-cut a distinction between them, was the scholarly class, the zawaya elerisy, whose main preoccupation was teaching and looking after the religious life of the community. The zawaya class was composed in the main but not exclusively of the Sanhaja educated élite, and in addition to teaching and preaching it was also involved in commerce, the organisation of the caravan trade and the supervision of well-digging. Furthermore, the zawaya for the most part did not carry arms and were dependent for protection on the Arab "warrior" class.

In addition to these two classes there were a number of other classes or castes below them in the social hierarchy, such as the white tributaries (lahma), the coloured tributaries (haratin), and lowest of all the artisans, the musicians, hunters, fishermen and slaves. All of these classes were obliged to work for their overlords and pay various taxes and tributes.[3]

The arrival of the Arab warriors in the western Sahara not only led to profound political and social change but also to a cultural change of immense significance for the western Sahara and neighbouring territories. The Arab emigration saw the establishment of Arabic, or more specifically what is known as the Hassaniya dialect of Arabic, as the lingua franca of the region. This, of course, not only anchored even more deeply Arabic culture in the western Sahara but also enabled many more people there to have access to works in Arabic, on Islamic law and the Islamic sciences and thereby contributing to the islamisation of the territory.

The Kunta.

The Kunta, who claim descent from 'Uqba b. Nafi, were and remain a remarkable group of families distinguished by, among other things, their learning.[4] They claim to have originated in Kairouan. From there families of Kunta migrated to Tuwat in Algeria, and then in the 15th century some of them, such as Sidi Muhammad al-Kunti, left Tuwat for the western Sahara. Others travelled to different parts of the Sahara and West Africa. Sidi Muhammad al-Kunti's move to the western Sahara occurred at the same time as the Arab warrior tribes were infiltrating the region and the latter came to respect Sidi Muhammad who earned a reputation as an outstanding scholar, an important religious guide and counsellor of the people.

Sidi Muhammad earned the respect of the Banu Hassan for other reasons as well. Although a scholar and holy man he was prepared to support the military action by the Banu Hassan against the 'Abd-u-Kal Sanhaja, a branch of the Lamtuna to whom he was related through his mother and who held sway in Zammur to the north of Adrar in the western Sahara. There had been a serious disagreement between Sidi Muhammad and his relatives among the

'Abd-u-Kal. With his advice and counsel the Arab warriors won a decisive victory over the 'Abd-u-Kal, and turned the survivors into tributaries, with the exception of the zawaya scholars, forcing them to pay the protection levy (gharama).

In addition to establishing strong ties with branches of the Banu Hassan, Sidi Muhammad also forged close links through marriage with the Tajakant, a group of Lamtuna Sanhaja who emerged at the time of the Almoravids and were still in the 15th century a powerful force in Adrar. Their headquarters were, as we have seen, at Tiniqi where they are said to have built 24 mosques. The Tajakant, in fact, became one of the leading Muslim intellectual and missionary groups in the western Sahara.

Among the other outstanding Kunta figures in the western Sahara was Sidi al-Bakka'i, son of Sidi Muhammad and his wife from the Tajakant. Sidi al-Bakka'i, who settled at Walata, is credited with being a man of great piety and learning, and also with introducing the Qadiriyya brotherhood into West Africa.[5] This brotherhood was founded by Abd al-Qadir al-Jilani (c. 1077 – 1166) in Baghdad, in modern day Iraq. The brotherhood spread from Iraq to Syria and to other parts of the Muslim world before reaching the western Sahara in the second half of the 15th century. The Qadiriyya brotherhood or *tariqa* trained its members in Islamic law and the Islamic sciences, and also in mysticism (*tasawwuf*). Those who became fully qualified mystics or Sufis were regarded as having been endowed with gifts of divine grace (*baraka*). Moreover the people believed that they had the power to pass on their baraka to others and to perform extraordinary actions or miracles.

Following the death of Sidi al-Bakka'i in Walata in c. 1515, the Kunta in the western Sahara began to disperse in different directions. One reason for this dispersal was the feud which occurred between members of Sidi al-Bakka'i's family. Meanwhile, other Kunta families, such as the Kunta al-Sharq, in alliance with Arab clans, combined missionary work and teaching with commercial ventures which took them all across the Sahara from Tuwat in Algeria to Timbuktu, Agades, Borno, Gobir, Katsina and the Volta Basin in search of salt, grain and kola nuts.

By the end of the 16th century, then, there were numerous groups or cells (zawaya) of Muslim scholars in the western Sahara, the majority of whom were devoted to the peaceful expansion of Islam. Arabic had become the lingua franca of the region, and the Muslim brotherhood, the Qadiriyya, had been introduced into the western Sahara. The social and political arrangements in Mauretania, moreover, with the Arab warriors as secular overlords and protectors of the zawaya and other classes, led to stress and tension. Some zawaya scholars eventually decided to resort to arms to revive Islam and establish a greater degree of equality between themselves and their protectors. One scholar has in fact suggested that the tension between these two groups lay at the root of the militant tradition of Islam, which emerged in the western Sahara and the Senegambia in the 17th century and continued on into the 18th and 19th centuries affecting the large areas of West Africa.[6]

Islam in the states of the Senegambia.

The Senegambia, for the purpose of this chapter, comprises that area of West Africa which is today covered by the Republics of Senegal, Gambia, Guinea Bissau and the coastal and central area of Guinea (Conakry). A number of states, such as Takrur and Jolof, were formed in this region during the period under discussion and in this section I will trace the development of Islam in these kingdoms and the rest of the Senegambia, beginning with Takrur.

Islam in Takrur: beginnings and development.

The kingdom of Takrur, the heart of which lay along the Senegal River and which today forms part of the Republic of Senegal, became a Muslim state in the first half of the 11th century. It was a Muslim state in the sense that one of its rulers, War-Dyabe, became a Muslim sometime before his death in 1040 A.D. and made Islamic law (the Shari'a) the law of the kingdom. A number of leading African Muslim scholars, among others, held the view that where the ruler of a state was a Muslim that state belonged to Islam. The Algerian Muslim scholar, 'Abd al-Karim al-Maghili, who taught in various parts of West Africa in the 15th century including Gao (Songhay), Air, Kano and Katsina and who advised rulers such as Askia Muhammad Ture I of Songhay, held this view. So too did Shaykh Usuman dan Fodio, the leader of the 19th-century Islamic reform movement in Hausaland in northern Nigeria.

The Arabic historian, al-Bakri, writing in 1068 A.D., provides us with a brief account of War-Dyabe's conversion and the creation of an Islamic state in Takrur. He states that the people of Takrur — the majority of the population were Tokolor — were adherents of the indigenous religion, worshipping such "idols" as Dukur, until War-Dyabe came to power. He became a Muslim and in al-Bakri's words "established among them (the Tokolor in Takrur) the laws of Islam, forcing them to obey these laws after his own eyes had been opened to the truth (Islam). He, War-Dyabe, died in 432 A.H./ 1040−1 A.D. . . . . today (1068 A.D. when al-Bakri wrote this account) the people of Takrur are Muslims."[1]

There is no indication here as to exactly when War-Dyabe became a Muslim, or about who was responsible for his conversion. Moreover, the conversion was clearly not the result of Almoravid pressure, since War-Dyabe was already a Muslim before 'Abdullah b. Yasin launched the Almoravid movement in the Sahara. War-Dyabe may have been influenced in his decision to become a Muslim by Tareshna al-Lamtuna, the Sanhaja leader who waged a holy war against a community of Sudanese in the Sahara. On the other hand it seems more likely that the ruler of Takrur came to his decision as a result of contacts with Muslim traders and religious guides who frequented commercial centres within Takrur's sphere of political influence.

Takrur controlled for a time the rock salt mines of Awlil in the west of the kingdom, and was relatively close to commercial centres such as Awdaghost, and the gold-producing region of Bambuk, which was situated near the confluence of the Senegal and Faleme rivers. All of this combined to make Takrur an important state both in terms of trans-Saharan and West African commerce, attracting Muslim traders from North Africa, the Sahara and from West African towns such as Koumbi-Saleh, capital of Ancient Ghana, and Gao, for several hundred years capital of Songhay.

Whoever was responsible for War-Dyabe's conversion to Islam, the latter turned out to be a strong-minded Muslim who was determined to spread Islam far and wide. Al-Bakri tells us that War-Dyabe spread Islam to the town of Silla, and the ruler of Silla in turn attempted to impose Islam on the "unbelievers" in the territories surrounding him. [2]

Although the Almoravid movement was not responsible for the introduction of Islam to Takrur it may well have played a part in the later development of Islam in that kingdom. Certainly close ties existed between Takrur and the Almoravids in the 11th century, ties which took the form of a military alliance in 1056 A.D., and perhaps also in 1087 A.D. It is possible that many of the West African soldiers who fought on the side of the Almoravids at the battle of al-Zalaga in Spain in 1087 A.D. came from Takrur.

Though it remained an important commercial centre under strong leadership Takrur declined in size and political importance in the 12th century. Moreover, the name Takrur itself came to be applied by Arabic writers from the Middle East and elsewhere not specifically to the kingdom we have been discussing but either to West Africa as a whole, or to different parts of West Africa, or simply to West African Muslims. [3]

Islam in the Jolof empire and other states of the Senegambia.

The Jolof empire in Senegal was established in the 13th century and according to tradition its founder was Ndiandiane N'Diaye. Jolof consisted of a number of states or provinces including Walo, Cayor, Sine and Saloum, all loosely knit together under the authority of the Bourba (king). The majority of the inhabitants were the Wolof who were noted for, among other things, their highly stratified societies, some ten castes being distinguished below the monarchy.

A Portuguese account of the Jolof empire compiled in 1507 A.D. provides us with some information about the state of Islam among the Wolof at the end of the 15th century. The account states that "The king and all the lords and nobles of the province of Gyloffa (Jolof, the heartland of the Jolof empire) are Muslims and have bischerys (marabouts) who are priests and preachers of Muhammad and can read and write. These marabouts come from far in the interior, for example, from the kingdom of Fez and of Morocco and they come to convert these Negroes to their faith by their preachers. These marabouts make amulets written in Arabic and put them on the neck of the negroes and also on their horses."[4] Marabout is the name given to Muslim religious notables in parts of French-speaking West Africa. To refer to them as priests as is the case in the above account can be misleading. Islam has no hierarchically ordained priesthood in the same sense as, for example, Christianity; consequently it would be perhaps more accurate to describe marabouts as religious guides, specialists, clerics or teachers rather than priests.

From the above account it is clear that Muslim religious teachers from

North Africa were working among the Wolof in the 15th century. Moreover, they appear to have been quite numerous and active. According to an earlier 15th-century source these religious guides were "constantly on duty in the mosques".[5] Their activities, however, were not confined to the mosques, or to writing amulets in Arabic for the Wolof. They in fact played a part in the life of the royal court and presided over important ceremonies, such as the sacred bathing ceremony performed on the occasion of the enthronement of the Damel (ruler) of the province of Cayor.

The development of Islam in the rest of the Senegambia.

With the rise of Mali in the 13th and 14th centuries to a position of great political and economic power in West Africa, Mande-speaking traders from the Upper Niger region began to extend their trading network throughout the length and breadth of the empire, which at the height of its power stretched over a very large area of West Africa from Senegal in the north-west to Air in the north-east, and south almost to the forest zone. Following the imperial flag of Mali, and in some instances preceding it, Mande traders, some of whom were Muslims and were known in parts of West Africa by various names such as Dyula, Yarse, Marka and Wangara, established themselves in towns and villages along the trade routes that criss-crossed West Africa. They also settled along the rivers Senegal and Gambia, and penetrated Gabu and elsewhere in the Senegambia and, as we shall see, the Volta basin and Hausaland. These traders were not traders pure and simple but also teachers and preachers of Islam, and wherever they went they were accompanied by a Muslim religious guide.

It would, of course, be wrong to give the impression that all or even a majority of the Mande merchants went about actively propagating Islam among the non-Muslim people among whom they settled. They did not do this; in fact, in some cases, they lived in relative isolation from the indigenous people and even went so far as to maintain that it was not part of their duty to convert non-Muslims to Islam. In their opinion members of other faiths, including traditional religionists, who lived an upright and honest life, could be saved without becoming Muslims in this life since after death they would enter a kind of purgatory where they would embrace Islam before entering Paradise.[6] Nevertheless the Mande-speaking traders did establish "pockets" of Islam in the Senegambia and by their performance of Islamic prayers and worship they must have given people some idea of the Muslim way of life.

The Jakhanke and Torodbe groups were more directly concerned with education and missionary work though they were also involved in trade. The Jakhanke produced some outstanding scholars and following their founder, al-Hajj Salim Suware, adopted a peaceful approach to the spread of Islam. The Torodbe on the other hand, related to the Tokolor who in turn are related to the Fulani, were not committed to pacifism and over the centuries developed into a very important intellectual and religious force in West Africa, counting among their members Muslim reformers of the calibre of Usuman dan Fodio and al-Hajj 'Umar. Already by the 16th century some of the Torodbe had set up separate Muslim villages in Futa Toro and in other parts of the Senegambia, while others became the religious guides of the Fulani pastoralists moving out with them from the Senegal valley across the savannah region of West Africa, and acting not only as their religious guides but also as mediators between them and other Fulani and non-Fulani groups. The Torodbe, as I mentioned above, unlike the Jakhanke, never disavowed the use of jihad of the sword or military holy war in defence of or for the propagation of Islam. Moreover, they tended to make a clear distinction between dar al-Islam (the land of Islam) and dar al-harb (the land of unbelief).

The Jakhanke are in some respects an exceptional body of Muslim scholars and here I will outline in very summary fashion their history and impact on Islam in the Senegambia up to the end of the 16th century, the point in time when this chapter closes.[7]

The Jakhanke.

A Muslim cleric, al-Hajj Salim Suware, established a community in the 13th century at Diakha Massina, and later re-established it in Diakha-Bambuk in the Senegambia. From these centres followers of al-Hajj Salim Suware moved out to set up Muslim communities in the Senegambia and elsewhere in West Africa. Among the first of these communities to be established were those of Gunjur and Didécoto in Senegal. In these communities people of servile status did the manual work while the educated taught in Qur'anic or *ilm* schools where the Qur'an and Islamic sciences such as *fiqh* (law) were studied. The size of the communities ranged from several hundred to several thousand members, and in addition to book learning one could also learn a trade and become a blacksmith or leather specialist.

The Jakhanke followers of al-Hajj Salim Suware, unlike some of the Mande whom we spoke about, made a point of going out among the people to convert them to Islam. However, as we have seen, they did not believe in the value of jihad of the sword as a means of spreading Islam, and instead preached the necessity of extending the frontiers of Islam by peaceful means. However, it should be pointed out that the tolerant approach of the Jakhanke, an approach similar to that of the Mande, to existing non-Muslim traditions, customs and beliefs helped to produce and foster an Islam that in some respects was regarded as "corrupt" by Muslim reformers belonging to the Torodbe tradition. The Jakhanke, for instance, practised divination with little reference to Islamic teaching, and allowed among other things marriage between a man and his brother's daughter, a practice prohibited by Islamic law.[8]

Islam in the Senegambia, then, remained during the period 1000—1600 the religion of a minority of people. Moreover, of those who became Muslims the majority came from the ruling and merchant classes, notable exceptions being the Torodbe religious guides and the Fulani pastoralists. Furthermore, Islam for most of these converts, excluding people like War-Dyabe of Takrur, appears to have been more of a supplement, an addition to their traditional religion than a replacement. This can be seen in the enthronement ceremony of the Damel (King) of Cayor, a province of the Jolof empire. A Muslim religious leader presided over the sacred bathing ritual, the Khouli-Khouli, and the king was turbanned in Muslim fashion. Not only was the ritual traditional but the Damel, a Muslim, continued to be regarded, and allowed himself to be so, as a sacred being responsible for the prosperity of the community. This responsibility was in fact clearly symbolised in the sacred bathing ceremony by the planting of seeds from local crops in a hole filled with water from the sacred bath. Again, in a number of Senegambian societies where the rulers were Muslims such un-Islamic practices as the matrilineal principle of inheritance and succession persisted.

In some societies Muslims were regarded as irrelevant and useless by rulers and warriors who dismissed them as people who knew nothing other than prayer. However, some rulers and ordinary people took a more positive view of Islam. Rulers valued the fact that Muslims were literate and numerate and could therefore exercise efficiently the functions of treasurer, accountant and historian. They realised clearly that a written language was a valuable additional means of communication, and appreciated the fact that Muslims could be important in terms of forging economic and diplomatic ties with other states, particularly the Muslim lands of North Africa.

Literacy was also esteemed and valued because of its apparent magical properties. As Goody points out "the instruments of writing easily became invested with a supernatural power, particularly where writing is a primarily religious activity. Especially is this true of the ink and other colouring used in writing on paper, papyrus, slates or skins for the material that actually gives concrete embodiment to speech is held to encapsulate the communicative power of the word. To wash the colour from off the writing surface and then swallow it down is to drink in . . . a power which would otherwise remain external to the observer."[9] Many Muslims in West Africa have drunk in the water which had been used to wash off the Qur'anic verses from their slates or writing boards, believing that the Holy Word of the Qur'an can be in some sense absorbed by this practice.

Al-Sa'di, the 17th-century author of the *Ta'rikh al-Sudan* (History of the Sudan), writes about the protective power of religious books such as the Qur'an and the Sahih of al-Bukhari. He relates, for example, the story of the ruler of Farma, who, seeking protection from a rival, put his books on his head and cried out "I place myself under the protection of these books".[10] And al-Idrisi (1100—c. 1166 A.D.) writes of the Tuareg belief in the magical power of the written word. The Tuareg, when they either lost their way or lost something, wrote in the sand and in this way discovered what they were looking for "as if they had seen what was lost in the writing".[11]

In addition to the attractions of literacy some people, such as the Torodbe, who appear to have been formed out of various deprived and dispossessed groups, saw in Islam a means of creating for themselves a cultural identity. Moreover, the Fulani pastoralists who roamed far and wide found in Islam a universal religion which knit them together regardless of space and time. Again as we have seen in the Portuguese account already cited, ordinary people valued the baraka possessed by Muslim missionaries, and looked on these men as being capable of providing them with health and prosperity. Furthermore, the Jakhanke communities and similar Muslim organisations performed a variety of functions relevant to people's needs serving as schools, hospitals, places of refuge, markets and law courts. Also, membership of the Muslim community could lead to the learning of a trade, or provide one with valuable commercial contacts. No doubt for some most important of all, although at times their practice of Islam may appear to have contradicted this, Islam offered a new and original vision of God, man and life which had great appeal.

Many of the points made here about the attraction of Islam for people in the Senegambia apply as we shall see to peoples elsewhere in West Africa.

Islam in Ancient Ghana.

A good deal has already been said about the origins and early development of Islam in Ancient Ghana (see Chapter 2). The kingdom of Ancient Ghana was founded probably as early as the 5th century. At the height of its power in the 11th century it covered a vast area from the southern limits of the Sahara in the north, southwards to within easy reach of the goldfields of Bambuk, and from the Niger River in the east to the Atlantic in the west. This region today forms part of the West African Republics of Mauretania, Senegal and Mali.

The ancestors of the Soninke were probably the founders of Ancient Ghana.[1] They were agriculturalists who once lived in the Sahara. The Soninke themselves, also known as the Sarakole, began to play a more active role in the trans-Saharan trade from the second half of the 8th century and by the 10th century along with Muslim traders from North Africa formed the majority of the floating population of the commercial centres of Sijilmasa and Awdaghost. Moreover, the fact that Ancient Ghana itself indirectly controlled the supplies of gold produced in the Bambuk goldfields located some eight days journey south of Ancient Ghana's capital, Koumbi-Saleh, led to an influx of Muslim merchants from North Africa into Ancient Ghana. These merchants built their own town within Koumbi-Saleh. Al-Bakri described the situation in 1067—8 A.D. when he wrote: "The capital of Ghana is made up of two towns one of which is inhabited by the Muslims. This Muslim town is a big town with twelve mosques, one of which is for public prayers on Fridays. . . . One finds there also Muslim lawyers and academics. . . . The other town, the royal town, is situated six miles away . . . there is also a mosque in the royal town, where Muslim delegations pray. The King chooses his interpreters, his treasurer and most of his ministers from among the Muslims. . . ".[2]

The king of Ancient Ghana was not a Muslim at this time, 1067—8 A.D., though he appointed Muslims to top government posts. Arabic scholars writing in the mid-12th century, however, almost 100 years after al-Bakri, state that the kings of Ghana were certainly Muslims by that time. Al-Zuhri, as we saw in the last chapter, indicates that the kings of Ancient Ghana were Muslims by 1076 A.D. (see Chapter 2, p. 18). Al-Idrisi, the Arabic geographer who wrote his "Book of Roger" in 1154, although he does not give any indication as to when the kings of Ancient Ghana became Muslims, repeats al-Bakri stating that the capital of Ancient Ghana is composed of two towns and goes on to describe it as the biggest city in the Sudan, with the most inhabitants and the most commerce, attracting merchants from all over north-west Africa. Al-Idrisi also states that both the king and the inhabitants of Koumbi-Saleh are Muslims, adding that prayer is said in the king's name. The king was also, according to al-Idrisi, a very just man, and known by people as far away as Morocco to be very wealthy.[3]

Although we remain uncertain as to exactly when and why the kings of Ancient Ghana began to convert to Islam (see Chapter 2, p. 22), it seems probable that the first king of Ancient Ghana to become a Muslim did so sometime in the last quarter of the 11th century or in the very early years of the 12th century. This conversion, moreover, could very well have been, as I mentioned earlier, the result of the influence exerted on the king by Muslims within Ancient Ghana.

As we saw from the accounts from the accounts of al-Bakri and al-Idrisi there were many Muslims in the capital, Koumbi-Saleh, some of whom were employed by the kings as interpreters and commissioners. In addition, there was a mosque close to the royal palace and the kings of Ancient Ghana must have observed Muslims practising their faith, and may well have been impressed by what they saw. Moreover, we have seen that Islam offered rulers, particularly those rulers who were involved in international affairs, like the kings of Ancient Ghana, many positive benefits.

Islam and the decline of Ancient Ghana in the 13th century.

In the 13th century Ancient Ghana was replaced by Mali as the most powerful and the wealthiest kingdom in West Africa. A number of reasons have been put forward to explain this decline of Ancient Ghana, such as its lack of political cohesion. Moreover, some historians suggest that Ancient Ghana's decline was occasioned in part by the fact that trade between Ancient Ghana and North African states slackened off with the result that the state became economically weak.[4] Several reasons are given for this fall-off in trade, one being that the gold mines of Bambuk upon which the strength of Ancient Ghana's economy was based had been partially exhausted of their supplies of gold. In addition, it has been suggested that the trade routes linking Ancient Ghana with North Africa through Awdaghost and Sijilmasa had become unsafe for commerce after Arab warrior tribes had captured Sus and Wadi Dar'a. In addition to the fact that the gold supplies from Bambuk had been depleted and the main trade route north from Ghana had become unsafe, the growing importance of the Taghaza salt mines north-east of Ghana is said to have encouraged traders and commercial firms to move out of Ancient Ghana and go further east to Walata, situated at the terminus of a trans-Saharan route which effectively by-passed Ancient Ghana. Therefore, the argument goes, Muslim merchants moved out of Koumbi-Saleh and other commercial centres in Ghana and settled elsewhere, taking their trade and business with them and contributing to the economic decline of the kingdom.

In addition to these political and economic reasons given for the decline of Ancient Ghana, it is also the opinion of some scholars that religion played a part in the collapse of the empire. These scholars maintain that Ancient Ghana, although she regained her independence later, was permanently weakened by the alleged Almoravid invasion in 1076 — 8 A.D. For example, the French historian, J.C. Froelich, wrote that although Ancient Ghana regained its independence from the Almoravids in 1087 A.D. on the death of 'Abu Bakr b. 'Umar the king "could not recover the power of his predecessors for his former vassal states . . . knew how to preserve their independence." Froelich also states that Islam was at this time proscribed in Ancient Ghana and that the kingdom returned to being a "pagan state".[5] These scholars go on to suggest that the Muslims in Ancient Ghana, inspired by the militant Almoravid type of Islam, acted as hostile agents and helped to undermine the authority of the government in Ancient Ghana. The eventual outcome was that Ancient Ghana, first weakened by the Almoravids, later recovered some of its political and military power only to be overrun again, first by the Susu kingdom to the south in the early years of the 13th century and finally by Mali in the middle years of the 13th century.[6]

This picture of events is not very convincing for a number of reasons. First of all we have seen in Chapter 2 that the evidence in support of the view that the Almoravids conquered and weakened Ancient Ghana is not by any means conclusive. In addition, it has been shown that the rulers of Ancient Ghana, even before they converted to Islam, were sympathetic to Muslims, and that after their conversion they formed alliances with the Almoravids and joined with them in the spread of Islam to Tadmakka (see Chapter 2, p. 20). There is no evidence, further, to suggest that Muslims inside Ancient Ghana acted against the interests of the government and people.

With regard to the suggestion that Ancient Ghana's economy declined as a result of the partial exhaustion of the Bambuk goldfields, here again it is doubtful if this was the case. One reason for this doubt is that the Almoravids received plentiful supplies of gold from West Africa until the middle of the 12th century, and these supplies of gold more than likely continued to come from Bambuk via Ancient Ghana before going north to the Almoravids.[7] Moreover, a number of Arabic sources indicate that Ancient Ghana, far from suffering decline, was strong politically and economically during the 12th and 13th centuries and that even when Mali was at the height of its power Ancient Ghana, though a province of Mali, was strong enough and powerful enough to obtain a number of privileges and concessions from Mali including a considerable degree of political independence. The writings of al-Harrani, an Arabic scholar who wrote in c. 1332 A.D., gives support to this view. He stated that Ancient Ghana was the largest and most important commercial town in the Sudan, and that gold was plentiful there, that its ruler had under him a large army and exercised authority over a number of other states.[8] Al-Umari, the Arabic geographer writing in c. 1337 A.D., asserted that "throughout the Mali empire no-one bore the title king except the ruler of Ghana who is, however, only the deputy of the king of Mali although he 'has the title of king".[9]

It is not clear, therefore, why Ancient Ghana was superceded by Mali as the dominant power in the Western Sudan, but it is reasonably certain that she was not, at least until sometime in the 14th century, a mere puppet of Mali.

Ancient Ghana never became in any real sense a Muslim state. It is true that its rulers became Muslims and assisted in the expansion and reform of Islam in surrounding areas, but they do not seem to have attempted to make Islamic law the law of their kingdom. Although they dressed as Muslims and allowed they daily activities to be in some respects regulated by Islamic practices, the indigenous legal system and a variety of other un-Islamic customs were retained. It was still necessary, for example, to prostrate and cover one's head with sand or dirt on entering the presence of the ruler, a practice which Islam objects to on the grounds that it gives exaggerated respect and importance to a human being. Moreover, rulers continued to be seen as "sacred" and in possession of supernatural or mysterious powers, while 'magic' was practised on a large scale.

Islam in Ancient Ghana, therefore, was at best an adjunct to the traditional religion. Furthermore, it was, in the main, the religion of the rulers, the court officials, the merchant class and the townspeople.

Islam in Mali.

Islam in Mali from c. 1050 to 1250.

Mallel was the name given to Mali by Arab geographers and historians. Al-Ya'qubi, writing in the 9th century A.D., states that Mallel, about 12 days distance from Ancient Ghana, was at war with Kanem.[1] Mallel or Mali was a Mandinka chiefdom at this time. Al-Bakri in 1068 A.D. made reference to Mallel and another Mandinka chiefdom, Do.[2] And again in the 12th century al-Idrisi, writing about the country of the Lamlam, by which he most probably meant Mandinka country, states that in the whole of Lamlam there are only two small towns, like villages, one is called Malal and the other Do.[3] In the 11th century the Keita clan, as we shall see, particularly under their ruler Mamadi-Kani and with the support of the hunters' association, gave a semblance of unity and cohesion to the Mandinka chiefdoms.

The Keita claim descent from a certain Bilali Bunama, who may well be Bilal b. Rahab, the black companion of Prophet Muhammad and the first *muezzin* (Mu'adhdin), the one who calls the people to prayer. Ibn Hasham, who wrote in the 9th century, was told by one who studied Islamic tradition that "when the apostle (Prophet Muhammad) entered the Ka'ba in the year of the conquest (630 A.D.) in company with Bilal he ordered him to call the people to prayer".[4]

A number of Mali traditions point to the descent of the Keita from Bilali Bunama. In one of these traditions, which recounts the role of Sundiata in the establishment of the Mali empire, we read that "Bilali Bunama, ancestor of the Keitas, was the faithful servant of Prophet Muhammad . . . . Bilali Bunama had seven sons of whom the eldest, Lawalo, left the holy city and came to settle in Mali; Lawalo had Latal Kalabi for a son, Latal Kalabi had Damul Kalabi, who then had Lahilatoul Kalabi. Lahilatoul Kalabi was the first black prince to make the pilgrimage to Mecca".[5] According to another account Bilali Bunama himself is said to have come from Mecca to Mali, and his grandson, Lalal Kalabi, is credited with establishing by conquest the Keita chiefdom situated between the Niger and Sankarani Rivers.[6] Ibn Khaldun, too, writing in the 1370s and 1380s, states that the rulers of Mali had been Muslim for quite some time, and that the first Muslim king of Mali to make the pilgrimage to Mecca was Barmandana, and that other rulers followed his example.[7]

Although on certain points these traditions appear to contradict one another, they all nevertheless indicate, as Levtzion states, "an early Islamic influence among the Keita before the rise of the empire of Mali".[8] It is clear in fact from al-Bakri's 11th-century account of the conversion of the king of Mallel that Islam had begun to penetrate the Mandinka chiefdoms some 200 years before Mali began to emerge as a strong, imperial power in the middle of the 13th century. According to al-Bakri the ruler of Mallel was converted to Islam by a Muslim missionary and trader who was staying with the king as a guest, at a time when the country was afflicted with drought. The king's guest promised to pray for rain if the king and his people became Muslims. The king, having already prayed for rain to the local gods without success, accepted the terms offered by the missionary. Al-Bakri's account finishes like this: "They prayed throughout the night, the Muslim reciting invocations and the King saying Amen. The dawn had just begun to break when Allah brought down abundant rain. The King then ordered that the idols be broken and the sorcerers expelled from his country. He together with his descendants and the nobility became sincerely attached to Islam, but the common people of the kingdom remained traditional religionists . . . the kings have ever since been given the title al-Muslimani (the Muslims)".[9]

Oral and written sources, therefore, indicate that Islam had begun to influence the leaders in some Mandinka chiefdoms by the first half of the 11th century. After these conversions, however, it seems that there was something of a reaction against Islam. Al-Idrisi wrote in 1154 A.D. that the people of the Mandinka chiefdoms were plunged in unbelief and ignorance, and described one of their initiation rites which involved marking with fire the face and temples of one who had reached the age of puberty.[10]

By the middle of the 12th century the Mandinka chiefdoms had not been welded together into one kingdom under a central government. Some progress, however, was being made, as I have pointed out, towards the greater consolidation and unification of these chiefdoms. Drawn into a wider trading network with the opening up of the Buré goldfields, chiefs like Mamadi-Kani of the Keita with the assistance of hunters' associations (donso-ton) began building up their military and political strength. By the beginning of the 12th century the Keita clan based on the Sankarani River had come to be regarded by other Mandinka chiefdoms as the most powerful and senior Mandinka clan.

Nevertheless, over a century later, in the first half of the 13th century, the Mandinka chiefdoms were not sufficiently united or strong enough to prevent their territory being overrun by Sumanguru, ruler of the Soso. It was not in fact until the reign of Sundiata (known also as Mari-Djata), c. 1230—c. 1255 A.D., that there is evidence of a strong, expansionist Mali kingdom composed of the different Mandinka chiefdoms.

Islam in Mali from Sundiata to Mansa Musa.

Sundiata, by his victories over the Soso ruler Sumanguru at the battles of Nequeboria and Kangique, had convinced a number of chiefs that their security and safety, threatened by Sumanguru, could only be guaranteed if they gave him their support. Consequently these chiefs, among them the kings of Do and Kri, Traore and Sibi, gathered on the plains of Sibi to pledge their support for Sundiata. "All the allies," the griot of Mali states, "had arranged to meet him in the great plain of Sibi and all the children of the Savannah were there about their kings. . . . Pennants of all colours fluttered above the sofas divided up by tribes." Sundiata was greeted "by all the sons of Mali . . . all those who say N'Ko . . . all who spoke the clear language of Mali were represented at Sibi and welcomed Sundiata shouting: 'Maghan Sundiata, Son of Sogolon, Son of Nane Maghan, assembled Mali awaits you. . . . You Maghan, you are Mali. . .'."[11] Here there is clear evidence of a greater unity and sense of Malian identity among the different, previously loosely knit, Mandinka chiefdoms.

It was not, however, until the battle of Krina in c. 1230 A.D. that Sumanguru was decisively defeated by Sundiata and his allies. This battle formed another landmark in the political history of Mali. It gave greater unity and cohesion to the Mali kingdom and placed Sundiata in a powerful position with regard to other states in West Africa. Having conquered the Soso, Sundiata was now free to establish the rule of Mali over a wide area of West Africa. The boundaries of Mali were pushed outwards into and beyond Futa Jallon to the lower Casamance in the Senegambia and further north and east.

After the battle of Krina and the wars of expansion the allies of Sundiata gathered at Ka-Ba. Sundiata, and this is a point to be noted, wore on this occasion the same clothes as a Muslim king. At this meeting, as at Sibi, rulers of different states pledged their loyalty to Sundiata. They even went further. They acknowledged that their authority and position as kings were a gift to them from Sundiata. In other words Sundiata had the right to appoint and dismiss them. He was their overlord and ruler. In his address to Sundiata at Ka-Ba, the King of Sibi emphasised this point. "It is from you," he told Sundiata, "that I derive my kingdom for I acknowledge you as my sovereign. My tribe and I place ourselves in your hands. I salute you supreme chief, Fama of Famas. I salute you Mansa." Twelve rulers at Ka-Ba proclaimed Sundiata Mansa. As the griot recalled, "He had become emperor".[12]

I mentioned that at Ka-Ba Sundiata wore Muslim dress and this he did, I believe, because he was anxious to be seen not as the ruler of one particular state within Mali or the chief-priest of one particular religion but as king of a whole federation of states. And since Islam would not be regarded as local and particularist by the assembled gathering of kings, some of whom were Muslims, but rather as a universal, international creed, Sundiata chose to present himself as a Muslim leader on this occasion. On other occasions, for example when he returned to the heartland of the Mali empire, he changed his Muslim dress for traditional clothing.

Sundiata was converted to Islam by the grandfather of a certain Mudrik

Ibn Faqqua. Ibn Battuta is writing about the unpopularity of Mansa Sulayman when he makes this reference to the conversion of Sundiata, "His (Sulayman) successor was Mansa Magha, and before him reigned Mansa Musa, a generous and virtuous king who loved whites and gave gifts to them. . . . I heard from a trustworthy source that he gave 3,000 mithqals on one day to Mudrik Ibn Faqqus, by whose grandfather his own grandfather, Saraq Jata (Sundiata) had been converted to Islam."[13] Sundiata was perhaps born a Muslim and turned to the traditional religion while in exile, and then, perhaps for the reasons mentioned above, turned back to Islam when he began to rule Mali.

Mansa Uli, Sundiata's son and successor, was also a Muslim and is believed to have made the pilgrimage to Mecca. It was during his reign that the important commercial and religious centre of Walata, situated at the southern end of a trans-Saharan trade route, came under Mali control. This control of Walata exposed Mali to greater Islamic influence by putting her in more direct and frequent contact with Muslim merchants and missionaries who frequented Walata or used it as a base. Later, other commercial centres such as Gao, Timbuktu and Jenne also came under Mali's authority and had a similar effect in terms of the diffusion of Islamic influence.

Mansa Sakura (1285 — 1300), a usurper who was assassinated while returning from the pilgrimage, provided Mali with some cohesion and this attracted Muslim merchants from many parts of North Africa. Nevertheless, the last years of the 13th century and the first years of the 14th century were ones of instability in Mali, an instability caused in the main by rivalry among potential rulers and the lack of a definite and acceptable procedure for succession to the office of Mansa.

Islam in Mali during the reign of Mansa Musa, 1307 — 1332.

According to the Arabic scholar al-Umari (1301 — 1349), who wrote in the 1340s and had a plentiful supply of information on West Africa, Mansa Musa did a great deal to promote the development of Islam in Mali. Al-Umari stated: "The present king of Mali is called Sulayman and he is the brother of Mansa Musa . . . it was in effect his brother (Mansa Musa) who built the places of prayer, the mosques and the minarets, and set in motion congregational prayer on Friday . . . it was he (Mansa Musa) who brought to his country Islamic lawyers of the Maliki school of law. He was regarded as the Sultan of the Muslims. He devoted himself to the study of religion".[14] Other authors give a similar account of Mansa Musa's efforts on behalf of Islam in Mali and describe him as a devout, virtuous and pious ruler.

One of the high points in Mansa Musa's reign was his pilgrimage to Mecca which took place, according to Ibn Khaldun, in 1324 A.D.[15] He was accompanied on this pilgrimage by a very large number of people, some authors put the number at 8,000, others at 12,000 and one put it as high as 60,000. The size of Mansa Musa's entourage was perhaps much less than any of these figures suggests but it was nevertheless very large and attracted the attention of many people at the time. In addition to the large entourage Mansa Musa also took with him vast amounts of gold which he disposed of by giving almost every ruler and important government official he encountered "a gift in the form of a load of gold". In fact he is reported to have distributed so much gold in Cairo that its value there fell.

The pilgrimage to Mecca seems to have inspired Mansa Musa to make considerable efforts to promote Islam in Mali. We have already seen from al-Umari's account some of the things which he did in this respect (see p. 43). In addition he began the practice of sending students from Mali to Islamic centres in North Africa for further education in Islamic studies. He is said to have commissioned the Spanish architect al-Sahili to design mosques and palaces. He bought large numbers of books on Islamic law, and brought to Mali from Egypt and Arabia Sharifs, that is Muslim missionaries who could claim descent from the family of Prophet Muhammad and his grandsons Hassan and Hussein. The Sharif, in his green turban which is a mark of distinction, performed many functions such as healing, praying and divining. They travelled widely and did a great deal to extend the frontiers of Islam. They enjoyed, moreover, considerable status in the eyes of ordinary Muslims, who saw them as the protectors of the orthodox Islam faith which they spread wherever they went. Coming from Mecca, the centrepoint of the Islamic world, they no doubt forged closer ties between the Islamic world of West Africa and that of North Africa and the Middle East.

Although the reign of Mansa Musa was important in terms of the development of Islam in Mali and other areas of West Africa, its impact should not be exaggerated. It was in the main, as in Ancient Ghana, the rulers, the court officials, the administrators, the merchants, the intelligentsia and the townspeople who were Muslims. Islam was the religion of the élite, and of the important commercial centres in Mali. Nevertheless, some of the ordinary people in the rural areas and the less important commercial centres may also have become Muslims. Al-Umari stated that the king of Mali had under his authority "pagans" some of whom converted to Islam. The Mali empire was all the same overwhelmingly non-Muslim at this time, a situation that led Mansa Musa into holy war against the non-Muslim population of his empire. He did not, however, attempt to convert the people in the gold-producing areas. Any attempt to convert or control these people met with resistance and would have led to a fall in gold production, thereby seriously affecting Mali's economy. There were, therefore, limits to what a Muslim ruler could do for the cause of spreading Islam.

Ibn Battuta and Islam in Mali.

Ibn Battuta (1304 – 1368/1377 A.D.) was a globe-trotter who travelled far more widely than the average person even today. Leaving his home in North Africa at the age of 21 he travelled until he was almost 50 years old. He went across North Africa on pilgrimage, visiting Morocco, Algeria, Tunisia, Egypt, and then on to Israel, Lebanon, Syria, Jordan and Arabia. He then visited among other places Somalia, Tanzania, Turkey, southern Russia, Iran, Pakistan, India, Ceylon, Malaysia, Indonesia, China, Spain, and ended up by crossing the Sahara to Mali in 1352 A.D. In his book "Travels" Ibn Battuta describes what he saw of Islam in Mali, and according to some scholars he has provided us with "one of the most reliable sources that has come down to us from pre-modern times".[16]

While in Mali Ibn Battuta met and discussed with Muslims, visited Muslims in their homes, attended the mosque for congregational prayer on Fridays, and was present at Muslim festivals and ceremonies. He also met the ruler of Mali who at that time was Mansa Sulayman, emperor from 1337 to 1359, brother of Mansa Musa, and on occasion attended the audiences he held for his people.

Among the things that impressed Ibn Battuta about the Muslims he met was the way in which they meticulously observed the times of the prayers (salat) and the attendance at congregational prayer on Friday. "On Fridays," he wrote, "if a man does not go early to the mosque he cannot find space to pray because of the large number of people there." People also showed great concern about cleanliness. Ibn Battuta says they put on good, white clothes on Friday and if a person had only a tattered shirt he washed it and wore it for the Friday service in the mosque. People, moreover, attached a great deal of importance to the learning of the Qur'an by heart. Parents made sure their children applied themselves seriously to this task, punishing them severely for laziness or indifference. Ibn Battuta visited a Muslim *qadi* (judge) on the occasion of an Islamic festival and saw that the judge's children were tied up. He asked the judge why he did not release them and was told that the children would remain tied up until they knew the Qur'an by heart. He also tells us that *zakat* or almsgiving, one of the five pillars of Islam, was practised in Mali.[17]

Nevertheless although people were conscientious about attending Friday prayers, and learning the Qur'an by heart, traditional customs and practices, some of them un-Islamic, persisted and to an extent were encouraged by the Muslim rulers of Mali. The practice of prostration in the presence of the king remained even though, as I have already mentioned, in the eyes of the orthodox Muslims one should only prostrate as a sign of dependence on and submission to God. Divination was widespread in Mali, and the matrilineal system of inheritance and succession continued on long after the rulers had become Muslims. Also, in a number of areas under Mali's sphere of influence, such as Walata, Ibadite views and practices still existed in Ibn Battuta's time. Again, almost all traditional titles given to court and government officials continued to be used. Finally, Islamic law and the Islamic system of justice were not fully applied in Mali at this time although there were many Muslim lawyers and experts in the capital. However, law and order were well maintained and security was excellent. No-one according to Ibn Battuta had any need to fear being molested or robbed.

The Muslim rulers of Mali, moreover, although they surrounded themselves with Muslim judges, scholars and holy men, also paid heed to the philosophers and priests of the traditional religion. Ibn Battuta made this point when he wrote about the poets of the traditional culture who stood before the king on a festival day and recited their poetry which he said was "a kind of preaching". Ibn Battuta continued, "In it (the poetry) they tell the Sultan that such and such were the good deeds of one and such and such of another (past king). 'So do good that good will be recounted of you.' "[18] The

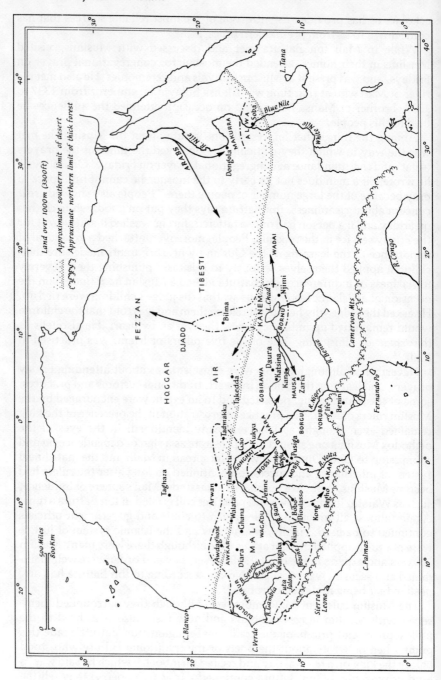

IV States of the Sudan in the 14th and 15th centuries

power and influence of the traditional culture was in fact so strong that a Muslim ruler even had he wanted to could not have disregarded it.

Islam in Mali, then, during this period was the religion of the ruler, of the royal court, of the élite, the merchants and the townspeople, and it was an Islam adapted to fit in with the traditional culture.

Islam in Songhay, c. 1000−1600.

The arrival and early development of Islam in Songhay.

During the second half of the 15th century Songhay replaced Mali as the strongest political and economic power in West Africa, and from the reign of Sunni Ali, which began in 1464, until the Moroccan invasion of 1591, Songhay was the largest and most powerful of the West African states.

According to one tradition, the first ruler of Songhay, Za al-Ayaman, was a Muslim. He is said to have ruled sometime in the 7th century.[1] Another theory put forward is that the first dynasty or ruling house was Christian of Berber stock from Libya.[2] It is impossible, given our limited knowledge of Songhay history, to substantiate either of these two viewpoints. Another theory on the origins of the Songhay kingdom suggests that Sorko fishermen from the Lake Chad region and Gow farmers possibly related to the Sorko fishermen moved up the Niger at some unknown date and formed the nucleus of a state centred on Kukiya, about 100 kilometres south of Gao on the Niger river. Gao itself was evidently quite well established by the 9th century and in 872 A.D. the Arabic scholar, al-Yaqubi, described it as the most important kingdom of the Sudan.[3] Moreover, by the 9th century Gao had made its first contacts with Islam. There was an expatriate Muslim community in Gao by this time composed of Muslim Arab and Berber merchants from North Africa.

The rulers of Songhay seem to have become Muslims sometime around 1000 A.D. One Arabic author writing in 996 A.D. mentioned that the king of Gao was a Muslim,[4] while in the history of West Africa written in the 17th century known as the "Tarikh al-Sudan" it is stated that Za-Kossoi, ruler of the Songhay in Kukiya, became a Muslim in 1010 A.D.[5] Za-Kossoi almost immediately after his conversion transferred the capital of Songhay from Kukiya to Gao, and Gao remained the capital until 1497 when Askiya Muhammad Ture I, ruler of Songhay from 1493 to 1528, moved it to Tendirma. Al-Bakri, writing in 1068 A.D., said the ruler of Gao professed Islam and that when he was enthroned he was presented with a copy of the Qur'an, a sword and a shield, all sent from the Caliph (leader) of the Muslim world who at that time resided in Baghdad, the capital of modern-day Iraq.

Although the ruler was a Muslim and appointed Muslims to top posts in government, the ceremonials at the royal court continued to be based on traditional customs and beliefs, and the majority of the people in Gao were non-Muslims. As with Koumbi-Saleh in Ghana there were two parts to the town of Gao. In one sector, the royal quarter on the east bank of the Niger, lived the king and the courtiers, and in the other sector were the rest of the population with the Muslim community living apart. There were at least two mosques, one of which was a Friday mosque.[6]

Islam made little progress over the centuries in Gao for, according to one account, the majority of the city's inhabitants were still adherents of the traditional religion in the 13th century.[7] Ibn Battuta's account of his visit to Gao in 1352 A.D. indicates that there were some local Muslims in an otherwise largely non-Muslim population. Gao was, according to Ibn Battuta, "a big city on the Nile, one of the best of the cities of the blacks", and he adds that there was one mosque there for the 'whites', the Muslim merchants from North Africa, implying thereby that there was another one for the local inhabitants.[8]

Gao, for a time in the 13th and 14th centuries a province of Mali, was turned into the capital of a large empire, the Songhay empire, during the reign of Sunni Ali who ruled from 1464 to 1492 A.D. Sunni Ali, further, by incorporating Timbuktu and Jenne into the Songhay empire, gave Songhay control over three of the most important commercial and Islamic centres in West Africa. Timbuktu, founded in the 11th century, had by the late 15th century virtually replaced Walata as the main terminus of the trans-Saharan trade route from North Africa. In Timbuktu there were many Muslim scholars and businessmen who had moved there from Walata to join others from Egypt, Fes, Tuwat, Dra'a and elsewhere. Not all the Muslim scholars and businessmen, however, were expatriates. There were many indigenous Muslims who engaged in trade and commerce, taught the Qu'ran and Islamic studies and held the position of *qadi* (judge) and *imam*. Timbuktu, moreover, prided itself on being a Muslim town and boasted of never having known "idol worship".

Jenne was similar to Timbuktu. According to Al-Sa'di the first ruler of Jenne to be converted to Islam was Kunburu around 1200 A.D. By this time, it is estimated, there were 4,200 *ulama* in the town.[9] This figure is probably an exaggeration but it does indicate that Muslim scholars were fairly numerous at this time in Jenne. Jenne became an important commercial centre attracting merchants from Muslim North Africa and elsewhere. From Jenne Muslim merchants carried Islam across the Volta Basin to the fringes of the tropical forest from the late 14th and early 15th centuries, colonising such towns as Begho, close to the Akan goldfields.

Sunni Ali's attitude to Islam and to the 'Ulama (teachers of Islamic law and theology).

Sunni Ali has been described as a tyrant, a persecutor of Muslim scholars and as little more than a nominal Muslim.[10] In 1469 he drove many Muslim scholars from Timbuktu believing that they were cooperating with his opponents, the Tuareg. He carried out another purge of Muslim scholars in the same city in 1486 A.D. These purges earned Sunni Ali the reputation of being a bloodthirsty dictator. Although it is true that he favoured and repected some 'ulama he was also accused of playing at being a Muslim, of making a joke of Islam. It is reported that he said the five daily prayers, normally said at different specific times of the day, in one prayer session and remained seated while he said them. We are told he simply sat down and prayed saying "This is the morning prayer, this is the midday prayer, this is the afternoon prayer, etc".[11] Furthermore, he never attended the congregational prayers at the mosque on Fridays, and refused to allow the members of his court to pray or keep the fast during Ramadan. He did, however, employ Muslims as secretaries and administrators, but rarely if ever did he give them key positions. Sunni Ali continued to believe in and practise the traditional religion, though he gave the appearance at times of being a Muslim. In many respects he resembled Sundiata of Mali.

Sunni Ali's attitude towards Islam can be explained to some extent by the fact that he found that the pathway to success and security as leader was through the traditional religion and culture and not through Islam. He made Songhay into a large empire, he had never lost a battle, and everyone agrees that he was a courageous and fearless man. He probably believed, therefore, that though Islam was important to a ruler offering him many skills such as literacy, and important in terms of trading connections, the powers and the knowledge gained from a thorough grasp of the traditional sciences such as divination and geomancy were even more important in terms of political success. As a descendant, moreover, of the Za kings he could claim before the majority of Songhay's non-Muslim population to be the lawful ruler of

I The famous centuries-old mosque in Jenne with mud walls many feet thick

Songhay and to have inherited extraordinary powers, skills and knowledge which would enable him to defend and protect their interests. Finally, there was the question of the Muslim population being by and large expatriate and therefore possibly siding with opponents of his regime. He believed this to be true of the Tuareg in particular, who had lost control of Timbuktu and were political and economic rivals of Songhay, and who in their mosques could give sanctuary to opponents of the regime.

After Sunni Ali relations between the rulers of Songhay and the 'ulama were to improve considerably although a certain tension was always there. One reason for this tension was the growing tendency among some of the 'ulama class to abandon the principle of neutrality and non-involvement in politics, a principle followed by the Jakhanke and other Muslim scholars, and to agitate for the establishment of a truly Islamic state and an end to all accommodation with and tolerance of non-Islamic laws and practices by Muslim rulers. Al-Maghili is a good example of such a trend among the 'ulama and he had many followers and supporters in Songhay and elsewhere.

Islam in Songhay from the reign of Askiya Muhammad Ture I (1493–1528) until the Moroccan invasion in 1591.

Sunni Ali was succeeded by his son, 'Abu Bakr Da'ud (Sunni Barou), who ruled Songhay for only a few months from January to April 1493 and refused during this time to declare himself a Muslim. This gave a former commander in Sunni Ali's army, Muhammad Ture, the opportunity to overthrow Sunni Barou. At the battle of Anfao in April 1493 Muhammad Ture defeated Sunni Barou, and taking the title Askiya Muhammad I, ruled Songhay from 1493 to 1528. He was forced to abdicate his throne in 1528 because it was said his blindness made him incapable of ruling. He died in 1538 A.D.

Like Sunni Ali, Askiya Muhammad I, known as Askiya the Great, expanded the political frontiers of Songhay. However, unlike Sunni Ali, he gave much more encouragement to Muslims and assisted in a number of ways the spread and development of Islam. In the first 25 years of his reign in particular he gave active support to Muslim scholars, listened to their advice, appointed them to government posts, allowed them a great deal of independence and gave them a number of privileges. One of the Muslim scholars whom Askiya turned to for advice was the well-known Muslim academic, al-Maghili from Tlemcen in Algeria. Al-Maghili's advice to Askiya was an important piece of advice in terms of its impact on West African history in general and Islamic history in West Africa in particular. It contained ideas and opinions which not only influenced the behaviour and outlook of Askiya Muhammad I but even more so perhaps the thoughts and actions of Muslim reformers such as Usuman dan Fodio of Nigeria (see chapters 4 and 5).[12] One of the important ideas which al-Maghili emphasised was the idea that every hundred years a Muslim reformer, a *mujaddid*, would arise and purify Islam, eradicating from it all traces of un-Islamic beliefs and practices. This idea played an important role in the Muslim reform movements of the 18th and 19th centuries in West Africa.

Al-Maghili advised Askiya with regard to what he should do about

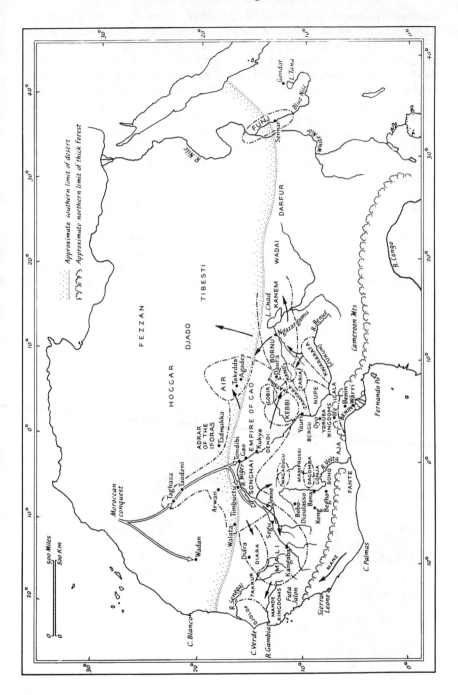

V States of the Sudan in the 16th century

Muslims who taught or practised Islam incorrectly, on when and in what circumstances a holy war (jihad of the sword) should be fought and on many other matters, such as the way to dispense justice according to the precepts of the Qur'an. Another important piece of advice that al-Maghili gave was that Askiya should in no circumstances allow half-educated, semi-literate Muslim teachers to teach and misinterpret the doctrines of Islam and earn a livelihood thereby. No-one, he stated, should treat the Islamic faith as a "commercial product", packaging it and selling it in order to make a living. It should not be watered down or changed to suit people's needs and circumstances, nor the needs and circumstances of rulers if these clashed with its true message. Askiya took some of al-Maghili's advice seriously while ignoring, perhaps for political reasons, the rest.

From the time of Askiya the Great's deposition in 1528 until 1537 Songhay went through a period of instability at the centre of government. Askiya Musa, the son of Askiya Muhammad whom he had overthrown, was himself ousted by a coup in 1531. His successor, Askiya Benkan, was in turn overthrown by another son of Askiya the Great, Askiya Ismail, in 1537. Askiya Ismail died in 1539. But this time there was no coup and Songhay entered a period of peace and stability which was to last about 40 years.

II The 16th-century Sankore mosque at Timbuktu which was restored in the 17th century

Askiya Ishaq I (1539 — 49) and Askiya Da'ud were Muslim kings along the lines of Askiya the Great. They gave Islam an important place in their thinking and political behaviour, but by no means to the exclusion of the traditional religion.

In 1591, during the reign of Askiya Ishaq II, a Moroccan army under its commander Judar Pasha invaded Songhay and brought about the collapse of the central authority of the empire. The various provinces of the empire seized this opportunity to assert their independence and Gao, Timbuktu and Jenne came under a system of Moroccan indirect rule. Songhay's failure to integrate many of the provinces of the empire into the political system and its internal disunity, brought about through a civil war in the 1580s and disputes over succession to the throne, helped to make the Moroccan invasion possible and successful.

The situation, then, of Islam in Songhay changed when Askiya Muhammad Ture I came to power in 1493. His attitude towards the Muslim community was much more positive than that of Sunni Ali. As we have seen Muslim support was far more important to Askiya than it was to Sunni Ali or any of his predecessors. The former set out to please the Muslim élite and was always frightened of losing their support. He was sensitive, moreover, to any adverse criticism made against him by the Muslim community. On one occasion, after losing a battle, he is said to have stated that the defeat was less painful to bear than the thought of what might be said of him by his critics in the Sankore mosque in Timbuktu.[13]

Askiya, nevertheless, believed that Islam had a great deal to offer in terms of education, religion, law and culture, and therefore treated the Muslim community well. He made the Muslim scholar, Umar b. Muhammad Naddi Koi, one of the most important dignitaries in the empire, giving him the right to possess a drum, the sign of a very important official. Muslims, moreover, were among the very few people allowed to dine with the emperor, and the only people he stood up to greet were the Muslim scholars and people return ing from the pilgrimage. While, therefore, Askiya Muhammad Ture I and some of his successors realised the valuable contribution Muslim scholars could and did make to the state, one also has the impression that they were at the same time suspicious of the scholars and that a certain tension existed between rulers and scholars, in particular between rulers and the highly educated scholars who had links with the wider Muslim world and were not directly involved in government or administration.[14]

Islam in Air.

Arrival and development.

Air, inhabited by a large number of Tuareg and situated to the east of the Songhay empire, today forms part of the West African Republic of Niger. Askiya Muhammad Ture I of Songhay passed through this region both on his way to Mecca in 1495 and on his return from Mecca in 1497. He also launched military campaigns against Air in 1500 A.D. and in 1514 — 15, and compelled the Sultan of Agades to pay tribute.[1]

The Tuareg, or Imashagen (noble and free) as they call themselves, are a very diverse group of people. They are found in many places in Africa including Algeria, Libya, Mali, Niger and Nigeria, and played an important role in the establishment of Islam in Air and also in its development in other parts of West Africa. It is not certain when the Tuareg themselves first came into contact with Islam. One historian thinks that groups of Tuareg in the Fezzan and the surrounding areas in southern Libya began to turn to Islam around the year 700 A.D., and that some of these Islamised Tuaregs had probably established themselves as the ruling group in Air as early as the 10th century.[2] These Tuaregs, while engaged in the commerce and trade carried on across the Sahara between North and West African states, would have encountered and been influenced by Muslim merchants and missionaries belonging to the unorthodox form of Islam known as Kharijism, or a milder form of this unorthodoxy espoused by the Ibadis.[3] Moreover, to the west of Air in Tadmakka in Adrar of the Iforas, now a part of Mali, a number of Tuaregs had become Muslims by the 10th century. Here again these Tuaregs had come under the influence of Ibadi Muslim merchants. This may explain why the Almoravids and Ancient Ghana probably waged a jihad against Tadmakka in the 1080s. They were not it seems aiming at establishing Islam for the first time in Tadmakka but at converting the Muslims there to orthodox Islam.

Over the centuries the Tuareg Muslim scholars known as Ineslemen, meaning Islam or Muslim, helped to make Tadmakka an important centre of Islamic learning and mysticism. In the 15th century, as Tadmakka declined, many of these Muslim scholars moved out and settled in Timbuktu, Takedda and Agades in Air. Ibn Battuta, the Arabic writer and indefatigable traveller, visited Takedda in 1352 and left us his impressions of the Tuareg inhabitants there. He informs us that their main preoccupation was commerce. He also said that a man who wants to marry a woman among them had to settle in the country near them (that is, near the woman).[4] In other words the people held to the matrilocal system of marriage whereby the man is obliged to go and live in the woman's home area. In addition to the matrilocal system of marriage the Tuareg of Takedda also kept to the non-Islamic matrilineal system of succession although their rulers were Muslims. For evidence of this we can turn again to Ibn Battuta who recalled that when he met Izar, the Sultan of Takedda, the Sultan was with his sister's sons "who will inherit his kingdom".[5] Again, from Ibn Battuta we can conclude that there must have been a fairly large North African Muslim community in Takedda for he tells us that he stayed near that part of the town inhabited by Muslims from North-west Africa who had their own Muslim shaikh, Sa'id b. Ali al-Jazul, and their own Muslim judge (qadi), 'Abu Ibrahim Ishaq al-Janati.[6]

Iferouan in the north and Agades in the south of Air were also centres of Islam. One of the most famous Muslim sanctuaries in Air was the great mosque at Agallal near Iferouan, built in 1480. It was about the same time as this mosque was built that Agades, founded around 1460 and capital of Air from that time onwards, had come to be regarded as a "land of Islam". Muslim scholars from the Middle East, and North and West Africa travelled to Agades to teach. Among them was Shaykh Zakariya b. 'Abdullah from Baghdad, in modern-day Iraq. This Muslim holy man and teacher is credited

III The Agades mosque

with the building of the great mosque in Agades between 1530 and 1550, a mosque which still today dominates the city and the surrounding landscape. Moreover, some 200 years after the building of this mosque Muslim students, such as Shaikh Usuman dan Fodio from Hausaland in northern Nigeria, continued to travel to Agades to study there under well-known Muslim scholars. Agades, therefore, enjoyed for several hundred years the reputation of being an important centre of Islamic intellectual and mystical life, and among those responsible for laying the foundations of this reputation were the Tuareg aided by the Egyptian scholar al-Suyuti.

Al-Suyuti (1445 – 1505) and Islam in Air.

Al-Suyuti, the Egyptian Muslim intellectual, was a liberal-minded scholar who gained the widespread respect and admiration of many Muslims in the Middle East, North Africa and West Africa. He reached the pinnacle of his profession when in 1497 he was appointed by the Caliph of Egypt as Supreme Judge over the Muslim world.

Al-Suyuti's writings were read fairly widely in West Africa from about 1475 onwards, and among the issues which he wrote about was the important and frequently debated one concerning the coming of the Mahdi and the End of the World. According to Ibn Khaldun, the Arabic scholar who wrote in the 14th century, many Muslims at every period in history, relying on certain traditions which he did not think were really worthy of acceptance, believed that at a certain point in time a Deliverer or Saviour would come to restore order, peace, justice and true religion to a morally degenerate world torn asunder by strife. This Deliverer or Saviour, who, it was believed would come from the Prophet's family, was called the Mahdi, the one rightly guided by God.[7] In restoring justice and peace the Mahdi would also renew and strengthen Islam for a period of time before the world came to an end.

The question asked by many Muslims in al-Suyuti's time, and again later in the time of Usuman dan Fodio in Hausaland, was when would the Mahdi appear? Scholars like al-Suyuti made their predictions. Al-Suyuti's view was that there would be twelve Caliphs of the Muslim community, accepted by Muslims as a whole as men who had ruled according to the teachings of the Qur'an. He maintained that by his time there had already been ten such Caliphs, leaving two more to follow, and that the last one would be the awaited Mahdi. According to al-Suyuti's reckoning the Mahdi would appear in either 1785 – 6 or 1789 – 90 and many people were later to look to these dates, and when they had passed as we shall see, they looked to others in expectation of the Mahdi.[8]

Al-Suyuti wrote about many other things apart from the Mahdi while at the same time assisting, advising and exhorting Muslim rulers and scholars who either went to see him or wrote to him. He arranged an interview for at least one West African ruler, Askiya Muhammad Ture I of Songhay, with the Caliph in Cairo in Egypt. He wrote letters of advice and guidance on matters of Islamic law to Muslim scholars in Air, and addressed letters to a number of rulers in West Africa, including the Sultan of Agades, in which he asked them to follow the Shari'a and to be just to their subjects.

From the letters written to al-Suyuti by Muslim scholars in West Africa it is clear that there was a good deal wrong with the way some Muslims in the region, including Muslim scholars, practised their faith. In one letter written to him by Muhammad al-Lamtuni, al-Suyuti was asked to answer 57 questions relating to the practice of Islam. It is not possible to state with any accuracy where Muhammad al-Lamtuni wrote from or where he was writing about, although one suggestion is that he wrote from either Agades or Takedda and that he was writing about Islam in Air and the surrounding areas.[9]

Muhammad al-Lamtuni, in his letter to al-Suyuti, gives a picture of Islam which resembles in some respects that given by Ibn Battuta when he visited the Tuareg town of Takedda in Air. He told al-Suyuti that the rulers of the region he was writing about adopted a system of taxation which was in some respects based on local custom and in other respects violated Islamic law. The taxes were heavy and imposed on Muslims and non-Muslims alike. Even firewood was taxed, for example. Furthermore, free men were being enslaved and their inheritance divided up arbitrarily and not according to Islamic law. Generally speaking, the Islamic laws on inheritance were not observed. Muhammad al-Lamtuni wrote, "What a man leaves when he dies goes to his sister's sons or to men of power and influence".[10] Again the rulers in some instances preferred the company of non-Muslims to that of Muslims and gave the former preferential treatment. Other un-Islamic and reprehensible practices mentioned by Muhammad al-Lamtuni were gambling, involvement in spirit possession — this was particularly true of the women — idol worship and the giving of false testimony.

There was also considerable slackness in the field of Islamic ritual, and denials of, or false ideas concerning, a number of important doctrines. In the sphere of ritual Muhammad al-Lamtuni alleged that some Muslims rarely performed the required ablution, namely the washing of the whole body, after what he called "major ritual pollution". Sexual intercourse, for instance, caused major ritual pollution and necessitated the washing of the whole body. In the field of doctrine some people denied the belief in the Resurrection. Furthermore, Muhammad al-Lamtuni criticised the custom of prostration before rulers which also existed as we have seen in Ancient Ghana, Mali and Songhay. He also accused scholars of neglecting the Qur'an, of failing out of fear to speak out against the un-Islamic behaviour of their rulers, and of partaking in the rulers' ill-gotten gains while explaining to others that the goods wrongfully acquired by the rulers were in fact legally acquired.

Many of the complaints made by Muhammad al-Lamtuni against the Muslim rulers and scholars in West Africa were also made by others such as al-Maghili and later by Usuman dan Fodio. Al-Suyuti replied to Muhammad al-Lamtuni's questions, pointing out to him what the Shari'a commanded regarding some of the issues raised while leaving him without a definite answer regarding others. Al-Suyuti did not answer, for example, the question about whether the patrilineal system of inheritance should be imposed in preference to the matrilineal system practised by some of the Tuareg. This lack of precision and "dogmatism" on al-Suyuti's part led some of the Muslim scholars of Air to regard him as a liberal-minded man who made concessions to local customs which someone of a more radical and fundamentalist frame of mind like al-Maghili would not have endorsed. While some scholars in Air were to adopt the more gradualist approach to reform characteristic of al-Suyuti, others followed the militant and direct approach of al-Maghili.

In Air, then, during the period under review the rulers, although they went on pilgrimage and attended the mosque, allowed the beliefs and practices of the traditional religion to continue, realising that the majority of their subjects were non-Muslim, and that even among the Muslim population many still adhered to traditional beliefs and customs. In these circumstances it might have been politically unwise to attempt to enforce to the letter Islamic law throughout the region under their control.

The actions of the Muslim scholars, however, are a little more difficult to understand. Perhaps al-Suyuti would have understood them better than al-Maghili. The latter deplored the mixing of Islam with traditional religion but he was equally indignant about such abuses as illegal taxation and extortion of goods and property from innocent people. He also deplored "venal" *mallams* who dedicated themselves to acquiring wealth, power and influence rather than to spreading the knowledge and faith of Islam. In the behaviour of the Muslim rulers and scholars of Agades and elsewhere in West Africa in this period one can detect some of the reasons for the 18th- and 19th-century reform movements. One must, however, avoid over-generalising. There were many outstanding Muslim scholars and mystics in Agades. Indeed the tradition of scholarship and mysticism was sound enough to give Agades a reputation as a centre of Islamic learning, a reputation which was still very much alive in the 18th century.

Islam in the Volta Basin.

From the late 14th and early 15th century Muslim traders from the Upper Niger region, known by various names such as Wangara, Dyula and Yarse, became increasingly involved in the gold and kola nut trade which was centred on the forest region to the south. The gold trade was stimulated by the increasing demand in the Muslim world and Europe for supplies of gold from West Africa, a demand that was to continue well into the 16th century and beyond. While gold was considered useful mainly because of its value as a currency, kola found in the forest zone was and still is valued as a thirst quencher, a stimulant and a present which a host might give to a guest or a subject to a ruler. Moreover, though grown in the forest zone mainly, kola were in great demand further north in the drier, hotter climates of the savanna and sahel regions.

To reach the gold and kola nut producing areas in the forest regions to the south the Muslim traders from Jenne and elsewhere in the Upper Niger region crossed the Volta Basin, a region bounded in the north by the River Niger and in the south by the Volta River and today covered by the West African Republics of Upper Volta, Ghana, the Ivory Coast and Togo. During the period with which we are concerned in this chapter a number of trade routes criss-crossed this region linking Jenne, an important market centre in the Upper Niger region, and Katsina and Kano in Hausaland with the forest zone.[1]

While traversing these routes Muslim traders from Jenne or Kano or Katsina broke their journey at certain points since the distances to be covered were long. The journey from Jenne, for example, to Begho, close to the gold-producing area in the Akan forest in the south, could take up to 50 days. At the points where they broke their journeys the Muslim traders established settlements. It was in this way that towns such as Bobo Dioulasso came into existence.

Among the convenient staging posts already in existence was Begho in Ghana close to the gold fields, and by the early years of the 15th century a number of Muslim traders had already settled there. The impact of these Muslim traders on Begho was twofold. On the one hand they contributed to the commercial development of the town, while at the same time they converted peoples such as the Hwela who lived in and around Begho to Islam. Then in the first quarter of the 18th century, as Begho declined due to the dislocation and disruption of trade caused by the Moroccan invasion of Songhay and European involvement in the gold trade, many Muslims left Begho to settle and establish Islam elsewhere in the Volta Basin.

Wangara traders who had settled in Hausaland in the 14th century also played a part in the establishment and development of Islam in this region. The impact of these Muslim merchants and de facto missionaries, however, varied from place to place. Unlike elsewhere in West Africa very few, if any, of the ruling élite in the Volta Basin became Muslims during the period 1000 — 1600. Indeed, the rulers of the Mossi kingdoms in Upper Volta showed themselves to be decidedly hostile to Islam. On a number of occasions the Mossi adopted a militant, aggressive approach towards Mali and Songhay, invading their territory and sacking towns such as Timbuktu. Songhay put an end to Mossi aggression when in 1493 Sunni Ali routed the Mossi forces. Askiya Muhammad Ture I, after requesting the rulers of the Mossi to become Muslims to no avail, launched a jihad of the sword against them in 1498. However, although the Mossi army was once again defeated, the Mossi rulers refused to convert to Islam and it was not until the 17th century that Muslim traders from the Upper Niger region, known to the Mossi as Yarse, were officially allowed to establish Muslim communities in the Mossi states of Wagadugu and Yatenga. Furthermore, we have to wait until the late 18th century for the first Muslim ruler of the Mossi.

Elsewhere in the region, while some rulers simply tolerated Muslims, others were even sympathetic to Islam. East of the Black Volta River, chiefs used Muslims as advisers and Muslims became an integral part of the political and social system. Few chiefs, however, converted to Islam. West of the Black Volta River Muslims tended to live apart from society and as a result preserved more of their Islamic identity while having relatively little impact on the peoples around them.[2]

Islam in Hausaland.

Beginnings and development to c. 1600.

Kasar Hausa, the land of those who speak the Hausa language as their mothe
tongue, covers in the main a large area of northern Nigeria and part of th
present-day Republic of Niger. Some scholars have suggested a northern
perhaps Saharan origin for Hausa, while more recently the view has been pu
forward that Hausa spread not from the Sahara in the north southwards, bu
from east to west across the savanna belt of northern Nigeria.[1] Agai
opinions differ as to when Hausa began to develop and spread as a cultur
and language. Some scholars have dated this process back several thousan
years, others see it as a much more recent development. It has been suggested
for example, that the spread of Hausa from east to west across Nigeria bega
about 1,000 years ago, reaching areas such as Zamfara and Kebbi in norther
Nigeria in the 15th century.[2]

   Not only is there an ongoing debate over the question of the origin
and chronology of the spread of Hausa but scholars are also re-appraisin
the evidence concerning such issues as the emergence of walled town
(*birane*) in parts of Hausaland.[3] There is also debate on the nature and th
extent of the governmental changes that took place in parts of Hausaland i
the second half of the 15th century. The question, moreover, of the rol
played by Islam in bringing about these changes is one that has attracted con
siderable attention in recent years.[4] Then there is the whole question of th
reliability of the source material used by historians and others. It has bee
suggested recently, for example, that the 17th-century author of the Kan
Chronicle, which provides so much of our knowledge of the history of Kanc
did not intend simply to write a blow by blow factual account of the histor
of Kano.[5] The Kano Chronicle is, it has been suggested, "a document c
intellectual history for 16th and 17th century Kano". And one of the mai
intellectual problems of the 16th century and one dealt with by the auth
of the Kano Chronicle was "the proper relationship between Muslim an
non-Muslim".[6] The Kano Chronicle, therefore, is "not just a mine fro
which to dig valuable facts".[7] Moreover, the historical accounts it provides c
the period prior to 1450 A.D. are "almost wholly legendary. . . .".[8] It i
therefore, against this background of the re-appraisal of Hausa history tha
wish to outline tentatively the history of Islam in part of Hausaland from i
arrival until c. 1600 A.D.

Islam in Kano.

According to the Kano Chronicle, which as I have indicated must be handle
with great care, there was a Muslim community in Kano by the middle of tl
14th century. The Chronicle states: "In Yaji's time the Wangarawa came fro
Melle (Mali) bringing the Muslim religion. Their leader was Abdurahma
Zaite . . . (they were) about forty in all. When they came they commande
the Sarki to observe the times of prayer. He complied and made Gurdam
his Liman (leader of the prayers in the mosque) and Lawal his Muezzin (tl
one who calls the people to prayer)".[9] Another document, again from tl

7th century, states that the Wangara brought Islam to Kano, not in the reign f Yaji, c. 1349 – 1385 A.D., but some one hundred years later in the reign of Muhammad Rumfa (1463 – 1499).[10]

One cannot, therefore, give a definite date for the arrival of Islam in Kano. t may well, however, have been the case that Muslim clerics and traders rom Mali did visit and even establish a Muslim settlement in Kano in the econd half of the 14th century. By Kano is meant here the Dutsen Dala area ut of which the "city state" of Kano had been forged by the second half of the 5th century.

Prior to the second half of the 15th century Islam made very little progress n Kano. Indeed there is some indication that Muslims may have met with a onsiderable amount of opposition from the adherents of the traditional eligion, and that there was great reluctance on the part of the local nhabitants to support or recognise the authority of a Muslim ruler. This may xplain why Sarki Kanajeji (1390 – 1410) revived the cult of Tsumburburai, he spirit of Dala Hill and the adjacent grove of Jakara.[11] And it may also xplain why Umaru, Kanajeji's successor, gave up being ruler in order to evote himself to the study and teaching of Islam and to prayer.[12] In support f this view that the local people opposed the introduction of Islam is the tory in the Kano Chronicle which relates how, when the Muslims had left the nosque after prayer, the Sarkin Garazawa who was "opposed to prayer . . . vould come with his men and defile the whole mosque and cover it with lth".[13]

In the second half of the 15th century during the reign of Muhammad umfa (1463 – 1499) the fortunes of Islam changed for the better. Increasing umbers of Muslim traders and scholars, including al-Maghili, settled in or isited Kano. Muhammad Rumfa himself may well have wanted to see Islam stablished in a real sense as the state religion, perhaps seeing in Islam a neans of bolstering his authority and of ensuring that Kano reaped the maxi- num possible benefit from its increasing involvement in international ade.[14] These factors, without excluding the possibility that he genuinely ccepted Islam, may explain why Muhammad Rumfa asked al-Maghili to rite a treatise on how a good Muslim ruler should govern.

I want now to consider both the treatise produced by al-Maghili for Muhammad Rumfa and the former's teaching and missionary activity in ano.

l-Maghili and Islam in Kano.

l-Maghili arrived in Kano in c. 1492 while on a journey that took him to Mecca as well as to Air, Gao and Katsina among other places. While in Kano, addition to organising and seeing to the religious needs of the North frican community there, al-Maghili, according to the Kano Chronicle vrote a Qur'an for the people of Kano, for he had not brought one with him, nd taught the Qur'an and the punishment of the law".[15] He also, on the quest of Muhammad Rumfa, wrote a treatise on how a good Muslim ruler ould govern, called "The Crown of Religion Concerning the Obligations of rinces". This document has had a considerable impact on the political and religious history of West Africa, and for this reason it is worthwhile looking at it in some detail.

Al-Maghili's "Obligations of Princes",[16] written not long before the Italian Niccolo Machiavelli wrote his influential treatise on government, "The Prince" in 1513, outlines the qualities and behaviour required in a good Muslim ruler, and equates the welfare of an Emir (a Muslim ruler/prince) with the welfare of his kingdom. Furthermore, almost all of the chapters of the "Obligation of Princes" end with the same words of advice or warning to the Muslim ruler: "Moreover the Height of Affliction is the Isolation of the Ruler from the Subjects", an admonition as valid today as it was in the late 15th century when al-Maghili compiled this treatise.

The first of the eight chapters in the treatise bears the title, "The Obligations of the Emir concerning Good Will", and here al-Maghili stressed that the ambition to dominate and rule others is not one of the characteristic of a good Muslim ruler. He writes: "It is an obligation for every sane person to be sure to avoid the Emirship unless it is unavoidable for him," and he continues, "Be mindful that you are merely one of God's creatures. Many would be more powerful than you were it not for the help of God. And let your ambition, all of it, be for the sake of God . . . and your concern, all of it be for the general welfare of the creatures of God. For God did not appoint you over them to be their Lord and their Master. Rather you were appointed to improve their faith and their welfare". Chapter 2, entitled "The Height of Affliction is the Isolation of the Ruler from the Subjects", points out that the two most shameful of shameful things are the pride of the poor and the lies of rulers, and so the ruler is advised: "if you speak, speak the truth. And if you make a promise, keep it". The general point is made: "the condition of the ruler and the condition of the subjects are two scales of a balance, so dispose wisely by increasing and decreasing (according to the situation) until the scales balance".

Chapter 2 and other chapters express some very different opinions from those expressed in Machiavelli's "The Prince" concerning the qualities required in a successful ruler. But on one issue their advice is similar: on the necessity of maintaining a good war machine. Machiavelli states, "The first way to loose your state is to neglect the art of war; the first way to win a state is to be skilled in the art of war".[17] Al-Maghili in Chapter 4 of the "Obligations of Princes" tells the ruler: "All your attention should be for brave men and for the implements of war". Al-Maghili saw war as justifiable not only when it was a question of self-defence but also as an instrument for ridding the country of corruption. He advises the Muslim ruler to "Uplift the country from the bareness of corruption with winds of battle and the lightning flashes of swords and the thunderous noise of sabres and the endless waves of soldiers. For indeed sovereignty is (won) by the sword and not by procrastination. And how can one dispel fear of the enemy except by intimidating him?" Al-Maghili had in mind the corruption brought about by such things as taking bribes, immorality, and in addition false religious beliefs and practices, and the adulteration and contamination of Islam by Muslims who mixed together Islamic faith and practice with the beliefs and practices of indigenous religions.

In other chapters of "The Obligations of Princes" al-Maghili outlines the duties of the good Muslim ruler concerning the appointment of government ministers, civil servants, spies and bodyguards. Al-Maghili's advice here is worth noting in the light of Muhammad al-Lamtuni's criticisms and future criticisms of Muslim rulers by reform-oriented Muslim scholars for appointing as ministers people who compromised their Islamic faith or people who were not even Muslims at all. All public officials, according to al-Maghili, were to be people of high moral standing and thorough going Muslims, and those found guilty of corruption were to be severely punished according to the full extent of Islamic law. The taking of wine was forbidden and anyone who showed signs of having drunk wine "in his odour, or speech or walk" was to be asked to breathe in the Emir's face, and if found guilty, the person was to be punished according to Islamic law. In fact, justice in general, as Chapter 6 of "The Obligations of Princes" implies, was to be dispensed according to Islamic law.

Chapters 7 and 8 of al-Maghili's treatise are mainly concerned with taxation and the distribution of wealth. Al-Maghili distinguishes between legal taxes "which God declared lawful for Emirs to collect", such as taxes on gold, precious metals, cultivated crops and on herds, and illegal taxes acquired by oppression. He regards the taking of bribes by the Emir when acting as a judge as oppression, and the illegal confiscation of the wealth of a thief or adulterer by the Emir he also regards as oppression "unless the crime of the criminal is directly related to that wealth". If, for example, someone dilutes milk with water to increase the amount of milk sold, then the Emir can seize the diluted milk and give it to the poor. On the distribution of zakat or alms al-Maghili stresses that "alms are for the poor, and the needy and those employed to administer the funds, and those whose hearts were recently reconciled (to the Truth of Islam) and those in bondage and debtors and (those engaging in jihad) in the cause of God, and travellers."

Although al-Maghili's treatise and his work as an educator did not lead to any revolutionary developments in the fortunes of Islam in Kano, this may well have been due once again to the strong resistance from the adherents of the traditional religion who were not prepared to see emerge a new type of government which weakened the power and authority of their religious leaders. The outcome, therefore, seems to have been a compromise. Muhammad Rumfa introduced a number of changes, such as, for example, the Muslim festival of Id al-Kabir, also known by the name Id al-Adha. This festival takes place on the 10th day of the 12th month, the month of pilgrimage (Dhu 'al-Hijja), and is marked by the sacrificing of animals by Muslims all over the world. Muhammad Rumfa also built a Friday mosque at the request of al-Maghili, and moved the seat of government to the Muslim sector of the city. But the Priest-Chief continued to play a role in the choice of the ruler.

For an overall view, finally, of al-Maghili's role in the development of Islam in Kano we can turn to the "Kano Chronicle". It states: "And when he (al-Maghili) had established the faith of Islam, and learned men had grown numerous in Kano, and all the country around had accepted the faith, Abdul Karim (al-Maghili) returned to Massar leaving Sidi Fara as his deputy to continue his work".[18] According to one estimate, which may well be an exaggeration, there were some 3,000 Muslim teachers in Kano at the time of al-Maghili's departure. Al-Maghili's influence lived on in Kano and elsewhere in Hausaland long after his departure, and his writings later influenced the thinking of the 18th- and 19th-century Muslim reformers such as Shaikh Usuman dan Fodio.

Islam in Kano, c. 1500 – 1600.

More Muslim scholars, we are told, came to Kano in Sarkin Kisoki's reign (1509 – 1565). Under Sarkin Kisoki mosques were built and the king himself is said to have waged war because it was the decree of Allah.[19] In other words, he used the idea of jihad as the motive for his campaigns. Other 16th-century rulers of Kano seem to have been just as dedicated to the spread of Islam as Kisoki, but they preferred to spread it by the pen rather then the sword. Sarkin Yakubu, for example, deposed after only four months as ruler, was more interested in Islamic learning than power and authority and so refused to be reinstated as king. Instead he went away to live with scholars and dedicate himself to the study of Islam.

Abubakar Kado, who ruled Kano from 1565 to 1573, was of the same temperament as the deposed Sarkin Yakubu, being more interested in praying than in ruling. According to the "Kano Chronicle", "He and all his chiefs spent their time in prayer". The king himself took on the role of Muslim teacher, making his sons, the princes, learn the Qur'an. His seven sons are said to have assembled every morning after prayer and each one in turn read a seventh of the Qur'an.[20] The king also built a centre for Qur'anic reading and learning.

Islam in Katsina, Zaria and Gobir.

There is a tradition that a group of Wangara Muslim clerics arrived in Katsina, as well as Kano, in the middle years of the 14th century. Al-Maghili also paid a visit to Katsina in 1493 and a few years later another Muslim scholar Makhluf b. 'Ali, who like al-Maghili had worked in Kano, came to Katsina to teach Islamic sciences.

Muhammad Korau (1466 – 1493 A.D.) is credited with being the first authentic Muslim ruler of Katsina. He, according to tradition, overthrew the Durbawa dynasty, the central point of the traditional religion. Then Muhammad Korau, perhaps influenced and supported by al-Maghili and the Muslim clerics and traders, attempted to introduce Islamic law on a wide scale.

Ibrahim, Muhammad Korau's successor, pursued the same policy of Islamisation, forcing his subjects to perform the five daily prayers on pain of imprisonment. However, although the Muslim community in Katsina was probably quite large and powerful, it does not appear to have been strong enough to overcome the resistance offered by the non-Muslim population to this policy of Islamisation. And as was the case in Kano, the Muslim rulers in Katsina had to compromise and accept a system of government over which

IV The Gobe mosque, Katsina

the leaders of the traditional religion continued to exercise considerable
influence.[21]

Unlike Kano and Katsina it would seem that Zaria, or Zazzau, did not have
a Muslim dynasty until the 17th century. Recent research on the early history
of Zaria suggests that Muhammad Rabbo, believed by some historians to

have ruled Zaria for a period during the second half of the 16th century, did not in fact reign until some 200 years later, that is from 1641 to 1658 A.D.[22] It is not, however, being suggested that there was no Muslim presence in the Zaria region prior to the 17th century. There were, it would seem, some Hausa-speaking Muslim settlements in what is today Zaria town and surrounds in the early 16th century. Muslim traders in the main lived in these settlements and exerted authority both within the settlements and in the area immediately surrounding them until the emergence of a new Hausa Muslim dynasty with its headquarters in Zaria in the 17th century.[23]

Gobir, situated to the north of Zaria and Katsina, was the home of Usuman dan Fodio. There is a great deal of speculation as to when and where the state of Gobir emerged. The view has been advanced that Gobir began as a state in the Air mountains in the 12th or 13th century. Leo Africanus, writing in the 16th century, states that Gobir was surrounded by high mountains and that Askiya Muhammad Ture I of Songhay killed its king and enslaved most of its inhabitants.[24] Suffering further onslaughts from the Tuareg, the Gobirawa then moved further south.

There is another view of events which, although it does not discount some form of migration southwards, suggests that this migration was not on a large scale but involved only one or perhaps a few families and that this took place in the 15th century. Moreover, these Gobirawa migrants may have been aliens who came to impose their authority over the local Zamfara peasantry.

There is also very little solid evidence concerning the beginnings of Islam in Gobir. Muslim traders probably visited and settled in the territory in the 15th and 16th centuries and possibly by the 16th century some of the rulers of Gobir were Muslims.

Islam, then, made faltering progress in Hausaland in the period under discussion. Muslim rulers, anxious for political as well as religious reasons to impose an Islamic system of government, met with stiff resistance. The outcome was a system of government which combined aspects of the traditional religio-political system with Islamic governmental principles and practice. In Hausaland in the 16th century a balance had to be kept between the Muslim clerics as advisers and councillors of the king and the priests of the Hausa religion. Both were skilled and knowledgeable: the former on account of their Islamic education, the latter because of their knowledge of the mysteries of the iskoki (the spirits). The kings were "chiefs" as it were, of both religions, a difficult position to maintain but made inevitable by the political realities of the situation. Though Muslims themselves, the kings of Kano and Katsina ruled over territories where the population was largely non-Muslim. They therefore needed the services of both Muslim religious specialists and the priests (bo'kaye) of the Hausa religion.

Islam in Kanem-Borno.

Beginnings and early development.

The state of Borno emerged out of Kanem and here I will deal first with the arrival and early development of Islam in Kanem. Situated to the north-east of Lake Chad, Kanem made its first contact with Islam through trade. Kanem had trade links with Tripoli in North Africa via Kawar and the Fezzan, and it was this trade route that provided the gateway for Islam to enter Kanem. According to al-Bakri, Muslim raiders led by 'Uqba b. Nafi came along this trade route as far as the Kawar region in 666 — 7 A.D. but withdrew north in a very short space of time. A more permanent Muslim presence was established on the Kanem-North African trade route in the second half of the 8th century with the establishment of the small states of Ajar Fazzan and further south, closer to Kanem, Zawila.[1] Zawila, a centre of Ibadite Islam (see Chapter 1, p. 7 and Chapter 2, p. 24), was overrun in 761 A.D. and its inhabitants massacred by Abbasid forces. The Abbasid descendants of the uncle of Prophet Muhammad, al-Abbas, became the Caliphs of the Muslim world in 749 A.D., after overthrowing the Umayyad dynasty.

The Abbasid attack did not spell the end of Zawila as an important Ibadite centre. Berber Ibadite Muslims continued to frequent and settle in Zawila which remained one of the more important departure terminals for caravans going to the Chad region and elsewhere in the Sudan. Zawila was also an important junction on the pilgrimage route.

It is possible that some Muslims, perhaps traders, came along this trade route to Kanem and settled there, at least for a time, and perhaps acted as advisers to the rulers. There is, however, no evidence that either the ruler or the people of Kanem accepted Islam prior to the second half of the 11th century. The Arabic geographer, al-Muhallabi, writing in the late 10th century, tells us that the people of Kanem "venerate their king and adore him in the place of God Most High. . .".[2] By the end of the 10th century, therefore, the indigenous religious system was still, it would appear, widely accepted in Kanem. Over half a century later, in 1067 — 8 A.D., al-Bakri commented that the people of Kanem were idolatrous blacks, among whom Umayyad refugees fleeing from Abbasid persecution had settled.[3] It is not at all certain that there were Umayyad refugees in Kanem, although one scholar believes there were and that they played an important role in the dissemination of Islam there.[4]

Shortly after al-Bakri made his comments on the people of Kanem a Muslim ruler, Humai Jilme of the Sefawa dynasty, was ruling in Kanem. Mai (King) Humai Jilme, who ruled from c. 1085 to 1097 A.D., was, according to some scholars, the first Muslim king of Kanem-Borno.[5] According to a Borno Mahram (a letter of privilege), Humai Jilme, with the assistance of a certain Muslim missionary Muhammad b. Mani, was responsible for the widespread dissemination of Islam in Kanem-Borno. One extract from the Mahram reads: "The first Muslim country in the Sudan which Islam entered was Borno. It came through Muhammad Ibn Mani. . . . Islam was spreading for two years before, through Muhammad Ibn Mani it became general . . . . Mai Umme (Humai) and Muhammad Ibn Mani spread Islam abroad to last until the day of judgment".[6] It has also been suggested, however, that two Muslim kings of the Dugawa dynasty ruled in Kanem in the late 1060s and early 1070s. There is also some reason to believe that the account which attributes such an important role in the dissemination of Islam to Muhammad Ibn Mani is an attempt by later orthodox Sunni Muslims to gloss over the role played by Ibadite Muslims in the early history of Islam in Kanem-Borno. Another view has been advanced that Humai Jilme was not a recent convert to Islam but was in fact a Berber and one of the Muslim business community, trading in Kanem. During a period of internal instability and declining trade with North Africa in the second half of the 11th century, a time when the Muslim Fatimid rulers of Egypt were pursuing expansionist policies which put pressure on Kanem, the Muslim community in Kanem displaced the Dugawa dynasty and established in power the Sefawa dynasty with Humai Jilme as Mai or King.[7]

We have, therefore, several different interpretations of how Kanem-Borno came to have Muslim rulers. It seems to me that in Kanem, as in Ancient Ghana, there was a relatively influential Muslim community, although numerically small in relation to the rest of the population, by the second half of the 11th century. Kanem's trading links with Muslim states to the north had in all likelihood led to the establishment of communities of Muslim traders and missionaries in Kanem from the 10th century. It is also possible, although the evidence here is flimsy, that Umayyad refugees had settled in Kanem. Instead, therefore, of emphasising the role played by one man, namely Muhammad Ibn Mani, or of external factors such as Fatimid expansionism in the early development of Islam in Kanem, it might be more accurate to ascribe the first royal conversions to Islam and the establishment of a Muslim dynasty to the growing importance and influence of the Muslim community of missionaries and merchants within Kanem itself.

For a considerable length of time after the establishment of a Muslim dynasty in Kanem, Islam remained confined for the most part to the royal court and the commercial centres. The Muslim rulers, however, soon after their conversion began to fulfil such duties as the pilgrimage to Mecca, and they also introduced aspects of Islamic law and began to wear the same style of dress as the Muslim rulers of North Africa. In the field of administration, moreover, the Muslim influence was felt with the emergence of a class of Muslim officials, among them *qadis* (judges), *talibs* (scholars) and *wazirs* (chief ministers), whose task it was to administer the empire. Muslims had the skills needed for the administration of an expanding empire, in particular literacy in Arabic. A letter written in 1391/2 by the Mai to the Mamluk Sultan begins with the words, "Praise be to God who has created writing for the purpose of communication between servants. ."[8] The kings of Kanem also valued prayer and requested Muslim clerics to devote themselves to praying for such things as rain, victory in battle and the security and safety of the kingdom.

During the reign of Dunama Dibbalemi (c. 1221−59) Islam seems to have made considerable progress in Kanem. The Arabic scholar Ibn Sa'id recounts that this ruler surrounded himself with experts in Islamic law, waged holy war, and opened a hostel for students and pilgrims in Cairo.[9] He is also said to have been in the words of the Diwan of the Sultans of Borno "the first to cut open a thing called Mune, the nature of which no-one save God Most High knows".[10]

What was the purpose of this action? Was Dunama Dibbalemi defending Islam against "paganism" or was he performing an irreligious or indeed sacrilegious act? According to Imam Ahmad Ibn Fartuwa, chronicler of the Kanem Wars fought by Idris Alooma, whom it must be remembered wrote in 1518 some 300 years after the event, the Mune was "a thing more acceptable than the purest water". It was something which the great Arab hero, Sayf b. Dhi Yasan, had possessed and whose descendants, according to certain traditions, established the Sefawa dynasty. The Mune was "a thing wrapped up and hidden away", and the Bani Sayf depended upon it for victory in war. Dunama's people warned him not to open the Mune, but he refused to heed their advice, and when he opened it "whatever was inside flew away impelling the chief men of the kingdom to greed for dominion and high rank".[11] The opening of the Mune not only led to strife, according to Ibn Fartuwa, but to infidels opposing Islam. In Ibn Fartuwa's view the Mune was not a symbol of "paganism" but something which "God had sent down to the children of Israel in the days of King Saul as is related in the Qur'an (2 v. 248), the ark in which was knowledge of victory."[12]

Smith suggests, on the basis of Ahmad Imam Ibn Fartuwa's account, that the breaking open of the Mune was not seen by the Muslim scholars in Kanem as a defence of Islam against paganism. The Mune, which once belonged to the *Kanuri* religion, had been incorporated into Islam in the same way as the Old Testament had been incorporated into Christianity, and its destruction Smith maintains was designed to bring about a conflict between the Sefawa and other interest groups both Muslim and non-Muslim.[13] Ibn Sa'id's almost contemporary evidence would, however, seem to contradict this, since it indicates that Dunama Dibbalemi took pains to seek advice and guidance from Muslim scholars and they may well have advised the breaking open of the Mune in defence of and for the purpose of establishing a more orthodox Islam in Kanem.

During Dunama Dibbalemi's reign and throughout the 13th century Kanem expanded its frontiers and took control of the trade route linking the Lake Chad region with North Africa. Perhaps the kingdom became too large to administer efficiently and it is also possible that economic prosperity led to the emergence of a governing class which demanded more privileges and a greater share of the wealth of the kingdom. The Diwan of Borno records with reference to the reign of Mai Dunama Dibbalemi (1221 — 1259): "In his time there occurred civil war through the greed of his children and in his time also the princes went apart into different regions. There was no discord before this time".[14] Several Mais in the first half of the 14th century ruled for just one year, dying in battle either against the So or some other group. In the last quarter of the same century war with the Bulala broke out and lasted intermittently for several centuries. Between 1350 and 1392 nine Kanem kings died in war with the Bulala and one was assassinated.

The Bulala, a branch of the ruling dynasty, forced the Sefawa to move out of Kanem towards the end of the reign of Mai Umar b. Idris (1386 — 1390). Mai Umar b. Idris called in his Muslim advisers to counsel him about what he should do concerning the Bulala threat and they reportedly told him: "Leave this place; our day is done here".[15] While the Bulala took charge of Kanem, the Sefawa moved west of Lake Chad to found the kingdom of Borno without, however, entirely giving up their claim to Kanem. The Sefawa met with strong opposition as they attempted to establish their authority over Borno and it was only after two civil wars between 1425 and 1444 and another between 1461 and 1476, and several coups d'etat and assassinations that they managed to create some form of stability and cohesion in the region. A revival in the fortunes of the Sefawa dynasty began during the reign of Mai ali b. Dunama (1476 – 1503), and after two major setbacks caused by famine in the middle years of the 16th century, the century closed with the relatively long and successful reign of Mai Idris Alooma.

Islam in Borno during the reign of Idris Alooma (1570 – 1602).

Idris Alooma's reign is noted for the emphasis he placed on updating and modernising the army and for the importance he attached to maintaining and extending contacts with Muslim states, from whom he imported weapons as well as military advisers and instructors. Idris was also, according to his biographer Ahmad Ibn Fartuwa, a devout and committed Muslim. We are told that among other things he sought to have justice dispensed according to the Shari'a (Islamic sacred law). On one occasion he wanted the issue of three towns seized by the people of Kanem from the Sefawa to be submitted to a decision of the Shari'a Court. The Sultan of Kanem refused because, in the words of the Borno chronicler, Ibn Fartuwa, "they (the Sultan of Kanem and his advisers) were unwilling to follow the Sunna".[16]

The account by Ibn Fartuwa of the Kanem wars — the seven expeditions of Idris Alooma against the people of Kanem to regain lost territory — contains a good deal of information about Idris Alooma's practice of Islam. There is frequent reference to the fact that he observed the Muslim prayers, saying them at the correct time of the day. During the first expedition, we are told by Ibn Fartuwa, "the Sultan dismounted for morning prayer and then continued on his way to Ikrima". He makes mention of the fact that Idris observed the celebration of the Muslim festivals of Id al-Fitr and Id el-Kabir, and of his observance of Ramadan. Alooma also visited the tombs of his ancestors in Kanem, accompanied by the emirs, 'ulama and captains and there had the Qur'an read three times, prayed to God and gave alms of minor offerings (horses and oxen).

The picture of Alooma given by Ibn Fartuwa is of a Muslim ruler guided and regulated in his political and military activities by Islam. We are told moreover, that he was recognised as a great Muslim leader by the Sultan of Turkey. "Have you ever seen a king equal to Our Father (Idris Alooma)" wrote Ibn Fartuwa, "when the Lord of Stambul (Istanbul), Sultan of Turkey, sent messengers to him . . . with favourable proposals indicating his desire to gain his affection and his eagerness for his society and friendship".[17]

Islam, therefore, did affect to some extent the way in which Idris and the other Mais ruled their kingdom. It did not, however, fundamentally affect the tradition of divine kingship, or the associated ritual of the seclusion of the monarch, which were un-Islamic. A Muslim praise-song in honour of Mai Humai, perhaps the first Muslim king of Kanem-Borno, sees him as a divine king in very much the same way as his non-Muslim predecessors. The song goes, "Hail all powerful! Today you are the world's health-giver, who holds destiny in your hands, today you have made the world a paradise. With whom lies the power for good or evil; today you are the world's sweetness; Islam's disposer, today you are the pillar supporting the world. . . . Protect us and we shall protect you on earth. O Sultan you are the Ark of the Qur'an. O Sultan Angel of God . . . we wait upon your blessing".[18] Ibn Battuta, writing in the 14th century, mentions the ritual seclusion of the king: "The people of Borno have a king called Idris who never shows himself to his people or talks to them except from behind a curtain".[19] This practice continued well into the 19th century.

Royal women, in particular the king's mother (Gumsu), his elder sister and his senior wife, had privileged positions and great power and influence long after Islam had been adopted by the rulers of Kanem-Borno. King Biri b. Dunama is reported to have been put in prison by his mother for executing a thief instead of carrying out the punishment prescribed in the Qur'an. Another gumsu is said to have had 60 courtiers, all nobles, 40 slaves who worked for her, and 20 men-at-arms who went out to fight for her and maintain her authority. Each one of these 20 men-at-arms commanded 1,000 slaves.

Islam thus had not lead to a radical transformation of political institutions, nor had it swept away all the beliefs and practices of the indigenous religions even among those who had become Muslims. The institution of divine kingship was perhaps the most notable but not, however, the only survival from the traditional politico-religious system. Nevertheless, the impact of Islam should not be underestimated. Certainly the introduction of literacy in Arabic and of a Qur'anic system of education had begun to have an important effect on the political, social and cultural life of the government and people of Borno. The Friday mosques and the Muslim festivals also played an important social and political role in Borno. N'gazargamu, capital of Borno, had in the 17th century four Friday mosques each with an estimated 12,000 worshippers. These mosques, moreover, were of political as well as religious importance to the rulers for it was there that they received public recognition through prayers said in their name. Furthermore, in the mosques the preachers would remind the people of their civil and other responsibilities.

Although Borno, therefore, was not a thorough-going Islamic state by the end of the 16th century, Islam played an important role in the intellectual, cultural, political and religious life of the towns, the rural areas remaining as elsewhere in West Africa predominantly non-Muslim.

Conclusions.

By 1600, therefore, some 850 years after it had made its first contacts with West Africa, Islam's main strength was among the privileged classes, the rulers, the administrators, the scholars and the merchants. Moreover, it was confined in very many parts of West Africa, the western Sahara being the exception, to the urban centres. The mass of the people in the rural areas had remained virtually untouched.

Even among the rulers some, like the Mossi, resisted Islam while others, like Sunni Ali, merely "played" with it. Moreover, for those kings, administrators and scholars who made the pilgrimage and built mosques and schools and waged jihad of the sword, the profession of Islam did not necessarily imply detailed adherence to its legal, moral, doctrinal and ritual demands.

With the exception perhaps of Takrur, about which we know very little, there were no thorough-going Islamic states in this period. Where ruling groups did seriously attempt to administer their kingdoms in accordance with Islamic principles they sometimes met with strong opposition. They therefore had to compromise and while appointing Muslims to important posts in the administration as ministers, interpreters and secretaries, they also had to allow room for non-Muslim participation in government and accept the continuance of many pre-Islamic rituals, institutions and practices, something which Ibn Battuta, for example, observed when he visited Mali.

Not all Muslims, however, strove or even wanted to establish an Islamic state. Some, moreover, did not believe that it was part of their duty to spread Islam. While some were expatriates and lived apart from the rest of the society, others held the view that there was no need to convert people since all who led a good life would become Muslims before entering Paradise and thereby be saved. This attitude of toleration and justification of the status quo may of course have been the result of an underlying feeling of resignation on the part of a Muslim minority that realised its inability to change the situation to its own advantage.

Rulers, whether Muslim or not, appointed some Muslims as advisers, councillors, administrators and secretaries. One of the main reasons for this was that Muslims were literate in Arabic. This had many advantages for rulers. A universalistic language like Arabic could be of assistance in establishing the conditions necessary for the smooth and efficient organisation of long distance trade, or in establishing and strengthening relations with Muslim states of North Africa. Arabic was also used as the medium for writing despatches and orders, for summoning military aid, for the issuing of administrative directives to provincial governors, for disseminating propaganda, for recording history. It was the language of learning, the language of the diplomat, the merchant, the lawyer and the teacher. Moreover, it enjoyed a "sacred" character. The written word in Arabic was considered to have a great deal of power to heal and protect.

Literacy in Arabic could also, however, have its disadvantages for Muslim rulers who were lax in their Islamic duties. For once Arabic became widely used among Muslims, in particular among those not in government, and people began to read Islamic texts and write in Arabic, it could be both an instrument for change and a means of preserving orthodoxy. By being able to read the standard orthodox Islamic legal and doctrinal texts Muslims in West Africa were able to compare the existing state of Islam in their own kingdom with the ideal Islamic state as presented in the texts. If Islam in their own state did not conform to the ideal they could demand that reforms be made. The pilgrimage, as we shall see, could perform a similar role.

Notes.

Islam in the south-western Sahara (Shinqit/Mauretania).

1   Mauretania disengaged from the war in the Western Sahara in August 1978.
2   A.D.H. Bivar and M. Hiskett, "The Arabic Literature of Nigeria to 1804: a provisional account", *Bulletin of the School of Oriental and African Studies* (B.S.O.A.S.) XXV (1962), pp. 104 — 148. See also P.F. Moraes Farias, *op. cit.*, pp. 855 *ff*.
3   For a fuller account of western Saharan society see H.T. Norris, *Shinqiti Folk Literature and Song* (Oxford, 1968), especially Chapter 2.
4   A.A. Batran in J.R. Willis, ed, *op. cit.*, pp. 113 — 146, provides an interesting account of the origins and history of the Kunta.
5   *Ibid.*, p. 120. This view contradicts that put forward by A.D.H. Bivar and M. Hiskett, *op. cit.*, p. 106, who suggest that al-Maghili introduced the Qadiriyya brotherhood into the western Sahara.
6   P.D. Curtin, "Jihad in West Africa: Early Phases and Inter-relations in Mauretania and Senegal", *Journal of African History* (J.A.H.) XII (1971), pp. 11 — 24.

Islam in the state of the Senegambia.

1   Al-Bakri (V. Monteil's translation), *op. cit.*, p. 68.
2   *Ibid.*, p. 68.
3   'Umar el-Nagar, "Takrur, the history of a name", *J.A.H.* X (1969), pp. 365 — 374.
4   From V. Fernandes, "Description de la Côte Occidentale d'Afrique", ed, T. Monod, A. Toxeira da Mota and R. Mauny (Bissau, 1951), pp. 7 — 11, and cited in *France and West Africa*, ed J.D. Hargreaves (London, 1969), pp. 15 — 18.
5   J.R. Willis, ed., *op. cit.*, p. 12.
6   Y. Person, *Samori: A Dyula Revolution*, (I.F.A.N. Dakar 1968), p. 134, Tomel.
7   Much of what I say here and elsewhere in this book on the Jakhanke is based on L.O. Sanneh's *The Jakhanke* (London, 1979).
8   Sanneh, *op. cit.*, p. 244.
9   J. Goody, ed, *Literacy in Traditional Societies* (Cambridge, 1968), p. 230.
10 Al-Sa'di, *Ta'rikh al-Sudan*, French translation by O. Houdas (Paris, 1900), p. 139.
11 Al-Idrisi in J. Cuoq, *op. cit.*, p. 153.

Islam in Ancient Ghana.

1   Levtzion, *op. cit.*, Chapter 2, and N. Levtzion, "The Sahara and the Sudan from the Arab Conquest of the Maghrib to the Rise of the Almoravids" in J. Fage, ed., *Cambridge History of Africa*, Vol. 2 (Cambridge, 1978), p. 665.
2   Al-Bakri (V. Monteil's translation), p. 70.
3   Al-Idrisi in J. Cuoq, *op. cit.*, pp. 133 — 134.
4   A. Boahen, *op. cit.*, pp. 9 — 13. And for a brief summary and critique of some of the reasons put forward for the collapse of Ancient Ghana see Moraes Farias, "Great States Revisited", Review Article, *J.A.H.* XV (1974), pp. 479 — 488.
5   J.C. Froelich, *Les Musulmans d'Afrique Noire*, (Paris, 1962), p. 26.
6   J.L. Triaud, *op. cit.*, especially Chapter 5. *Ghana* provides a number of citations from different scholars who have put forward this view. See also Boahen, *op. cit.*, pp. 9 — 13; Levtzion, *Ancient Ghana and Mali*, *op. cit.*, pp. 51 — 52, 185 — 6, p. 195. And see Moraes Farias, "The Great States Revisited", *op. cit.*, pp. 481 *ff*,

and Conrad and Fisher, *op. cit.*, Part I, pp. 1 *ff*, for a critique of these views.
7   Moraes Farias, "The Great States. .", pp. 484 *ff*.
8   Al-Harrani in J. Cuoq, *op. cit.*, pp. 249−250.
9   *Ibid.*, p. 265.

Islam in Mali.

1   Al-Ya'qubi in J. Cuoq, *op. cit.*, p. 52.
2   Al-Bakri (V. Monteil's translation), p. 74.
3   Al-Idrisi in J. Cuoq, *op. cit.*, p. 130.
4   Cited in P.J. Ryan, *Imale: Yoruba Participation in the Muslim Tradition*, (Harvard, 1978), p. 1.
5   D.T. Niane, *Sundiata, an Epic of Old Mali*, translated by G.D. Pickett (London, 1965), p. 2.
6   Levtzion, *Ancient Ghana and Mali*, *op. cit.*, p. 56.
7   Ibn Khaldun in J. Cuoq, *op. cit.*, p. 355.
8   Levtzion, *op. cit.*, p. 56.
9   Al-Bakri (V. Monteil's translation), p. 74.
10 Al-Idrisi in J. Cuoq, *op. cit.*, p. 130.
11 D.T. Niane, *op. cit.*, p. 55.
12 *Ibid.*, pp. 73 *ff*.
13 Hamdun and King, *op. cit.*, p. 46.
14 Al-'Umari in J. Cuoq, *op. cit.*, p. 263.
15 Ibn Khaldun in J. Cuoq, *op. cit.*, p. 346.
16 Hamdun and King, *op. cit.*, pp. 1 *ff*.
17 *Ibid.*, pp. 47−8.
18 *Ibid.*, p. 42.

Islam in Songhay.

1   Al-Sa'di (O. Houdas' translation), *op. cit.*, p. 6.
2   M. Delafosse's opinion discussed in J.O. Hunwick, "Religion and State in the Songhay Empire, 1464−1591" in I.M. Lewis, ed, *Islam in Tropical Africa*, (London, 1980), p. 125.
3   J.O. Hunwick, *op. cit.*, p. 124.
4   Triaud, *op. cit.*, p. 135.
5   Al-Sa'di (O. Houdas' translation), *op. cit.*, p. 5.
6   Al-Bakri (V. Monteil's translation), pp. 79−80.
7   Triaud, *op. cit.*, p. 141.
8   Hamdun and King, *op. cit.*, p. 55.
9   Al-Sa'di (O. Houdas' translation), p. 23.
10 *Ibid.*, p. 103.
11 *Ibid.*, p. 110.
12 M. Hiskett, "An Islamic Tradition of Reform in the Western Sudan from the Sixteenth to the Eighteenth Century", *B.S.O.A.S.* XXV (1962), pp. 577−596.
13 M.F. Dubois, *Timbouctou la Mystérieuse*, (Paris, 1897), p. 304.
14 N. Levtzion, "Islam in West African Politics: Accommodation and tension between the 'ulama and the political authorities", in *Cahiers d'Etudes Africaines* XVIII (1971), pp. 333−345.

'slam in Air.

1 H.T. Norris, *The Tuaregs, Their Islamic Legacy and its Diffusion in the Sahel,* (Wilts, England, 1975), p. 56.
2 *Ibid.,* p. xiv.
3 *Ibid.,* p. 13.
4 Hamdun and King, *op. cit.,* p. 56.
5 *Ibid.,* p. 59.
6 *Ibid.,* p. 56.
7 Ibn Khaldun, *The Muqadimmah,* translated by F. Rosenthal, edited and abridged by N.J. Dawood (London, 1967), p. 259.
8 M.A. Al-Hajj, "The Thirteenth Century in Muslim Eschatology: Mahdist Expectations in the Sokoto Caliphate", *Research Bulletin,* Centre of Arabic Documentation, Ibadan, III (1967), p. 108.
9 H.T. Norris, *op. cit.,* pp. 45 — 7; and Hunwick, "Notes on a late fifteenth-century document concerning 'al-Takrur' " in C.H. Allen and R.W. Johnson, eds, *African Perspectives,* (Cambridge, 1970).
10 Hunwick, "Notes on. . ." *op. cit.,* p. 13.

'slam in the Volta Basin.

1 I. Wilks, "A Medieval Trade Route from the Niger to the Gulf of Guinea", *J.A.H.* III (1962), pp. 337 — 341.
2 N. Levtzion, *Muslims and Chiefs in West Africa,* (Oxford, 1968).

'slam in Hausaland.

1 For a discussion of these issues see J.E.G. Sutton, "Towards a less orthodox chronology of Hausaland", *J.A.H.* XX (1979), pp. 179 — 201.
2 *Ibid.,* p. 201.
3 A. Smith, "The Early States of the Central Sudan" in J.F. Ade Ajayi and M. Crowder, eds, *History of West Africa,* Vol. 1 (London, 1971), pp. 177 ff; and F. Fuglestad, "A Reconsideration of Hausa History before the Jihad", *J.A.H.* XIX (1978), pp. 319 — 339; and D.M. Last, "Before Zaria. . .", African History Seminar paper, University of London (S.O.A.S.), January 1981.
4 See, for example, H.J. Fisher, "The Eastern Maghrib and the Central Sudan" in R. Oliver, ed, *Cambridge History of Africa,* Vol. 3 (London, 1977), pp. 241 — 330; and Fugelstad, *op. cit.*
5 D.M. Last, "Historical Metaphors in the Kano Chronicle", *History in Africa* VII (1980), pp. 161 — 178.
6 *Ibid.,* p. 171.
7 *Ibid.,* p. 161.
8 *Ibid.,* p. 163.
9 H.A.R. Palmer, "Kano Chronicle" in *Sudanese Memoirs,* Vol. 3, (Lagos, 1928), pp. 104 — 5. (Kano Chronicle will henceforth be abbreviated to K.C.)
10 M.A. Al-Hajj, editor, "Chronicle on the origins and missionary activities of the Wangarawa", *Kano Studies* IV (1968), pp. 7 — 16.
11 K.C., *op. cit.,* pp. 107 — 8.
12 K.C., *op. cit.,* p. 108.
13 K.C., *op. cit.,* p. 105.
14 Fugelstad, *op. cit.,* p. 335.
15 K.C., *op. cit.,* p. 111.
16 The text of the "Obligation of Princes" used here is "Taj Aldin Fima Yajib Ala Al

Muluk" or "The Crown of Religion Concerning the Obligations of Princes" trans lated by K.J. Bedri and P.E. Starratt in *Kano Studies* I (1974/77), pp. 15–28.
17   Machiavelli, *The Prince*, translated by G. Bull (London, 1961), p. 87.
18   K.C., *op. cit.*, p. 111.
19   *Ibid.*, p. 113.
20   *Ibid.*, p. 114–5.
21   Fugelstad, *op. cit.*, p. 330.
22   D.M. Last, "Before Zaria. . .", *op. cit.*, for an account of the names and early history of Zaria. On the dates of Muhammad Rabbo's reign see p. 15 of thi article.
23   *Ibid.*, p. 9.
24   Leo Africanus, *Description de l'Afrique*, translated by A. Epaulard (Paris, 1956) p. 437.

Islam in Kanem-Borno.

1   B.G. Martin, "Kanem, Borno and the Fezzan: Notes on the Political History of Trade Route", *J.A.H.* I (1969), pp. 15–27. This article provides a concise an interesting account of the Muslim Ibadite activities in the Fezzan and of Kanem North African trading links.
2   Al-Muhallabi in J. Cuoq, *op. cit.*, p. 78.
3   Al-Bakri in J. Cuoq, *op. cit.*, p. 82.
4   D. Lange, "Progrès de l'Islam et Changement Politique au Kanem du XIe au XIII siècle: Un Essai d'Interprétation", *J.A.H.* XIX (1962), pp. 495–513.
5   See, for example, J.S. Trimingham, *A History of Islam in West Africa, op. cit.* p. 115.
6   Palmer, *Sudanese Memoirs, op. cit.*, Vol. 3, p. 3.
7   Lange, *op. cit.*
8   J. Cuoq, *op. cit.*, p. 377.
9   Al-'Umari in J. Cuoq, *op. cit.*, p. 209.
10   H.A.R. Palmer, *Borno, Sahara and Sudan* (London, 1936), p. 92.
11   Palmer, *Sudanese Memoirs, op. cit.*, Vol. 1, pp. 69–70.
12   *Ibid.*
13   A. Smith, "The Early States. .", *op. cit.*, p. 167, n. 41.
14   Palmer, *Borno. . ., op. cit.*, p. 92.
15   *Ibid.*, p. 93.
16   Palmer, *Sudanese Memoirs, op. cit.*, Vol. 1, p. 19.
17   *Ibid.*, p. 69.
18   Palmer, *Borno. . ., op. cit.*, p. 161.
19   Levtzion, N. and Hopkins, J.F.P., eds, *Corpus of Early Arabic Sources for Wes African History* (Cambridge, 1981), p. 302.

4

c. 1600 – 1800: widening horizons.

During the period c. 1600 – 1800 Muslims in many parts of West Africa, though often linked together by family ties and education, nevertheless constituted a minority in the areas in which they settled or worked. They adopted different responses to the surrounding society and took different approaches to the spread of Islam and the building up of the Muslim community. There were those among them who held the opinion that the various existing cultures and belief systems including their own could co-exist side by side in the same society. These constituted what might be termed the pluralists or the "pluralistic" Muslim minority. There were others who either wanted or were obliged to participate in the political, cultural and social life of the dominant group and these made up the "accommodationists". Finally, there were increasing numbers of Muslims, mainly scholars, who sought religious and political authority and took militant means to achieve these ends.

Throughout this period, however, Muslims in general, including a majority of the scholars, adopted a pacific approach to the spread of Islam. The militant approach did have its supporters in southern Mauretania, the Senegambia and Air, and in the 19th century, as we shall see, it came to be regarded in many parts of West Africa as the only viable approach to the reform and spread of Islam.

Although the 17th and 18th centuries have been described as an age of Islamic stagnation and pagan reaction",[1] it is the view of a growing number of historians and one which I share that Islam, although experiencing a number of setbacks, made considerable progress in many parts of West Africa during these centuries. By 1800 most of West Africa it is true was still non-Muslim. Islam's greatest advances were made in the 19th and 20th centuries. Nevertheless, in the 1600 – 1800 period Islam spread into areas where it had not previously existed. Moreover, this period witnessed important developments in the educational, legal and intellectual side of Islam. If development was slow and imperceptible at times and even accompanied on occasion by decline, it was nonetheless real and played a vital part in charting the course Islam was to take in the 19th century.

Islam in the south-western Sahara (Shinqit/Mauretania).

A new society emerged in the western Sahara as a result of the process of

Arabization which we discussed in Chapter 3. The Hassaniya dialect o
Arabic became the lingua franca and the Arab immigrants took over as the
dominant political group, leaving the literate, formally educated Sanhaja to
look after the religious and commercial life of the society. Moreover, the 15th
century saw the emergence in the western Sahara of the Kunta and the
Qadiriyya Muslim brotherhood, both of which were to prove very effective
instruments in the spread of Islam, although at first the Qadiriyya was no
popular among the Sahaja because of its strong North African connections.

During the 18th and 19th centuries the Zawaya scholars, in building on the
already existing tradition of learning in the south-western Sahara, increased
Mauretania's importance as a centre of Islamic learning, mysticism and mis
sionary activity. With regard to learning Mauretania and certain district
around its borders became the most influential Arabic cultural centre in the
Sahel, producing at the Arabic colleges, such as the one at Boutilimit in
Mauretania, a wide range of high quality Arabic literature, much of which
was concerned with Islamic law and mysticism.[2]

The Senegambia was among those areas of West Africa most directly
influenced by the missionary zeal of the Zawaya from Mauretania. One
Mauretanian Zawaya group, the Idaw al-Hajj, was responsible for the estab
lishment of the Muslim brotherhood known as the Shadhilliyya among th
Wolof of Senegal. Other Mauretanian religious educators took up residenc
in Senegalese villages and gained a reputation for themselves as scholars an
holy men. It was not, however, all one-way traffic: the Senegambians also
made a contribution to the advancement of Islamic learning in the western
Saharan region. Mauretanians such as Ahmad al-'Aqil went, according to
tradition, to study in Futa Jallon in central Guinea (Conakry) in the
Senegambia. It is interesting to note in connection with Ahmad al-'Aqil tha
his sister Khadija was an Islamic scholar and, according to tradition, had a
one of her pupils at her school in Mauretania the well known 18th-century
reformer and jihadist Abd al-Qadir, who took over from Sulayman Bal a
leader of the Muslim reform movement in Futa Toro in northern Senegal in
1776.

Among the Mauretanian Zawaya groups which perhaps contributed mos
to the dissemination of Islam in the northern part of Senegambia was th
Idaw al-Hajj. Members of this body of religious teachers and guides such a
Hamdi b. Mukhtar Mahjub (d. 1802) and his three sons converted man
inhabitants in the villages along the Senegal river and further south to Islam
The Banu Dayman was another Mauretanian Zawaya group that influence
the course of Islam's development both in southern Mauretania and in th
Senegambia. But whereas the majority of the religious specialists of th
Zawaya chose to pursue their objective of disseminating Islam by peacefu
means, one of their associates, Nasir al-Din, a member of the Banu Dayma
Zawaya, decided to embark on a series of military campaigns to throw off th
authority of the Arab overlords, and to reform Islam. Nasir al-Din by doin
this was not only high-lighting the stresses and strains in the relationshi
between the Zawaya class and the Arab aristocracy, but was also rejectin
the idea, generally accepted by scholars in the region from the 15th centur
and perhaps even earlier, that religious specialists ought not to use arm

either in defence of their own and their communities' interests, or for the purpose of reforming or disseminating Islam.

The Jihad of Nasir al-Din, c. 1673—77.

Prior to the military phase of his holy war in the 1670s, Nasir al-Din attempted to bring about an Islamic revival through preaching and teaching. He hoped that a renewed and revived Islamic society, founded on Islamic law and governed through Islamic institutions, would put an end to the political and military domination of the south-western Sahara by the Hassani aristocracy. Nasir al-Din also intended to reform Islam in the Senegambia and to overcome the political, economic and other divisions there by uniting people in a true Muslim community. It is also worth bearing in mind that Nasir al-Din's campaign for the reform of Islam took place during a period when the Atlantic slave trade was contributing along with the gum trade to the polarisation of Senegambian society between slave-trading warrior élites and a Muslim community which participated minimally in the trade.[3] Realising the opposition to the slave trade among the ordinary people, Nasir al-Din included an anti-slave trade provision in his reform programme.

To show that his intentions were religious Nasir al-Din took the titles al-Imam (leader of the faithful in prayer) and Amir al-Mu'minin (Commander of the Faithful.) The taking of these titles has led some scholars to think that Nasir al-Din was inspired by the tradition of the reformist, intellectual and militant brand of Islam established by the Almoravids in the Sahara.[4] In support of this view it can be said that Nasir al-Din prided himself on his descent from the Lamtuna who were involved in the Almoravid movement. Nevertheless, it still remains problematic as to whether there was a direct link between Nasir al-Din's jihad and that of the Almoravids. One scholar sees little resemblance between the doctrinal issues in Nasir al-Din's movement and those which preoccupied 'Abdullah b. Yasin.[5]

For more than a decade Nasir al-Din tried to win over rulers and people in southern Mauretania and the Senegambia to his reform movement. He did gain quite a large following among the ordinary people who were told by his missionaries that if they converted to Islam and accepted the toubenan (religious conversion), they would be spared such tasks as planting grain. Moreover, the missionaries emphasised that the End of Time was close and that the Mahdi would soon appear and rid the world of injustice and every sort of evil and assure the triumph of Islam.

There is a contemporary account of the preaching activities of Nasir al-Din. In this account he is described as going from village to village in Senegal in 1673, and without consulting the ruler, he is said to have preached openly to the people that he was sent by God to reform Islam. In addition he declared that God clearly disapproved of and would bring to an end the evil practices of the kings which included killing, pillaging and enslaving their people. He emphasised that the rulers were there to serve and protect the people, and apparently the people listened to this charismatic leader, at the time only about 30 years of age, who with shaven head and clothes discarded, preached the necessity for everyone to repent and obey God's law.[6]

Some of those who listened to Nasir al-Din responded to his call for reform by modelling their appearance on that of their leader, that is shaving their heads and discarding their clothes. They also redoubled their prayers, reformed their lives, abandoned their work and took up arms against their rulers. It was in 1673 that Nasir al-Din decided to resort to military jihad to bring about his reform and establish his Islamic state. He enjoyed some success initially, securing control of Futa Toro, Walo and Cayor. In both Walo and Cayor internal dissension among the ruling élite enabled Nasir al-Din to gain control. Leaders acceptable to Nasir al-Din were appointed in the conquered kingdoms before he moved into southern Mauretania for the purpose of establishing his authority there. In southern Mauretania, however, the Hassaniya, united behind their leader, Haddi b. Ahmad b. Daman, refused to recognise Nasir al-Din's authority, and in the battle at Tirtillas in August 1674 Nasir al-Din was killed. Within a few years of his death the reform movement which he had initiated had almost completely collapsed. The Denianké rulers returned to Futa Toro, and Walo and Cayor reasserted their independence.

Although Nasir al-Din's reform movement lasted for a relatively short period of time its long term significance should not be underestimated. Nasir al-Din was a Muslim scholar who demonstrated his opposition to the practice of accommodating Islam to existing non-Muslim beliefs and practices. He was also prepared to go against the approach of many Muslim scholars, by taking up arms and stepping into the political arena to further his campaign for the reform of Islam, the elimination of injustice and the preservation of the economic and political interests of his own people. He was, in fact, one of the first examples — there was another case of a militant Muslim scholar in Air at about the same time (see p. 92) — in West Africa since the Almoravid movement of the Muslim intellectual-cum-warrior to decide to solve the political, religious and economic problems facing his people by recourse to jihad of the sword. Soon after the collapse of Nasir al-Din's jihad other Muslim scholars in Senegal and elsewhere in West Africa, living in societies which they believed discriminated against them and their followers, societies, moreover, which experienced the tensions brought about by the Atlantic and trans-Saharan slave trade, the importation of firearms and ammunition, and the growing competition from European powers for control of trade and commerce, were to follow his path and take up arms for the purpose of creating Islamic states and reforming Islam.[7]

Islam in the Senegambia.

By the 17th century a number of Islamic beliefs and practices had become widespread in certain parts of the Senegambia, in particular amongst the Wolof, Tokolor and Fulani. In the above mentioned contemporary account of religion in Senegal written in 1674, for example, it is stated that the people are Muslims, obey the precepts of the Qur'an, perform the prayers (salat), observe Ramadan (the fast), do not eat pork or drink wine, participate in the Muslim festivals and some make the pilgrimage to Mecca. Muslim judges, according to this report, dispense justice according to Islamic law. However, it is clear from the account, if the author observed things correctly, that a number of the above mentioned Islamic rites were not performed correctly. We are told, for example, that the people performed the prayer three or four times a day, instead of the required five times.[1] There were, of course, exceptions like the Siratik (ruler) of Futa Toro who did not drink wine or brandy and obeyed "the law of Muhammad more religiously than others".[2]

The Jakhanke, religious educators and missionaries, had set up Muslim centres in many places in the Senegambia, including Diamou, Bafoulabe, Kayes, Bakel and Guemou. By the mid-18th century the Jakhanke "holy town" of Gunjur had acquired a reputation as an important religious centre. Muslim scholars there were advisers to the ruler of Bundu, in whose territory the town was situated, and helped in the establishment of Qur'anic schools throughout the kingdom. Jakhanke missionaries and scholars were also active in Futa Jallon in modern Guinea (Conakry). One of the most influential Jakhanke scholars in Futa Jallon in the 18th century and early 19th century was Karamoko Ba (1730 – 1824). Wherever he travelled, and he travelled widely, he was followed by students. He settled in Kankan in Guinea for three years and gained a formidable reputation as a scholar. Later he founded the town of "New Touba" in Futa Jallon, and this town played an important role in developing and expanding Islam in central Guinea and beyond. As its reputation spread, students from Mandinkaland and elsewhere flocked to New Touba.[3]

The Torodbe, like the Jakhanke, founded strong Muslim communities in areas of the Senegambia where Islam had not previously existed. Unlike the Jakhanke, however, they made a very clear distinction between dar al-Islam (the land of Islam) and dar al-harb (the land of war). Non-Muslims were excluded from Torodbe communities whereas the Jakhanke offered their services to Muslims and non-Muslims alike. The Torodbe, moreover, allowed trade between Muslims and Christians only if the Christians accepted the status of a "protected people" and paid a tribute known as the *jizya* in recognition of Muslim authority. This tax had to be paid by Christians who wanted to trade with Bundu in the Senegambia after Bundu had become an Islamic state in the 1690s. The well-known Torodbe religious leader and Jihadist, al-Hajj 'Umar Tall, who created the Tokolor empire in the mid-19th century, demanded that the French in the Senegambia pay the *jizya*, since in his view they were Christians living and trading in areas ruled by Muslims like himself and were therefore obliged by Islamic law to pay tribute in recognition of Muslim authority.

The Muslim traders, the Dyula, were also active in settlements in the Senegambia, for example, at Soundouta near Tambacounda in Senegal and another just south east of Kankan in Guinea (Conakry). Like the Jakhanke and the Torodbe, the Dyula opened schools and undertook additional tasks such as the organisation of the pilgrimage to Mecca, thereby increasing West African contacts with the intellectual influences and ideas prevalent in the rest of the Muslim world. The pilgrimage, moreover, not only drew West African Muslims into the orbit of North African and Arabian Islam but also made it possible for West Africans to make a comparison between the state of Islam in West Africa and the state of Islam in the rest of the Muslim world. At times such comparisons, as we shall see, reflected unfavourably on Islam in West Africa and motivated West African Muslim pilgrims to purify and reform the Muslim community in West Africa on their return home from the hajj.

Without the financial resources and initiative of the Dyula the considerable advances made in Islamic education and learning in many areas of West Africa would not have been possible. The Dyula initiative was so successful because it was so well organised.[4] In every Dyula settlement students were trained to teach in and administer the schools, while others worked to provide the money. The Dyula system of social organisation was flexible and adaptable enough to allow both the survival and multiplication of educational institutions. The Dyula were organised into work units known as *lu*, and then into wider units such as the So and Kabula (tribe). The male lu consisted of a set of brothers, their father, their children and in addition some cousins or slaves. When such units were economically strong the father would send his senior son for advanced studies, and indeed most of the members of the lu would be allowed to go for higher education. However, where the lu was not economically strong only the younger sons would be allowed to pursue their studies to a higher level. The system of social organisation, therefore, was arranged in such a way that the members could take the opportunity to go to school without undermining the commercial or economic interests of the work unit (lu).

In the Senegambia, therefore, there was a network of Muslim centres, villages, colleges and schools in the 17th and 18th centuries. The people of the villages looked to the Muslim religious specialists for leadership and guidance, and the colleges and schools produced an educated élite, some of whom were critical of and challenged the authority of the rulers of the states in which they lived. According to tradition one of these Muslim colleges, Pir Saniokhor, in Cayor in Senegal, produced the leaders of the Muslim revolt which took place in Futa Toro in 1776. In addition, a number of other revolts, linked in some respects as we shall see to the Nasir al-Din reform movement, occurred in the Senegambia in the 17th and 18th centuries.

Militant Islam in the Senegambia in the 17th and 18th centuries.

Militant Islam in the Senegambia and elsewhere in West Africa was the product of a variety of forces, social, political, economic, educational and religious. The emergence of a group of educated Muslims, such as the Torodbe, has already been mentioned. The Torodbe were not inclined passively to accept a situation in which the Muslim community was discriminated against or obliged to undertake duties which were contrary to the tenets of Islam, such as military service under a non-Muslim or a "lapsed" Muslim ruler. On the contrary, they accepted the necessity of defending and advancing their rights by military jihad or holy war. Moreover, they received support from the Muslim peasant population who were frequently subjected to plunder and pillaging by the warrior class, the *tyeddo*, and those involved in the trans-Atlantic slave trade. Moreover, the development of trade with Europe contributed significantly to the bringing about of important economic, social and political change in the Senegambia. With increasing trade and commerce came increasing supplies of weapons and ammunition which enabled the traditional ruling élite, the tyeddo, and also the opponents of the ruling élite, to battle more effectively for political power and wealth. It also assured the warrior groups of power over the masses, in whose eyes they were no more than plunderers and thieves who lived by pillaging. The result was greater political instability and tension, and only a minimum of protection and security for the farmers, fishermen and other less powerful groups.

It was in this situation that Muslims in the villages began to look to Muslim leaders among the Torodbe for political as well as religious guidance. It was, moreover, in this situation that an "oppositional" Islam began to emerge and challenge the traditional authority. It would not, of course, be correct to imply that all Muslims set themselves in opposition to the traditional rulers and the tyeddo, for some of the rulers and the tyeddo were themselves Muslims after a fashion and enjoyed the support of other Muslims who were involved in the slave trade and the pillaging, and in the competition for control of commerce and land. Nevertheless, there were Muslim leaders with wide-ranging contacts and who, knit together by marriage alliances and by the fact that they had been educated in the same schools, were prepared to defend and promote the interests of their followers by military jihad.

What I have outlined here is the general context in which the military jihads of the 17th and 18th centuries took place. This context changed over time and sometimes dramatically. The military jihads of the second half of the 19th century, for instance, took place as we shall see in Chapter 5 at a time when the trans-Atlantic trade was being replaced by "legitimate" commerce and at a time when the European colonial powers had begun to extend their political and economic control over the Senegambia.

The Jihad of Malik Sy and the creation of the Imamate of Bundu, c.1696.

Malik Sy created an Islamic state in the Senegambia known as Bundu which lasted for almost 200 years. Born near Podor in Futa Toro in the 1640s, Malik Sy was the son of a Muslim teacher. After attending Qur'anic school he continued his studies at the Muslim college at Pir in Cayor in Senegal. After completing his studies, Malik Sy, like so many others, travelled far and wide in search of further knowledge, eventually taking up a post as governor of the southern region of the kingdom of Gadiaga in Senegal. The region was inhabited by a variety of different peoples such as the Mande-speaking agriculturalists and the land-hungry Fulani refugees from Futa Toro. Moreover, it had scarcely been touched by Islam.

Joined by increasing numbers of Fulani and Tokolor refugees from Futa Toro, Malik Sy strengthened his forces and, resorting to arms in what has been considered a holy war, he severed his allegiance to the ruler of Gadiaga, imposed his authority by force on the southern region of the kingdom, and proceeded to extend the frontiers of his newly established Islamic state. Bundu, the capital of this Islamic state, was conveniently situated on a trade route along which passed gold and kola nuts.

Malik Sy ruled over Bundu for 13, or possibly for 17, years. Like Nasir al-Din he came from a family of religious teachers who had connections with people in the same profession in southern Mauretania, Nasir al-Din's homeland. Moreover, Malik Sy may have been in Futa Toro during the time of Nasir al-Din's takeover there, and possibly joined his army. As Curtin suggests, therefore, Malik Sy was probably influenced by Nasir al-Din's militant reform movement.[5]

The establishment in Bundu of an Islamic state by a member of the Muslim intellectual élite from Futa Toro, supported by pastoral Fulani who were anxious to change the social order and by business people, was followed by several other military jihads in different areas of the Senegambia in the 18th century.

The Jihad of Alfa Karamoko in Futa Jallon.

As I indicated in Chapter 2, it is not always clear what the motives were for launching or sustaining a jihad of the sword. According to one historian the jihad of the sword waged in Futa Jallon in the 18th century soon became little more than a cover for slave raiding.[6] However, as another historian points out, although slave exports do appear to have been relatively high during the period c. 1720—1750 when the jihad was under way, and again in the 1780s, it is by no means certain as to whether "the demand for slaves caused the wars of the jihads, rather than the jihads creating a supply of prisoners for sale".[7] Although, the transatlantic slave trade may well have played a part in bringing about the jihad of the sword in Futa Jallon in the 1720s, there were nevertheless a number of other antecedents which combined to give rise to this jihad.

At one time the population of Futa Jallon (in present-day Guinea Conakry), was composed in the main of Dialonke, Susu and Mandinka. These people were mainly hunters and farmers. In the 15th century Koli Tengella from Termes, assisted by Fulani, established the nucleus of a state in the region. Then a new wave of Fulani immigrants entered the territory from Masina in the 16th century, followed by a much larger wave of Fulani towards the end of the 17th century.

Over a period of time clashes between the Dialonke, the masters of the land, and the new arrivals, became more frequent and increasingly violent. One of the main reasons for this was that the Dialonke, the resident farmers, were demanding a payment from the Fulani herdsmen whose cattle were damaging the land and destroying their crops. Some of the settled Fulani supported the Dialonke, both groups being at this stage non-Muslim. Then the Dialonke placed a ban on public prayer, which affected the local Muslim Mandinka merchants and many of the new immigrants from Masina who were either Muslims or sympathetic to Islam as a form of protest against the Dialonke.

It was in this situation that Alfa Karamoko, otherwise known as Musa Ibrahima or Alfa Ibrahima Sembegu, emerged, supported by the chief of the Council of Elders of Timbo, an important town in the south-east of Futa Jallon. Alfa Karamoko had been a Muslim student in Kankan under the respected Jakhanke scholar, Qadir Sanusi. He appears to have been a charismatic leader with a wide appeal. Professor Curtin has tried to demonstrate school and family ties between Alfa Karamoko and Malik Sy, the leader of the jihad in Bundu. Curtin in this way draws the conclusion that there was a connecting chain linking the jihad in Futa Jallon with that in Bundu, and ultimately with Nasir al-Din's jihad in Mauretania. He also suggests, as we shall see, that the jihad in Futa Toro in northern Senegal was likewise part of this militant Islamic tradition of reform.[8]

Alfa Karamoko died in c. 1751 and was succeeded by his cousin Ibrahim Sori, a man with great ambitions in both the political and economic spheres. It was under Ibrahim Sori's leadership that the jihad lost whatever remained of its religious inspiration.

The Muslim community in Futa Jallon which had supported the jihad during the days of Alfa Karamoko, now split into two factions, one of which was the keenly orthodox Islamic faction known as the Alfaya, and the other was the Soriya or followers of Ibrahim Sori, who were more intent on political and commercial control of Futa Jallon than on the creation of the ideal Islamic state. In 1776 Ibrahim Sori abandoned the title Imam al-salat, leader of the Muslim community in prayer, and took on that of Imam al-ta'a, commander of obedience.

This division in Futa Jallon persisted after Ibrahim Sori's death in c. 1781, and to all intents and purposes the struggle to create a united Islamic community administered according to Islamic principles was unsuccessful. Still, Futa Jallon exercised great influence as a centre of Islamic education, and the holy war itself brought many non-Muslim communities, tributaries of Futa Jallon, within the sphere of Islamic influence. These wars also gave rise to a good deal of upheaval and migration which resulted in Muslim communities being established in Sierra Leone and Liberia to the east and south-east of Futa Jallon.

The jihad in Futa Jallon, however, like those that were fought elsewhere, was to some extent, counter-productive. It created a hostile reaction to Islam among some non-Muslim communities and even on occasion alienated Muslim sympathisers. In Futa Jallon, for instance, the Solima people whose leaders had become Muslims were at first in alliance with the jihadists but later, disenchanted with the course of the jihad under Ibrahim Sori, withdrew their support and moved into Sierra Leone where they established the non-Muslim state of Falaba.

The Jihad of Sulayman Bal in Futa Toro.

Once ruled by the Tokolor, the kingdom of Futa Toro was taken over by the Denianke dynasty founded by the warrior Koli Tengella. The Denianke rulers, who bore the title Siratik (leader of the way), ruled in the late 16th and for most of the 17th century not only over northern Senegal but also over southern Mauretania, and this partly explains why Nasir al-Din waged his *jihad* against Futa Toro.

The Denianke rulers of Futa Toro, although they recovered somewhat from their defeat at the hands of Nasir al-Din in the 1670s, were no longer as powerful in the 18th century as they had been between 1590 and 1670. During the 18th century the Denianke rulers of Futa Toro were constantly challenged by Moorish and other political factions and as a result the kingdom was a prey to lawlessness and political instability. King after king was driven out by internal and external rivals, struggling for power and a monopoly of commerce and trade. In the main it was the Moorish faction that gained the upper hand particularly in the second half of the 18th century and were regarded by the Tokolor and the other inhabitants of Futa Toro as responsible in great measure for causing distress all along the Senegal river.

It was in this situation of virtual anarchy that Sulayman Bal, a Tokolor and a Muslim scholar who had schooled in Futa Jallon, emerged and gathered around himself a party of Muslims dedicated to the reform of Islam, the creation of political stability and the establishment of law and order. Once these objectives had been achieved Sulayman Bal believed that the people of Futa Toro would be able to resist the threat to their independence from the Moors to the north. It was against the Moors in Trarza in particular, in the southwestern province of Mauretania, that Sulayman Bal launched his campaigns in the 1760s and 1770s. The Trarza emirate, and further east the Brakna emirate, were established in the 17th century. In addition to being the main centre of the Berber zawaya groups such as the Banu Dayman to which Nasir al-Din belonged, Trarza also had forests of gum trees, gum being a much sought after commodity in Europe.

In the course of fighting against the Moors Sulayman Bal overthrew the Denianke dynasty in Futa Toro and opened the way for the establishment of an Islamic state in the territory. He himself was killed while engaged in combat with the Moors in 1776 and was succeeded by 'Abd al-Qadir, who was elected to the office of Almamy (leader of the faithful in prayer and of the Muslim Community).

Under 'Abd al-Qadir the wars against the Trarza Moors continued until 1786 − 7 when the Moors were defeated. The Almamy also extended the war to Bundu and Cayor, but was taken prisoner during the attack on Cayor in 1796 − 7. He was released, however, and on returning to Futa Toro he entrusted authority over the various provinces to those who had fought in the jihad. 'Abd al-Qadir also carved out territory which he placed under the authority of the deposed Denianke in return for the payment of tribute. He believed that in showing such leniency to the Denianke he would ensure their support against his other rivals. It seems, however, that he miscalculated in this. It is not certain what exactly led to the downfall of 'Abd al-Qadir but it appears that the Denianke played a part in his overthrow. According to one account he was overthrown in 1805 by a coalition comprising the Denianke, the Almamy of Bundu and the Bambara ruler of Kaarta, and then in 1806 he was put to death by the Almamy of Bundu aided by Kaarta.

Militant Islam in the 18th century: an assessment.

The Muslim scholars turned militant reformers in the Senegambia established relatively strong Muslim communities in areas where Islam had either been non-existent or was only superficially adhered to by those who professed to be Muslims. Moreover, they created what might be termed a more scholarly form of Islam, which was also an Islam opposed to much of the culture and attitudes of the surrounding society. Mungo Park, for example, who visited Bundu in the late 18th century, stated that a large majority of the inhabitants of Bundu were Muslims and that "the authority and laws of the Prophet (Muhammad) were everywhere looked upon as sacred and decisive". He also wrote about how Islam was spreading throughout the schools and mentioned that most of the people had some knowledge of Arabic.[9]

Islam was emerging as a counter-tradition, so to speak, whereas previously it had been accommodationist, assimilationist and prepared to coexist peacefully with the non-Muslim community. Instead of turning completely to mysticism and messianic theories, these Muslim scholars in parts of the Senegambia came to insist on the necessity of assuming political authority. This occurred partly for the reason that as a minority some Muslims felt that they were being discriminated against and subjected to intolerable pressures, such as the payment of heavy taxes and service in the armed forces of non-Muslim states. Furthermore, as I have indicated, society was being turned upside down by the slave trade, the importation of arms and ammunition, the pillaging and devastations wrought by the tyeddo, and people were crying out for protection, stability and law and order.

Moreover, in addition to improving the quality of Islamic life and education — and I realise that I am generalising here and that there were exceptions and even at times a decline in these spheres — the Muslim scholars, in particular the Torodbe of the Tokolor, who were behind most of these militant Islamic movements, also gained for Islam control of the land. The new Muslim rulers of Bundu, Futa Jallon and Futa Toro, while leaving intact all rights prior to the conquest, nevertheless as Imams came to hold the land in trust for the people and had the right to assign plots for people to cultivate. Furthermore, people only had the right to work the land on payment of the zakat, and this ensured the administration of land within a Muslim framework.

Having begun, however, with the intention of democratizing society and making it more egalitarian, some of the Muslim reformers allowed these ideals to slip out of sight and ended up turning the Imamate, an elected office open to all freemen, into the preserve of a few families. The artisans, slaves and other deprived groups, at first encouraged to participate in the new order, were soon once again to have to rest content with their lot.

Islam in the Upper and Middle Niger region.

The greater part of the Upper and Middle Niger region situated today in the West African republics of Mali, Niger and Nigeria, was under Songhay's control at the time of the Moroccan invasion in 1591. This invasion, as we have seen, led to greater political instability and a decline in trade in the region as the Songhay empire broke up into a number of smaller, independent kingdoms in which Islam was no longer the official state religion. This situation persisted until the 18th century when the Mande-speaking Bambara people, whose rulers were either non-Muslim or like Sundiata and Sunni Ali only nominal Muslims, came to dominate large areas of the region. The main centres of Bambara power were at Segu on the Upper Niger, and at Nioro in the breakaway Bambara state of Kaarta to the north-west of Segu.

By the second half of the 18th century, during the reign of N'Golo (c. 1753 — 90) the Bambara had extended their authority over such renowned centres of Islamic learning as Timbuktu. This was a blow to Islam that may, however, have been softened by the fact that Timbuktu was no longer as influential or prestigious as an Islamic centre as it had been in the 16th century, and also by the fact that some of the Bambara rulers of Segu appointed Muslims as judges, advisers and government officials, and even claimed to be Muslims themselves. Mungo Park observed when he visited Segu in 1805 that there were mosques in every quarter of the town.

The collapse of Songhay and the rise of the even more superficially Islamic Bambara kingdoms did not put an end to the spread of Islam in the upper and middle Niger region as a whole. In certain parts of the region Islam did suffer setbacks and the indigenous religions either regained some of their adherents who had converted to Islam or they remained unchallenged and unopposed even by those Bambara rulers who claimed to be Muslims. The latter regarded Islam very much as an addition to and not a substitute or replacement for the indigenous religion. Nevertheless, the diffusion and development of Islam continued. The Muslim brotherhoods, such as the Qadiriyya, played a major role in this continued expansion and development, and so too did the wandering Muslim teacher, highly mobile and close to the people whose needs he understood and who valued him for his advice as healer, interpreter of dreams and man of prayer.

Mungo Park's diaries of his expeditions to the upper and middle Niger region in 1795 — 6 and in 1805 — 6 contain many examples of the value to the local communities in the region of the Muslim religious teacher and holy man. He recorded, for example, how a group of mallams helped a mother who was torn with grief on seeing her son, a young herdsman, who had been badly wounded in the leg by a shot fired by the Moors. Park, since he trained as a medical student, had some knowledge of surgery and recommended that the leg be amputated. The boy's mother and the rest of his family refused, and asked some Muslim preachers to prepare the boy for the next life. They got the boy to profess faith in the One God and in Muhammad as God's messenger, and then assured the boy's mother that the boy would be happy in a future life. The boy died the same evening and the mother's anxiety Park tells us was alleviated.[1] This event, and many others recorded by Park in his diaries, shows the direct appeal and relevance of the Muslim holy man and missionary to the ordinary people.

I want now to look in a little more detail at the Kunta, and at one Kunta leader in particular, in relation to Islamic expansion and development in the upper and middle Niger region in the period 1600 — 1800.

The role of the Kunta in the dissemination of Islam in the upper and middle Niger regions.

The Kunta, successful as Muslim religious teachers and as business people, were one of several zawaya groups to play a dominant role in the expansion and development of Islam in the upper and middle Niger regions during the

17th and 18th centuries. I realise that one cannot provide an adequate account of the influence and impact of the Kunta or any other movement or group of people by examining the ideas and activities of only one member of the movement or group. I want nevertheless to provide some idea of the role of the Kunta in the expansion and growth of Islam through a consideration of the career of a very influential Kunta leader, Shaikh Sidi al-Mukhtar al-Kabir "the Great" al-Kunti.

The spiritual jihad of Shaikh Sidi al-Mukhtar al-Kabir al-Kunti (1729 — 1811).

Shaikh Sidi al-Mukhtar "the Great" was born near Arawan to the north of Timbuktu in the Sahara in 1722 or 1729, and by way of contrast to Nasir al-Din and other Muslim reformers he continued to insist throughout on the necessity of the Greater Jihad, the spiritual jihad, as the best means of reforming and spreading Islam, and he enjoyed remarkable success. A great deal of what we know about his early life is legendary rather than historical. Legend can often, of course, be a more important influence in the shaping and moulding of a career or a movement than historical fact, however pure. While a young man Shaikh Sidi al-Mukhtar "the Great" gained a wide reputation as a Muslim scholar and attracted the attention of many students who decided as a result to go and study under him. He also aroused the envy and jealousy of a number of Muslim experts in the Islamic sciences who frequently challenged him to debate certain aspects of Islamic law. According to one history of the Shaikh's life, he won all these debates.[2]

The most important victory he gained was success in a debate against the leader of the Kel Antassar. The latter, Tuareg scholars living in and around Timbuktu and along the route to Gao, had gained a reputation as outstanding scholars and Muslim missionaries among the peoples to the north, east and west of Timbuktu. However, after the debate they appear to have been superceded as the most prominent exponents of the Islamic faith by that branch of the Kunta led by Shaikh Sidi al-Mukhtar "the Great".

The Shaikh wrote a great deal; according to one account he wrote over 300 books and treatises, and in his writings he emphasised the importance of the greater jihad, that is, jihad or holy war of the heart, mind and tongue, over against military jihad, or jihad of the sword, referred to as lesser jihad. In his view a Muslim who wanted to make progress should place himself under the direction and guidance of an accomplished spiritual guide or shaikh, and learn to empty himself of all attachment to material things. He did not mean by this that a person should not work hard to acquire wealth, on the contrary he insisted that engagement in commerce was Sunna — something one should do since Prophet Mohammad had recommended it by his own actions, being a merchant prior to his call to prophethood. This attitude towards wealth is in some respects very similar to that of the Calvinist as described by Max Weber, the sociologist, and to that of Ahmad Bamba, founder of the Muridiyya brotherhood in Senegal (see Chapter 7).

A variety of different claims to knowledge and sainthood were made by Shaikh Sidi on his own behalf and were accepted by his followers. He claimed, for example, to be by descent a Wali, that is a person who sees himself and is seen by his followers as close to or a friend of Allah. According to certain Muslim mystics one can become a Wali by fair different ways, through descent, or by right of birth, or by what is known as "divine attraction" whereby God draws a person to himself without any effort being made by the individual concerned, or by following certain religious exercises which demand a great deal of personal effort.[3]

As a Wali, Shaikh Sidi believed, and so did his followers, that he was not only near to God, but was also guided and protected by God. It was understood that spirits (jinn) and human beings would be loyal to such a person. In his capacity as Wali Shaikh Sidi claimed to be able to exercise a considerable influence over peoples' lives and on the course of history. He claimed, for instance, to have been requested to save the Muslim Ottoman army in the war against Russia, and to have been requested by people to recover stolen property from bandits.[4]

A man noted for the simplicity of his appearance, Shaikh Sidi regarded himself and was regarded by others as in some senses an extraordinary figure, being described by Muhammad Bello, who succeeded his father Usuman dan Fodio as Caliph of the Sokoto Empire in northern Nigeria, as "the legal expert, the mystic, the upright Wali, the Pole of Poles . . . the last of the Sufi Imams who were well versed in the Shari'a (Islamic sacred law) and the sciences of Haqiqa (Truth)".[5] Others asserted that Shaikh Sidi could see far beyond the normal distance, revive the dead, appear in two places at the same time (the gift of bilocation, a claim made on the behalf of many Christian saints), predict the future, and transform himself into another object or being. Many believed him when he claimed to be the mujaddid, the renewer of Islam for the 13th century.

Shaikh Sidi was a charismatic figure in the sense outlined in Chapter 2, and his influence was felt in the Middle Niger region and beyond in the 18th century and for a long time afterwards. He is, in fact, credited with having had an influence on Islam over a vast area stretching from Air in the east across West Africa to Senegal in the west, and from southern Morocco in the north as far south as Nigeria. One writer states that throughout this area there were to be found followers of Shaikh Sidi among the celebrities and notables, including such important Muslim leaders as the reformer Usuman dan Fodio of Hausaland, his brother Abdullah, and his son and successor Muhammad Bello.[6] Moreover, as leader of the Qadiriyya in West Africa, Shaikh Sidi did a great deal to revive and strengthen this Muslim brotherhood. Among those he initiated into the Qadiriyya order was Alfa Nuhi, a Jakhanke from Masina in the upper Niger region. Alfa Nuhi in turn initiated Karamoko Ba, the Jakhanke Muslim scholar who, as we mentioned previously, travelled widely in the upper and middle Niger area, teaching in places such as Kankan and Jenne, and establishing Muslim centres such as New Touba.[7]

While it is possible to dismiss some of Shaikh Sidi's claims, such as his claim to be able to see beyond normal distances or to have the ability to be in two places at the same time, it is important to remember that his followers accepted these claims and regarded him as an extraordinary individual, and it is this fact that matters most in terms of his impact on history. Furthermore, Shaikh Sidi's insistence on the pacific approach to the reform and dissemiation of Islam should not lead one to regard him as lacking in conviction. He directed a great deal of harsh criticism against Muslims both high and low on account of the unsatisfactory way in which they practised their religion.

The commercial rivalry, moreover, between the different Zawaya groups, and the fact that they challenged each other for religious and intellectual supremacy, and at times supported different political factions, made for disagreements and differences between the Shaikh and others. However, while Shaikh Sidi al-Muhktar "the Great" and his followers insisted on the pacific approach to the reform and spread of Islam, there were others, like the Tuareg Kel Antassar, who were in the process of moving towards the position of accepting that the scholar was justified in taking up a militant stand in defence of his interests and in the cause of Islam.

Islam in Air.

Apart from extending their authority over Adrar and their occasional military victories over Borno and Gobir, Zamfara and Katsina, the Tuareg sultans of Agades experienced numerous disasters of a political, economic and natural kind during the 17th and 18th centuries. Among the natural disasters were the epidemic of 1687, the drought of 1697–9 which was followed by treacherous rains in which people, homes and crops were destroyed, and the plague in Agades in the 1680s in which many people lost their lives. On the political front divisions and disputes among the different branches of the Tuareg led to political instability and forced the Sultans to flee the capital on many occasions. These internal conflicts and the wars with neighbours to the south, disrupted trade and commerce and thereby weakened Air's economy.

Through all of this, however, rulers and ordinary people found time to perform some of their duties as Muslims such as the pilgrimage to Mecca. In one contemporary account, for example, we are told that al-Hajj Akanfay, the son of the Sultan Muhammad al-Mubarak, made his third pilgrimage to Mecca in 1681. "He performed it (the pilgrimage)", the account states, "with a company of the people of Agades and its fuqaha" (Muslim legal experts) and the tribe of the Kel Away.[1] The Kel Away or Owi were an important Tuareg group who entered Air in the 16th century and may have been involved in the martyrdom of the mystic and scholar, Shaikh Mahmud al-Baghdadi.

Shaikh Mahmud al-Baghdadi's martyrdom tells us something about the power struggles and the attitude of some Tuareg groups in 16th-century Air Islamic mysticism (Sufism).[2] It appears that the Muslim jurists and the sultans of Air viewed with suspicion what they considered to be the unbridled mysticism and strong appeal of the Sufi orders and their leaders. In addition to the real or imaginary threat to their position and authority from mystics like Shaikh Mahmud al-Baghdadi, rulers and Muslim officials in many parts of West Africa were faced with Islamic reform movements led by zealous Muslim leaders who in some instances branded other Muslims as infidels deserving of death.

Viewing Sufism at a more general level it may well be that it appears as a threat to a regime or society whether religious or political, which places great

emphasis on the correct observance of specific ritual and legal enactmen
and where these are regarded as the main criteria of allegiance and fidelity. .
Sufi, or Muslim mystic, might argue, for example, that the only real pilgrim
age is not the pilgrimage to Mecca but the pilgrimage of the soul to God alor
the path marked out by qualified shaikhs or religious guides. If this type o
advice is not correctly understood it could lead to a devaluation of the pilgrim
age to Mecca and other observances which constitute the foundations of Islam

Furthermore, in the 18th and 19th centuries and even as early as the 17t
century as we have seen, Muslim rulers who were either unconcerned o
unwilling to establish an Islamic society had reasons to fear the mystics ar
the Muslim brotherhoods that trained people in mysticism. When one lool
back it is the case that virtually every challenge to the existing political ar
religious authorities came from a Muslim scholar who had received trainir
in mysticism and was a member of a Sufi brotherhood. Not all mystics, o
course, were radical, militant reformers. Shaikh Sidi al-Mukhtar al-Kabir a
Kunti provides a good example of one who was not. Moreover, many of th
Zawaya groups and the Jakhanke communities remained committed to th
pacific approach to the spread and reform of Islam, even though they pra
tised mysticism.

Nevertheless in the West African setting and elsewhere in the Musli
world, the following, the organisation and the appeal of the Muslim mysti
in addition to his sometimes considerable economic power acquired by h
organisation's involvement in commerce and the gifts received for his he
and prayers, have led rulers to regard mystics as rivals and a force to l
reckoned with. It is possible that Shaikh Mahmud al-Baghdadi fell into th
category and was therefore martyred.

Among the Tuareg, as was the case among the Sanhaja of the sout
western Sahara, communities of scholars emerged devoted to the study of t
Islamic sciences and the dissemination and development of Islam by peacef
means. These Tuareg scholars were known as Ineslemen (Muslims) and, li
their counterparts in the western Sahara, had ruled out militant holy war a
means of reforming society. However, as I have already mentioned, by t
17th century some groups of Ineslemen began to think again about the
approach to reform and came to the conclusion that Muslim scholars li
themselves could and should resort to militant jihad or holy war.

One Tuareg scholar influenced by this thinking was Hadahada, an aml
tious man who dreamt of creating an Islamic empire which would stret
across West Africa from Timbuktu to Air, and in which Arabic would be t
lingua franca.[3] It is worth noting in relation to Hadahada's aims that t
movement of Arab peoples from North Africa into the Air and upper a
middle Niger regions had not led to a process of Arabisation on anything li
the same scale as was the case in the western Sahara among the Sanhaja.

Hadahada launched a holy war in the 1640s which brought about t
destruction of towns such as Taduq on the border of Air and the destructi
of several holy places like Jikat both on the borders and inside the Sultana
itself. Hadahada justified his actions by claiming to be the mujaddid, t
Muslim reformer, whom as we have seen al-Maghili among others ma
tained would appear once every hundred years, and he accused the Musl

ilers of Air of being infidels and therefore no longer commanding the
bedience of their subjects.

There was strong opposition from a number of Muslim scholars and holy
en to Hadahada's attack on the Sultans, and to the aims of his *jihad*. One
oly man charged him with having launched his attacks "against Islam
one", attacks which could not be considered as constituting a *jihad*. Other
ilitant Islamic reform movements followed that of Hadahada, one of the
ore notable being that organised and led by Muhammad al-Jaylani in Adrar
the first half of the 19th century (see Chapter 5).

By 1800, therefore, although free of Borno control, Air was experiencing
rious economic and political problems. However, in the midst of these
oblems centres like Agades retained their reputation as places of Islamic
arning and scholarship, attracting scholars and students from Sokoto and
ano. In some respects Islamic influence was becoming stronger: the matri-
real form of succession for example, unacceptable to Islam, was on the
ane, although it never completely died out. Many compromises continued
be made, however, between Islam and non-Islamic Tuareg customs, com-
omises made necessary in the opinion of some by the nomadic existence
the Tuareg. As we shall see in more detail later, some Tuareg refomers
e Muhammad al-Jaylani, whose views were backed up by Muhammad
llo, the Muslim reformer and Caliph of Sokoto, were of the opinion that
e life of a settled existence in a town was more favourable to the develop-
ent of an Islamic community than the nomadic life of the desert (see
apter 5).

am in the Volta Basin.

am in Mossi society in the upper Volta Basin.

we saw in Chapter 3, the inhabitants of the Mossi kingdoms of Wagadugu
d Yatenga had been in contact with Islam since the 14th century. Very few
them, however, had become Muslims by 1600. Moreover, I pointed out
t in the 15th century the rulers of the Mossi states had strongly resisted
nghay's attempts to convert them to Islam. On being requested by envoys
m Askiya Muhammad Ture to convert to Islam, the Moro Naba (ruler of
: Mossi) replied: "Return to your master and tell him that between him and
there will be only war and combat".[1] Askiya Muhammad reacted by
acking the Mossi in 1497—8. In this war many Mossi men were killed,
iers had their fields destroyed, while others were taken captive along with
men and children. However, apart from the conversion of the Mossi
otives taken by Songhay, Islam made no headway in the Mossi states, the
ers and people preferring to remain for political and religious reasons non-
uslims.[2]

What proved to be impossible to achieve by means of holy war was accom-
shed, although very gradually, by peaceful means. Mande-speaking
uslim traders from Timbuktu and Jenne, known among the Mossi as Yarse,
;an settling, albeit unofficially, in Wagadugu, capital of present-day Upper
lta, in the 16th century. By the 18th century not only had they been given

permission to build a mosque in Wagadugu but some of the rulers ha
decided to convert to Islam. These conversions, however, did not lead t
anything like a complete break with the indigenous religious tradition,
central feature of which was ancestor veneration. The rulers continued t
regard the traditional religion as a vital support of the political system
providing it with a certain degree of stability and legitimacy.

Even in the 18th century, then, rulers like Moro Naba Dulugu, although h
allowed mosques to be opened in Wagadugu and in/the surrounding village
and appointed the first Imam to the royal court, still had reservations abou
Islam. They were particularly concerned that it might lead to a breakdown
the traditional political system which depended for its survival and smool
functioning on the maintenance of a ritual bond between the rulers and the
ancestors. As a result of this fear the Mossi rulers, including those who we
sympathetic to Islam and had turned to Islam themselves, refused to allo
their eldest sons to become too committed to Islam. Their ideal Muslim rul
was one who could balance his commitment to Islam with a continui
adherence to some of the fundamental tenets and practices of the indigeno
religious system.

Islam east of the Black Volta River.

Here I will consider briefly the development of Islam in Gonja, Mamprus
Dagomba and Wa.

Gonja.

There are a number of traditions concerning the founder and the origin
Gonja. According to one of these traditions a group of warriors from t
middle Niger region of Bambara origin imposed their authority over t
people in the Gonja region and established the state of Gonja with Gbuipe
its capital. This invasion probably took place some time in the 16th centu
and already at that time there may have been Muslims in the Gonja area w
had arrived there from Begho, Hausaland and Borno.[3] The founders of t
state, moreover, prior to the invasion had probably had contact with Musl
traders and missionaries in the upper and middle Niger region, and once th
had taken control of the Gonja area they recruited Muslims to assist them
administering the new state.

One of the functions performed by these Muslims was that of keeping "f
mal lists of past chiefs and their imams".[4] This was extremely important giv
the problems and conflicts arising from succession disputes. The Muslims
Gonja would read out the list of names of past chiefs in the presence of t
ruler and the people on the occasion of the festival of Damba, held on t
anniversary of Prophet Muhammad's birth (*Mawlid*). By drawing up th
lists the Muslims were recording history and by reading them out in pub
they were corroborating the claim of the ruler to govern. In return t
Muslims expected and received assistance and support from the rulers.

In addition to keeping formal lists of chiefs and imams, Gonja Musli
also studied and recorded the history of the kingdom as a whole. Al-H
Muhammad b. Mustafa, for instance, chronicled events in Gonja fr
c. 1710 to 1752, and this history was added to by Imam Umar Kunar

b.'Umar. Goody suggests that this interest in history may have been stimulated by contact with the Middle East.[5] Al-Hajj Muhammad b. Mustafa made the pilgrimage to Mecca in 1733/4. There is also the possibility that Gonja Muslims were influenced by the tradition of historical writing that had developed in Timbuktu. As Ivor Wilks has shown there was a route which linked Gonja's central provinces of Gbuipe and Daboya not only with Kumasi to the south but also to Jenne and Timbuktu to the north.[6]

In addition to the existence of Muslim communities in the main commercial centres such as Gbuipe, there were several independent Muslim villages in Gonja such as Larabanga and Dokrupe.[7] Moreover, all along the trade routes to the north and south there were numerous "staging posts" where Muslim and other traders rested. The people at and around these points must have come into contact with and have been influenced by the Muslim traders, who would have manifested their faith by, among other things, praying in public. Gonja Muslims were also active in the administration and court life in Kumasi, the heartland of the Asante empire, exercising an influence in Kumasi, as Wilks points out, "quite incommensurate with their numbers".[8] And this continued to be so after the Asante conquest of the western, central and eastern provinces of Gonja in 1751–2.

Mamprussi.

There are no reliable dates for the early beginnings of Mamprussi, and various centuries from the 11th to the 16th have been suggested as the period when this state was formed.[9] With regard to the advent of Islam in Mamprussi, it seems that this occurred in the 17th century before the long reign of Na Atabia, c. 1688–1741.[10] During this reign the trade between Hausaland and the Volta Basin increased in importance leading to the establishment of numerous Hausa Muslim trading settlements in the state. Muslims in Mamprussi tended on the whole to exercise less influence over the chiefs than their counterparts in Gonja, and this may have been due in some measure to the fact that there was less political unity and cohesion in Mamprussi than in Gonja. Muslims in Mamprussi were regarded by the chiefs as men of learning and prayer and ordered to keep out of politics.

Dagomba.

Islam probably entered Dagomba sometime in the 17th century, but it was not until around 1700 that it began to exercise any real influence there. The early Muslims in Dagomba were Mande-speaking Muslim traders from the upper Niger region who were later joined by Muslim traders from Hausaland.[11] It was not, however, until the reign of Na Zangina (c. 1700–1714) that a strong and influential Islamic community began to emerge in Dagomba. Part of the reason for this was that Na Zangina sought the support of the Muslims in his attempt to fend off Gonja, whose leaders said that one of the reasons for their success against the Dagomba was that they had the support and prayers of their Muslim followers. Na Zangina, realising perhaps that he too would benefit from Muslim support, drew closer to the Muslims and in 1713 defeated an invading Gonja army. His successors followed a similar policy but they did not present themselves as Muslim leaders for fear that they might alienate their non-Muslim supporters. By 1800 Islam had made some progress but Dagomba had not been transformed by this time into an Islamic state. Indeed Usuman dan Fodio, writing in 1806, said of Dagomba that it was a country "where infidelity is overwhelming and Islam rare." He advised all Muslims to emigrate since the rulers there were unbelievers.[12]

Wa.

To the west of Dagomba lies the kingdom of Wa, founded about 1650 by chiefs of Dagomba origin. The first Muslim settlers in the Wa region were Mande-speaking traders known as Wangara, who set up Muslim villages probably in the 16th century before the establishment of the kingdom of Wa. These traders were attracted to the area as we have seen by the gold of the nearby Lobi goldfields. The traders were followed by Muslim religious specialists who seem to have taken up residence in villages in the Wa region by the middle of the 17th century.

As was the case in Gonja and to a lesser extent perhaps in Mamprussi and Dagomba, the Muslims in Wa forged close ties with the chiefs and took on the language and many of the customs of the local people. They also allowed Islam to be adapted to a very considerable degree to the local culture.

Islam west of the Black Volta River.

Families of Mande-speaking Muslim traders and scholars from the late 14th and early 15th centuries, as we have seen, established commercial and educational centres in the region west of the Black Volta River. These Muslim traders created their own wards or quarters in the market towns of Bonduku, Banda, Bouna and Kong. Over time the Muslim community grew to form the majority of the population in places like Bonduku and Kong, so much so that these towns came to be regarded as Muslim Dyula towns.

Generally speaking Muslims west of the Black Volta River, as I have already pointed out, were not involved to anything like the same extent as their counterparts to the east of the river in state formation, nor were they integrated or assimilated into the political and social system to anything like the same extent. The Muslims west of the Black Volta in the state of Banda, for example, were valued for their ability as merchants and educators and although they were given many privileges by the rulers they always remained to a greater extent than the Muslims east of the river a group apart. This distinctiveness was also fostered by the Muslim education system. In Banda, Kong, Bonduku and elsewhere virtually every Muslim was assured of a basic Islamic education, and the more advanced students were tutored by well qualified scholars.[13] Very little effort was made, however, to extend this education to the non-Muslim population.

The collapse of such important Mande centres as Begho in the early 18th century had important consequences for Islam in the region. This collapse was brought about by several developments including the rise of the Asante, the diversion of the gold trade to the south as a result of increased European activity on the coast, and internal disputes between non-Muslim and Muslim in Begho. Among the consequences was a major shift in the Muslim Mande population in the Volta Basin. Some of the Mande moved north from Begho to Bonduku, Bouna, Gyaman and Kong. Those who went to Kong played an

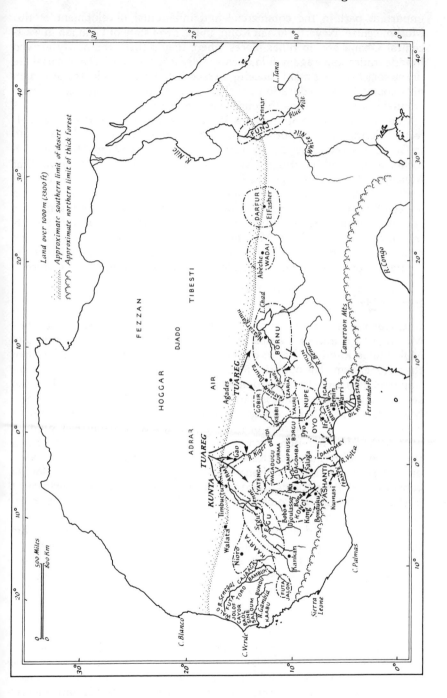

VI States of the Sudan and Guinea in the 18th century

important part in the commercial and intellectual development of this Muslim centre. Nevertheless in Kong, in the Bron state of Gyaman in west-central Ghana and in other places where they settled, the newly arrived Mande traders once again did not enter fully into the political and social life of the society. Their main concerns were as before with trade, the provision of a sound Islamic education for their own people and anyone else who wanted it, and organising the pilgrimage to Mecca.

Consequently, west of the Black Volta River there emerged a more intellectual, scriptural, pure form of Islam when compared with the Islam found in Gonja, Dagomba and Mamprussi where Islam was adapted to fit in with local customs and traditions. One main reason for this difference was that Muslims in Gonja and Dagomba were among the founders of these states and were therefore part of the political system from the beginning, whereas the states of Kong, Bouna and Gyaman were founded by non-Muslims, the Muslims arriving later as immigrants and never actually looking for or wanting a central role in politics. Muslims west of the Black Volta, therefore, were generally less prone than Muslims east of the river to take on either the "material" or the spiritual and ideological aspects of non-Muslim culture.

Islam in Hausaland.

In Chapter 3, in the section on Hausaland, we saw that Muslim rulers like Muhammad Korau of Katsina and his immediate successor Ibrahim, and Muhammad Rumfa in Kano, tried without complete success to make Islam the state religion. The opposition from the adherents of the indigenous traditional religion forced a compromise. Not only did they do this but they also seem to have regained some ground lost in the 16th, 17th and 18th centuries. Meanwhile, the Islamic education system continued to expand and to produce increasing numbers of Muslim scholars who, from their position outside the administration, became increasingly critical of the "mixed" Islam prevalent in government circles and in the wider society and which the rulers and their Muslim advisers often condoned by their actions. I want now to consider these two trends, the waning influence of Islam in government circles and the emergence of a more radically-minded Muslim intellectual élite in Hausaland.

However, before discussing the growth of this radically-minded Muslim intellectual élite I want to provide a more complete picture of the political, social and religious situation in Hausaland in the 17th and 18th centuries, highlighting some of those issues which caused concern among certain groups of Muslim scholars and many ordinary people.

Religion, politics and society in Hausaland, 1600—1800.

From contemporary documents such as the "Kano Chronicle" and the writings of Muslim scholars like Usuman dan Fodio we can arrive at some understanding of the attitude towards Islam adopted by Muslim rulers, 'ulama (scholars in the Islamic religious sciences) and the Muslim teachers known popularly today as mallams. With one or two notable exceptions the

"Kano Chronicle" gives a less than flattering account of the Muslim rulers of Kano in the 17th century. They allowed the Qur'an to be covered in goat skin and to be venerated and regarded as a lucky charm rather than seeing it as God's word to be used for their guidance. They imposed and collected un-Islamic taxes such as the cattle tax, the *jangali*, imposed upon and resented by the Fulani pastoralists. Another tax was imposed upon the merchants which was not only un-Islamic but so heavy that it curtailed trading activities and almost completely undermined the prosperity of a market in one area. Apart from taxation, rulers are alleged to have been guilty of extortion. Muhammad Sharefa, ruler of Kano, is said to have "introduced seven practices in Kano all of which were robbery" and to have "invented many other methods of extortion".[1]

The criticisms of Muslim administrators, government officials and mallams were just as harsh. Usuman dan Fodio, the leader of the Islamic reform movement in Hausaland in the early 19th century, made repeated attacks on "venal mallams" who preached and taught Islam although they were inadequately trained and presented people with a variety of misleading interpretations on points of Islamic doctrine. This was something al-Maghili protested about, as we have seen, and in one of his works Usuman dan Fodio quotes passages from al-Maghili on the question of the inadequately educated Muslim teacher. In his book, "Lamp of the Brethren", for example, Usuman dan Fodio cites the following extract from al-Maghili which is a criticism of poorly trained Muslim educators: "One of their characteristics is that they are not Arabic-speaking; they understand no Arabic, except a little of the speech of the Arabs of the town in an incorrect and corrupted fashion, and a great deal of non-Arabic so they do not understand the intentions of the scholars."[2] In Usuman dan Fodio's view and in al-Maghili's it was vital for a Muslim teacher to understand the writings of the respected orthodox Muslim scholars in order to be able to give the correct interpretation on points of Islamic doctrine and ritual.

Political and social conditions in Hausaland in the period under review did not make it any easier for potential Muslim reformers and opponents of the existing authorities to sit idly by and passively accept the status quo. No doubt some groups prospered from the fact that Kano, Katsina, Gobir, Kebbi, Zazzau and other states became more involved in the trans-Saharan and inter-state trade in West Africa from the 16th century. Nevertheless, the region experienced the adverse effects of the commercial and political rivalry between the states. Borno continued to exercise a relatively weak form of suzerainty over Hausaland during the 17th and 18th centuries, but this did not prevent the Sultanate of Air to the north from attempting to dominate the Hausa states, nor did it prevent these states from battling with one another for overall supremacy in Hausaland.[3]

At different times one state emerged as the most powerful to be displaced in a relatively short space of time by a rival. In the first half of the 18th century Zamfara was probably the strongest power in Hausaland, but this situation changed when Gobir, Usuman dan Fodio's state, rose to a position of dominance in the second half of the 18th century. Gobir was then challenged by Zamfara, Kebbi, Katsina, Kano and Air. Political stability and unity were not, therefore, characteristics of 17th- and 18th-century Hausaland, although states occasionally entered into what might be termed "alliances of convenience" which provided some integration and stability for short periods. The Kano Chronicle summed up the situation, with a little exaggeration, thus: "If the Gobirawa defeated the Kanawa one day, the Kanawa defeated them the next. This state of affairs continued for a long time."[4]

Meanwhile as the rulers fought for supremacy and the business community profited from the increased trade and commercial activity in the region, some of the less fortunate experienced the disastrous effects of famine, slave raiding and extortionate taxation. There was also a degree of tension between pastoralists and peasant farmers and between Muslim scholars outside the government and those who served in and sustained governments of Muslim rulers, who were either unwilling or incapable for a variety of reasons of ruling according to Islamic law. If the Muslim rulers did not heed al-Maghili's teachings and advice there were a growing number of Muslim scholars in Hausaland in the 18th century who did take him and other Muslims of the same intellectual standing and reforming zeal very seriously. Hausaland was not an intellectual backwater, cut off from the ideas and writings of the rest of the Muslim world. On the contrary, for the interested Muslim scholar in Hausaland, as we shall see, there were many books from which he could find out how a Muslim ruler should govern, what taxes he should impose and what un-Islamic practices and customs he had a duty to stamp out.[5]

The emergence of the Muslim reform movement in Hausaland.

In the 15th century, as we have seen, the foundations of a viable Islamic system of education had been laid in Hausaland. At this time the system was organised and maintained largely by Muslim scholars from North Africa and other parts of West Africa such as Mali and the Senegambia. Groups of Fulani and closely associated Torodbe religious specialists, for example, known in Hausa by their patronym Toronkawa, arrived in Hausaland from the Senegambia in the 15th century. Usuman dan Fodio's family belonged to the Toronkawa.

In the pre-colonial era an educated Muslim had a good chance of being employed in government service or of gaining a livelihood from teaching, just as in the colonial period an education in a Christian mission or western-style school often led to a career in government service or teaching. By no means all educated Muslims went into government service, however, and those who preferred to teach and preach joined or established Islamic communities where they studied and carried on missionary activity. Students and scholars did not necessarily stay in one particular place and attend one particular educational institution. The Islamic education system did not work like that. There were some schools and colleges on permanent sites, so to speak, and of course every Muslim community would have had its Qur'anic schools. However, in addition to schools and colleges there were certain well-known individuals and families who had a high reputation for scholarship and holiness, and the interested Muslim student would go and seek tuition and guidance from these people. Often this could mean a journey of hundreds of kilometres, and years away from home. Once a person had completed his studies and acquired his diploma (*ijaza*) he might travel far and wide to teach. One of Usuman dan Fodio's teachers, Jibril b. 'Umar, not only taught in Gobir but also in Agades.

Ideas and inspiration, moreover, came from the writings of orthodox scholars such as al-Maghili. Al-Maghili clearly stated that a ruler who imposes unjust and illegal taxes must be regarded as an unbeliever.[6] He also fully supported the belief that God would send in every century a reformer who would renew the faith and eradicate injustice. This belief influenced the thinking of Usuman dan Fodio, as did al-Maghili's militant stand against Muslims who mixed the Islamic faith with the indigenous religion. "There is no doubt," al-Maghili wrote, "that Holy War against them is better and more meritorious than Holy War against unbelievers".[7]

Usuman dan Fodio did not confine himself to the writings of al-Maghili. He had a large collection of books concerned with Islamic history, law, tradition, mysticism and theology. He read the commentaries on the Hadith compiled by al-Bukhari in the 9th century, and he read some of the works of the famous Iranian theologian and philosopher al-Ghazali (1058 — 1111). In addition, on his travels he met many scholars, including the Kunta scholar and mystic Shaikh Sidi al-Mukhtar al-Kabir al-Kunti. Like Shaikh Sidi, Usuman dan Fodio was a member of the Qadiriyya brotherhood.

Mysticism also played an important part in Usuman dan Fodio's life and like other members of the Qadiriyya brotherhood he believed that God made his will clear to some people through dreams and visions. From his middle thirties Usuman dan Fodio began to experience dreams and visions in which he claimed God spoke to him using Prophet Muhammad as his mouthpiece. In one such vision the founder of the Qadiriyya order, Abd al-Qadir al-Jilani, whom Usuman believed was his intermediary with Prophet Muhammad, girded him with the "Sword of Truth", telling him to use it against God's enemies.[8] This vision took place in the 1790s at a time when Usuman dan Fodio's community was being harassed by the rulers of Gobir.

Usuman dan Fodio did not follow slavishly the opinions and advice of his teachers and of the scholars whose works he read. He argued against Jibril b. Umar, for example, over whether a Muslim reverted to the status of an unbeliever by committing certain wrongdoings such as marrying more than four wives.[9] He quoted al-Suyuti, the Egyptian scholar, who said that "in truth wrongdoing does not cause faith to lapse, nor does innovation".[10] Usuman dan Fodio wrote and preached a great deal and in his writings and preaching he continually reminds Muslims in clear, simple language of the correct orthodox Muslim position on matters such as inheritance, marriage, fasting, prayer, almsgiving and other issues, while pointing out the various incorrect practices existing in Hausaland.

By the 1790s, therefore, Usuman dan Fodio was leader of a large community of Muslims settled at Degel in Gobir. Many of the members of his community were Muslim scholars, some of whom came from outside Gobir. The community was in some respects a state within a state and was critical of the rulers of Gobir for their failure to govern according to Islamic law.

Islam in Borgu and Nupe.

To the east of Hausaland was situated the kingdom of Borgu which consisted of three states, Bussa, Nikki and Illo. Bussa, the largest of the states, was located on the River Niger at a point where the trade routes from Hausaland to Gonja and Asante, and from Badagry north to Hausaland, crossed this river. According to a local tradition Bussa was founded by Kisra who had emigrated there from western Arabia after refusing to accept Prophet Muhammad's reforms. Whether or not this tradition is true, the Bariba inhabitants of Borgu, like the Mossi to whom they are related, steadfastly resisted several attempts by Songhay to convert them to Islam. Even when Askiya Da'ud of Songhay destroyed Bussa in 1555/6 the ruler and inhabitants refused to become Muslims.

However, as was the case in the Mossi states, the rulers of Borgu allowed Muslim traders into their kingdom and eventually consented to participate in a very limited way in Islamic worship. They agreed, for instance, to say the Muslim prayers twice a year at the two principal Muslim festivals of Id al-fitr and Id al-Adha. These rulers, however, and the Bariba population in general, continued to be regarded as non-Muslims, the name Bariba being synonymous with that of "unbeliever". In the main it was the Dendi settlers from the Illo and Gaya areas on the Niger River who along with traders and scholars from Hausaland formed the majority of the Muslim population in Borgu. The Dendi, in particular, who spoke a dialect of Songhay, were responsible for building up the Muslim community in Borgu to the extent that it constituted the majority of the population in such centres as Parakou, conveniently situated on the trade route from Hausaland to Gonja. Here the Muslim leader had considerable power and influence. In Nikki, on the other hand, the Muslims were in the minority and lived outside the town.

Nupe, situated to the south of Hausaland, came into existence as a state in the 15th century. According to tradition Tsoede, also known as Edigi, from Idah was the founder of this kingdom which from the 16th century became an important distribution centre for trade between the savannah states to the north and the forest kingdoms to the south. It was also an important industrial centre, where glass beads and brasswork among other things were produced and were in great demand. Muslim traders and teachers from Songhay and the upper Niger region were in Nupe in the 16th century, but it was not until the 18th century that a relatively large and influential Muslim community emerged in Nupe.

Islam in Borno, Bagirmi and Wadai.

Islam in Borno.

With the collapse of Songhay in 1591, Borno became the most powerful state in the western Sudan. Much of the credit for the political, economic and military strength of Borno has been given to Mai Idris Alooma (1569/70 — 1603), who, according to contemporary accounts, was a shrewd diplomat and a devout Muslim who did much to promote Islam in Borno. Mai Idris' reign has been presented by historians as the high point in Borno's political, economic and military fortunes and they maintain that after him a decline set in which lasted for most of the 17th and 18th centuries.[1]

However, there is little evidence of real decline in Borno until the 18th century. Before this time Borno seems to have remained a stable and powerful kingdom despite frequent attacks from the Tuaregs from Air in the north and the Kwararafa from the south. The Kwararafa were successfully held at a distance by successive Mais and completely turned away by Mai Ali b. Hajj (1640—1680) in 1668. The Tuareg from Air proved to be a more enduring menace to Borno. Anxious to control the trade route from Borno to Tripoli they persisted in their attempts to wrest it from Borno and achieved some success in this in 1759. In that year the Tuareg launched a partially successful attack on Borno, forcing Borno to allow Air to have access to the salt trade centred on Bilma. This Tuareg victory showed other states that Borno was not invincible. In 1781 Mandara, a state to the south of Lake Chad and under Borno's control, staged a successful revolt.

Other states within Borno's sphere of political influence, such as Bagirmi, also asserted their independence. By 1800, as a consequence, Borno's influence and authority in the western Sudan had shrunk considerably. This decline was not necessarily the result of poor leadership but could have been brought about by a succession of natural disasters such as famines. There was one disastrous seven-year famine during the reign of Mai Dunama Ali (1696—1714), another two-year famine between 1731 and 1747, and another described in the records as "a severe famine" during the reign of Sultan Dunama Gana (1747—1750).[2]

Although there was a decline in Borno's power and influence in the 18th century, particularly from 1759, there does not seem to have been any dramatic halt to the progress and development of Islam in the kingdom. Contemporary accounts describe a number of the Mais as being famous for their love of Islamic learning and for the help they gave to the Muslims. Mai Hamdun b. Dunama (1717—1731) was noted for his devotion to study; Ali b. Dunama (1750—1791) was, according to one account, "among the just and good", and his time the account continues "was famous for its love of learned men".[3]

If one looks at what was happening in the towns there is little sign that Islam in Borno was on the wane during this period. N'Gazargamu, had several Friday mosques in the mid-17th century with thousands of worshippers attending each one for Friday prayer.[4] In addition the Mais attempted to rule the kingdom according to Islamic principles and to replace the traditional ritual and worship by Islam. Mai Ali b. Hajj Umar (1644—1680) for example surrounded himself with experts in *fiqh* (Islamic jurisprudence) and consulted them as to whether certain practices were in accordance with Islamic law. He also seems to have had quite a good library containing among others books on Islamic jurisprudence written by Muslim scholars at the Islamic University of al-Azhar in Cairo, Egypt.

Moreover, Borno kings continued to bestow privileges and authority on Muslim scholars and religious leaders. They were often exempted from the payment of tax, for example, and obligations such as military service. A certain Muslim, a Fulani, by name Gabidama and his family were exempted from these obligations by successive Mais. Gabidama was made the most distinguished man in Borno by Mai Dunama Idris b. Hajj Ali (1699–1717). These scholars, furthermore, were active and highly regarded outside Borno. Muhammad Bello, son and successor of Usuman dan Fodio and a critic of the Muslim rulers in Borno, stated with reference to Borno Muslim scholars "there are not found in our towns (in Hausaland) students and writers of the Qur'an equal to theirs".[5] Muslim scholars in Borno, moreover, made N'Gazargamu into a centre of Islamic learning and trained a number of students who later joined the Muslim reform movement in Hausaland. Some of them like Mallam Zaki, Emir of Katagum and educated in Borno, became leading figures in the jihad.

Other Muslim scholars from Borno travelled widely, teaching in Hausaland, Nupeland and elsewhere. Many made the pilgrimage to Mecca and so also did the Mais of Borno. Ali b. Hajj, Mai from 1640 to 1680, made the hajj five times and at least six other Mais went on pilgrimage to Mecca during the 17th and 18th centuries. Judges and holymen were often consulted before policy decisions were taken or laws enacted. Nevertheless, the traditional religion still exercised a strong hold over many, particularly in the rural areas and even among those who professed to be Muslims. However, compared with other kingdoms in West Africa, Borno was in many ways in the 17th and 18th centuries the most advanced Islamic state.

Islam in Bagirmi.

The rulers of Bagirmi, to the south-east of Lake Chad and part of the present-day republic of Chad, became Muslims in the second half of the 16th century beginning with Abd-Allah Hajj (1568–1608).

At one time a province of Borno, Bagirmi gained its independence for a time after the death of Idris Alooma in 1603. The Borno Mai, it would seem, was responsible in large measure for laying the foundations of Islam in Bagirmi. According to tradition, however, Muslim scholars and pilgrims also played a part in the origins and growth of Islam in this region. One tradition relates that a Fulani mallam on his way to Mecca to perform the hajj stopped in Bagirmi and set up a centre of Islamic learning at Bidderi. This is said to have happened sometime around the beginning of the 16th century.[6]

Later other Muslim clerics from Borno came to settle in Bagirmi and among those there was a certain Waladaidi, who seems to have been influenced by the teachings and writings of such Muslim scholars as al-Maghili. On his arrival in Bagirmi in the late 16th century Waladaidi began to prophesy, and here one can detect the al-Maghili influence, that a Muslim reformer, a mujaddid, was about to appear to reform and purify Islam.

There seems little doubt that Islam in Bagirmi needed to be reformed, for though 'Abd-Allah (1568–1608) had introduced a number of Islamic laws and institutions, the Muslims on the whole ignored them. The Muslim rulers indeed openly ignored some of the basic tenets of Islam. 'Abd-al-Rahman (1785–1806), for example, contrary to the Qur'an, married his own sister. It was not in fact until the Tijaniyya, and to a lesser extent the Sanusiyy a brotherhood, began to capture the allegiance of the masses in the 19th century that Bagirmi began to resemble in practice a Muslim state.

Islam in Wadai.[7]

Wadai, situated to the east of Air, today forms part of the Republic of Chad. Islam came to this region rather late, and it was not in fact until the 17th century that a Muslim government was established in Wadai. According to one tradition the first person to preach Islam in Wadai was a Muslim scholar called by the name Jame or Salih. It was a relation, probably a nephew of this teacher, 'Abd al-Karim, known also as Muhammad al-Salih, who set up a Muslim form of government in Wadai. 'Abd al-Karim set up a small Muslim community at Bidderi in Bagirmi before moving into Wadai. He founded the capital of Wadai, Wara (in the middle of the 19th century the capital was moved to Abeshé), and ruled the country from 1635 to 1655.

'Abd al-Karim named the dynasty which he created Kolak al-Abbasi, indicating that in origin he was an Arab. This title would also leave no doubt in people's minds that the dynasty which continued in existence until 1911 was Muslim. From Wara, the capital, 'Abd al-Karim and his successors launched military expeditions against traditional religionists to the south. These expeditions, for slaves as much as for anything else, helped to spread Islam. Muslim scholars and merchants also implanted Islam in and around Wadai. Among these scholars was Abu Za'id b. Abd al-Qadir who taught there in the late 17th and early 18th century. One of the better known Muslim merchants was Hassad wad Hasuna who, in the middle years of the 17th century, organised a number of trading expeditions to various parts of Wadai, Borno and Hausaland.

By 1800 Wadai was becoming quite well known as a centre of Islamic learning. Muslim scholars from such places as Sennar, south of Khartoum, went to Wara, the capital, to teach, among other things, Islamic jurisprudence. These scholars and those whom they trained made Islam into an important religious, cultural and political force in Wadai.

Islam in the forest and coastal zones of West Africa.

So far we have concentrated on the expansion and development of Islam in the Saharan, Sahelian and Savanna regions of West Africa, with an occasional mention of the situation in the forest and coastal zone to the south. We noted that in the 15th century Mande-speaking Muslim communities from the upper and middle Niger regions began travelling across the Volta Basin along the trade routes and set up Muslim communities close to the gold and kola producing areas of the Akan forest. This situation continued in the 17th and 18th centuries. Among those people in the forest zone who came into contact with Islam for the first time in this period or perhaps a little earlier were the Yoruba (Nigeria), the Asante (Ghana) and the Temne (Sierra Leone). Here I will consider the development of Islam among the Yoruba and Asante of the forest zone in particular, confining myself to a few comments at the end on Islam in Sierra Leone and Liberia.

Islam among the Yoruba, 1600 — 1800.

Scholars are not in agreement concerning the date of Islam's arrival among the Yoruba in western Nigeria. The Nigerian Muslim scholar 'Abd Allah al-Iluri maintains that Islam came to Yorubaland from Mali in the first half of the 14th century, while others hold to the view that Muslim traders from Mali, the Wangarawa, entered the region in the 15th century. Then there are those who suggest a 16th-century date for the advent of Islam in Yorubaland.[1] A number of Muslim scholars, probably of Songhay origin but resident in Nupe to the north, may have entered northern Yorubaland in the 16th century, their purpose being to request the Alafin of Old Oyo, Ayibode, to treat a group of his subjects, believed by the Alafin to be responsible for the death of his son, in a more just way.

By the first half of the 17th century there were in all likelihood Muslims living in Yorubaland.[2] Some of these were teachers, others were merchants and others slaves. The latter were brought to Oyo from further north and eventually sold to Europeans on the coast. By the 18th century, though still a relatively small and largely "expatriate" community, the Muslims in Yorubaland had become quite an influential group. This can be seen from the fact that Bashorun Gaha, one of the foremost political figures in the Oyo Empire in the second half of the 18th century, and Afonja, the commander of the Oyo army, relied a good deal on the support of the Muslim community in Old Oyo in their struggles with the Alafin.

Also in the 18th century further south in Lagos the foundations of a Muslim community were laid by Muslim slaves from Hausaland. By 1775 this community had prevailed upon Adele, ruler of Lagos, to grant it a degree of official recognition. Some of the elders in Lagos did not, however, approve of Adele's tolerance and mounted a campaign which led to Adele being exiled in Badagry in 1780. One of Adele's successors, Kisoko, showed himself to be as tolerant and open-minded as Adele and he too was exiled, this time to Epe on the Lagos lagoon. Many of the Lagos Muslims followed Kisoko to Epe and set up a Muslim community there.

Islam in Asante.

Muslims began arriving in Kumasi, capital of Asante in modern Ghana, in the 18th century. These Muslims came from further north, from Gonja, Mamprussi, Dagomba and from centres in the upper and middle Niger region and even from North Africa. Some of these states, as we have seen, became tributaries of Asante as a result of Asante expansion northwards during the reign of Opoku Ware (1717 — 1750), and the Muslims who travelled south from these states and settled in Kumasi came to represent their own commercial and political interests and those of their states. The Mande-speaking traders and other Muslim traders from North Africa were also attracted to Asante by its natural resources, in particular its gold and kola. The Bey and his Mamluk in Tunis in North Africa were said in the 1840s to be consuming great quantities of kola nuts.

By about 1800 the Muslim community in Kumasi, situated in the centre of the town close to the main market and the royal palace, was made up of several hundred people some of whom were scholars and religious specialists while others were merchants. It was a community, then, with a considerable amount of talent and expertise, something the Asantehene and the chiefs were not slow to recognise. The rulers were particularly interested in availing themselves of the talents and gifts of the sharifs, those Muslim holy men who claimed descent from Prophet Muhammad's family and were endowed with baraka, that is, a blessing and spiritual power which many people believed enabled them to heal and ensure success or failure.

Muslims in Kumasi became the advisers to the rulers on important matters of state and they also came to control the distributive trade in gold, kola, salt and slaves, while at the same time securing a monopoly over the cattle industry. Thus they wielded considerable economic and political power. They were also allowed to preach and teach Islam. The involvement of Muslims, however, in the life of the court as advisers to the rulers meant that they were obliged to make compromises. They had, for example, to attend royal ceremonies involving traditional religious ritual and sacrifices. They did try, however, as we shall see, to change some of the un-Islamic ritual and worship performed at the royal court.

Islam in Sierra Leone and Liberia.

Islam had reached as far as the Sierra Leone coast by the 18th century. It was brought into what is today Sierra Leone by the Soso, Fulani and Mandinka from Futa Jallon in central Guinea who decided to leave their homeland and to migrate around the time of the holy war launched by Alfa Karamoko in 1726 (see Chapter 4, p. 84), and later after the destruction of Kankan by Konde Briama in 1765.

In Sierra Leone some of the Fulani settled in the east among the Limba, while the Mandinka took over the government of Port Loko from the Temne people of Sierra Leone and made it into an Islamic centre. A number of Sierra Leonean chiefs decided to become Muslims and considered it worthwhile to employ as secretaries Muslims literate in Arabic, and in this way Muslims gained access to positions of influence and power. By 1800, however, only very few of the indigenous people of the forest and coastal region of Sierra Leone had become Muslims. What existed in Sierra Leone was in essence a small Muslim community consisting mainly of local chiefs and expatriate Muslim merchants and warriors.

Islam likewise came to Liberia from the upper Niger region. Among the people of Liberia first influenced by Islam in this period were the Vai, Manding and Gola. The movement of Muslims from Futa Jallon towards the coast for purposes of trade and land, particularly in the 18th century, made for a stronger and more widespread Muslim presence in Liberia.

Conclusions.

In the period 1600−1800 Islam in some areas lost ground for a time in and around Songhay, for example, after the Moroccan conquest in 1591, and at the centre of government in some of the Hausa states.

Speaking generally, however, Islam did not stagnate or regress, but using essentially the same approach as in the early period, the peaceful, quietist approach, made considerable headway in many parts of West Africa in the 17th and 18th centuries. Literally thousands of Muslim communities, some no doubt small and very temporary, were established along the trade routes and in the commercial centres. Moreover, there was the important contribution made by the many wandering mallams and sharifs like those encountered by the Portuguese in the Senegambia or by Mungo Park as he travelled in search of the course of the Niger. Park also wrote of Muslim poets roaming around, singing hymns, and of the Muslim chiefs such as the one who "acted as chief magistrate of the town and school master to the children", most of whom were non-Muslim.

Although Islam was spread mainly by peaceful means this period also saw the emergence, or re-emergence, of an aggressive approach to the reform and expansion of Islam particularly among some of the intellectual élite. Frustrations of many kinds, in addition to their Islamic beliefs and the historical memory of past glory, pushed many scholars towards militancy. Moreover, the developments in education, the spread of literacy in Arabic, the social, political and economic upheavals occasioned by the trans-Atlantic slave trade were in part responsible for the re-emergence of this militant, revivalist tradition, not seen since the days of the Almoravids. The use of militant means in the struggle for the ideal society was to be continued, as we shall see in the next chapter, in the 19th century.

Notes.

Islam in the south-western Sahara.

1 Trimingham, *A History of Islam, op. cit.*, Chapter 4.
2 Norris, *Shinqiti Folk Literature, op. cit.*
3 B. Barry, "Le Royaume de Waalo" and J. Suret-Canale and B. Barry, "The Western Atlantic Coast to 1800" in J.F. Ade Ajayi and M. Crowder, eds, *History of West Africa, op. cit.*, Vol. 1, pp. 101−131 and pp. 456−511 respectively.
4 J.R. Willis, ed, *Studies in West African Islamic History, op. cit.*, Vol. 1 pp. 7−11.
5 H.T. Norris in Willis, ed, *Studies. . .*, *op. cit*, p. 10. Norris also maintains that the Almoravids did not use the title Amir al-Mu'minin (Commander of the Faithful) but only the title Amir al-muslimin (Commander of the Muslims) personal communication, 12/2/1981.
6 C.I.A. Ritchie "Deux Textes sur le Sénégal", *B.I.F.A.N.* XXX (1968).
7 P. Curtin, "Jihad in West Africa: Early Phases and Interrelations in Mauretania and Senegal" in *J.A.H.* XII (1971), pp. 11−24.

Islam in the Senegambia.

1 Ritchie, *op. cit.* p. 314.
2 M. Klein, "Social and Economic Factors in the Muslim Revolution in the

Senegambia", *J.A.H.* XIII (1972), p.427. Klein is quoting from Le Maure's *Voyage to the Canaries, Cape Verde and the Coast of Africa (1862)*, which was translated from the French by E. Goldschmid (Edinburgh, 1877).

3 Sanneh, *op. cit.*, Chapter 3.
4 I. Wilks, "Islamic Learning in the Western Sudan" in Goody, ed, *Literacy in Traditional Societies, op. cit.*, pp. 162—197.
5 Curtin, *op. cit.*, p. 18.
6 W. Rodney, *A History of the Upper Guinea Coast, 1545—1800*, (Oxford, 1970), pp. 236—9.
7 Curtin, *op. cit.*, p. 23.
8 Curtin, *op. cit.*, p. 22.
9 R. Miller, ed, *Mungo Park's Travels in Africa* (London, 1954), p. 45.

Islam in the upper and middle Niger region.

1 Miller, *op. cit.*, p. 77.
2 Batran, *op. cit.*, p. 129.
3 *Ibid.*, p. 132—133.
4 *Ibid.*, p. 138.
5 *Ibid.*, p. 136.
6 A.A. Batran, "An Introductory Note on the Impact of Sidi al-Mukhtar al-Kunti (1729—1811) on West African Islam in the 18th and 19th centuries", *Journal of the Historical Society of Nigeria* (J.H.S.N.) VI (1973).
7 Sanneh, *op. cit.*

Islam in Air.

1 Norris, *The Tuareg, op. cit.*, p. 80.
2 Norris maintains that Shaikh Mahmud was martyred in the 16th and not in the 17th century as is sometime suggested; personal communication, 12/2/1981.
3 Norris, *The Tuareg, op. cit.*, pp. 118 *ff.*
4 *Ibid.*, pp. 118 *ff.*

Islam in the Volta Basin.

1 Al-Sa'di, *Ta'rikh al-Sudan, op. cit.*, pp. 121 *ff.*
2 *Ibid.*
3 Levtzion, *Muslims and Chiefs, op. cit.*, pp. 51 *ff.*
4 J. Goody, "Restricted Literacy in Northern Ghana" in Goody, ed, *Literacy in Traditional Societies, op. cit.*, p. 213.
5 *Ibid.*, p. 214.
6 Wilks, "A Medieval Trade Route. . .", *op. cit.*, pp. 337—8.
7 Levtzion, *Muslims and Chiefs, op. cit.*, pp. 72 *ff.*
8 I. Wilks, *Asante in the 19th century* (Cambridge, 1975), p. 256.
9 Levtzion, *Muslims and Chiefs, op. cit.*, pp. xxiii—xv, 85 *ff*, 124.
10 *Ibid.*, pp. 124—125.
11 *Ibid.*, pp. 51—77.
12 Levtzion, *Muslims and Chiefs, op. cit.*, p. xxv *et passim.*
13 I. Wilks, "The Transmission of Learning in the Western Sahara" in Goody, ed, *Literacy in Traditional Societies, op. cit.*, pp. 161 *ff.*

Islam in Hausaland.

1   K.C, *op. cit.* pp. 116–123.
2   Cited in M. Hiskett, *The Sword of Truth*, (Oxford, 1973), p. 128.
3   R. Adeleye, "Hausaland and Borno, 1600–1800" in Ade Ajayi and Crowder, *op. cit.*
4   K.C., *op. cit.*, p. 124.
5   See on this M. Hiskett, "An Islamic Tradition of Reform in the Western Sudan" *B.S.O.A.S* XXV (1962), pp. 577 *ff.*
6   *Ibid.*, p. 585.
7   *Ibid.*, p. 584.
8   Hiskett, *The Sword of Truth, op. cit.*, p. 66.
9   D.M. Last and M.A. Al-Hajj, "Attempts at Defining a Muslim in 19th century Hausaland and Borno", *J.H.S.N.* III (1965), p. 233 *et passim.*
10   Hiskett, "An Islamic Tradition. . .", *op. cit.*, p. 589.

Islam in Borno, Bagirmi and Wadai.

1   Trimingham, *A History of Islam, op. cit.*, p. 151.
2   Palmer, *Borno, Sahara and Sudan, op. cit.*, p. 95.
3   *Ibid.*, p. 95.
4   *Ibid.*, p. 33.
5   M. Hiskett, "The State of Learning among the Fulani before their Jihad" *B.S.O.A.S.* XIX (1957), p. 572.
6   Trimingham, *op. cit.*, pp. 138–9, on Islam in Bagirmi, and G. Nachtigal, *The Sahara and Sudan*, Vols 1 and 4, translated with introduction and notes by A.G.B. and H.J. Fisher (London, 1974 and 1971 respectively).
7   See notes 1 and 6 above for references to early Islam in Wadai.

Islam in the forest and coastal zones.

1   See Ryan, *Imale, op. cit.*, chapter 3, for a summary of the various opinions concerning the advent of Islam in Yorubaland. Also G.O. Gbadamosi, *The Growth of Islam among the Yoruba* (London, 1978), pp. 1 *ff*; and R.C.C. Law, *The Oyo Empire, c. 1600–1836* (Oxford, 1977), p. 75.
2   Law, *op. cit.*, p. 65, makes the interesting point that the Hausa scholar Ibr Massanih of Katsina (d. 1667) wrote a book on the method of determining the time of sunset and addressed it to "The Learned men (*fuqaha'*) of Yoruba". This would suggest that there was a fairly well-established Muslim community in Oyo by the second half of the 17th century at the latest.

5

The militant struggle for the ideal Islamic state in West Africa in the 19th century.

We saw in the last chapter that a minority of Muslims in West Africa, for the most part scholars who once made what amounted almost to a dogma out of pacifism, came to regard jihad of the sword as a fitting and even necessary means for them to employ for the purpose of defending their own and their followers' interests and creating the ideal Islamic society. In the 19th century, although it was not the only strategy adopted, this "militant approach" found support among an ever increasing number of Muslim intellectuals.

The turn towards militancy, at times a last resort and a necessary defensive rather than a positive, aggressive measure, was prompted by a variety of overlapping and interrelated political, social, economic and religious developments, some of which I referred to in Chapter 4 and will discuss again in this chapter. Here I simply want to point to one such development which I believe was crucial to the emergence of what I have termed the "militant struggle for the ideal Islamic state", and that was the increasing tendency among Muslim scholars to place a greater emphasis on the written sources of the Islamic faith as the guide to the way a Muslim should live or the way a society should be administered.

This tendency, when contrasted with the pluralistic and accommodationist responses to society mentioned in Chapter 4, made for tension and confrontation. Islam for these Muslim scholars became a set of accessible and clearly stated laws and doctrines to defend, and this fact, given the other social and political problems of the time, projected them headlong into a struggle for the creation of the ideal society. With the expansion and development of the Islamic education system, of literacy in Arabic, and the more frequent contacts with the Muslim world of North Africa and the Middle East brought about by the pilgrimage, study abroad and the increasing supply of books and writings on Islam, an increasing number of Muslims in West Africa in areas with a long tradition of Islam, but where rulers had either been unable on account of opposition or unwilling to rule according to Islamic principles, had access both as individuals and communities to the ideals of Islamic civilisation as laid down in the Qur'an. They also had access to commentaries and explanations of these principles and ideals provided by such scholars as al-Ghazali, al-Suyuti, al-Maghili and others.

Some Muslim scholars took the decision, therefore, to step back to the Qur'an and to revive these ideals and principles, by militant means if necessary, while maintaining that by adopting this approach they and their

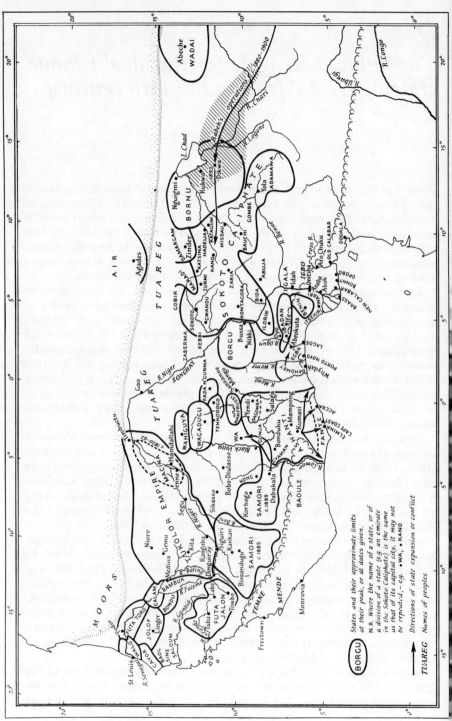

VII States of the Sudan and Guinea in the 19th century

supporters would not only fulfil their religious obligations but would also enable Muslims and those who accepted this new ideal Islamic society to live contentedly in a world which previously had been hostile and inhospitable.

The Islamic reform movement in Hausaland.

During the last decade of the 18th century and the early years of the 19th century tension was mounting between Shaikh Usuman dan Fodio's Muslim community in Gobir in the north-west of Hausaland and the Hausa rulers of that kingdom (see Chapter 4, p. 101). Successive rulers of Gobir, first Nafata and then Yunfa, were anxious to curtail the growing influence of Usuman dan Fodio and his followers and to this effect Nafata issued a proclamation in 1797 — 8 which prohibited all but Usuman dan Fodio himself from preaching and made it illegal for a son to adopt a religion different from that of his father. The wearing of the turban or veil, garments by which Muslims identified themselves, was also proscribed. Furthermore, Nafata's successor, Yunfa, once a student of Usuman dan Fodio, not only attempted to assassinate his former teacher but also in 1803 ordered both him and his family to leave their Muslim community at Degel. This order was given, it appears, because some of Usuman's followers had rescued 'Abd al-Salam, a Hausa Muslim, and his colleagues who had been taken prisoners by government troops.

At first Shaikh Usuman dan Fodio refused to obey Yunfa's order, and then Yunfa withdrew it. The Shaikh, however, reconsidered his decision and in February 1804, following the example of Prophet Muhammad who made the *hijra*, the planned withdrawal, from Mecca to Medina in 622 A.D, he decided to withdraw from Degel to Gudu some 50 kilometres away to the northwest. Many people, Fulani, Hausa and Tuareg, although harassed and prohibited by Yunfa from doing so, joined the Shaikh and formally elected him as Imam, prayer leader, and overall leader of the community, that is Amir al-Mu'minin, Commander of the Faithful. The Muslim community prepared to defend itself, and the jihad of the sword commenced when the community was attacked by a punitive expedition from Gobir in the early months of 1804. Usuman, fifty years of age at the time, was the leader of the jihadists (those who fight in God's path) although he was never involved in the actual fighting.

Before outlining the course of his jihad I want to consider the doctrinal justifications given by the Shaikh for the jihad of the sword. There will be some repetition here of what has been said in Chapter 4.

Manifesto of the jihad (Wathiqat ahl al-Sudan).[1]

Shaikh Usuman dan Fodio wrote a great deal and during the early months of 1804 a letter outlining his motives and intentions for launching the jihad in Hausaland was circulated among his supporters and others whom he hoped would join his movement. This letter or document is known as the "Wathiqat ahl al-Sudan" and constitutes the manifesto of the jihad in Hausaland. The purpose of the manifesto was to make it clear to Muslims what was from the

Muslim standpoint lawful and what was unlawful, and what an individual Muslim or a Muslim community was obliged to do in situations where Islamic practices and principles were either not being observed or implemented, particularly in those states where the rulers professed to be Muslims.

In the manifesto, which lays down 27 principles of action, Usuman states that according to the unanimous agreement of qualified Muslim lawyers the upright and conscientious Muslim has the duty to make holy war (jihad of the sword) on non-Muslim rulers who refuse to acknowledge and profess belief in One God, in other words, refuse to pronounce the Shadada, the Muslim confession of faith, "There is no god but Allah . . . Muhammad is the Messenger of Allah". It is also obligatory for Muslims to take over the government of a kingdom where the ruler, a Muslim, abandons Islam for what Usuman calls "heathendom". Moreover, the same obligation exists where a Muslim ruler, although he continues to profess his faith in One God and other Islamic doctrines, nevertheless combines the practice of Islam with other un-Islamic religious observances. This was commonplace among the rulers and ordinary Muslims in Hausaland according to Usuman.

The Shaikh also points out that it is wrong for a Muslim to attack Muslims residing in Muslim territory, a point to be borne in mind when one considers his attacks on Borno in 1809, and al-Hajj Umar's conquest of Masina (see p. 135). Moreover, it is unlawful, Usuman states, "to enslave the freeborn amongst the Muslims whether they reside in the territory of Islam or in enemy territory". Furthermore a Muslim must not make war or take away the property of a non-Muslim who has accepted the peace terms offered by the Muslims. It is the duty of a Muslim to launch a holy war against oppressors, and finally, a central theme in Usuman's teaching, the Muslim has the duty to "command what is right and forbid what is evil".

In the manifesto the Shaikh gives the impression of being quite forthright, militant and decisive, but his decision to launch a jihad of the sword was only reached after much careful consideration and in the end his mind was made up with the help of his brother Abdullah and other influential members of his community, who appear to have been more militant than himself.

In other writings attributed to him Shaikh Usuman dan Fodio provides us with a more detailed account of what he considered to be the un-Islamic observances and beliefs encouraged or tolerated and in some cases practised by Muslim rulers and ordinary Muslims in Hausaland.

Shaikh Usuman dan Fodio on government and religion in Hausaland.

In his book on the "difference between the governments of the Muslims and the governments of the unbelievers", the "Kitab al-Farq",[2] the Shaikh explains how a Muslim government should be organised and the role and function of some of its officials. The Caliph, for example, in accordance with the Shari'a should appoint a qadi, a Muslim judge, to supervise all the other judges in the provinces and towns under his rule. Usuman then goes on to list the failings and misdemeanors of the non-Muslim and nominally Muslim Habe rulers. He states that they impose taxes such as the jangali or cattle tax without any reference to the Shari'a. They take bribes, and fail to observe the

Islamic law on matters of inheritance and succession. Furthermore, the rulers "compel the people to serve in their armies, even though they are Muslims, . . . and whosoever does not go, they impose upon him a money payment not imposed by the Shari'a".

In one of his other books, the "Ta'lim al-Ikhwan" (Educating the Brethren), Usuman dan Fodio writes of the non-Muslim religious beliefs and practices which were fairly widespread in Hausaland. He mentions and condemns as polytheistic the practice of venerating trees and rocks on which libations were poured or sacrifices carried out. He also condemns the belief, and the ritual associated with the belief, in spirits who were regarded as inhabiting wells, streams and rivers. Again he regards various forms of divination, such as divination by sand, by the stars and by spirits, as unlawful. All these beliefs and practices were un-Islamic in the sense that they implied respect for and veneration of supernatural beings and forces other than Allah.

Usuman dan Fodio's description of the state of government and religion in 18th- and early 19th-century Hausaland was in substance correct even though some of what he had to say not based on first-hand experience. These and other writings, therefore, of the leader of the Islamic Reform movement in Hausaland provide us with an insight into the doctrinal justification he gave for launching the jihad of the sword in Hausaland.

The course of the jihad.

The first moves in the jihad as we have seen were made in 1804 when Yunfa attacked Gudu, only to find that the Muslims had evacuated their stronghold. The two sides, however, met in a major head-on collision for the first time in June 1804 at Lake Kwotto (Tabkin Kwotto). This was a battle in which swords, axes and arrows played as important a part as cavalry charges and muskets. The Muslim forces, less numerous than the Gobir army which included some Tuareg supporters, won a resounding victory at Tabkin Kwotto, and compared the victory here to the one won by Prophet Muhammad at Badr in 624 A.D. Tabkin Kwotto, however, was followed by a defeat at Tsuntsua in December 1804 when an estimated 2,000 Muslim scholars fighting on the side of Usuman dan Fodio lost their lives.[3]

Despite this defeat the Muslim party overran Birnin Kebbi, capital of Kebbi, in 1805, and also in the same year captured a number of towns in Zamfara and penetrated into Katsina. But in November 1805 they were once again defeated by Yunfa at the battle of Alwassa and just managed to beat off an attack on their new headquarters at Gwandu in Kebbi. Nevertheless, during the period 1806—1808 Usuman dan Fodio's army gained considerable ground and support. In 1808 his forces had captured Alkalawa, the capital of Gobir, and by this time also Katsina, Kano, Daura and Bauchi were ruled by Muslim leaders loyal to Usuman dan Fodio. Also in 1808 attacks were made on Borno, a Muslim state, which resulted in the capture of Birnin N'Gazargamu, the capital.

The jihad against Borno.

Because of the important matters of principle and doctrine that it raised, it is necessary to look at the reasons why Usuman dan Fodio and Muhammad Bello supported and justified the jihad against Borno.

Islam in Borno had by 1800 reached an advanced stage of development. The Mai (ruler) bore the title Amir al-Mu'minin (Commander of the Faithful), and there were numerous Muslims in the administration holding such posts as state imam and state judge (qadi). Moreover, Muslim scholars and teachers played an important role as advisers to the Mai and were very active in preaching in the mosques and teaching about Islam in the schools.

Before considering why the Muslim reformers in Sokoto sanctioned the jihad against Borno I want to look in a little more detail at what actually happened between the two sides. A Fulani leader in western Borno, Ardo Lerima, led a rebellion against Mai Ahmad, ruler of Borno, soon after the uprising in Gobir. The rebellion was put down but Ardo Lerima rose up again and captured Nguru, capital of western Borno, and this success generated a whole series of Fulani revolts which resulted in Borno loosing a considerable amount of her territory in the west and south-west. Out of this captured territory were created the emirates of Hadejia, Katagum, Misau and Gombe.

In 1808, with Borno in a weak position and having to fend off an invasion from Wadai in the north-east, the Sokoto jihadists captured N'Gazargamu, capital of Borno. With the assistance of a Muslim scholar from Kanem, Muhammad al-Amin Muhammad al-Kanemi, widely known simply as al-Kanemi, the Mai of Borno, at the time Dunama, recaptured N'Gazargamu. The Fulani supporters of the jihad retook it again in 1809, but al-Kanemi, with his mercenary army of Shuwa Arabs who formed the cavalry and Kanembu who were the spearmen, won back N'Gazargamu in the same year. Hostilities continued between the Borno rulers and the Fulani within and close to their western frontiers until 1827. In 1827 a settlement was worked out with Sokoto whereby Borno accepted the loss of Katagum and Hadejia, and Sokoto returned to Borno the region stretching from close to Maiduguri to Damaturu in the present-day Borno State of Nigeria.[4]

The grounds on which Usuman dan Fodio and Muhammad Bello justified the jihad against Borno were given in their correspondence with al-Kanemi which went on over a period of three years from 1809 to 1812.[5] Letters first passed between the Sokoto leaders and the Fulani leaders of the uprising in Borno. It seems that Goni Mukhtar and other leaders of the Fulani uprisings in Borno wrote to Sokoto justifying their rebellion on the grounds that Borno was a land of unbelief where people squandered the money of orphans, took bribes, passed false judgements in the law courts, made sacrifices in certain places for alms, and where women did not veil themselves. Al-Kanemi accepted that these practices existed in Borno, but added that they did not make Borno a land of unbelief, but rather constituted violations of Islamic law. He added that wherever one went in the Muslim world one would find people who disobeyed the law, and he insisted that it was a far greater offence to kill or enslave Muslims as the Fulani were doing in Borno. Usuman dan Fodio did, it should be mentioned here, write a letter in 1807 asking the Fulani leaders of the uprisings in Borno to cease hostilities. He also invited Mai Ahmad to join the jihad, but the letter refused and said that the rebels would be punished for attempting to undermine his authority.

Al-Kanemi stated that there were four types of people in Borno: unbelievers, apostates, Muslims who simply paid lip service to the teachings of Islam, and devout and sincere Muslims. These four types were to be found, he maintained, in all the surrounding countries also. Then he asked: how does one distinguish (when waging a jihad) between the devout Muslim and the insincere Muslim? Does one not risk in waging a jihad against a state like Borno killing or enslaving sincere Muslims along with the rest?

In their reply, the Sokoto leaders rejected the idea that they had sanctioned rebellion in Borno on the grounds that the non-Muslim practices mentioned by Goni Mukhtar made Muslims in Borno unbelievers. Muhammad Bello, in a letter to al-Kanemi in 1809, argued instead that the reason why he and the Muslim reformers in Hausaland approved of the fighting in Borno was because the Mai of Borno had given assistance to the non-Muslim Hausa forces who opposed the reform movement. Borno did, it seems, agree to assist the Hausa opposition in Daura, Hadejia, Katsina and elsewhere, and it was this action, in Bello's view, that made it lawful for the Muslim reformers to wage the jihad against Borno.

Muhammad Bello developed his arguments further as time went on. Later on he was to imply that the Fulani attack on Borno was justifiable on the grounds that people there sacrificed to rocks and trees, and built shrines to house their idols. Al-Kanemi was not convinced by these arguments and Sokoto did not accept the former's point of view either. As we have seen, a definite settlement was reached in the 1820s. Finally, it is worth pointing out here that a very similar debate took place between al-Hajj Umar b. Sa'id, founder of the Tokolor empire, and the Kunta-backed rulers of the Islamic state of Masina (see p. 135).

The division of responsibilities.

In 1809 Muhammad Bello, son and successor of Usuman dan Fodio and a leading strategist in the jihad, established the headquarters of the reform movement at Sokoto. In 1812 Usuman dan Fodio divided his recently established Muslim state in Hausaland into two spheres of responsibility, giving Muhammad Bello charge of the eastern sphere, which was to be administered from Sokoto, while his brother Abdullah took charge of the western region of the Caliphate, directing affairs from Gwandu. Responsibility for the north and the south was allotted first to local supporters of Usuman dan Fodio such as his army commander 'Ali Jedo, and later these areas were to come directly under Sokoto. Usuman dan Fodio himself, who held the official titles of Amir al-Mu'minin (Commander of the Faithful) and Caliph but was usually referred to simply as the Shaikh, held overall responsibility for the Caliphate until his death in 1817, when he was succeeded by Muhammad Bello.

Muhammad Bello, Caliph of Sokoto, 1817–1837, and the extension and consolidation of the Sokoto Caliphate.

When Usuman died in 1817 the work of the Muslim reformers had by no means been completed. Usuman dan Fodio's main objective was, he said, to establish a system of government based on Islamic law and Islamic ideals to replace those non-Muslim or only superficially Muslim systems of government in the Hausa states and neighbouring territories.

Within the ranks of the Muslim community of Sokoto itself there was already a certain amount of discontent and opposition and unlawful activity during Shaikh Usuman's own lifetime. Usuman himself complained about the illegal actions of some of his followers, and 'Abdullah his brother and Muhammad Bello his son made similar complaints. Bello stated in a pamphlet that of the ten types of people in the community nine were not sincere, genuine members. Some, he said, sought only worldly benefits, did not attend the mosque or the study sessions but spent their time in the market, while others cared only for horses and fighting.[6]

In 1817 there was a revolt of mainly Hausa elements led by 'Abd al-Salam. Another revolt followed in 1818, and indeed, for a period of years, no sooner was a revolt suppressed in one area than others sprang up elsewhere involving Muhammad Bello in numerous campaigns against dissident emirs and factions in Zamfara, Gobir, Kebbi and elsewhere. In order to prevent or at least contain these revolts Bello had *ribats* (fortified camps) built on the frontiers of the rebellious states such as Kebbi, Zamfara and Gobir.

In addition to quelling uprisings and consolidating the gains made during the early phase of the jihad Muhammad Bello also extended the frontiers of the Sokoto empire. In the 1820s and 1830s the emirates of Nupe, Ilorin, Misau and Muri were firmly established, and Kontagora followed in 1859.

Developments in the Sokoto Caliphate: 1837–1903.

There was never a time during the history of the Caliphate when its leaders could say that they had achieved their goal of establishing a completely stable, just society administered in strict accordance with the principles of Islam. This does not mean, as we shall see, that the Sokoto reformers achieved nothing at all but simply that their achievements were limited. One reason for this was that throughout the 19th century the reformers were pre-occupied with problems arising from administration, emigration, succession disputes, internal revolts, external aggression and the formation of rival reformist states such as the Mahdist state in Adamawa.

In various emirates of the Caliphate political rivalry among different factions began to emerge quite early on in the history of the reform movement. Kano is a case in point. Here competition for power among those Fulani clans and other Muslims who had participated in the jihad began as early as 1807. It broke out again in 1819 and was only solved when Muhammad Bello created the separate emirate of Kazaure and appointed as emir Dan Tunku. The latter was a prominent leader in the jihad in Kano, Katsina and Daura. He was also the leader of the opposition in Kano and obviously believed, like so many others who had actively participated in the jihad, that he deserved to be rewarded with high office. This sort of attitude, which was quite widespread, made it difficult for reformers like Usuman dan Fodio to create the ideal Islamic state which they believed should be governed by Muslim scholars and holymen who, as al-Maghili had said, should not be ambitious for power, status and prestige.

Rivalry of the same sort occurred in Adamawa, Muri, Nupe, Zaria and elsewhere. In some cases the rivalry and ambition led to serious and long drawn out rebellion. The Emir of Hadejia, Bukhari b. Muhammad Sambo, for example, led a rebellion which began in c. 1850 and went on for some 15 years, with the assistance of Borno. Fortunately for Sokoto, this revolt failed mainly because it never received the support of other emirates within the Caliphate. In fact it was actively opposed by Katagum, Kano, Bauchi and Zaria, who sent troops against Hadejia. This opposition to the rebellion indicates that the Caliphate did enjoy a certain degree of unity and cohesion.[7]

The revolt in Kano in the 1890s, known as the Tukur or Yusuf revolt over the question of succession to the office of Emir of Kano, was a much more serious affair than the one in Hadejia.[8] It led to famine and starvation in Kano and involved many of Sokoto's traditional opponents, such as Ningi and Gumel, and a number of emirates such as Katsina. Sokoto appointed, against the wishes of Yusuf and supporters, first Muhammad Bello and on his death in 1893, Tukur as Emir of Kano, overlooking Yusuf. This sparked off the revolt which Sokoto, because it never received adequate military assistance from the emirates, failed to suppress. Sokoto's failure here indicates one of the main reasons why it had difficulty enforcing its authority, the lack of a large, adequately equipped standing army.

The problem of Mahdism in the Sokoto Caliphate.

Elsewhere in this book I have discussed the idea of and widespread belief among Muslims in the advent of both the mujaddid or renewer who would appear every 100 years, and the Mahdi, the God-guided one (see for example Chapter 3, p. 56). The belief that a Mahdi would come and assist in the destruction of *dajjal* (the Anti-Christ), wipe away injustice, ensure prosperity and peace and revive and bring about the triumph of Islam was deeply rooted in the minds of many Muslims in West Africa in the latter half of the 18th century, and continued to be so throughout the 19th and into the 20th century.[9] In fact a historian of the Sokoto Caliphate maintains that the most important theme in popular Muslim thought in West Africa forming the background to the major Islamic reform movements such as those led by Usuman dan Fodio, Shaikh Ahmadu Lobbo I of Masina and al-Hajj 'Umar Tall, founder of the Tokolor Empire, was Mahdism. This historian adds, indicating its force and appeal, that "it (Mahdism) has been responsible for large scale migrations eastwards and the movement of countless individuals in West Africa towards the Nile".[10] The Mahdi, it was believed, would emerge in the east and in 1856/7 a Muslim jurist, Ibrahim Sharif al-Din, on his way through north-eastern Nigeria to Mecca, is said to have been followed by so many people (in search of the Mahdi) that the population of the region was substantially diminished.[11]

Usuman dan Fodio and Muhammad Bello, like so many others, accepted the idea that a Mahdi would come. It seems in fact that Usuman saw himself as the forerunner of the Mahdi, basing this assessment on the tradition well known in West Africa since the 15th century that after Prophet Muhammad there would be twelve Caliphs, the twelfth being the Mahdi.[12] Ten had already appeared, and Usuman probably saw himself as the eleventh Caliph. Many of his supporters claimed that he was in fact the Mahdi, a claim the Shaikh did not vigorously deny until after the jihad. Muhammad Bello stressed the connection between Usuman's jihad and the advent of the Mahdi, stating that the jihad would not end until the Mahdi appeared. Many people expected him to appear in the 13th Muslim century, that is, sometime between 1785 and 1882 A.D.

The fact that people thought of Usuman as the Mahdi no doubt motivated them to support his jihad. This may explain why Usuman was slow to deny the claim, until after the major battles of the holy war had been fought and won. Usuman then categorically denied that he was the Mahdi realising no doubt that those who constantly think about the Mahdi and the End of Time are not usually prepared to settle down and concentrate on the routine business of living, and that they can also be very critical of any form of authority that appears to them to be too bureaucratic and concerned with anything other than the reform and total triumph of Islam. Consequently, from 1808 onwards, after the important victories over the Hausa rulers had been achieved, Usuman began to make it clear that neither the advent of the Mahdi nor the End of Time were close at hand.

Nevertheless, the idea that the advent of the Mahdi was imminent would not go away. Even Muhammad Bello had "spies" sent east from Adamawa to find out if the Mahdi had come so that the Muslim community of the Sokoto Caliphate could go to meet him. And in Adamawa and elsewhere in northern Nigeria in the 19th century what were known as Mahdist states were established. The creation of these Mahdist states in the second half of the 19th century were in part inspired by the advent of the Sudanese Mahdi, Muhammad Ahmad al-Mahdi, who proclaimed himself in 1881. They were also born of disputes over succession and other disagreements within the Sokoto Caliphate.

Hayatu b. Sa'id and Mahdism in Adamawa, c. 1878 – 1898.

Hayatu b. Sa'id, a great grandson of Usuman dan Fodio, was born in Sokoto in 1840, and left Sokoto for Adamawa in 1878. One of his reasons for leaving Sokoto was his disappointment at the fact that his father Sa'id, a scholar, lost the election to become Sultan of Sokoto in 1877. This of course lessened considerably Hayatu's own chances of becoming Sultan himself. Certainly Hayatu appears to have entertained hopes of being the ruler of "a vast Muslim Empire", and the appearance of the Sudanese Mahdi in 1881 gave him the inspiration he needed to set about creating his own Muslim state at Balda in northern Adamawa.

In 1883 Hayatu sought and obtained from the Mahdi of the Sudan the appointment as his deputy "over all the people of Sokoto who were subjects of your great-grandfather Usuman dan Fodio".[13] Hayatu's next move was to communicate to his followers and the rulers of the various districts in and around Adamawa, that he believed the Mahdi had come in the person of Muhammad Ahmad al-Mahdi, Mahdi of the Sudan, and that all should acknowledge this fact and submit to his authority. The authorities greeted Hayatu's appeal with scepticism, believing him to be politically ambitious. The ordinary people, however, from Bauchi, Gombe and other parts of the Sokoto Empire joined Hayatu's Mahdist community, which by 1890 covered a fairly large area of Adamawa from Mandara in the north to Mubi in the south. The members of this community were identified by the dress they wore, in particular the patched jubba, and the fact that like the followers of the Mahdi in the Sudan they placed their hands across their chest while at prayer.

The Mahdist community was obviously a threat to the Sokoto establishment and in particular to its representative in Adamawa, the emir, whose authority Hayatu had rejected by the early 1890s. Perceiving that conflict was inevitable, Hayatu tried to obtain the support of the Mai of Borno and made an alliance with the Sudanese warrior Rabeh, who also believed that the Mahdi had come in the person of the Mahdi of the Sudan. Rabeh was also intent on making a Mahdist state.

In 1892 Hayatu successfully defended Balda from an attack by the Emir of Yola, Zubeiru, and then in alliance with Rabeh conquered Borno in October, 1893. The conquest of Sokoto was to follow, but the alliance between Hayatu and Rabeh, under stress almost from the beginning, broke down and Hayatu and all of his sons except Sa'id b. Hayatu were killed by Fadl-Allah b. Rabeh (Rabeh's son) in 1894. Hayatu's son Sa'id b. Hayatu took over the leadership of his father's section of the Mahdist movement in the Sokoto Caliphate. Exiled to Buea in the Cameroon in 1923 by the British colonial administration, always fearful of Mahdist uprisings, Sa'id returned to Kano in 1946 and was placed in detention there until his release in 1959. From his Kano headquarters and assisted by two of his eleven children Sa'id continued to preach to his followers about the Mahdi, claiming that his opinions on this subject of the Mahdi differed in no way from those of Usuman dan Fodio, except for the fact that the Mahdi had now come in the person of Muhammad Mahdi of the Sudan in 1881, something Usuman did not live to witness.

Mallam Jibril Gaini and the Mahdist state in Gombe.

Known by many names such as Mallam Jibrilla, Mallam Zayi, Mallam Burmi, Mallam Jibril Gaini, as I shall call him here, was born in Katagum emirate to the east of Kano in c. 1835, and settled in the early 1880s at the town of Zai on the borders of the Katagum and Fika emirates. With followers from as far away as Damagaram and Sokoto, Jibril began to attack non-Muslim villages around Zai and proved to be both an embarrassment and a threat to the Emir of Fika who started moves to get rid of him. Jibril then left Zai and settled at Burmi in the Gombe emirate and again attracted quite a large number of *talakawa* (common people) who were impressed by his ability to perform extraordinary feats such as levitation, and perhaps also by his lack of ostentation and simple life style.[14] Once again he began attacking the surrounding villages. He had meanwhile become a supporter of Hayatu b. Sa'id and a follower of the Mahdi of the Sudan. He was in fact appointed as a commander of the Mahdist army by Hayatu.

During the period c. 1885—1895 Mallam Jibril extended his control over a large area of the Gombe emirate. Later in 1896—7 he began raiding east into Borno, at the time under Rabeh's control. The latter was defeated and killed by the French at the battle of Kusseri in April 1900, and Fadl-Allah, his son, also died at the hands of the French at Gujba in October 1901. Meanwhile, the British, who were at the time extending their control over northern Nigeria, organised an expedition under Colonel Morland which had the aim among other things of "breaking the power of Mallam Jibrilla" if necessary. Although he put up strong resistance Jibril's forces were overcome and he was captured and taken to Lokoja where he probably died in 1902.

For almost two decades Jibril was able to attract numerous supporters to the Mahdist cause and with their help impose his authority over a fairly wide area. This indicates both the continuing strength of the Mahdist idea and its appeal in parts of the Sokoto Caliphate and the problems the rulers of Sokoto had in controlling uprisings led by charismatic figures.

Achievements of the Islamic reform movement in Hausaland.

Usuman dan Fodio, 'Abdullah his brother, Muhammad Bello his son and the other leaders of the Islamic reform movement were not out and out visionaries who believed they could transform Hausaland into an ideal Islamic state overnight. Usuman, moreover, was neither an extremist nor an intolerant man. He preferred to win people to his point of view by preaching, teaching and discussion rather than by force, and was not prepared to condemn and outlaw Muslims whose beliefs and practices he knew to be in certain respects reprehensible. Unlike one of his teachers, Mallam Jibril b. 'Umar, he did not classify as an unbeliever a Muslim who had more than four wives. Moreover, he was not, like some Muslim teachers whom he criticised, an inquisitor who continually questioned people about their Islamic beliefs and on receiving unsatisfactory answers categorised them as unbelievers and targets for the jihad. Nevertheless, he and his successors did set out to reform Islam in Hausaland, extend it far and wide, and establish an Islamic state. What success did they have?

One of the more significant changes effected by the Muslim reformers was the setting up of an Islamic administration which consisted in the creation of a central imamate. The Sultan of Sokoto became the Supreme Commander of all the Muslims in Hausaland, and he gave the emirs the task of administering the Caliphate at the provincial level. A chief qadi or Muslim judge was also appointed to supervise the administration of justice based on Islamic principles throughout the Caliphate. There was also an army commander (Amir al-jaish), a chief of police and a wazir or chief minister of state and head of the Muslim civil service. The wazir, moreover, linked the rest of the emirates with Sokoto and acted as moderator in disputes within and between the emirates.

The administration introduced by Usuman dan Fodio, Muhammad Bello and other leaders of the reform was not Islamic in every aspect. A number of pre-jihad Hausa offices, such as the office of K'ofa, were either retained or reintroduced. The K'ofa was responsible for the collection and organisation of tax receipts and for vetting all representations made to the Caliph. Furthermore, the Islamic law on taxation was not fully implemented, un-Islamic taxes continued to be collected such as the Hausa *Kudin K'asa* (landtax) and the unpopular *jangali* or tax on cattle.

In the educational sphere the reform movement did achieve a good deal. Through it literacy in Arabic was spread over a much wider area, and so also was literacy in Hausa and Fulani, making it possible for far greater numbers of people to become acquainted with the actual text of the Qur'an, Islamic history and the Islamic sciences in general. The reform movement also gave rise to a greater interest in and concern for the education of women, to the establishment of more Muslim schools and the training of ever-increasing numbers of Muslim teachers who enjoyed considerable moral and religious authority in the towns and villages transforming the attitudes and in general the style of living of the people.

The reform movement, however, did not lead to the conversion of all the people of Hausaland and the other areas it touched to Islam. Many people, particularly those in the rural areas, in the emirates of Sokoto, Bauchi, Kano and elsewhere, remained non-Muslim, and some still are to this day. Furthermore, in some, and only in some, of these emirates respect for Shari'a (the sacred law of Islam) had virtually ceased to exist by the late 19th century. Nevertheless, the ideals for which the jihad was fought were by no means dead by the end of the 19th century. People continued to be inspired by Usuman dan Fodio's reform movement and many resisted the British occupation of northern Nigeria not only to preserve their independence but also to retain and improve the legal administrative and educational system established by the Muslim reformers. Finally, through their writings the reformers provided later generations with a fund of valuable historical material for the reconstruction of part of West Africa's literary, intellectual, political, social and religious history.

Islam in Air.

The reform movement of Muhammad al-Jaylani: background and aims.

In Air, as in other parts of West Africa, from the 17th century some groups of Tuareg scholars and religious guides began to reject pacifism in favour of change and reform brought about by jihad of the sword (see Chapter 4, p. 92). Muhammad al-Jaylani (c. 1777−1840), a Tuareg Muslim scholar (Ineslemen), was one of those who had begun to think in this way. The Kel-es-Suq, however, an important group of Ineslemen claiming descent from Prophet Muhammad, still rejected military jihad. A brief look at the history

V Interior of the Zaria mosque built in 1862

of Muhammad al-Jaylani's people, the Kel Dennek, at his educational background, his connections and at contemporary events in Hausaland in particular, but also elsewhere in West Africa, provide some indication as to why Muhammad al-Jaylani turned to militancy.

The Kel Dennek formed the eastern branch of the Iwillimeden, a large confederation of Tuaregs, who today reside mainly in the Republics of Mali and Niger. The Kel Dennek were a group of Ineslemen who experienced tension and strain in their relations with their overlords, the Tuareg nobles known as the Imashaghen. They had, however, by the first half of the 18th century obtained the right to levy certain taxes, to carry weapons and to join in raiding expeditions. Consequently, they were equipped, trained and prepared to launch a jihad of the sword if the right circumstances and the right leadership presented themselves. Both the circumstances and the leadership emerged in the early years of the 19th century.

Muhammad al-Jaylani had read the writings of al-Maghili, who as I mentioned in a previous chapter, had spent time in Air. In a letter to Muhammad Bello in Sokoto, al-Jaylani quotes opinions of al-Maghili on, among other things, the question of the correct Muslim position with regard to the property of apostates, and concerning the motives lying behind a person's behaviour and actions. On this last mentioned point he asks Muhammad Bello whether or not he had read the words of al-Maghili which were "Your motive for action is linked inseparably to your act. If such be good, then the reward and recompense is due to you on both accounts. But if it be evil, then the punishment is likewise on account of both."[1] Here we have an important principle of behaviour laid down which guided some Muslim reformers like Muhammad al-Jaylani and which also can be of assistance when discussing such topics as the motives behind the 19th-century West African Islamic reform movements.

Although influenced by the opinions, ideas and activities of Muslim reformers in Hausaland, Muhammad al-Jaylani turned out to be more radical than his Sokoto counterparts. Moreover, Muhammad al-Jaylani's reform movement was in some respects different from other 19th-century West African reform movements. All of these reform movements were, it is true, concerned with political, social and moral as well as religious issues, but Jaylani seems to have placed greater emphasis on the social, economic and political issues. He was, for example, convinced of the necessity to abolish distinctions. He regarded the Tuareg nobility as being no higher socially than the labourer or slave, and planned to establish among the Tuaregs of Adar, which he conquered and tried to turn into a Muslim state, a classless urban society.

It is interesting to consider why Muhammad al-Jaylani wanted to create an urban society when so many of the Tuareg were cattle herders and desert nomads. One of the reasons that prompted him to insist on urban or village life in preference to a nomadic, wandering life as a cattle herder was that it was easier to build up the ideal Muslim community in an urban or village setting. Muhammad al-Jaylani sought advice on this subject from Muhammad Bello of Sokoto and was informed that, although Prophet Muhammad did not lay down a hard and fast rule which obliged his followers to live in an urban environment, the Prophet did seem to him to recommend it. Bello pointed out that in a town it was easier for Muslims to assemble for congregational prayer, to implement the Shari'a and make sure it was observed, and to collect taxes. Moreover, he believed that people were naturally suited to living in towns, and that it was only in towns that they could reach the height of perfection and civilisation. The desert on the other hand, was only useful as a place to retire to, or as somewhere to escape to when under attack.[2]

The defeat of Muhammad al-Jaylani in 1816 and the alliance with Sokoto.

After conquering Adrar and gaining several successes against Tuareg groups such as the Kel Geres of Air, Muhammad al-Jaylani's forces were heavily defeated in 1816, at a place called by some Shendewenka and by others Jibale, by the Tamezgidda (the people of the mosque) and the Kel Geres, led by the scholar-turned-warrior, Ibrahim.[3] Muhammad al-Jaylani himself escaped from this battle with a number of his followers and sought refuge in Sokoto. However, 20 years later in 1836, with the support and assistance of Sokoto, he returned to the battlefield and routed Ibrahim and his allies, who included the Sultans of Gobir and Katsina.

It is worth pointing out here, in the context of Muhammad al-Jaylani's links with Sokoto, that different Tuareg groups adopted different positions with regard to the Muslim reform movement in Hausaland. Contacts between the Muslim reformers in Sokoto existed prior to 1804, the date of the outbreak of the Sokoto jihad. Moreover, many Tuareg scholars joined Usuman dan Fodio's community and took part in his jihad.[4] Others however, like Ibrahim, were consistent opponents both of the Sokoto reform movement as well as that led by Muhammad al-Jaylani. Ibrahim's Tamezgidda group had close ties with certain sections of the noble and chiefly Iwillimeden Tuareg and this may explain its opposition to the egalitarian principles of Muhammad al-Jaylani.

Conclusions.

Muhammad al-Jaylani was an inspiration to many Tuareg in the 19th century. According to some accounts his supporters claimed that he was the Mahdi while others believed he possessed extraordinary powers.[5] He came to accept that a Muslim scholar, traditionally a pacifist, could and should resort to jihad of the sword for the purpose of redressing their grievances, reforming and restructuring society, and purifying and spreading Islam. He nevertheless failed to establish his urban, classless, ideal Muslim society by means of jihad of the sword and it would appear that the peaceful approach to reform pursued by the Kel es Suq continued to exercise the stronger influence on the thinking of the majority of Tuareg Muslim scholars.

Finally, given the view of Muhammad al-Jaylani and Muhammad Bello that the urban centre, the town, was a more appropriate setting than the village or the desert for the establishment of the ideal Muslim community, it is worth mentioning here what a well-known contemporary scholar, Ernest Gellner, has described as the main characteristics or central tradition of Islam.[6] I should point out that I do not intend to provide a critical analysis of Gellner's views, but simply to state them, leaving the reader to consider them and to come to his or her own conclusions about them.

In Table I, I have listed the characteristics which Gellner states "are more favoured by an urban than by a rural setting in view of their requirements of literacy, and perhaps for other reasons".[7] Table II lists the characteristics which according to Gellner "are more favoured by a rural than by an urban society".[8] A little further on in his article, after stating that the set of characteristics presented in Table II are central in the Christian religious tradition, he adds that in Islam the position is reversed. It is the set of characteristics presented in Table I that form the central religious tradition in Islam. To use Gellner's words: "The urban, literate or literacy oriented, at least theoretically egalitarian Islam of the 'ulama (Muslim scholars/teachers) of the towns is somehow identical from one end of orthodox Islam to the other, and . . . is also somehow continuous over time". On the other hand Gellner claims that the characteristics in Table II "are inevitable for tribal Islam, at least in most circumstances".[9]

More so than in the rural areas, people in the towns, in Gellner's opinion, tend to be literate or close to people who are literate. Therefore urban dwellers are more likely than those in rural areas to depend for guidance on

TABLE I: *Main characteristics of Islam in the urban setting.*
1. Strict monotheism
2. Puritanism
3. Stress on scriptural revelation and hence on literacy
4. Egalitarianism between believers
5. (As a consequence of 4. above) absence of special mediation, which of course on its this worldly side would involve hierarchy
6. Minimisation of ritual or mystical extravagance; correspondingly moderation and sobriety
7. Stress on the observance of rules rather than emotion states.

TABLE II: *Main characteristics of Islam in the rural setting.*
1. Tending towards hierarchy both within this and the other world
2. (As a consequence of 1. above) priesthood or ritual specialisation and a multiplicity of spirits in the other (world)
3. The incarnation of religion in perceptual symbols or images rather than the abstract recorded words
4. (As a consequence of 3. above) the tendency towards the profusion of ritual and mystical practices rather than sobriety and moderation
5. Similarly an ethic of loyalty towards personality rather than respect for rules.

the written word (of the Qur'an) than on mystical experience or dreams or "spirits", or on Shaikhs or charismatic leaders. Gellner is not saying, of course, that there is no mysticism or "personal", as opposed to literate, abstract, religion in the towns. He is simply suggesting that these forms of religion are not central to the urban religious tradition, and where they exist in the towns it is not for the same reasons as they exist in the rural or tribal setting. He states, for example, that mysticism in the towns "is essentially an escape from life; in the countryside it confirms the local forms of life". [10]

In Gellner's opinion, then, and in that of the sociologist Max Weber[11], urban life in contrast with rural or desert life provides an individual with greater facilities for becoming literate, for becoming acquainted with the written, authentic version of his or her faith, with the Qur'an for example. It also tends to create an environment less favourable for mysticism to develop and form the basis of a whole way of life. Moreover, for these and other reasons the urban setting, where the inhabitants are literate and which is generally more impersonal and anonymous, is less likely to provide any would-be prophet or charismatic leader with a large, ready-made clientele who can change, adapt or interpret the religion in whatever way he/she believes is necessary. There is, furthermore, less chance of people in the towns relying on mediators, or "lesser" gods and spirits, since they can read about and find answers to their questions in books or in the "Holy Book," or from the scholars whose task it is to study and know the doctrinal, legal, moral and other aspects of the religion.

As we have seen, Muhammad al-Jaylani and Muhammad Bello put forward reasons why it was preferable for Muslims to live in towns rather than rural or desert settings. According to them it was easier for Muslims in the towns to implement the Shari'a, to assemble for congregational prayer, and in general to observe the tenets and practices of Islam, which seems to indicate that the ideal Muslim society is an urban one.

Much more research on Islam in West Africa is required before we can appreciate whether or not Gellner's opinions hold true for West Africa. I will add simply that a literate, relatively orthodox Islam has flourished in the desert conditions of the western Sahara on occasion, while the urban centres of West Africa have presented a picture of Islam more typical of the rural/desert areas as depicted by Gellner. Nevertheless, in the light of the rest of the material in this book and other research, the views of Muhammad al-Jaylani, Muhammad Bello and Gellner on the proper setting for orthodox Islam to develop are worth considering.

Islam in the upper and middle Niger regions.

In the 17th and 18th centuries in the upper and middle Niger regions Islam was spread in the main by peaceful means, an approach encouraged by Muslim leaders such as Shaikh Sidi al-Mukhtar al-Kunti "The Great" (1729–1811) (see Chapter 4). Although Islam continued to develop in this way in the 19th century, militant means were also used both to reform Islam and to extend its frontiers. There were two major military jihads or holy wars in the upper and middle Niger region in the 19th century: the first was waged by Shaikh Ahmadu Lobbo of Masina, and the second by al-Hajj 'Umar Tall. Although the main concern of this section is with these two jihads I will also consider the campaigns and activities of Samory Ture, founder and ruler of the state of Wasulu, and their bearing on the development of Islam in the region.

The Islamic reform movement of Shaikh Ahmadu Lobbo I of Masina.

Masina, in the upper and middle Niger region, was subjected to Songhay rule by Sonni Ali in the second half of the 15th century, and then after the collapse of Songhay in 1591 it came under a non-Muslim Fulani dynasty, the Rari. In the 17th century Masina became a vassal state of the Bambara kingdom of Segu, and in fact continued to be governed by the Rari in dependence on Segu until 1818. In 1818 Shaikh Ahmadu Lobbo I, a Muslim scholar, launched his militant Islamic reform movement which put an end to the Rari dynasty, threw off Bambara overlordship and turned Masina into an Islamic state. Inspired to a degree by the reform movement in Sokoto, Shaikh Ahmadu overcame the combined resistance of the Rari and their Bambara allies,

VI Arabs and Tuaregs praying on route

routing them finally at the battles of Nokouma and Geri.

After establishing his authority in Masina Shaikh Ahmadu attempted to extend his control over Jenne and Timbuktu where there were large Muslim communities. Jenne was incorporated into Masina but the Tuareg Muslim community in Timbuktu put up strong resistance to Ahmadu's expansionist aims until 1846. In that year the leader of a Kunta group in Timbuktu, Sidi Ahmad al-Bakka'i, arranged a compromise between the Tuareg of Timbuktu and the authorities in Masina. This allowed Timbuktu to retain a considerable degree of internal self-government and the right to keep a portion of the taxes collected in the town and surrounding areas in return for recognition of Masina's overall sovereignty. Moreover, in accordance with the terms of the compromise Masina agreed that there would be no military occupation of Timbuktu.

The Masina authorities also attempted, without much success, to impose their authority on the Mossi to the south-east, and on the Bambara kingdoms of Segu and Kaarta to the south-west and west. The campaigns against the Bambara continued intermittently for many years and only ceased with the conquest of Masina in 1862 by al-Hajj 'Umar Tall, the well-known Muslim reformer and founder of the Tokolor empire.

Although the reform of Islam was not the sole motive for the Masina campaigns against the Bambara and others it did play an important part in the thinking of Shaikh Ahmadu Lobbo I and his associates. Their imaginations were fired by the long-standing and widespread tradition in the upper and middle Niger region that a renewer of Islam would appear there in the 13th

Muslim century to recreate the ideal Islamic state as a prelude to the advent of the Mahdi.

References to these events were contained in the "Tar'ikh al-Fattash", a history written in the first half of the 16th century by Muhammad al-Kati from Timbuktu. Shaikh Ahmadu Lobbo I, according to some accounts, based his claim to be the mujaddid, the renewer of Islam, on a passage in the "Tarikh al-Fattash" which stated that the twelfth Caliph, the orthodox Caliph and Renewer, would be called by his own name Ahmadu.[1] He is also said to have referred to himself as "the Commander of the Faithful" whose task it was "to restore the faith of the Lord and to do battle for God in the Sudan".[2]

Although, therefore, Shaikh Ahmadu and his associates were concerned to protect and defend trade and commerce by providing proper policing on the trade routes and by combatting excessive taxation of market activities, they also saw themselves very much in the same light as Usuman dan Fodio and his associates in Hausaland, that is as reformers committed to the renewal of Islam. Moreover, a considerable amount of correspondence passed between Shaikh Ahmadu Lobbo I of Masina and the reformers in Hausaland.[3] It seems that Sokoto wanted at one stage to extend its authority over Masina, but then Shaikh Ahmadu declared himself to be Amir al-Mu'minin and turned Masina into a Caliphate, and refused to acknowledge the leadership of Sokoto.

Shaikh Ahmadu's dedication to Islamic reform was not in fact questioned by Muslim reformers like al-Hajj 'Umar. The latter, however, did not regard Shaikh Ahmadu's successors, namely his son Shaikh Ahmadu II, who ruled Masina from 1844 to 1852, and his grandson Shaikh Ahmadu III, ruler from 1856 to 1862, the year in which Masina was conquered by al-Hajj Umar, as committed and genuine Muslim reformers.[4] In fact Umar saw them if anything as an obstacle to the forward march of Islam in much the same way that the Sokoto Muslim reformers saw the leaders in Borno.

What really convinced Umar of this was the fact that the Masina rulers in 1856 and 1861 were prepared to make alliances with the non-Muslim and mixing Muslim rulers of the Bambara states of Kaarta and Segu in an effort to block his own advance in the middle Niger region. It was this that provided Umar with what he believed was a doctrinal justification for conquering the Islamic state of Masina in 1862, regarded by some historians as the most complete or thoroughgoing Islamic state in 19th-century West Africa. We will return to Umar's justification for his attack on Masina in the next section. Meanwhile, after putting up strong resistance to Umar's authority in 1863–4, Masina became a province of the Tokolor empire until that empire itself collapsed with the French occupation of Bandiagara in 1893.

The achievements of the Islamic reform movement in Masina.

Ahmadu Lobbo I established in Masina one of the most thoroughgoing of the Islamic states to emerge in West Africa in the 19th century. He enforced aspects of the Shari'a (Islamic sacred law) to the letter. The government consisted of a council of 40 elders with Shaikh Ahmadu Lobbo acting not as an arbitrary dictator but as the first among equals. The provinces were administered by provincial governors, and Muslim scholars exercised authority at district or local level. Masina, however, suffered from considerable political disunity and this no doubt partly explains why al-Hajj Umar found it relatively easy to overrun it in 1862.

A major cause of this political disunity was the fact that Ahmadu Lobbo appointed his son, Ahmadu b. Ahmadu, to succeed him instead of following a Fulani tradition and appointing one of his brothers. Consequently, his brothers Ba Lobbo and Abd al-Salam, resentful at being overlooked, served Shaikh Ahmadu Lobbo's successors, his son and grandson, without conviction or enthusiasm and regarded al-Hajj Umar's invasion of Masina as a means of obtaining the power and authority which they believed they had been deprived of by Shaikh Ahmadu Lobbo I. They were, however, further disappointed when al-Hajj 'Umar disregarded their claims and appointed one of his own sons as governor of Masina, a move which resulted in Ba Lobbo and Abd al-Salam joining the resistance movement which fought unsuccessfully to overthrow Tokolor rule in Masina and the rest of the middle Niger region.

The Islamic reform movement of al-Hajj 'Umar b. Sa'id Tall and the establishment of the Tokolor empire.

Along with Usuman dan Fodio, al-Hajj 'Umar b. Sa'id Tall is perhaps the best known of all the 19th-century West African Muslim reformers. He was born in c. 1794 near Podor in Futa Toro, northern Senegal, at a time when Futa Toro was undergoing an Islamic reform movement (see chapter 4, p. 85). 'Umar, like Usuman dan Fodio, Ma Ba Diakhou and so many other Muslim reformers, was the son of a Muslim teacher. His father, a Tokolor, belonged to that group of religious leaders whom we have already spoken about, the Torodbe. After being taught the Qur'an and the Hadith, 'Umar, as was the custom among many Muslim students who wanted to improve their education, left home when he was about 15 and went in search of a Muslim scholar who was known to be well qualified in the subjects the student wished to specialise in. 'Umar's preference was for someone competent in mysticism (tasawwuf) rather than but not to the exclusion of Islamic law (fiqh).

While travelling around and teaching in Futa Jallon, today part of Guinea (Conakry), 'Umar met members of the Tijaniyya brotherhood, and in c.1823 one of his teachers 'Abd al-Karim b. Ahmad al-Naqil conferred upon him membership, though not full membership, of this brotherhood. Two years later in c. 1825 'Umar set out on his long pilgrimage to Mecca following a route which passed through Masina, Kong, Sokoto and Gwandu, Air, Borno, the Fezzan and Egypt. From Egypt he crossed the Red Sea and arrived at Jedda in Saudi Arabia in 1828, and then went on to Mecca. 'Umar spent three years in Mecca and in addition to performing the hajj three times he studied under Muhammad al-Ghali Abu Talib, the head of the Tijaniyya brotherhood in the Hijaz (the centre of Islam in western Arabia).

Muhammad al-Ghali not only made al-Hajj 'Umar a full member of the Tijaniyya brotherhood but also appointed him as one of the spiritual and temporal leaders of the order. Moreover, he advised 'Umar to go back to West Africa and sweep away all the remaining traces of "paganism" and convert the people to Islam.[5]

This advice was given in c. 1831, at a point in time when it seems that 'Umar had already decided to dedicate himself to the reform of Islam by holy war, holy war of the heart, mind and tongue as well as holy war of the sword. This can be seen from some of his writings completed between 1828 and 1831 while in Mecca in which he encourages Muslims to have greater faith and to commit themselves more to prayer, fasting, almsgiving the pilgrimage and to holy war.[6]

On his way back from Mecca 'Umar spent some time in Borno where he had differences of opinion with Muhammad al-Kanemi, the ruler of Borno, who was a member of the Qadiriyya brotherhood and who refused to allow members of the Tijaniyya to assemble together for the recitation of their litanies. Al-Kanemi also criticised the idea, accepted by 'Umar, that an individual could be a friend of or specially close to Allah (a Wali) because of his spiritual achievements.

In addition to visiting Borno, 'Umar spent several years in Sokoto, from 1832 to 1838, where he forged close ties with Muhammad Bello and, according to some accounts, convinced the latter to leave the Qadiriyya and join the Tijaniyya brotherhood.[7] 'Umar married one of Muhammad Bello's daughters, Miriam, who gave birth to Ahmadu, his eldest son and his successor as ruler of the Tokolor empire. Al-Hajj 'Umar also married into the Borno ruling family and his wife, in this case Mariatu, bore him a son Aquibu, who again played a prominent role in the Tokolor empire.

After leaving Sokoto 'Umar spent several months in Masina as the guest of Shaikh Ahmadu Lobbo I. Then, after being held captive by the Bambara in Segu, he finally arrived in Futa Jallon after passing through his homeland Futa Toro. In Futa Jallon, with the permission of the Muslim ruler, Bubakar, 'Umar established a centre of religious learning and missionary activity at Diaguku in 1840. From his base at Diaguku, and later at Dinguiray, 'Umar concentrated on preaching and teaching about the Tijaniyya order, on writing and on trading. He traded with British merchants in Sierra Leone and with the French merchants at St Louis and those at the French trading posts along the Senegal River, supplying them with, among other things, gold dust in return for guns and ammunition. Meanwhile, his followers cultivated the land and produced large quantities of grain.

Al-Hajj 'Umar, therefore, as a result of his pilgrimage to Mecca, his learning, his close association with Muslim leaders from Sokoto and elsewhere, his wealth and his large following, became a man of considerable authority and influence, and was called upon to arbitrate in both political and religious disputes. He also came to be regarded by the Almamy (political and religious head of a Muslim community) of Timbo in Futa Jallon as a threat to his authority and later the French were to view him in the same light.

What probably frightened the Almamy of Timbo most was not so much 'Umar's economic strength but the radical and what no doubt appeared as the threatening tone of his comments while preaching which attracted widespread support. According to one contemporary account 'Umar would tell the people, "In our country people think they have fulfilled their whole religious duty when they have said *salaam* (the prayers), but soon I shall set out to convert the world, and then Futa will see a real Muslim". His preaching, according to this account, endeared him to the oppressed who believed that if he became their leader the tyranny of their chiefs and the oppression of the Moors would end. 'Umar's language was strong; he is said to have threatened to "wipe out" those people who refused to convert to Islam and follow his leadership.[8]

As tension increased between his community and the Almamy of Timbo 'Umar decided to follow the example of Prophet Muhammad and make a planned withdrawal (*hijra*) from Diaguku to Dinguiray, situated in the forest region to the east of Futa Jallon but outside the Almamy's sphere of influence. This withdrawal probably took place in 1851, and at Dinguiray 'Umar, though he continued his preaching and teaching, began in earnest to prepare his community (*jama'a*) for military jihad by forming a standing army. The military jihad began officially after an attack on his community by Yimba, the non-Muslim ruler of the Tamba, capital of Tamla. After this incident Umar is said to have announced on 6 September 1852 that Allah had informed him that he was authorised to undertake the jihad against the infidel.

Several major forces were to work against the success of al-Hajj 'Umar's militant Islamic reform movement. There was opposition, for instance, from the nominal Muslim and non-Muslim states such as the Bambara states of Segu and Kaarta, from the French, from Muslim states such as Masina and from prominent members of the Qadiriyya brotherhood, such as Shaikh al-Bakka'i, a descendant of Shaikh Sidi al-Mukhtar al-Kabir al-Kunti and leader of a branch of the Kunta in Timbuktu. I will consider each of these opposition groups as I outline the course of 'Umar's jihad.

The first stages of the jihad.

In 1853 'Umar subjugated Tamba which he renamed Taibatu, one of the names which the early Muslims gave to the town of Medina in Arabia, and then went on to attack and overrun a number of other areas in the Senegambia. By 1854 he had subdued Bambuk and then took control of a number of provinces in the state of Khasso. The next major campaigns were fought against the Bambara kingdom of Kaarta between 1855 and 1857. By February 1857 'Umar had conquered Kaarta, placed it under the control of his *talibes* (disciples/followers) and set out again for Khasso. Meanwhile the French had become positively hostile to 'Umar and his jihad, seeing in it an obstacle to their own political and economic interests and expansionist aims in the Senegambia.

Al-Hajj Umar's jihad and French opposition in the Senegambia.

During the 1840s al-Hajj 'Umar met a number of French officials and traded with French merchants. At this stage, it seemed that in the interests of trade and commerce the French might support 'Umar's plans to "pacify" the Senegal valley and the rest of the Senegambia where wars in defence of sovereignty and trading rights were adversely affecting his own commercial interests, those of the French and the commercial interests of the area as a whole. The French did not have the manpower in the 1840s to perform the task of "pacification" themselves. With the arrival in 1854 of Louis Faidherbe as governor of Senegal the situation changed. Faidherbe, who had two terms as governor of Senegal from 1854 to 1861 and from 1863 to 1865, has often been regarded as the architect of French imperialist policies in West Africa. Faidherbe did not regard 'Umar as too great a threat to French interests during his first couple of years in Senegal, 'Umar was at this time involved in campaigns in Kaarta to the east and was not affecting French commercial interests which centred on gum, groundnuts and gold. In fact the French even decided to inform 'Umar that they recognised his right to rule over Kaarta. 'Umar, however, did not reply and the French began to fear that after the conquest of Kaarta he would begin waging a campaign in areas closer to their commercial and political interests. They therefore set about strengthening existing French forts along the Senegal River and building others. Faidherbe, moreover, entered into alliances with rulers opposed to 'Umar, such as Sambala of Khasso, obtained permission to build forts in their territory and assisted them in their resistance to 'Umar.

Faidherbe also instigated an anti-'Umar propaganda campaign with the aim on the one hand of making the French government aware of the danger posed by 'Umar's jihad to their political and economic interests and on the other of turning people in Senegal against the Muslim reformer. In 1858 Faidherbe wrote that the French in West Africa had two enemies to fear, "the king of the Trarza with his pride, and among the blacks, al-Hajj 'Umar with his Muslim fanaticism, which he seeks to arouse against us wherever he goes". The French authorities in Senegal, moreover, began to characterise al-Hajj 'Umar in their official bulletin for Senegal and Dependencies as an "impostor" and a false prophet.[9]

The first direct military encounter between al-Hajj 'Umar and the French and their Senegambian allies took place in April 1857 when the Muslim leader attacked the French fort at Médine situated in that part of Khasso ruled by Dyouku Sambala, an opponent of 'Umar. This encounter lasted three months and resulted in a defeat for 'Umar, and while it left the Muslim reformer in need of reinforcements, it left Sambala even more dependent on the French.

After his defeat 'Umar decided to recruit more troops in Futa Toro, but while en route there he found he was opposed by the Almamy of Futa Jallon. Further, when he arrived in Futa Toro in July/August 1858 he discovered that Faidherbe's hostile propaganda had weakened support for his cause and he was even opposed by the Muslim leadership in his own home area of Toro. Moreover, French alliances with those states bordering on Futa Toro meant that both in and outside of Futa Toro 'Umar was surrounded by hostile rulers. The Damel of Cayor was an exception. He was willing to cooperate with 'Umar in return for help against the Bourba (ruler) of Jolof. 'Umar, however, realising that his chances of success in Futa Toro and the Senegambia as a whole were slim, decided to move east towards Kaarta and consolidate his position there while continuing his struggle against the French by using the economic weapon.

From his fortress at Guémou 'Umar was able to prevent the gum supplies carried by the Moors from reaching the French fort at Bakel. The French, therefore, to protect their economic interests, attacked Guémou in October 1859. 'Umar at this point was planning his conquest of the Bambara state of Segu and decided to negotiate for peace terms with the French. The latter agreed to send envoys to 'Umar but these envoys, Captain Mage and Dr Quintin, did not set out until 1863 and the treaty between the French and the Tokolor was not signed until 1866, almost two years after 'Umar's death. In practice, however, in 1860 'Umar accepted out of necessity the French presence in the Senegambia, and the French for their part decided not to interfere with 'Umar's plans for the development of his Tokolor empire in the upper and middle Niger region. However, 'Umar continued to encourage Muslims in the Senegambia to emigrate to Muslim territories since the French were non-Muslims. He told the Senegambia Muslims that no true Muslim could live under a non-Muslim ruler. 'Umar did not, however, object to non-Muslims living and trading in a Muslim country. He had in fact in 1847 told French officials at Bakel that the French could trade in the Senegambia if they paid the *jizya*, a tribute payable by non-Muslims living under Muslim rule and a sign that the non-Muslims accepted Muslim authority. The French never agreed to pay this tribute.[10]

'Umar, therefore, left the Senegambia to the French for the time being and went on to consolidate and expand his empire in the upper Niger region. The Bambara state of Segu fell to his forces in April 1861, and the Muslim state of Masina was overrun in June 1862 after a campaign lasting three months. The reasons given by al-Hajj 'Umar for the conquest of Masina were, as I have mentioned, virtually the same as those given by the Muslim reformers in Hausaland for their jihad against Borno. The war of words over Masina was carried on in the main between Yarki Talfi, a scholar and ally of 'Umar, and Shaikh Ahmad al-Bakka'i of the Kunta in Timbuktu and a leader of the Qadiriyya brotherhood there. Ahmad al-Bakka'i had given both moral and physical support to the rulers of Masina and Segu in their attempt to prevent 'Umar from taking over their territories. Moreover, he advised Shaikh Ahmad III of Masina to proclaim himself the ruler of the people of Segu both Muslim and non-Muslim, and thereby deprive 'Umar of any excuse for attacking the Bambara states. Ahmad al-Bakka'i was in this instance following the principle that if the ruler of a state is a Muslim then the land he rules is Muslim land and cannot therefore be attacked by another Muslim. 'Umar, nevertheless, attacked both Segu and Masina on the grounds that their rulers were unconcerned about the reform or expansion of Islam in territories over which they claimed sovereignty and that in addition they opposed his Islamic reform movement. Masina and some of the Kunta in Timbuktu did in fact assist Segu against the Tokolor, and 'Umar did find evidence of "idol" worship in the Bambara states.[11]

'Umar's end came soon after the conquest of Masina. In 1863 a revolt broke out against his rule in Masina, a revolt backed by some elements in Timbuktu, and in February 'Umar was killed in a battle against the rebels. The forces of Masina and Timbuktu were defeated in 1864, however, by 'Umar's nephew and the Tokolor empire, which covered a vast area of the upper and middle Niger region, continued in existence under the overall leadership of 'Umar's eldest son Ahmadu until 1893 when it was overrun by the French.

The Tokolor empire under Ahmadu, 1864—1893.

The creation of such a vast empire as the Tokolor empire and the fact that it lasted for 30 years was a quite remarkable achievement in itself, and was a tribute to the qualities of leadership demonstrated by al-Hajj 'Umar. However, as we saw, 'Umar died before he had had time to provide the empire with a strong central administration based on Islamic principles. While he was alive his charismatic leadership gave a certain unity and cohesion to the state but, as is virtually always the case when charismatic leaders die, after his death the enthusiasm which he engendered among his followers for his cause waned.

On the death of 'Umar a crisis occurred over the succession, some wanting his successor to be elected while others claimed that 'Umar had appointed his eldest son, Ahmadu, to succeed him and had therefore passed on his baraka, his blessing and charismatic powers, to Ahmadu. The result was that Ahmadu's authority was never universally accepted. In fact it was confined for most of the life of the empire to Segu, while his cousin Ahmadu Tijani ruled Masina, one brother ruled Kaarta and another Dinguiray. The disagreement over the succession and the consequent lack of unity resulted in a civil war in 1870 which lasted in the first instance for two years. This was a war in which Ahmadu fought Abibu and Mukhtar, his two half brothers, over the question of the control of Kaarta.[12]

Although he eventually established some control over Kaarta Ahmadu was never able to do the same in Masina, which remained for all practical purposes an independent province of the empire until 1893. Ahmadu also had to contend with the French who, until they decided to make a full scale assault on the Tokolor empire in the late 1880s, found other ways of destabilising the empire. While appearing to collaborate with Ahmadu, for example, they assisted Bambara and other resistance movements and put pressure on chiefs within the empire to work against Ahmadu.

For most of the 1880s Ahmadu was faced once again with a revolt against him in Kaarta led by the governor Muhammad Muntaga. The French then began their conquest of the Tokolor empire by invading and over-running Segu in 1890, Kaarta in 1891 and Masina in 1893. Although Ahmadu continued to resist for several more years, nevertheless by 1893 the French had effectively put an end to al-Hajj 'Umar's Tokolor empire.

Al-Hajj 'Umar's achievements: an assessment.

Al-Hajj 'Umar's reform movement did not lead to the establishment of an "ideal" Islamic state and society in the upper and middle Niger regions. Those parts of the empire once under Bambara rule continued to be organised and administered in much the same way as they had been under the Bambara rulers. However, the reform movement did result in the spread of Islam, particularly in the form of the Tijaniyya brotherhood, among the non-Muslim and nominal Muslim Bambara and others. This is clear from French reports written in the late 1880s in which the French colonial officials like Gallieni and Archinard, Governor of what was then called the French Sudan, stated that any Christian mission established in his sphere of authority would have to be sited in a non-Muslim area to avoid offending those of the Bambara who had converted to Islam.[13] Furthermore, 'Umar's reform movement, although it also turned some groups away from Islam, contributed to the development of the Islamic education system in the upper and middle Niger region, a fact testified to again by the French who on their arrival in the area were struck by the many Muslim schools in existence.

Samory and Islam.

Samory Ture is one of the best known of the 19th-century West African nationalists.[14] He was a talented military strategist and tactician and an able administrator, and during the last quarter of the 19th century he established in the upper Niger region and the Milo valley to the south the kingdom of Wasulu by uniting together under one central authority numerous independent Mandinka states. In 1894, however, Samory was forced by the French military advance in the western Sudan to abandon the heartland of his Wasulu empire. This was not the end of Samory's state-building activities. Between 1894 and 1898 while resisting French imperialism he established another state east of Wasulu in a region which today forms part of the Republics of Upper Volta and the Ivory Coast. The French forces caught up with Samory in 1898, took over his empire and sent him into exile in Gabon.

Samory has never been regarded as a Muslim leader dedicated to the reform and spread of Islam in the way that, for example, Usuman dan Fodio, al-Hajj 'Umar and Ma Ba Diakhou were. Instead he has been presented as a military genius and an ardent nationalist, who adopted an extremely matter-of-fact, pragmatic approach to the cause of Islam. Certainly when it was wise to do so from the political and military point of view Samory never hesitated to make alliances with non-Muslims against Muslims. At the beginning of his career as an empire builder he justified all his military exploits not by reference to the Qur'an and the need to reform Islam but on the grounds that they were necessary for the protection of trade and commerce and in order to provide merchants with stable government. Moreover, when Samory began to build up an army in the 1860s with a view to welding into a single state the various Mandinka kingdoms in the Milo valley, he assumed the title "fama", that is, "one who carries the sword" and by implication "one who takes power by military conquest".

Samory's indifference to Islam for much of his career as a soldier and ruler, which spanned the best part of 40 years, can be explained in part by his early upbringing and the political and social context in which he operated. He was born in Konya in the Milo valley to the south of the Islamic centre of Kankan and the Islamic state of Futa Jallon in about 1830. His father, Laafiya, was only a nominal Muslim at best, and continued to practise the indigenous religion. Through his mother he was related to the non-Muslim rulers of Konya. This was a very different environment from the one in which Usuman dan Fodio and al-Hajj Umar were raised.

Samory in fact knew next to nothing about Islam until at the age of about 20 he became a trader and met some Muslim merchants, one of whom, Shaikh Nyonsomoridugu, taught him the basic tenets of Islam. When, however, he left trading for a career as a soldier in the early 1850s he seems to have lost interest in Islam. He joined the Sisé army as a volunteer in the hope that they, the Sisé, would release his mother whom they had taken as a captive during a raid on Konya in 1853. The Sisé themselves were Muslims who in 1835 had established the Islamic state of Moriuledugu to the south of Konya. The founder of this state, Mori Ulé, was born in Kankan and was probably influenced by the military jihad in Futa Jallon (see Chapter 4, p. 84).

Samory was forced to leave the Sisé army in 1861 and began to think in terms of establishing his own empire. However, he needed support and he also needed to be able to provide people with good reasons for following him and accepting his leadership. He therefore presented himself as the only one who could defend Konya against militant Muslim groups such as the Sisé and in this way obtained a following with which he formed an army. However, he failed to keep out the Sisé, who in 1865 pushed him from his base at Sanankoro further south towards the forest zone. Samory returned to Sanankoro in 1867.

Between 1867 and 1885, using Sanankoro as his capital until 1873 and from then onwards Bisandugu, Samory extended his authority over Toron, Kankan and up as far north as the southern boundary of the Tokolor empire in the upper Niger region. In the west his sphere of influence stretched as far as the British colony of Sierra Leone and in the east as far as the kingdom of Sikasso. Although many Muslims fought alongside Samory during this period of rapid conquest and expansion the army was not a Muslim army and Samory did not see himself as the champion of Islam. He in fact allied with non-Muslims in 1880 when he made an attack on the predominantly Muslim centre of Kankan. Indeed Samory and his Muslim supporters, many of whom were Dyula merchants, appear to have fought mainly to protect and expand their economic and commercial interests.[15] Nevertheless Samory did at one stage attempt to form an Islamic state.

Samory and the creation of an Islamic community.

In the 1880s Samory did attempt to turn his kingdom into something resembling an Islamic community. A beginning was made in this direction when he assumed the title of Almamy (imam) which although it means simply prayer leader was also used, as in Futa Jallon, to describe the leader of the Muslim community as a whole. In fact Samory may well have been influenced in his decision to set up a Muslim community or jama'a by his contacts with the Islamic state of Futa Jallon, and perhaps even more so as a result of his conquest of Kankan in 1881. After overrunning Kankan he appointed a number of Muslim scholars to his council and gave them responsibility for, among other things, the administration of justice. Islamic law, however, was applied to only a very limited number of people, the majority of the population continuing to be tried according to customary law. Moreover,

Samory reserved to himself the right to decide the penalties for certain criminal cases such as plotting against the regime, sabotage on the trade routes, the mistreatment of foreigners, and in these and other cases he recommended penalties derived from customary law.

In addition to introducing the Shari'a at least in a limited form, Samory also banned the taking of alcohol. He also withdrew the right of non-Muslims to assemble for worship and enforced the five daily prayers and obliged all parents to send their children to Qur'anic schools. Samory himself again took up the study of the Qur'an and was by 1886 qualified to lead his people in prayer. Furthermore, all of his councillors and administrators and the leading families in the state who were non-Muslims were obliged to convert to Islam. Samory in fact wanted all his subjects to become Muslims and established a network of Muslim schools throughout his empire and staffed them with Muslim teachers who were paid from a tax collected at the village or local community level.

This policy of Islamisation which was pushed ahead at a rapid pace met with strong opposition. Samory's own father, Laafiya, opposed it by performing the indigenous religious rites in public. Samory reacted by having him taken into custody. He also demonstrated his desire to have the Shari'a implemented and respected by having his daughter stoned to death for acts of immorality. The opposition to the creation of an Islamic community was too great, however, and Samory, pre-occupied with the problems created for him by the French and by stiff resistance from Sikasso had to reverse a number of his decisions.

While beseiging Sikasso to the east, a rebellion involving large numbers of his subjects broke out in the heart of Samory's empire. The rebellion was put down in August 1888 but not before many lives had been lost and good agricultural land destroyed. After quelling the rebellion Samory abandoned the idea of making conversions to Islam compulsory and of rigorously enforcing the Shari'a. Moreover, non-Muslims were no longer forced to send their children to Qur'anic schools and they were once again allowed to assemble for worship. In addition people educated and trained in the traditional education system were again appointed as administrators. Further, Samory himself, although he kept the title of Almamy and encouraged the pursuit of Islamic learning and the maintenance of Islamic culture, no longer presented himself as being first and foremost a Muslim leader. Instead he began to stress his role as the defender of the nation's independence against French imperialism and other hostile forces.

Samory's attempts to create a Muslim community in the 1880s may have been made partly from a personal commitment to Islam. As one of the best known scholars of Samory's life and times puts it, "His devotion to Islam must not be underestimated".[16] There were no doubt other motives as well. Islam offered a great deal to a leader like Samory who was in the process of attempting to create out of a number of small-scale and diverse societies a single state or nation. Muslims were literate, they possessed skills in accountancy, book-keeping and in other fields. Moreover, Islam offered a formal education system and a wide-ranging commercial network. It also offered a leader like Samory whose empire was bounded in the north by

Muslim states a means of legitimating his authority. Samory, according to his biographer, not only believed that Islam was intellectually and morally superior to indigenous religions but probably also felt that no one particular indigenous religion or combination of these religious was able to provide a foundation for his authority as ruler of a vast territory.[17] Islam, on the other hand, was not the religion of any particular group of people, and by attempting to present himself as a Muslim ruler and by basing his claim to authority on Islam Samory possibly believed that people would come to regard him as belonging to and favouring no particular indigenous religious or political system, but rather as a ruler with a "national" or international outlook and policy.

Ironically Kong, one of the most famous and prestigious Dyula centres of Islamic learning, was destroyed by Samory, himself a Dyula, in 1897. In 1889 the ruler of Kong, Karamoko Ule Wattara, had placed the kingdom of Kong, which covered an area stretching from Bobo-Dioulasso in the north in present-day Upper Volta almost as far as the forest zone in the south, under French protection. After moving east in the direction of Kong in 1894 Samory forced the French troops sent to relieve the area to withdraw. Then in 1897, in order to deprive the French of the use of Kong as a base and because the inhabitants of Kong were allies of the French and refused to fight in his army, Samory ordered its destruction. Many of the Muslim scholars and ordinary people in Kong were put to death because, it is said, Samory accused them of knowing nothing about war. Some of the Dyula managed to escape and went on to establish Muslim settlements such as Dar-as-Salaam in and around Bobo-Dioulasso, while others migrated to the region of Odienne.

Samory was, then, above all else, a military man and an administrator. He became more committed to Islam at a personal level as time went on, and this may have had something to do with his decision to govern his state according to Islamic principles. It seems, however, that the desire to give his authority greater legitimacy and to give his kingdom greater unity and cohesion by making Islam the official state religion were the stronger, more compelling reasons for this decision. The venture had to be almost entirely abandoned as we have seen. However, the system of Islamic education which he developed led to the emergence of numerous, small Muslim communities among the Mande-speaking peoples to the south and east of Futa Jallon and the Tokolor empire.

Finally, Samory gave a rather more indirect impetus to the spread of Islam. His campaigns against the French and against opponents in the upper Niger and Volta Basin, and his destruction of Kong, caused considerable upheaval and dislocation, forcing people, among them Muslims, to migrate. In some instances, as we have seen, these Muslim migrants settling in the region of Odienne in the Ivory Coast and elsewhere established Islamic centres where they had not previously existed and in this way became agents for the dissemination of Islam.

Islamic reform movements in the Senegambia.

The jihad of Ma Ba Diakhou Ba, 1861–1867.

The tradition of militant Islam was relatively old in the Senegambia by the

19th century (see Chapter 4). Here I begin with the militant Islamic reform movement of Ma Ba Diakhou Ba, having decided to consider al-Hajj 'Umar's jihad as part of the militant Islamic reform movements of the upper and middle Niger region, although as I indicated it was born in and had an impact on the Senegambia.

Ma Ba Diakhou Ba (1809 – 1867) was, like his father and grandfather who came from Futa Toro in northern Senegal, a Muslim teacher by profession. His grandfather Ibrahima Mapate Ba established a Muslim school in Jolof, and his father N'Diogu Ba not only established a Muslim school but also a Muslim village called in Wolof, Kir Ma Ba, or Hambacunda in Mande. Ma Ba Diakhou, born in 1809 in Kir Ma Ba, studied the Qur'an in his father's school and after his secondary education in Cayor began teaching in the state of Baddibu, also known as Rip, situated between the rivers Saloum to the north and the Gambia to the south and governed at the time by the Mandinka.[1]

Sometime before launching his military jihad in 1861 Ma Ba Diakhou met al-Hajj 'Umar Tall and was initiated by him into the Tijaniyya brotherhood. He also received encouragement from 'Umar when he announced his intention of waging a holy war in Badibu (Rip). The immediate cause of Ma Ba's holy war was the tension that existed between the various interest groups in and around Badibu. Pastoralists wanted more grazing rights, and the farmers, though they welcomed the manure supplied by the pastoralists, resented the fact that the latters' cattle were allowed to trample over their farms in search of pasture. Furthermore, merchants and rulers were in conflict. One of the causes of this conflict was that the rulers, having lost a considerable source of revenue with the abolition of the trans-Atlantic slave trade, imposed heavier taxes on the merchants who had begun to benefit from the growing trade in groundnuts.

Another important factor contributing to tension and conflict in the region was the presence of British traders on the Gambia who, after some of them had been molested by the people of Baddibu, attacked the area. Ma Ba Diakhou, to the annoyance of the ruler of Baddibu, negotiated peace terms between the British and Baddibu. Then, after the ruler of Baddibu attempted to assassinate him, Ma Ba, with the assistance of the pastoralists and merchants, launched his jihad against Baddibu in 1861.

After conquering Baddibu Ma Ba succeeded in imposing his authority over the Serer state of Saloum in 1864. He also entered into an alliance with both the French governor of Senegal, General Faidherbe, who recognised him as Almamy of Baddibu and Saloum, and with the Damel(ruler) of Cayor, Lat Dior, who was an opponent of French imperialism. However, Ma Ba's alliance with Lat Dior and his desire to create throughout the Senegambia a Muslim state eventually brought him into conflict with the French and contributed to his downfall in 1867. The French had driven Lat Dior from Cayor in 1864 because they alleged that Dior had broken an agreement made in 1859 which allowed the French to build a telegraph line through his territory linking St Louis with Dakar. Lat Dior took refuge with Ma Ba at the latter's capital of Nioro and became a Muslim. The French insisted that Ma Ba expel Lat Dior, but Ma Ba refused on the grounds that Lat Dior was a Muslim.

Although Ma Ba had made a treaty with the French which recognised the right of the French to trade in the Senegambia, he did not acknowledge French claims to political authority in the region. He told General Faidherbe that he could see no reason why the French should interfere in the affairs of the people of the Senegambia. He also regarded the French as Christians who were opposed to Muslims, and went on to point out to Faidherbe in a letter in 1864 that he regarded it as his duty to make war on infidels in an attempt to convert them to Islam.[2]

The French at first approved of Ma Ba's activities, seeing in them the best means of unifying politically the different peoples of Saloum and elsewhere, even if the form of administration established was Muslim. What they could not accept, however, was Ma Ba's intention to carry on his jihad until all the people of the Senegambia had been converted to Islam. This would, they believed, disrupt trade and commerce, the main reason for the French presence in the Senegambia. Moreover, they probably felt that if Ma Ba became too powerful he might attempt with success to expel the French from the Senegambia and thereby put an end to their economic and imperialist ambitions in West Africa.

In 1865, after extending his influence north beyond Saloum in defiance of the treaty made with the French in 1865, Ma Ba had to return to Nioro to put down a revolt. This he did, but he was then faced almost immediately with a French attack in November 1865. He held off the French and consolidated his hold over Baddibu and Saloum during 1866. However, in 1867 he invaded Sine and lost his life at the battle of Somb.

Ma Ba's jihad caused severe hardship to many of the people of Baddibu and Saloum. Many were displaced or fled from their homes to the coastal towns such as Jaol and took refuge there. He did, however, manage to impose an Islamic form of government on large areas of the Senegambia previously untouched by Islam. He appointed Muslim judges to administer the Shari'a and made provisions for the establishment of Muslim schools throughout his kingdom.

The Jihad of Alfa Molo: 1870.

Ma Ba Diakhou Ba was succeeded by his brother, Mamour N'Dari, who continued with his father's plans to reform Islam and build a Muslim state in the Senegambia. He failed, however, to extend his authority over the Mandinka-ruled states to the south of the Gambia river, some of which probably dated back to the 14th century and even earlier. The cradle of Mandinka influence in the region was Gabu (also written Kaabu, Cabo or Ngabu). From Gabu other states were founded such as Combo on the south bank of the Gambia river. Moreover, there were Fulani settlements within or close to these Mandinka states, for example in Combo, such as Kantora, Tomami and Jimara. One estimate puts the number of Fulani in the last three mentioned settlements in the 19th century at around 55,000 and they probably possessed several hundred thousand cattle.[3]

The Fulani who had come from Futa Jallon and elsewhere acknowledged the authority of the Mandinka rulers and paid tax in return for grazing rights, taxes which were at times so heavy that the Fulani would either revolt or move away in search of a better deal. Meanwhile French and British traders and officials were becoming more involved in the commerce of the region, and in this context Alfa Molo and his son Musa Molo, supported in the main by other Fulani, staged a revolt against their Mandinka overlords.

After five years of combat they imposed their authority over Tomari, Jimara and several chiefdoms and forged out of them the relatively large Islamic state of Fuladu, which covered some 5,000 square miles in the upper reaches of the Gambia with its capital at N'Dorna. Alfa Molo died in 1881 and, although he was succeeded by his brother Ba Kary, his son Musa became the power behind the throne. It was, it seems, Musa's dictatorial behaviour which contributed to the eventual collapse of the state in the 1890s, when even his own supporters, led by Muslim religious leaders, rose up in rebellion against him.

The jihad of Fode Kaba: 1870s.

One of the Muslim clerics who rebelled against Musa Molo was the Mandinka Muslim leader, Fode Kaba. After settling in Fuladu in the 1870s, Fode Kaba built up a strong following before launching a holy war in the name of Islam. His primary objective was the defeat of Musa Molo who had attacked his settlement, killed his father and kidnapped his women and children.

The struggle between these two men, which brought devastation to numerous Diola settlements and indeed to villages all over the lower Gambia and Casamance region, prevented the creation of a viable Muslim state on the south bank of the Gambia river. Fode Kaba did, however, conquer Gabu and also managed to impose his authority over Combo. From Combo he organised several religious wars. Combo had been influenced by Islam from the time of its foundation as a state. According to one tradition Mandinka migrants from Gabu, some of whom were Muslim, established the state of Combo in the 14th century. By the middle of the 19th century there was considerable discontent and instability in the state. Moreover, Muslims were pressing the rulers to take measures to preserve their control over trade and commerce and to prevent land from falling into the hands of foreigners and non-Muslims. Eventually they rallied behind Fode Kaba and took power, and then by a combination of peaceful persuasion and force converted many of the remaining non-Muslim population to Islam, while others fled the country.

Much maligned in European records and eventually defeated by a three-pronged British, French and Fulani assault in 1901, Fode Kaba nevertheless is presented in some oral traditions as a great Muslim leader, as a man endowed with miraculous powers who, among other things, could command rivers to dry up so that his troops could cross in safety and escape the enemy.

Lat Dior and the development of Islam in Cayor in the 1870s.

Lat Dior, a hero of Senegalese resistance to French imperialism, was born in Cayor in Senegal in 1842. Although provinces of Cayor such as N'Diambour in the north of the state were by this time heavily Islamised and influential centres of Islamic learning such as Pir Saniokhor had been in existence in Cayor for over a century, Lat Dior was nevertheless born into a non-Muslim environment. He was from an aristocratic family, and many such families in Cayor were hostile to Islam. What they actually disliked was the fact that Muslim leaders, sometimes harbouring political ambitions, had encouraged and organised the peasants, burdened by the harsh demands made upon them by the princes and tyeddos (slaves of the Crown who were recruited by the Damel as soldiers), to revolt.

The rulers of Cayor, therefore, although they welcomed the educated Muslims' advice and employed them as secretaries, generally speaking were not committed Muslims themselves nor did they foster the development of Islam, and some ruling, aristocratic families like Lat Dior's family had not even by the 19th century converted to Islam. Lat Dior himself, as we have seen, became a Muslim while in exile with Ma Ba Diakhou between 1864 and 1869. Lat Dior eventually returned to Cayor in 1869 and was recognised by the French as the legitimate king or Damel in 1871. Between 1871 and 1882 he did a great deal towards turning his country from a semi-Muslim to a completely Muslim state.

Supported by Muslim religious guides and teachers, known as *marabouts*, and among others a Muslim judge, Momar Anta Sali M'Backe, father of Ahmadu Bamba who founded the Senegalese Muslim brotherhood the Muridiyya (see Chapter 7), Lat Dior used the machinery of government and a good deal of persuasion in an effort to turn Cayor into a Muslim state. He was also assisted by the Muslim traders of St Louis and by many, though by no means all, of the local Muslim chiefs. Not only were some of the traders and chiefs anxious to convert their own people to Islam but they also wanted the European missionaries whose activities in the Senegambia had expanded considerably since the 1840s, to become Muslims.

According to one missionary account written in the 1840s the Muslim chief in Dakar did not want the French Roman Catholic missionaries to build a school in his territory because as he explained "it might destroy the religion of Islam". The chief then went on to ask the missionaries to change their religion and become Muslims. The missionaries replied that they would do so if they found the chief's religion better, and added that the chief must also be prepared to become a Christian if they convinced him that Christianity was a better religion than Islam. The chief then showed the missionaries a Qur'an with a leather cover, a drawing of Prophet Muhammad's tomb and a plan of Mecca and Medina, and the missionaries gave the Muslim chief among other things statues of the three kings who in Christian tradition went to adore Christ at his birth, and pointed out that one of those kings was black. But on hearing that the missionaries referred to Christ as the Son of God, the chief returned the statues of the three kings, telling the missionaries that they were instruments of magic. He did, however, accept some medals of the mother of Jesus.[4]

The chief here was simply following Islamic teaching in which Jesus is regarded with respect and counted as one of the prophets but is not regarded as the son of God. Belief in Jesus as the son of God constitutes shirk, that is the association of something human with the divine, or the giving of partners to God. This sort of belief amounts, in the Muslim's view, to a denial of the unity of God, the basic doctrine of Islam contained in the Shahada, or confession of faith, which reads: "There is no god but Allah and Muhammad is his messenger".

To return to Lat Dior. He opposed the French plans to construct a railroad through his territory linking St Louis with Dakar, and was once again forced by the French to leave Cayor in 1882. Between 1882 and 1886 he waged a guerilla war against the French but was killed in a battle against them at Dekkilé in October 1886.

By becoming a Muslim, employing Muslim judges and teachers and persuading chiefs to turn to Islam Lat Dior made a significant contribution to the development of Islam in Cayor. Moreover, in Jollof to the east of Cayor Lat Dior's nephew, Alboury N'Diaye, embarked in the 1870s on a policy of islamisation similar to that pursued by Lat Dior in Cayor, while in Walo to the north Muslim traders from St Louis and Muslim missionaries were enjoying great success in converting the tyeddo, the class once most hostile to Islam. Furthermore in the south, in Bathurst (Banjul), established as a "Christian" town in 1816, Islam had by the 1880s become the predominant religion mainly as a result of the influx of Wolof and Mandinka Muslim traders and missionaries and through the jihads of Ma Ba Diakhou and Fode Kaba. The majority of the inhabitants of the commercial centres in the Casamance region such as Ziquinchor, Sedhiou and Carabane were also Muslim. In his report on the Roman Catholic mission in Bathurst (Banjul) for 1899, the missionary in charge stated that almost all the Wolof, Mandinka and Sisé people in the town were Muslims, leaving him with very few potential converts to Christianity.[5]

However, although Islam had made giant strides forward in the Senegambia by the 1880s, there was in the view of Muslim scholars like Mamadu Lamine a great deal still to be done. He, and no doubt, others who were not Tokolor themselves disliked the fact that the Tokolor had come to wield so much authority, power and influence in the Senegambia and upper and middle Niger regions.

The jihad of Mamadu Lamine, c. 1885−87.

Although his jihad lasted less than two years, Mamadu Lamine, a Soninke, played an important role in the history of Islam in West Africa in the last quarter of the 19th century. He acquired, moreover, a reputation for holiness and learning and as a nationalist. His renown was due in part to the fact that he travelled widely, going on pilgrimage to Mecca, and studied and taught in various parts of the Senegambia and upper Niger.[6] Moreover, his jihad was seen by many as a war against French imperialism.[7]

Mamadu Lamine, like al-Hajj 'Umar Tall whom he had met, and Ma Ba Diakhou, was a member of the Tijaniyya brotherhood. Although his relations with al-Hajj 'Umar appear to have been quite cordial, this cannot be said of his relations with Ahmadu, al-Hajj 'Umar's son and successor as head of the Tokolor empire. On his way back from Mecca in 1880 Mamadu

Lamine stopped off at Segu, capital of the Tokolor empire, and on several occasions Ahmadu allegedly attempted to have him assassinated.

This may have been because Mamadu's reputation as a scholar and a man believed to be endowed with extraordinary gifts and powers, had begun to spread far and wide in the region of the upper Niger and the Senegambia, causing Ahmadu to see in him a potentially dangerous and subversive force. Mamadu was after all a Soninke who resented Tokolor domination in part of the Senegambia and the upper and middle Niger region. Furthermore he seems to have criticised Ahmadu's failure to rule in strict conformity with the Shari'a. In addition, Mamadu Lamine probably angered Ahmadu by claiming to be the leader of the Tijaniyya brotherhood in West Africa and by speaking of al-Hajj 'Umar Tall as though he were dead. Al-Hajj 'Umar had in fact been killed in battle in 1864 but Ahmadu and many of his followers held the view that 'Umar had not died but had simply vanished and would return in the hour of greatest need.

Mamadu left Segu early in 1885 and made his way back to his birthplace and centre of Islamic learning, Gundiuru in Khasso. The French authorities knew about him and kept an eye on him but at first they were not too worried about him. In fact when Mamadu Lamine arrived at the French fort at Bamako on the River Niger he was given permission by the French to travel freely in what they now considered to be their sphere of influence. Mamadu then travelled home, visiting French forts en route, and reached Gundiuru in July 1885. At this time he gave no indication of being hostile to the French, simply appearing to them as an opponent of Ahmadu of the Tokolor and as a man with wide religious appeal. Mamadu was at pains to preserve the image the French had of him as a peacemaker and even wrote to the French governor of Senegal in August 1885 outlining his plans to work for peace among his fellow countrymen. However, a month later, in September 1885, he began diplomatic and military preparations for a jihad. Envoys were dispatched to various parts of the Senegambia including Bundu, and arms and ammunition were bought and soldiers enlisted for a holy war against the people of Gamon who were his enemies from his student days and who, according to Mamadu Lamine, did not pray or know the true religion.[8]

Meanwhile Mamadu Lamine, and this was a very unusual thing for a Muslim reformer to do, asked the French for permission to wage his jihad against Gamon. He met a French army officer at Kayes in November 1885 and told him that he had no hostile ambitions towards the French but on the contrary would like to join in an alliance with them against Ahmadu of the Tokolor empire. Then he requested French permission to attack Gamon and some British factories in the Gambia.

Whether or not the French approved of Mamadu Lamine's plans it is difficult to say. The Muslim religious leader appears to have been under the impression that although the French were not ready to form an alliance against Ahmadu and the Tokolor empire, since their main concern at the time was to destroy Samory, they nevertheless recognised him as an ally and as the spiritual and temporal leader of the Sarakole people. By means of his preaching tours and the way he used traders and others to get the people's support and allegiance he had in actual fact become spiritual and temporal leader of the Sarakole people throughout the region from Futa Toro right along the Senegal River to Kayes by the end of 1885. Some of the Sarakole regarded him as a prophet, a miracle worker, while others saw him as the Mahdi, the God-guided one, who had arrived to destroy the anti-Christ, rid the world of injustice, reform Islam and usher in an age of peace, justice and plenty. Mamadu Lamine referred to himself as the Commander of the Faithful, the leader of the Muslims, the Reformer of Islam and as the one who would implement fully and perfectly the Shari'a. In other words he saw himself in the same light as Usuman dan Fodio, Ma Ba Diakhou, al-Hajj 'Umar and other West African reformers saw themselves.

Mamadu Lamine's career as a militant Muslim reformer, as I have said, lasted a very short time. In 1886 the French, with the support of the people of Gamon, of the British, of Musa Molo, of the ruler of Bundu and others, gradually isolated Mamadu Lamine and in December 1887 cornered him in the district of Niani. Soldiers then beheaded him and presented his head to the French authorities as a trophy. This was done before Mamadu Lamine had achieved any of his aims with regard to the Tokolor or the people of Gamon. The French, like the Sissibé rulers of Bundu, obviously feared the growing military strength of Mamadu Lamine. By February 1886 he was in command of an army about 5,000 strong and this army had enabled him to defeat the Sissibé rulers of Bundu and to begin turning Bundu into a Sarakole state. The French, however, felt he was too strong to be allowed to remain in Bundu, a strategic state from the point of view of their imperial ambitions in the Senegambia and upper and middle Niger region, and so early in 1886 they began their attempt to undermine his leadership and destroy him before his power and authority reached uncontrollable dimensions. This task was accomplished, as we have seen, by the end of 1887.

Mamadu Lamine, though he did not create an Islamic state like al-Hajj 'Umar, Usuman dan Fodio and others, nevertheless belongs in the class of West African militant Muslim reformers. His reformist aims met with a great response from many traders and in particular from the ordinary Sarakole people while many established rulers opposed him. His reform movement, however, suffered from a number of serious setbacks: it received support by and large from the Sarakole only, and it was launched at a time when the French colonial conquest in West Africa was in its most vigorous phase.

Conclusions: a general assessment of the achievement of militant Islam in the 19th century.

Scholars hold different opinions concerning the achievements of the militant Islamic reform movements of the 19th century. In his conclusions on what he refers to as the Tokolor experiment, the jihad of al-Hajj 'Umar, Professor Oloruntimehin writes: "Turning people into good Muslims from their various primordial religions and cultures has never been achieved by the sword: it requires a long period of proselytizing and educating in order to tune the minds of those concerned in the right direction. For all this the sword could create the opportunity by giving the revolutionaries power to control and direct society."[9]

The same author maintains that both politically and from the point of view of the spread and development of Islam al-Hajj 'Umar's jihad enjoyed only very limited success. For although it created for a relatively short time the political framework, in the form of the Tokolor state, for the spread of Islam the movement "not only engendered violence in non-Muslim areas, but also had the effect of fracturing the Muslim community itself and undermined the idea of 'Umma (community) which emphasised the essential oneness of Islam."[10] Oloruntimehin then goes on to point out that there is a certain irony in the fact that "it was mainly after the Tokolor had been divested of political power that they achieved remarkable success in their other role of spreading Islam", by "personal contact" and peaceful means.[11]

Commenting on al-Hajj 'Umar's jihad and more generally on the contribution made by other Tokolor Muslim reformers in the 18th and 19th centuries to the "cultivation" of Islam in West Africa, the historian Willis is of the opinion that 'Umar, whom he describes as "the great Torodbe mujahid of the mid-19th century", enabled through his reform movement the "rootless individuals of all ethnic backgrounds" to look to Islam as a source of cultural identity. He adds that in 'Umar's reform movement "the ties of Islam and the community of faith came to supplant the old threads of allegiance among believers. Superiority in faith or stricter observance of its precepts presented a new passport to honoured status."[12]

Recently it has been convincingly argued that the jihad in Hausaland was not the result of a clash between ethnic groups, but a "revolutionary movement within a traditional Muslim society".[13] It has also been pointed out that the Sokoto jihad did not have for its main aim the conversion of the non-Muslims of Hausaland to Islam, but the revival of Islamic orthodoxy. Consequently, it is implied, its success is not to be decided solely or even primarily on the basis of the numbers of people converted to Islam.[14] If we take the view that the primary aim of the Sokoto jihad was the creation of the ideal Islamic state administered according to the Shari'a, then allowing for a certain measure of failure at the level of ideals and practice, it is nevertheless clear that the jihad was to some extent successful. Hiskett sums up the outcome of the jihad aptly when he states that although "the theoretical ideal set out by the Shehu (Usuman dan Fodio) in his writings . . . may not always have functioned exactly as intended . . . there is . . . no reasonable doubt that the reform movement brought about a real change."[15] These changes occurred in the educational, administrative, constitutional and legal spheres. Among other things a central imamate was created, the Shari'a court was introduced throughout the emirates, and Muslim officials were appointed. However, it was in the educational or intellectual sphere, Hiskett believes, that the biggest advances were made. Literacy in Arabic spread much more widely throughout society and led to the emergence of literacy in the vernacular languages. This in turn meant that writings on Islam contained in the Arabic sources could be channelled through to a much wider public.[16] With regard to the militant Islamic movements in the 19th century in the Senegambia, the opinion has been expressed that, for example, the jihad of Ma Ba Diakhou Ba "succeeded in a primary objective: the spread of Islam to pagan and religiously pluralistic communities". Doctrinally, it is argued, Ma Ba's jihad succeeded, politically it failed.[17] As I have suggested, however, it did alienate some people, putting a divide between them and Islam. With regard to Samory and Islam, some of the Muslim scholars in the Ivory Coast who witnessed his destruction of Kong, maintain that his activities "did not accomplish a true and lasting conversion to Islam."[18]

There is, then, obvious room for debate regarding the outcome of the militant struggle for the ideal society in the 19th century. I believe it would probably be easier to assess the outcome if there was some agreement as to whether those involved saw themselves as "reformers" or as "revolution-aries". Although the reformist and the revolutionist responses, *in the context of religion*, to change and society have characteristics in common, there are nevertheless differences between them.[19] The reformist approach, for example, although it seeks to amend or change society, accepts that this will only come about gradually. The revolutionist, on the other hand, believes that society will be turned upside down in a flash, so to speak, by divine action. Here in the revolutionist's approach it is not a question of changing people's attitude through education and training and the correct application of the law. It is my opinion that, although at stages in these militant Islamic movements, particularly at the beginning, there were revolutionist hopes and aspirations, the dominant attitude and perspective of the leaders of these movements was reformist rather than revolutionist. This is not, however, to suggest that the aim was not a radical transformation of society, but rather that the belief prevailed among the reformers that this would be accomplished gradually through teaching, preaching and education once the right framework had been created by jihad of the sword.

Notes.

The Islamic reform movement in Hausaland.

1   A.D.H. Bivar, "The Wathiqat Ahl al-Sudan: A Manifesto of the Fulani Jihad" *J.A.H.* II (1961). All the following citations from the manifesto are from this source.
2   M. Hiskett, "Kitab al Farq: A Work on the Habe Kingdoms attributed to 'Uthman dan Fodio", *B.S.O.A.S.* XIX (1957). All the following citations from the Kitab are from this source.
3   D.M. Last, *The Sokoto Caliphate* (London, 1967), p. 31.
4   L. Brenner, "Muhammad al-Amin al-Kanemi and Religion and Politics in Borno" in J.R. Willis, ed, *Studies in . . . op. cit.,* pp 160—176.
5   T. Hodgkin, ed, *Nigerian Perspectives* (Oxford, 1975), pp. 261—267 provides the al-Kanemi — Bello correspondence in which the case against and for the jihad are outlined by al-Kanemi and Muhammad Bello respectively.
6   D.M. Last, *The Sokoto Caliphate, op. cit.,* p. 59.
7   R. Adeleye, *Power and Diplomacy in Northern Nigeria, 1804—1906,* (London, 1971), Chapter 4 *et passim.*
8   *Ibid.,* pp. 97 *ff.* See also Adamu Muhammad Fika, *The Kano Civil War and*

British Over-Rule, 1882—1940 (OUP/Ibadan, 1978), especially Chapter 3, pp. 50 ff.

9   P.B. Clarke, "Islamic Millenarianism in West Africa: A Revolutionary Ideology?" *Religious Studies* 16 (1980), pp. 317—339.

10   D.M. Last, Forward, *Research Bulletin*, Centre of Arabic Documentation, Ibadan, III (1967), p. 1.

11   H.J. Fisher, "The Western and Central Sudan and East Africa" in P.M. Holt, A.K.S. Lambton and B. Lewis, eds, *Cambridge History of Islam* (Cambridge, 1970), Vol 2, p. 373.

12   Al-Hajj, "The Thirteenth Century . . .", *op. cit.*, pp. 109 ff.

13   Martin N. Njeuma, "Adamawa and Mahdism: the Career of Hayatu ibn Sa'id in Adamawa, 1878—1898", *J.A.H.* XII (1971), pp. 67—8.

14   J. Lavers, "Jibril Gaini: a Preliminary Account of the Career of a Mahdist Leader in North Eastern Nigeria", *R.B.C.A.D.* Ibadan, III (1967), p. 24.

Islam in Air.

1   Norris, *The Tuaregs* . . ., *op. cit.*, p. 149. The advice of Muhammad Bello, Norris states, "was vital in shaping the policy of Muhammad al-Jaylani".

2   *Ibid.*, p. 150.

3   Dr H.T. Norris in a personal communication, 19/2/1981, pointed out that in some Tuareg traditions the 1816 battle took place at Shedewenka. See, for example, Ghoubeid Alojaly, *Histoire des Kel-Denneg avant l'arrivée des Français* (Copenhagen, 1975), p. 46. Jibale in some Tuareg traditions is put at a later date. Dr Norris in *The Tuareg* . . ., *op. cit.*, suggests 1816 for Jibale, p. 155.

4   Last, *The Sokoto Caliphate, op. cit.*, p. 16 ff.

5   Norris, *The Tuareg, op. cit.*, p. 158.

6   E. Gellner, "A Pendulum Swing Theory of Islam" in R. Robertson, ed, *Sociology of Religion, op. cit.*, pp. 127—138.

7   *Ibid.*, p. 130.

8   *Ibid.*, p. 130.

9   *Ibid.*, p. 131.

10   *Ibid.*, p. 135.

11   R. Bendix, *Max Weber: An Intellectual Portrait* (London, 1966), p. 114.

Islam in the upper and middle Niger Regions.

1   M.F. Dubois, *Timbouctou la Mystérieuse, op. cit.*, pp. 135—137.

2   *Ibid.* See also W.A. Brown "The Caliphate of Hamdullahi, c. 1818—1864", Ph.D. thesis (Wisconsin, 1969).

3   A.M. Kani and C.C. Stewart, "Sokoto-Masina Diplomatic Relations", *R.B.C.A.D.* II (1975/6, Ibadan), pp. 1 ff. See also Last, *The Sokoto Caliphate, op. cit.*, p. 232.

4   J.R. Willis, "The Writings of al-Hajj 'Umar al Futi and Shaykh Mukhtar b. Wadi'at Allah: Literacy, Themes, Sources and Influences" in Willis, ed, *Studies* . . ., *op. cit.*, pp. 177—210. Also J.R. Willis, "Jihad Fi Sabil Allah: Its Doctrinal Basis in Islam and some Aspects of its Evolution in 19th century West Africa", *J.A.H.* VIII (1967), pp. 395—415.

5   Willis, "The Writings of . . .", *op. cit.*, p. 178.

6   *Ibid.*, p 178 ff, and "Jihad fi Sabil Allah . . . ", *op. cit.*, pp. 406 ff.

7   J. Abun-Nasr, *The Tijaniyya* (Oxford, 1965), p. 108, supports the view that al-Hajj 'Umar initiated Muhammad Bello into the Tijaniyya, so also does Amadou

Hamphate Bá and Jacques Daget in "L'Empire Peul de Macina 1818 — 1853" Mali (1962), p. 245. Last, *The Sokoto Caliphate, op. cit.* disputes this claim. For an examination of the different views held on this subject see J. Paden, *Religion and Political Culture in Kano* (California, 1973), pp. 76 — 9.

8 J.D. Hargreaves, ed, *France and West Africa* (London, 1969), pp. 128 *ff*.

9 C. Garesch, "Jugements du Moniteur du Sénégal sur al-Hajj 'Umar de 1857 à 1864", *B. de l'I.F.A.N.* XXXV (1973) ser. B No. 3.

10 Hargreaves, *op. cit.*, p. 131.

11 B.O. Oloruntimehin, *The Segu Tokolor Empire* (London, 1972), p. 728 *ff*.

12 *Ibid.*, pp. 178 *ff*.

13 The Under-Secretary of State at the French Ministry of the Marine and Colonies wrote to the head of the Roman Catholic Mission in Senegal, Bishop Picarda, in 1887 concerning the establishment of a Catholic Mission in the former French occupied Sudan (Mali): "Any measure which tends to create the belief that we are prepared to interfere with Islam would entail the gravest consequences. . . . Missionaries must therefore set themselves up in a "pagan" area and must present themselves not as the propagators of a new religion but as educators of the indigenous in the French language and in the different *métiers* that we want to introduce into the Sudan." These and other conditions relating to the establishment of a mission were recommended to the Under-Secretary by Gallieni, Commander of the French-occupied Sudan. See C.S.Sp. Archives (i.e. Archives of the Holy Ghost Fathers), Paris, Sénégambie, 1880 — 1890, Boîte No. 159, 1887 — 1888.

14 Y. Person, *Samori . . .*, *op. cit.*, p 267.

15 *Ibid.*, p. 269.

16 *Ibid.*, p. 269.

Islamic reform movements in the Senegambia.

1 C.A. Quinn, "Ma Ba Diakhou and the Gambian Jihad 1850 — 1890" in Willis, ed, *Studies . . .*, *op. cit.*

2 M. Klein, "Moslem Revolution in 19th century Senegambia" in D.F. McCall, N.R. Bennett and J. Butler, eds, *Western African History*, Boston University Papers on Africa, Vol IV, (F.A. Praeger, 1969), p. 85.

3 C.A. Quinn, "A Nineteenth Century Fulbe State", *J.A.H.* XII, 3 (1971), pp. 427 — 440.

4 C.S.Sp. Archives, Paris, Senegambia, Boîte No. 152, Doss B, Lettres Divers, 1840 — 1846.

5 *Ibid.*, Boîte No. 163, Doss B. Letter of 25 April 1899 from the Superior of the Roman Catholic Mission of St Mary of the Gambia to the Superior of Congregation of the Holy Ghost, Paris.

6 H.J. Fisher, "The Early Life and Pilgrimage of al-Hajj Muhammad al-Amin the Soninke", *J.A.H.* XII (1967).

7 See B.O. Oloruntimehin, "Muhammad Lamine in Franco-Tokolor Relations 1885 — 1887", *J.H.S.N.* IV (1968), and Oloruntimehin, "Senegambia — Mahmahdou Lamine" in M. Crowder, ed, *West African Resistance* (London, 1971).

8 See L.O. Sanneh, *op. cit.*, pp. 67 *ff et passim* on Mamadu Lamine's relations with the people of Gamon.

9 Oloruntimehin, *The Segu Tokolor Empire, op. cit.*, pp. 316 — 7.

10 *Ibid.*, p. 324.

11 *Ibid.*, p. 325.

12 J.R. Willis, ed, *Studies . . .*, *op. cit.*, Introduction: The Diffusion of Islam, p. 31.

13 See for example M.A. Al-Hajj in Y.B. Usman, ed, *Studies in the History of the Sokoto Jihad* (Sokoto, 1980).
14 D.M. Last in Levtzion, N, ed, *Conversion to Islam* (New York, 1979), chapter 13.
15 Hiskett, *Sword of Truth, op. cit.*, p. 152.
16 *Ibid.*, pp. 152 *ff.*
17 Quinn, "Ma Ba Diakhou . ." in Willis, *Studies . . ., op. cit.*, p. 255.
18 R. Bravmann, *Islam and Tribal Art in West Africa* (Cambridge, 1974), p. 73.
19 B.R. Wilson, *Magic and the Millenium* (Paladin, England, 1975), pp. 23−4.

6
The peaceful penetration of Islam in West Africa in the 19th century.

In much of West Africa in the 19th century the quietist, pacific approach to the spread of Islam persisted. This was the case in the south-western Sahara, Borno, the forest and coastal zones and the Volta Basin. This is not to say that these areas were not in any way affected by militant Islamic reform movements. In the Volta Basin region, for example, in the Boromo region north-west of Kumasi, a certain al-Hajj Mahmud Karantan waged a jihad of the sword in the 1860s.[1] Moreover, Muslims in the south-western Sahara, Borno, Asante, Yorubaland and the Volta Basin were indirectly affected by the jihads in Hausaland, the Senegambia and the upper and middle Niger regions. On the whole, however, Islam in the parts of West Africa discussed in this chapter, where it did expand and attempt to change society, did so by the use of pacific means, even if in certain cases these means were dictated by circumstances rather than by principle or doctrine.

Islam in the south-western Sahara (Shinqit/Mauretania).

In the 19th century in the part of the western Sahara which today forms the Islamic Republic of Mauretania, a number of developments took place which assisted the growth and expansion of Islam both in the region itself and beyond its frontiers. There was, for instance, what one scholar has termed a Zawaya "renaissance" which consisted in the emergence of "a remarkable series of Arabic scholars who drew political and spiritual strength from the Maghrib (north-west Africa) and the Arab east . . . (whose) grasp of Arabic was to be a precious legacy for Moorish generations to come".[1] Among the outstanding and influential Mauretanian Muslim scholars and religious leaders of the period were Sidi 'Abdallah b. al-Hajj Ibrahim of Tijikja, Shaikh Sidiyya al-Kabir, founder of the Islamic University at Boutilimit in southern Mauretania and promoter of the Qadiriyya brotherhood, and Muhammad al-Hafiz b. Mukhtar who established the Tijaniyya brotherhood in Mauretania. There was also the scholar and leader of a resistance movement against French imperialism Shaikh Ma' al-Aynayn of Smara in what was formerly the Spanish Sahara and part of which was until August 1978 claimed by Mauretania.

These scholars and others, building on a tradition of scholarship dating back many centuries, made Islam in the 19th century an even stronger intellectual, political, economic, social and religious force in the south-western

Sahara and beyond. Here I will limit myself to a consideration of the work and impact of Shaikh Sidiyya al Kabir, leaving to the next chapter a discussion of the jihad of Shaikh Ma' al-Aynayn of Smara. I will also consider in this section the development and impact of the Qadiriyya and Tijaniyya brotherhoods in Mauretania in the 19th century.

Shaikh Sidiyya al Kabir (The Great), 1775–1868.

Shaikh Sidiyya al Kabir (The Great) is credited by some Mauretanians with having accomplished more than any other man in Mauretania's history, while others are content to stress his central role in Mauretanian history in the 19th century, maintaining that prior to the emergence of Shaikh Ma' al-Aynayn he was the country's most outstanding and dynamic leader.[2]

Shaikh Sidiyya was born into a small, relatively influential Mauretanian tribe, the Awlad Ibiri, which had become by 1868, the year of his death, one of the most powerful political, economic and intellectual groups in southern Mauretania. This transformation was due in no small measure to Sidiyya's own personal religious and political activities, which, according to one historian, had an impact on people not only in Mauretania but all over the vast area stretching from Morocco in the north to Futa Jallon in the Senegambia in the south, and east as far as Timbuktu. This historian adds that "Sidiyya was in correspondence with men in Mecca and governors at St Louis (Senegal), with two successive Sultans in Marrakesh (Morocco) and with two (and possibly four) of the leaders of the 19th-century jihads in West Africa. He had become a "kingmaker" in Mauretanian politics, and his religious influence was unique in Shinqit."[3] Shinqit is the name not only of the once prosperous caravan town in the province of Adrar in northern Mauretania but also of the western Saharan region from the Atlantic in the west to the River Niger bend in the region of Timbuktu, and from Morocco in the north to the Senegal River in the south.

The Awlad Ibiri group to which Shaikh Sidiyya belonged was one of the zawaya communities who renounced the use of force in the settlement of disputes, and acted as the guardians of the intellectual, religious and cultural heritage of the Moors of the western Sahara. The zawaya also engaged in other activities, such as pastoralism, trade and commerce. Shaikh Sidiyya, for example, organised a long distance, large-scale commercial caravan operation which transported salt, millet and dates to various parts of the western Sahara. He was also involved in the harvesting, transporting and selling of gum to European traders on the Atlantic coast and on the Senegal River in return for cloth (guinée) and paper. Firearms and paper were also exchanged for gum but it seems very unlikely that Shaikh Sidiyya showed any interest in these items.[4]

Shaikh Sidiyya never excluded religion from his commercial and economic activities. His followers who under his supervision administered and operated the caravan trade and the economic side of his activities were also charged with looking after the religious life of the community in which they lived and worked, and as a result his economic power and religious influence were to an extent interconnected.

Shaikh Sidiyya enjoyed a large following. In addition to the numerous noble families and zawaya groups in Mauretania who regarded themselves as his disciples, he also had followers among the leaders and ordinary people in Senegal. Some people were impressed by his mystical powers which they believed enabled him to protect or destroy someone from a distance simply by lifting his finger. Others were attracted to him on account of his expertise in Islamic law and mysticism, while others saw him as the successor of Sidi al-Mukhtar al-Kunti al-Kabir (See Chapter 4, p. 89). Shaikh Sidiyya did in fact study under Shaikh Sidi al-Mukhtar in the Timbuktu region known as the Azawad, and on the death of the latter in 1811 his son Sidi Muhammad took over as Shaikh Sidiyya's teacher.

In 1826/7 at the age of 48 Shaikh Sidiyya returned home to Mauretania with an education that was firmly grounded in the Kunta intellectual tradition. He had concentrated in his studies on Islamic law (*fiqh*) and mysticism (tasawwuf), and he was also a member of the Qadiriyya brotherhood which Shaikh Sidi al-Mukhtar had done so much to establish in West Africa. After Sidi al-Mukhtar's death some of the Kunta groups looked to Shaikh Sidiyya as one of the foremost leaders of that brotherhood. Shaikh Sidiyya was obviously an important and respected Muslim figure and this much can be gathered from the fact that he was called upon to adjudicate in the territorial dispute between Usuman dan Fodio of Hausaland in northern Nigeria and Ahmad Lobbo I of Masina.[5] In southern Mauretania in the 1840s and 1850s he was frequently involved in settling succession disputes and in mediating between the warrior hassani and the zawaya groups. The fact, moreover, that those whom he put forward as leaders of the Trarza and Brakna peoples in southern Mauretania were by and large accepted as the rightful rulers is an indication of the respect in which he was held and the influence he exercised in political as well as religious affairs. Furthermore, many who were in trouble with their leaders or with authority of whatever kind took refuge with Shaikh Sidiyya and he granted them asylum. In fact people from all parts of Mauretania, Morocco, Algeria and the Senegambia put themselves under his protection and guidance.

In addition to his involvement in politics and commerce, Shaikh Sidiyya found time to travel, to teach, to read and to write. He wrote poems in praise of Usuman dan Fodio, his brother 'Abdullah and his son Muhammad Bello. He also wrote on aspects of Islamic law and mysticism and read the works of well-known Muslim scholars such as al-Ghazali who wrote many books including "The Revival of the Religious Sciences" and "The Beginning of Guidance". He was also familiar with the writings of al-Suyuti and al-Maghili. In addition to furthering his own education the Shaikh established a centre of Islamic studies at Boutilimit in southern Mauretania. Boutilimit still exists and attracts Muslim students from many parts of West Africa, and for a number of years graduates from Boutilimit have occupied prominent positions in the government and administration of the Islamic Republic of Mauretania.

Although perhaps not the greatest of Mauretanian scholars and educationists Shaikh Sidiyya's achievements consisted, according to some

Mauretanians, in bringing "knowledge to the people of his country" and in protecting "the people of his time".[6]

Muhammad al-Hafiz b. Mukhtar and the advent of the Tijaniyya in the western Sahara (Mauretania).

The Tijaniyya brotherhood which had a profound impact on West African Islam in the 19th century was founded by the Algerian, Ahmad al-Tijani (1737/8 — 1815), in 1781/2. The brotherhood took root in North Africa and was then carried into the western Sahara by the Mauretanian Muslim missionary, Muhammad al-Hafiz b. Mukhtar (d. 1830).[7]

Muhammad al-Hafiz heard about the Tijaniyya while in Mecca in 1789, and he then travelled to meet the founder of the order Ahmad al-Tijani in Fes in Morocco. Ahmad al-Tijani appointed him as a muqaddam (leader or representative) of the brotherhood in the western Sahara among his own people, the Idaw 'Ali, one of the zawaya groups in Mauretania which claimed descent from the family of Prophet Muhammad. By 1830, the year he died, most of the Idaw 'Ali group had joined the Tijaniyya brotherhood.

The Idaw 'Ali, although it only enjoyed limited success in its attempt to extend the Tijaniyya to other groups in Mauretania, did introduce the brotherhood into the Senegambia where they made some important converts. It was the Senegalese Muslim, al-Hajj 'Umar Tall, founder of the Tokolor empire, who made the Tijaniyya brotherhood widely known in West Africa in the middle years of the 19th century (see Chapter 5, p. 131).

Organisation of the Tijaniyya, Qadiriyya and other Muslim brotherhoods.

In general outline the brotherhoods differed little from each other in terms of organisation and ritual. They all have, for instance, an initiation ritual in which specific prayers, litanies and rules of a confidential, esoteric nature are revealed to the novice or new recruit. The new member is also endowed with a portion of that baraka (divine grace) possessed by the founder.

There are different degrees of membership of a brotherhood and the initiation rites differ for each stage depending on whether the person intending to join the brotherhood is to be a "professional" full-time member or simply a "lay" member of the order. The former is obliged to carry out more rigorous spiritual duties than the latter.

Most brotherhoods, moreover, are organised on the basis of zawaya, that is into communities under a shaikh, all of which are linked spiritually and through officials (muqaddams and *wakils*) to a "mother-*zawaya*" or headquarters of the order at a regional or international level. In West Africa, for example, in the 19th century zawaya of the Qadiriyya order at Touba in Futa Jallon, at Kankan and N'Diassane (Senegal) were linked spiritually to the Kunta Qadiri Zawaya in Timbuktu.

The recognised head of a brotherhood, the founder and his successors, has to have a *silsila* (isnad), or chain of authority or mystical genealogy. The founder of the Tijaniyya brotherhood Ahmad al-Tijani produced "a one-link silsila" which connected him directly with Prophet Muhammad. To be acceptable the silsila normally has to be much longer than this. Usuman dan Fodio, for example, had a very long silsila.[8] Furthermore, the successsor of the founder of an order is believed to have inherited his baraka or "divine grace or spiritual blessing with which the founder was endowed by Allah". Differences and disputes have tended to emerge on occasion within and between the brotherhoods. Differences within brotherhoods have also tended to emerge when the founder dies without leaving specific, definite instructions concerning the succession or the path to be followed. Even where this existed, for example in the Tijaniyya and the Muridiyya of Ahmadu Bamba of Senegal, disputes occurred leading to a certain degree of fragmentation.

There have been and still are disputes between brotherhoods. We have seen that Shaikh Ahmad al-Bakka'i of the Qadiriyya brotherhood disagreed with al-Hajj 'Umar Tall over certain practices and opinions adhered to and professed by the Tijaniyya (see Chapter 5, p. 153). Some Muslims, for instance in present-day northern Nigeria a group known as the Yan Izalla Bida (those who withdraw from "unlawful" innovation), disagree with what they regard as the excessive respect and honour given to the founder of the Tijaniyya movement by some of the members of this brotherhood.

Political, economic and religious rivalry either within or between brotherhoods have also tended to create friction or breakaway groups. There have been several breakaway groups or dissident movements in the Tijaniyya order, one of them being the Hamalliyya (see Chapter 7). There are also numerous examples of cooperation between members of different brotherhoods. The Tijani muqaddam al-Hajj 'Umar Tall, for example, developed close personal ties with the Muslim reformers in Hausaland who belonged to the Qadiriyya brotherhood.

The brotherhoods, some of which tended to draw into their zawaya whole groups of people at a time rather than an individual here and another there, played a very significant part in the development of Islam in West Africa, in particular the Qadiriyya from the 18th century onwards and the Tijaniyya from the 19th century. In the 20th century other brotherhoods like the Muridiyya have come to play a vital role, though on a more limited geographical scale, in the conversion of many West Africans to Islam. These brotherhoods provided people with a community to belong to, work, training, education, guidance, security and, if trading the resources and opportunities, to participate in a well organised commercial network. In southwestern Mauretania (the Gebla), for instance, this was the role played by the Qadiriyya under the leadership of Shaikh Sidiyya al-Kabir.

The 19th century, therefore, saw a revival in Islamic scholarship in Mauretania and the expansion and development of Islam through the activities of men like Shaikh Sidiyya and Muhammad al-Hafiz, both of whom had the organisation and support of branches of the Qadiriyya and Tijaniyya brotherhoods respectively.

Islam in Borno, Bagirmi and Wadai.

Borno.

The state of Islam in Borno at the beginning of the 19th century was described by al-Kanemi in his letters to the Sokoto reformers (see Chapter 5, p. 117). Not everyone was a Muslim, and the beliefs entertained and the religious practice of some of those who were Muslims fell far short of what was required of them by the precepts of Islam. Furthermore, the rulers appeared to tolerate and condone a number of un-Islamic practices.[1] This was not, however, as we have seen, the main reason why the Muslim reformers in Hausaland sanctioned the jihad against Borno (see Chapter 5, p. 116).

The Sokoto jihad had very little impact on the development of Islam in Borno in the 19th century. Indeed what impact it did have was more political than religious, contributing to the further decline of Borno's imperial influence. In a relatively short space of time, starting in the second half of the 18th century, Borno had lost control over Agades, Bagirmi and Damagaram, and had suffered serious defeats at the hands of the armies of Mandara and Wadai. By 1810 it had lost territory in the west, such as Hadejia.

Any further loss of territory and political influence was prevented by the Muslim scholar, Muhammad al-Kanemi. Al-Kanemi, as I have already mentioned, retook N'Gazargamu and went on to become a powerful force in the political and religious life of Borno. He has been described by one historian as "a man of deep religious conviction".[2] Being a scholar he was well versed in Islamic law and the Islamic sciences generally. Furthermore, from his correspondence with the Sokoto reformers it is evident that although he was fully aware of the existence of un-Islamic beliefs and practices in Borno and the fact that some Muslims tolerated and even participatd in these beliefs and practices, he did not believe it was necessary or even right to resort to military jihad to reform Islam in Borno. In this correspondence, as we have seen, he rejected the use of military jihad in a state such as Borno on the grounds that there was no satisfactory means of discriminating between those Muslims who made every effort to practise their faith in accordance with the teaching of the Qur'an and those who wilfully and consciously disregarded this teaching. By waging jihad of the sword, therefore, one would endanger the life of innocent Muslims.

However, although al-Kanemi believed that the pen was more effective than the sword where the reform and development of Islam were concerned, and was prepared to tolerate to an extent failure, he could be absolutely rigid in his enforcement of certain aspects of Islamic law. For example, Captain Denham and his companions who visited Borno in the early years of the 1820s recorded how he commanded a man and a woman to be hanged for committing adultery, and how on another occasion he ordered two girls, both under 17 years of age, to be sentenced to death for immoral conduct. However, after it was pointed out to him by a scholar that such a sentence as the last-mentioned was *haram* (forbidden) since it was not strictly in accordance with the Qur'an, and after much pleading for mercy from many people, the Shehu, as al-Kanemi was known, commuted the death sentence to that of head-shaving which was carried out in public.[3]

Although the Mais were allowed to remain as the legally constituted rulers of Borno, al-Kanemi was in fact from 1820 until his death in 1837 the most powerful man in the kingdom. He was regarded as a scholar, a miracle worker and an outstanding military tactitian and strategist who prevented not only the jihadists from Hausaland but also the Bagirmi army from over-runing Borno. Al-Kanemi was succeeded by his son 'Umar in 1837 who, according to the German visitor to Borno, Nachtigal, was a cultivated, humane but weak man.[4] By 1846 'Umar had become the sole ruler of Borno bringing to an end the Sefawa dynasty. The dynasty collapsed ironically just at the time when the Mais were attempting to regain some of the authority and power which they once enjoyed but which had passed into the hands of al-Kanemi. What seems to have happened was that while Shehu 'Umar was preoccupied with disturbances in Damagaram, Mai Ibrahim sought support from Wadai in his bid to strengthen his position in relation to 'Umar. Ibrahim's secret dealings with Wadai, however, were discovered and he was executed. Wadai, nonetheless, invaded Borno, sacked Kukawa and installed Ibrahim's son Ali as Mai. Later Shehu 'Umar was able to negotiate his return to Borno and the withdrawal of Wadai. Meanwhile Mai Ali was killed in battle, and no new Mai was ever appointed to succeed him, thus bringing the Sefawa dynasty to an end.

Shehu 'Umar, although Wadai was independent and challenged Borno for control of the vital trade routes to the north and east, took little interest either in foreign or domestic policy, devoting most of his time to scholarship. Borno was still renowned in the late 19th century for its scholarship. In the capital, Kukawa, there were several thousand students and, according to Nachtigal, "scholars from all countries and nations" went there to study and teach.[5] However, like Bagirmi, Borno was to be overrun by Rabeh in the 1890s, and then it was taken by the French before finally becoming, as we have seen, part of the former British colony of Nigeria.

Bagirmi.

Throughout the 19th century until its defeat at the hands of Rabeh in the 1890s there was little change in the situation of Islam in Bagirmi. The Muslim reformers in Sokoto did entertain hopes of reforming and expanding the frontiers of Islam in Bagirmi, and for this purpose placed it under the authority of Adama, Emir of Adamawa. They also appointed a flag-bearer, Muhammad al-Hajj al-Amin, to lead a campaign for the reform and spread of Islam in Bagirmi. One of the main reasons why the leaders of the jihad in Hausaland were so interested in Bagirmi was on account of its geographical position to the east of Hausaland. As Last points out "a friendly Bagirmi was important to Sokoto owing to the expectation that with the coming of the Mahdi everyone would emigrate to the Nile, and attempts were made to keep the road east always open".[6]

However, things did not work out exactly as the reformers in Hausaland had wanted. In Usuman dan Fodio's day according to his own reckoning, some of the most outstanding and well-known Muslim scholars in West

Africa came from Bagirmi.[7] But political tensions and wars, and the fact that Bagirmi, in the words of one historians, became a "slave reservoir"[8] made it difficult for this tradition of scholarship to flourish. Moreover, rather than acting as a "gate" to the east for pilgrims and those who wanted to go to meet the Mahdi as the reformers in Hausaland had hoped, the authorities in Bagirmi, at least on occasion, opposed pilgrimage traffic through their territory. There was for example the case in 1856—7 when the ruler of Bagirmi tried to prevent Sharif-al-Din, the Fulani scholar and mystic who was regarded by his many fellow pilgrims and followers as the Mahdi, from travelling from the west through his territory to Mecca.[9]

Wadai.

In the 19th century Wadai's political and religious life was characterised, as was the case in Bagirmi and some other West African states in this period, by a tense intermixture of Islamic and traditional religio-political precepts and observances. At the level of government, for instance, the belief in divine kingship was still adhered to, while at the same time it was expected of the ruler that he be a devout and committed Muslim. Nachtigal described the system of government in Wadai and although he pointed out that the Sultan need not be literate, he stated that he nevertheless both must be and be seen to be a committed Muslim. Nachtigal put it this way: "Though the observance of the external marks of Islam and principally the performance of the five daily prayers and the Ramadan fast are indispensable, a mere outward show of religion without a way of life in conformity with it would damage the ruler seriously in the estimation of the people".[10]

The Islamic education system was in Nachtigal's view more developed in Wadai than in Borno. He remarked on the fact that elementary schools were to be found in every village and added that in Wadai "compulsory schooling is no less stringent than in our own country (Germany)".[11] By elementary schools Nachtigal meant Qur'anic schools. There were also, according to the German traveller, some 30 advanced (*ilm*) schools in the various regions of the country where the Islamic sciences were studied using "text books" imported from North Africa, in particular Egypt.

In the 19th century, then, Wadai had large numbers of trained Muslim school teachers and lawyers. Not all of its inhabitants, however, were Muslims, but gradually the non-Muslim elements were being won over to Islam. The Tamazan, for example, were turning to Islam, although at the time Nachtigal visited Wadai in 1873 they were not as yet, in his words "deeply attached to it". The same comment applied to the Zoghawa people.[12]

Wadai not only trained but also exported Muslim missionaries and scholars. There was, for instance, the scholar and missionary Yums, mentioned by Fisher, who was born of Meccan parents in Wara, at one time capital of Wadai, in c. 1850. Later in life he travelled west to the Tokolor state, and then on to the Casamance region of Senegal in the early years of the 20th century. There he established the Ha'idara Sharifs of Casamance.[13] The reputation of Wadai scholars like Shaikh Yums was high, and they were widely known throughout West Africa and beyond. It was the opinion of

Barth, given in the middle years of the 19th century, that "the Wadai fakihs (Muslim legal experts) and the ulama (Muslim scholars) are the most famous of all the nations of the Sudan for their knowledge of the Qur'an".

Many of these Muslim scholars, often claiming descent from the Prophet's family and bearing the title of sharif, belonged to the Muslim brotherhoods such as the Qadiriyya, Tijaniyya and Sanusiyya, and drew people in large numbers to these brotherhoods. There are many instances in West Africa where membership or affiliation to a brotherhood or conversion to Islam was accomplished on a group rather than an individual basis. With regard to group affiliation there is the example of the Kunta who joined the Qadiriyya, and with regard to group conversion I have cited in this chapter the conversion in Ijebu-Ode, western Nigeria, of Chief Kuku and his household (see p. 168). Part of the appeal of the brotherhoods to groups or communities, as I have mentioned already, lay in the fact that they provided economic, commercial, agricultural and social as well as religious benefits.

The Sanusiyya brotherhood, for example, founded in the early 19th century by the Algerian Muhammad b. Ali al-Sanusi, not only brought educational and religious benefits but also beneficial agricultural and commercial ones as well to parts of North Africa and the western and central Sudan. In the second half of the 19th century the Kufra oases in the Libyan desert became the headquarters of the Sanusiyya brotherhood. From Kufra, an important junction of desert crossings, the order expanded south towards Darfur and Wadai. At the same time as Sanusi religious guides were moving into these states and into Kanem, Air and elsewhere the order was making the trade route from the south through Kufra to Cyrenaica (Tripoli) one of the most important late 19th-century trans-Saharan crossings from a commercial and cultural point of view. This led to closer ties between the rulers of Wadai and the Sanusiyya brotherhood and stimulated the cultural and commercial life of the state. However the Sanusiyya connection with Wadai did not lead to any major expansion of Islam there. One reason for this was that this brotherhood tended to keep itself apart from non-Muslims in order to preserve the purity of its own Islamic faith. The state of Wadai, after surviving the destruction caused to its southern provinces by Rabeh in 1889−90, was finally overrun by the French in 1911.

Islam in the Volta Basin.

Islam in Mossi society.

Between the 16th and 18th centuries, as we have seen, the attitudes of the rulers of the Mossi changed from one of hostility to one of tolerance, and in some instances of sympathy and respect for Islam. Generally speaking, however, they still had reservations about Islam, believing that it could undermine the indigenous political system. Some of the Mossi rulers, therefore, who became Muslims, were opposed to their eldest sons, their heirs, becoming "devout" Muslims. In the late 18th century this was the case with Moro Naba Dulugu who, although a Muslim himself, was concerned about the fact that his eldest son, Sawadogo, was showing signs of becoming a sincere Muslim. His concern centred on the fact that Sawadogo might refuse on becoming ruler to participate in the animal sacrifices offered to propitiate the ancestors. Failure to participate in these rites, it was believed, would destroy one of the strongest forces binding not only the Mossi rulers with their ancestors but also with their subjects.

Apart from a few notable exceptions, this indeterminate, equivocal attitude of the Mossi rulers towards Islam persisted throughout the 19th century. Sawadogo, despite his father's objections, remained after becoming Moro Naba a devout Muslim and helped to spread Islam. Moro Naba Koutou, who reigned from c. 1850 to 1871 and is said to have been "truly Muslim", also encouraged the development of Islam in his kingdom. Nevertheless, Koutou, like Dulugu, did not want his eldest son Sana to take Islam too seriously, and therefore, although he sent his other children to Qur'anic schools he did not allow Sana to attend. Like Dulugu, Koutou thought that Sana, if he became too strict a Muslim, would on taking over as Moro Naba disrupt the vital relationship between the Mossi royal family and their ancestors.

Other 19th-century Mossi rulers were far less tolerant and sympathetic to Islam than Sawadogo and Koutou. Moro Nanamsé, for example, refused to allow Muslims to pray in public places.[1] Nevertheless, throughout the 19th century Muslims continued to work in the royal court and to advise the rulers. They also, despite Moro Nanamsé's prohibitions, celebrated Muslim festivals and were joined in these celebrations by non-Muslims.

Moro Nanamsé's prohibitions imply that Muslims, although not very numerous, were becoming influential in Mossi society. Their influence derived in part from the fact that chiefs had begun to employ them as advisers and interpreters, and also because of the important role they played in trade and commerce. Muslims did not, however, show any overt hostility to the existing regime or manifest any intention of challenging the status quo. The Imam of Wagadugu, for example, agreed to receive from the Moro Naba, whether the latter was a Muslim or not, the insignia of the office of Imam, the turban and white robe. The Imam also took an oath testifying before Allah and Muhammad to obey and be loyal to the ruler.

During the 19th century the Muslim community in Upper Volta, though small in relation to the rest of the population, had grown substantially. There were then, by c. 1900, about 30,000 Muslims out of an estimated total population of 400,000 in the region of Ouahigouya in the north-east, and an estimated 7,000 Muslims in Wagadugu out of an overall population of c. 300,000.[2]

Islam in the northern states of the Asante Empire.

In the 18th century several states east of the Black Volta River in what today forms part of northern Ghana, including Gonja and Dagomba, were conquered and annexed by the Asante. However, with the defeat of the Asante by the British in 1874 these northern states regained their independence.

During the 19th century, as was the case in the 17th and 18th centuries, Muslim merchants from the Upper Niger region and Hausaland settled and traded in the most important commercial centres in northern Asante. The

19th century in fact saw an increase in the number of Hausa traders in this region, and one reason for this was that the Asante, with the abolition of the slave trade, began increasingly to look to the north for the goods they needed such as cloth, beads, leatherwork and natron. Muslim traders from Hausaland obtained these goods from Nupe or further afield in West Africa and brought them along the trading routes to Salaga. One of the safer and more frequently used of these routes in the 19th century was the one that passed through Nupe and Borgu to Salaga. At Salaga the Hausa exchanged their goods for, among other things, kola and gold.

Muslim communities in Salaga as a result emerged and developed around the market, and although they did not contribute a great deal to the spread of Islam among the local population they did create an effective and prestigious educational system in the town. This attracted scholars to Salaga like al-Hajj 'Umar al-Salagawi, who arrived in the town from Kano in c. 1870.[3] This scholar wrote on theological and historical subjects and composed a number of poems of a polemical nature on Christianity. However, even before the arrival of al-Hajj 'Umar al-Salagawi, Gonja had its quota of Muslim intellectuals. Mention has already been made of al-Hajj Muhammad b. Mustafa, a historian who wrote a history of Gonja in 1752 (see Chapter 4). Education, moreover, was not confined to the wealthy. In Salaga all males seem to have had a right to education and to have benefited from it, for as one observer commented in 1877, "in this strongly Muslim town . . . almost every man can read and write Arabic".[4]

Salaga was rent by civil war in the 1880s and in the same decade and through the 1890s it became a victim of the increasing competition among the European powers for the most economically and strategically important areas in Africa. Meanwhile the town declined as a commercial centre and the Muslim population moved on to places like Yeji, in this way spreading Islam to other parts of the region.

Islam west of the Black Volta River.

For most of the 19th century, indeed until the 1890s when Samory appeared in the region, the Mande-speaking Muslims, the Dyula, in Kong, Bonduku and other centres in the region west of the Black Volta River maintained their well organised and impressive Islamic education system. This system, however, was designed, as I have pointed out, more for the purpose of preserving and developing the faith and knowledge of the Mande themselves than as an instrument for the conversion of the indigenous people of the region in which the Dyula lived. Consequently, by the end of the 19th century while the Mande, who formed the vast majority of the 10,000 inhabitants of the canton of Kong, were Muslims, very few of the non-Mande population had been converted to Islam. The same situation obtained in the town of Bonduku and its dependent villages. Here again the Mande constituted about 60 per cent of the population at the beginning of the 20th century and they were virtually the only Muslims in the region.[5] Very few of the Senufo, Kulango, Nafawa and the other indigenous peoples had been converted to Islam by the Mande-speaking Muslim traders and teachers.

It was of course the case, and this also in part explains the very slow, almost imperceptible growth of Islam among the Senufo, Kulango, Nafawa and others, that whereas these peoples were rural based and agriculturalists, the Muslim communities were in the main urban based and oriented towards commerce and long distance trade.

Muslims, moreover, west of the Black Volta River showed very little enthusiasm for any form of militancy in the cause of Islam. The majority of them in fact refused to respond to Samory's appeal for assistance in his campaigns against the towns of Bonduku, Banda and Sorhobango in the 1890s. I mentioned above and in Chapter 4 the tendency of Muslims west of the Black Volta River to disassociate themselves from the social, political and cultural life of the surrounding society. I do not, however, want to exaggerate the extent of this isolation from the surrounding society. It is in fact only meaningful to talk in terms of the relative isolation of the Muslim communities west of the Black Volta when comparing and contrasting these communities with those east of the Black Volta. The Dyula west of the Black Volta came increasingly as time went on to play a part in the political and cultural life of the societies in which they lived. In the court of the Bron paramount chief of Gyaman, for example, no important decision was taken without first consulting the Muslim scholars. Again, although through their education system among other things the Muslims preserved to an extent their Islamic identity, there was nevertheless a limited amount of cultural exchange between Muslims and non-Muslims west of the Black Volta, particularly in the sphere of art.[6] And here I want to make a few general comments on the attitude of the Muslims of the Black Volta and in West Africa generally to traditional art.

Islam and traditional art in West Africa.

The Qur'an and the Hadith (the body of transmitted actions and sayings of the Prophet Muhammad) give the Muslim position with regard to imagery and art forms in general. AL-Bukhari's and other "sound" collections of the Hadith state quite clearly that image and idol makers will be punished,[7] and there are many instances in West African history where Muslims following this guidance have collected together and publicly burnt images and idols, or ordered their destruction. The four orthodox schools (Madhahib) of Islamic law, the Hanafi, the Shafi'i, the Hanbali and the Maliki schools, give very little attention to the question of representational art, although generally speaking they follow the position outlined in the Hadith.

Some Muslim scholars, however, have interpreted the teaching of the Qur'an and Hadith and of the schools of law on representational art and imagery to mean that the making of a representation in itself is not forbidden, but what is absolutely forbidden is the worship of images, idols or representations of any sort.[8]

Shehu 'Umar of Borno, son and successor of al-Kanemi, provided us with an explanation of Islamic doctrine concerning representational art. In July 1870 he was presented with gifts from the King of Prussia by the German traveller, Gustav Nachtigal. Among the gifts was a mantlepiece clock decorated with "a lightly clad allegorical figure", and three life-size portraits, one of the King of Prussia, one of the Queen and the third of the Crown Prince, which Nachtigal realised were, in his own words, "in contradiction to the tenets of Islam".[9] Nachtigal explained to Shehu 'Umar, who incidentally for this audience had removed his *litham* (veil), something he rarely did, that the King of Prussia had sent these portraits because he himself could not visit 'Umar and meet him in person. The Shehu, "a sensitive prince", was a little concerned but in "the most admirable way" explained what in his view constituted Islamic teaching on representational art. He said to Nachtigal: "I myself know well that Islam condemns *only those representations of the human form which are produced in a way which enables a shadow to be cast, statues or pictures in relief for example;* a picture drawn on flat paper or a smooth canvas, however, is not classed in the category of sins."[10] The Shehu was in fact summarising the teaching of the Maliki school, the one most widely followed in West Africa, on the subject of representational art.

It is known from the correspondence between al-Maghili and Askiya Muhammad, from the writings of Usuman dan Fodio on the state of religion in Hausaland before the jihad, from al-Kanemi's correspondence with Sokoto and from al-Hajj 'Umar Tall's discoveries in the Bambara states that both the interpretation of Islamic doctrine on representational art given by Shehu 'Umar and the teaching of the Qur'an and Hadith on this subject were at times ignored in West Africa.

The Muslim communities west of the Black Volta River have shown great tolerance towards indigenous representational art, and in some instances have even contributed to its maintenance and development. In Bonduku in the Ivory Coast, for example, Muslims have not only participated in the Gbain cult, an anti-witchcraft masking tradition, but have also generally assumed positions of responsibility and control over this cult.[11] There are other masking traditions in this area such as the Do tradition which, it is believed, is Muslim in inspiration. The Do masquerade, moreover, is said to be "ultimately tied to Islamic holy days and Muslim functionaries". Some of the masques, moreover, used in the Do masquerade have been carved by Muslims.[12]

There have been, on the other hand, Muslims in Bonduku who have objected to Muslims participating in non-Muslim masquerades on the grounds that such participation at whatever level is contrary to Islamic teaching. But even these Muslims do not condemn participation in the Do masquerade which is considered to be Islamic in inspiration and where some of the masques are in the form of human faces and contain scarification marks. Two of the principal occasions on which the Do masquerade is performed are the end of Ramadan and on the festival of Id al-Kabir.

This tolerance and at times approval of aspects of indigenous representational art shown by the Mulsim Dyula in the Ivory Coast and Ghana has parallels elsewhere in West Africa. It indicates not only that some Muslims were and are prepared to accept elements of the non-Islamic culture and environment which surrounded them, but that they also helped to maintain, shape and develop aspects of the artistic and cultural life of West Africa.[13]

The above comments are worth bearing in mind when we come to discuss the Islamic reaction to traditional culture in Nigeria in the 1970s (see Chapter 8).

Islam in the forest zone and coastal regions of West Africa.

Islam in Yorubaland.

By the beginning of the 19th century there were only a few relatively small Muslim communities in Yorubaland in places like Old Oyo, Ilorin, Badagry, Epe and Lagos (see Chapter 4). These communities consisted in the main of Muslim merchants, missionaries and slaves from Hausaland, Borno and further north. Many of the slaves had escaped from their masters and, according to one account, some of them banded together to constitute "a formidable force of about 20,000 who annoyed the whole country".[1]

Islam in Yorubaland in the first half of the 19th century and for much of the second half of the same century, was a minority religion with little organisation and cohesion. It was also regarded as a threat to the existing political and cultural system. It was a threat in the sense that the body of knowledge, beliefs and practices which it brought with it into Yorubaland were considered to be both irrelevant and to constitute a danger to the existing and generally accepted Yoruba views on politics, art, religion and education.

The Yoruba, who can be divided into a number of sub-groups such as the Ijebu, the Oyo, the Ekiti, the Ondo, the Egbe, the Egbado and others, were to an extent united by the belief that they were descendants of Oduduwa of Ife, who in some myths is presented both as a primordial divinity and a deified ancestor.[2] They also believed in a Supreme Being known by a number of names such as Olodùmare, Olórun, Alààye and others. The Supreme Being, moreover, was regarded as being among other things the Creator, as unique, immortal, omnipotent, omniscient, transcendent and King and Judge. This belief in the Supreme Being and other interrelated beliefs, practices and rituals according to one historian "permeated the whole fabric of Yoruba life and culture".[3] Moreover, the Yoruba peoples believed, like many other peoples in Africa and elsewhere, that their strength, welfare and to an extent survival were linked with the close, correct and continual observance of their traditional beliefs and practices. As we have seen, the Mossi took a similar view with regard to the survival of their own political and social system.

Islam was also seen as a threat to stability and independence in Yorubaland because of its association with what has been termed "Ilorin imperialism".[4] Ilorin in northern Yorubaland was incorporated into the Sokoto Caliphate and thereby became part of dar al-Islam, the land of Islam, in the first half of the 19th century. The first steps in this process of incorporation into dar al-Islam were taken when Afonja, the Ara-One-Kakanfo, leader of the Oyo forces, staged a revolt against the Alafin (ruler) of the Oyo empire whose capital was at Oyo Ile, "home Oyo", in north-eastern Yorubaland. Oyo, a strong power in northern Yorubaland as early as the 14th century, went on to establish its authority not only over much of Yorubaland to the south but also over parts of Nupeland and Borgu to the north, and over parts of Benin

(Dahomey) to the west and southwest. However, during the late 18th century Oyo suffered a number of military defeats, for example, at the hands of Borgu (1783) and Nupe (1791), and started to decline. In the 1790s Afonja began his rebellion by refusing to pay tribute to the Alafin. From his base in Ilorin and with the assistance of the Muslim Solagberu, leader of the Yoruba Muslims in and around Ilorin, and Salih b. Muhammad b. Janata, better known as Alimi and leader of the Fulani and Hausa Muslims in Ilorin, Afonja built up an army which enabled him to resist any attempt by the Alafin to crush his rebellion. This situation prevailed until 1823 — 4 when, with Alimi now dead, a split occurred between his son Abd al-Salam and Afonja. The former challenged Afonja's leadership and in the battle that ensued Afonja was killed. Later Abd al-Salam was installed as the first Emir of Ilorin, thus making Ilorin part of the Sokoto empire.

Abd al-Salam and his brother Shitta, who succeeded him as Emir of Ilorin, went on to wage military jihad against Oyo and areas to the north and south. By 1835 Old Oyo, capital of the Oyo empire, lay in ruins and its inhabitants had fled to the south and east in search of new homes. The Ilorin advance, however, was checked when the Ibadan forces defeated the Ilorin army at the battle of Osogbo in 1840.

This militant brand of Islam manifested by Alimi and in particular his sons Abd al-Salam and Shitta heightened the sense of uneasiness that many of the Yoruba already entertained about Islam. They saw Islam now as a form of imperialism. In other ways too, the Ilorin campaigns had an adverse effect on the development of Islam in other parts of Yorubaland. It led, for instance, to a concentration of Muslims in Ilorin either to take part in the campaigns or to ensure their safety and security. Some Muslims it seems had been persecuted and put to death by the Alafin after threats had been made against him by the *babalawo*, priests of the indigenous religion, that he would lose his empire if he allowed the Muslim missionaries to continue teaching about Islam in his kingdom.[4] Muslims then came to Ilorin, weakening the existing Muslim communities in the rest of Yorubaland. This situation, however, was partly offset by the fact that after the fall of Old Oyo in 1835 a number of Muslims once resident there made their way to towns such as Ilaro, Ibadan, Ede, Osogbo and Ogbomoso. Moreover, Ilorin itself became "a sort of Islamic lighthouse, a local Mecca to which the Yoruba Muslims turned for study and guidance."[5]

The hostility to Islam provoked by the Ilorin campaigns subsided and Islam began to make a certain amount of solid progress in the second half of the 19th century, although in certain areas it had to compromise a great deal with the indigenous traditional beliefs and practices. It was still, moreover, the religion of the minority and as the Muslim missionary in Ibadan stated in 1855: "Muslims must conform a little to heathen fashion because they are not yet enough in power and number to get on without".[6] In Ijebuland Islam was prohibited, as was Christianity, until the last quarter of the 19th century because as Awujale (King) Fidipote, who ruled from 1841 to 1886, explained the indigenous religion "ministered satisfactorily to all the needs and aspirations of his country, making his people prosperous, peace-loving, virtuous, law-abiding and honest in its dealings with other people".[7]

However, during the period 1890—1910 nothing short of a religious revolution was to take place in Ijebu-Ode, capital of Ijebuland, which led to the establishment of a strong, large Muslim community in the kingdom.

Islam was brought to Ijebu-Ode in the late 1870s by Hausa domestic slaves and Ijebu merchants.[8] At first the community practised its faith in secret because of the opposition from the local people. However, by the late 1880s many of the chiefs and influential people in and around Ijebu had not only become sympathetic to but were also prepared to become Muslims. One of the most significant conversions in terms of the growth of Islam in Ijebu-Ode was that of the former Christian Chief Kuku in 1902. On this occasion several hundred members of Chief Kuku's household are said to have become Muslims along with him, and by the end of the first quarter of the 20the century there were well over 50,000 Muslims in what was then Ijebu Province.[9]

In addition to the chiefs becoming Muslims, a great asset in terms of the expansion of Islam since many people followed the example of the local rulers, the success of Islam in Ijebuland was also due to the fact that in many respects it was tolerant of local customs and traditions. It took over many of the organisational and administrative structures of the local society and without any radical alteration adopted them for its own purposes. What Dr Gbadamosi states with reference to Islam throughout Yorubaland at an earlier period in the 19th century applies equally to Ijebu-Ode in the late 19th century: "Very soon almost the whole complex of the system of Yoruba traditional organisation was, in the main, taken over by the Yoruba Muslims . . . with the coming of the new culture Islam about which knowledge was just growing among the Yoruba Muslims there was a remarkable tendency to borrow from and strike parallels with their own cultures and traditions."[10]

This tendency to borrow and strike parallels, however, was resisted by some who wanted Muslims to present themselves as a clearly distinct community with a unique message and way of life. This can be seen from the writings of some Muslim scholars in Osogbo who believed that since the practice among the non-Muslim Yoruba was to level their tombs, Muslims should raise theirs up, otherwise people might think that "Muslims were imitating the traditional people".[11] I will return later to what I have referred to elsewhere as the development of a counter-cultural Islam in Yorubaland.[12]

Despite the attempts by some Muslims to reform Islam and present it as a real alternative to the indigenous religious, political and social system, many continued to be satisfied with borrowing and, to use Dr Gbadamosi's phrase, "striking parallels" with their own culture and traditions. Moreover, in many parts of Yorubaland Muslims were loyal supporters of the local rulers, respected their authority and even in a sense enhanced it. In Ijebu-Ode, for example, chiefs played a part in choosing the Imams, and on the occasion of the election of a Chief Imam the Muslims presented their candidate to the Awujale (King), who, whether Muslim or not, publicly indicated his approval and then attended the prayers that followed. This procedure indicated quite clearly that the Muslims had no desire to usurp authority but in fact recognised as their ruler whoever was chosen in the traditional manner.

By the last quarter of the 19th century, then, and in some parts of the region even earlier, many traditional rulers in Yorubaland, in contrast with those in the upper and middle Niger region, had come to realise that they had little to fear from Islam, indeed they began to regard it as in some ways a source of strength insofar as their status and authority were concerned.

There were also other factors which facilitated the growth of Islam in Ijebuland and elsewhere in Yorubaland, and one of them was the close links between urban and rural areas. The Yoruba are widely known as builders of large towns. Most Yoruba lived in towns but had frequent contact with the rural areas. Some had farms in the villages. Villagers for their part frequently visited the towns to go to the market or for social reasons. In this way ideas spread quickly from the towns to the rural areas and to quote Dr Gbadamosi once again "this city village life style . . . proved important for the spread and growth of Islam in Yorubaland".[13]

Islam's development in the second half of the 19th century was also assisted by the fact that people were beginning to appreciate what the Islamic education system had to offer. As the Christian missionary in Ibadan, Anna Hinderer, wrote in 1855, "Abudu was destined by Ifa to be a book boy and so his father gave him a Muslim name".[14] Here, in the verses of the "Ifa Oracle", which reflects to an extent local attitudes and opinions, Islam is seen as offering people a worthwhile education. Of course, as scholars of Islam in Yorubaland point out, the general level of learning and education in the Muslim community itself was low and needed to be improved, and by the end of the 19th century movements had emerged within Islam in Yorubaland which aimed at raising the standard of education among Muslims.[15]

In addition to Ijebu-Ode, Islam made steady progress in many other Yoruba urban centres in the second half of the 19th century. In Ibadan the Muslim community grew from being in the 1820s and 1830s a small, loosely-knit community of mainly non-Yoruba Muslims whose first mosque was pulled down by Oluyole, ruler of Ibadan (1836 – 50), into a fairly large influential body by the 1870s. By this time Muslims were in senior positions in the Ibadan political and administrative hierarchy, and one of them, Muhammad Latosisa, was the Are-Ona-Kakamfo, the most senior official in Ibadan, from 1871 to 1875. By 1900 Muslims made up about 10 per cent of the population.[16]

Similar developments took place in Iwo, where by the 1860s the Oba (King) and most of the government and military officials were Muslims. Epe was almost entirely Muslim by the 1870s and Islam in Abeokuta and Lagos made significant gains between 1850 and 1900.[17]

The Muslim freed slaves, who began returning home to Nigeria in the 1840s, played an important role in the development of Islam in Lagos and the surrounding areas during the second half of the 19th century. Moreover, some with their knowledge of English and others with their knowledge of Portuguese, and their skills, gave Islam a certain prestige and status which previously it did not have.

Many Muslims from West Africa were among those sold into slavery during the era of the trans-Atlantic slave trade. Among the Mande speaking Muslims enslaved, some ended up in Brazil, and took part in the rebellion in Bahia in north-eastern Brazil in 1835. During the rebellion they carried or wore on their persons bits of paper or parchment which contained verses of the Qur'an. The non-Muslims regarded these as a form of "magic" designed to protect them, and eventually the term Mandinka came to be used in Brazil to mean magic.[18]

While enslaved many Muslims continued to practise their faith as best they could. Those in Georgia, in North America, according to their descendants, said the five daily prayers and some of them, such as the Fulani, given the name "Old Tom", remained strict Muslims. Others, however, like 'Umar b. Sa'id, a slave in North Carolina, became a Christian. 'Umar recalled in 1831 how he practised his faith in Africa. He recounted that in Africa, "I prayed at noon, prayed in the afternoon, prayed at sunset, prayed in the evening. I gave alms every year . . . went on pilgrimage to Mecca". He continued, "Now I pray 'Our Father in the words of Our Lord Jesus the Messiah'. " Others, while remaining Muslims, adapted Islam to Christianity, explaining that "God is Allah, and Jesus Christ is Muhammad . . . the religion is the same but different countries have different names".[19] However, some Muslims who had converted to Christianity while away turned back to Islam almost immediately on arriving home.

In the 1830s a movement began among freed slaves of all religious persuasions, Muslims, Christians and adherents of the indigenous African religions, to return home. Many of these people had been living in Sierra Leone after being recaptured from slave ships which were bound for the West Indies and North and South America. Among the Muslim freed slaves and recaptives who returned home were some who settled at Badagri in 1844. They appointed Salu, a Yoruba freed slave, as their Imam and he was succeeded by Muhammad Shitta, born in Sierra Leone in 1824 or 1830. Muhammad Shitta, widely known as Shitta Bey, Bey being a title conferred upon him by the Sultan of Turkey in 1894, moved to Lagos with his family and some of his associates in 1852.

The Lagos Muslim community at the time was mainly composed of non-Yoruba Muslims. Shitta Bey and other freed slaves turned it into a much more "local" community while at the same time preserving and even strengthening its cosmopolitan image. When Richard Burton, the traveller, visited Lagos in 1860 he observed that "a few Muslims have already risen to political importance".[20] He wrote also of the presence in Lagos of North African and Hausa mallams and their followers "some of whom had learnt to speak Portuguese in Brazil".[21] One North African from Tripoli, Shaikh Ali, had come to Lagos via Borno, Adamawa and Sokoto.[22] According to one estimate made by Burton there were between 700 and 800 Muslims in Lagos in 1861, and this number had increased to c. 1,200 by 1865 and to c. 10,000 by 1880. There were also 27 mosques.[23] 1894 saw the opening of the famous Shitta Bey mosque, an opening attended by the British Governor of Lagos and Muslims and non-Muslims from abroad.

The success that came to Islam in the second half of the 19th century brought its own problems. By accommodating so readily to the traditional political, social and cultural life of Yoruba society Muslims had made it much more difficult to establish a Muslim society with its own distinct identity and its own laws based on the Shari'a. Moreover, just as Islam was beginning to

VII A Lagos mosque showing Brazilian influence

make steady progress it was faced with competition from the Christian missions. The Christian missions had control over the new western system of education, and Muslim parents felt, often justifiably so, that pressure was put on the children attending these schools to become Christians. This was one of the main reasons why they boycotted schools run on western lines. Eventually in 1896 the colonial authorities in Lagos Colony, with the advice and assistance of Dr Edward Wilmot Blyden, the West Indian scholar and writer, opened a Government Muslim School where Islamic and western sciences were taught. Another was opened in Epe, but the scheme was a failure and Muslims who wanted an education in the western sciences had to attend schools run by Christians. One Muslim, now a very old man, recounted how he became the most outstanding pupil in his school in Bible Knowledge while never actually turning to Christianity.[24] His father taught him the Qur'an and kept him strong in his faith. In the next chapter we will look at how the Muslims coped with the problems presented by western education and Christianity (see Chapter 7).

During the 19th century, then, Islam in Yorubaland moved from its position as the religion of a low status minority group to one where it was accepted by all the different social strata in Yoruba society. As the Muslim community developed it took on many of the "material" and some of the non-material characteristics of Yoruba society, adapting for its own use Yoruba political, social and religious practices and ideas. The general tendency among Muslims was to conform and only very rarely did they resort to aggression or rebellion. The end of the century, however, saw the emergence of an Islamic movement, discussed in the next chapter, which aimed at preserving an Islamic identity in the face of pressure from the western system of education, the Christian missions and colonialism.

Islam in Dahomey (The People's Republic of Benin) in the 19th century.

The kingdom of Dahomey, situated to the west of Nigeria, once for a time formed part of the Old Oyo Empire. Under its Fon rulers Dahomey began to emerge as a centralised state in the 17th century.[25] Although it never expanded its frontiers to anything like the same extent as the Old Oyo or the Asante kingdoms it was by the 19th century a strong, well organised state with an efficient standing army and was able to offer very stiff resistance to the French colonial forces in 1892. The French, however, eventually subdued the Dahomeans, occupying the capital Abomey. In 1894 Agohagbo, brother of Behanzin who had led the resistance, became the ruler of Dahomey, and was prepared to negotiate with the French. Behanzin did not surrender until much later, and when he did he was deported first to Martinique and then to Algeria where he died in 1906.

Today Dahomey forms part of the Peoples Republic of Benin. This Republic stretches from the Gulf of Guinea in the south as far north as the southern frontier of the Republic of Niger. The majority of its three million inhabitants live in and around Cotonou, Whydah and Porto Novo situated on the coast in the south, and Parakou in the centre of the country.

Islam first entered the kingdom of Dahomey from the north. In the northern region of the country many of the inhabitants, known as the Dendi, had become Muslims by the 19th century. According to one early 20th-century estimate c. 10,000 of the 16,000 Dendi in northern Dahomey were Muslims at that time.[26] Although relatively small in numbers, the Dendi Muslims, who first came into contact with Islam in the late 15th century, have nevertheless exercised a great deal of influence over their neighbours. From their bases at Illo and Gaya in the middle Niger region they spread out over the northern region settling in commercial centres such as Djougu, Parakou and Nikki, all situated on the trade route linking Hausaland with Gonja. Eventually, all the Muslims in the area adopted the Dendi language, a dialect of Songhay, as their lingua franca. Moreover, the name Dendi became synonymous with the term Muslim among the Muslims in the Volta Basin, and later it was used in the same sense by the French colonial administration. By way of contrast the term Bariba came to mean unbeliever, pagan or non-Muslim.

The Bariba, as we have seen, formed the majority of the inhabitants of Borgu and are said to have resisted, like the Mossi, all attempts by Songhay to convert them to Islam. Again in the 19th century the Sokoto reformers sent out expeditions against Borgu but they failed to convert the Bariba to Islam. Islam did, however, make some headway among the Bariba. Muslim traders from Hausaland exerted a limited influence over a number of Bariba chiefs and ordinary people, and by the early years of the 20th century an estimated 4,000 out of the 125,000 Bariba were Muslims.[27] There were also some 40,000 Muslim Fulani in and around areas frequented by the Bariba.[28]

A few Muslim traders had reached the south of Dahomey by the very early years of the 18th century. They probably arrived at the port of Whydah after travelling through Oyo, and were also very probably involved in the slave trade. By the beginning of the 19th century the number of Muslims in southern Dahomey had grown, and it appears that several hundred of them from Hausaland and Yorubaland who had settled at Whydah were sold into slavery for allegedly plotting against the Dahomean ruler, Gezo.[29]

Some of these Muslims, now freed from enslavement, returned to Whydah and rebuilt their Muslim community. In the 1840s, 50s and 60s the Muslims returning from slavery in Brazil and others from Sierra Leone, where they had been settled as recaptives, helped to develop the already existing Muslim community in Porto Novo to the east of Whydah. One of the better known of this group was José Paraiso, of Yoruba ancestry and once a slave in Brazil. He and his family played an important role in the Muslim community in Porto Novo.[30]

Many of the freed slaves had become Roman Catholics while in Brazil and one is reported to have told a missionary in Dahomey, "I was a slave when I was baptised; I was in the power of my master, I allowed this to be done."[31] On returning home, however, though they retained their Brazilian names such as Paraiso, Marcos, Lopez and Da Silva, they re-converted to Islam although it seems that their faith was in the end a mixture of Islam and Catholicism. Moreover, the ties of friendship made in exile persisted; those who remained Catholics accompanied others once their companions and fellow-slaves in Brazil to the doors of the mosques on Fridays, while the Muslims or those who had re-converted to Islam went along on days of service with their Catholic friends to the doors of the Catholic Church.[32]

By the 1880s Porto Novo had a large and impressive central mosque and many of the Muslims like Ignacio Paraiso, son of Jose Paraiso, had become important and influential businessmen.

The Muslim community in Grand Popo on the coast was founded in the second half of the 19th century by Hausa and Nupe traders from Nigeria. Cotonou, present-day capital of the Republic of Benin, had a very small floating Muslim population in the 19th century. The Muslims in Cotonou came in the main from Senegal, and from northern and western Nigeria, arriving for the most part in the 1890s after the French conquest. The then Chief Imam, for example, was born in Lagos of Nupe parents and ran an Islamic secondary or ilm school, which had only a few pupils, and a small Qur'anic school.

By the end of the 19th century there were Muslim communities in all the main towns in southern Dahomey (Benin Republic), the largest and most highly developed being the one in Porto Novo. In Porto Novo, as we have seen, there was an impressive central mosque as well as other mosques and numerous Qur'anic schools. However, it was this same Muslim community in Porto Novo which experienced the most serious tension and conflict, occasioned to an extent by the attitude and behaviour of those Muslims who had returned home from slavery or exile. Some of them, literate in Portuguese or English, and highly skilled, tended to look down upon the rest of the Muslim community, regarding them as illiterate. As I have indicated they seemed to live in far greater harmony with their Christian associates who had been their companions in exile than with other Muslims who had not had a similar experience.

Another source of tension was the emergence of a small group of young Muslims who, on returning from the pilgrimage to Mecca, began the attempt to reform what they considered to be the lax and corrupt form of Islam either tolerated or practised by the Muslim leadership, a leadership made up in the main by the former exiles and slaves. They also wanted Muslims to be much more active in propagating Islam among the non-Muslims of southern Dahomey, for even by the end of the 19th century the rulers of the country, the subordinate chiefs and the majority of the people had not become Muslims and showed little signs of doing so.

Islam in Togo.

The northern region of Togo, situated between the Benin Republic (Dahomey) to the east and modern Ghana to the west, and bounded by the upper Volta in the north and the Atlantic in the south, had its first known contacts with Islam in the 18th century. Islam came to the south of the country in the second half of the 19th century.

The main centre of Islam in the north of the country was the Chokossi state, and more specifically Sansanne-Mango, the capital, situated on a trade route linking Hausaland with commercial centres in the Volta Basin and forest zone. Like Kong, the Chokossi state was founded by Wattara chiefs of Mande origin in the second half of the 18th century. Soon after its foundation Muslim traders from Kong and others from Hausaland settled there.[33]

Towards the end of the 18th century Muslim traders also spread among the Kotokoli or Temba people of northern Togo. It was not, however, until the 1860s that the Muslim community was given recognition by an important Kotokoli chief. Until that time Muslims were regarded as "strangers". Then in the 1860s the chief Uro Djobo II, influenced by his brother who was associated with al-Hajj 'Umar Tall, converted to Islam and gave Muslims the right to own land which previously had been denied them. Moreover, he even considered making Islam the state religion.[34] Uro Djobo's new measures in favour of Islam, however, met with strong opposition which was only appeased when his son and successor, Uro Djobo III, agreed not to follow his father's Islamic policy. Uro Djobo II seems to have believed that Islam would be a unifying cohesive force which would bind together the loosely-knit confederation of Kotokoli chiefdoms of which he was the head.

Islam arrived in central and southern Togo in the late 19th century brought there by Hausa traders from Salaga in the state of Gonja. The Muslims in these areas, never very numerous, were concentrated in Atakpame and Lomé and lived apart from the rest of the population in what is known as a *zongo*, or separate quarter of the town. A similar situation obtained elsewhere in West Africa where Muslims formed the minority in a non-Muslim state. Indeed the situation of the Muslims in southern Togo in the 19th century resembled very much that of the Muslims in Ancient Ghana as described by al-Bakri in 1068 A.D. (see Chapter 3).

Islam in Metropolitan Asante in the 19th century.

During the second half of the 19th century the Asante empire, which covered what is today part of modern Ghana, began to fall apart. The northern states regained their independence and the British, after suffering defeat at the hands of the Asante in 1824 and 1863 – 4, won a victory over them in 1874 and went on to turn the southern states into the British Crown Colony of the Gold Coast. By 1880 the Asante empire consisted simply of Metropolitan Asante, that is Kumasi and the surrounding region, and Brong Ahafo. Here I will concentrate on the development of Islam in Metropolitan Asante since I have considered its development in the rest of the empire elsewhere in this chapter (see p. 162).

In the early years of the 19th century there were over 1,000 Muslims settled in Kumasi under the leadership of Muhammad al-Ghamba, popularly known as Baba, who came from Gambaga, capital of the northern kingdom of Mamprussi.[35] This community, it is worth noting, followed the Shari'a "privately", that is they applied it in their own homes, mosques and schools. The same situation prevailed, and still prevails today, in many Muslim communities in, for example, western Nigeria.

Most of the Muslims in Kumasi, like Muhammad al-Ghamba, were "strangers" from Mamprussi, Gonja, the Senegambia, the upper and middle Niger region, Hausaland and North Africa, who had come there in search of gold and kola, or to teach or missionise. Muslim missionary activity in Kumasi, although permitted, could be a delicate and difficult task especially if there were signs that it was having what was considered to be too strong an influence on the Asantehene (King of the Asante). According to one account the Asantehene, Osei Kwame, was deposed in 1798 because of his attachment to the Muslims and his inclination to make Islamic law the civil code of his empire.[36] Muhammad al-Ghamba, the Imam of the Muslims in Kumasi, summed up the difficult situation in which Osei Kwame found himself in this way: Osei Kwame, he explained, was a believer at heart but he could not confess this publicly otherwise he would lose his throne.[37] To what extent Osei Kwame was a devout Muslim at heart is difficult to say. On the one hand he prohibited festivals at which human blood was spilt, while on the other he was deeply committed to the rites associated with the veneration of the ancestors.

Muslims certainly seem to have regarded Osei Kwame as a potential convert and gave him their loyalty and support. After his deposition in 1798 there were uprisings in the north-west of the country which were aimed at restoring him to power. The rebels, however, were defeated at the battle of Barbanou (Boaben) and among the prisoners taken by the government forces were an estimated 5,000 Muslims. All of them, however, regained their freedom eventually, some buying it, others being ransomed and the remainder were freed by the government in 1808.[38]

Providing they were tactful and diplomatic the relations between Muslims and rulers in Metropolitan Asante were good. Joseph Depuis, one-time British envoy and consul in Asante, wrote in his journal published in 1824 that many of the Muslims in Kumasi "enjoyed rank at court, or were invested with administrative powers, entitling them even to a voice in the Senate".[39] Muslims were highly influential people. They were among the leading trading families in Kumasi, they were literate in Arabic, and had contacts with the northern provinces of the empire. Recognising their skills, talents and influence, Asantehenes appointed them as envoys and advisers. Muslims were among Osei Bonsu's councillors when he negotiated with the British in 1807, and in 1820 Muslims again played a part in the negotiations concerning the revision of the 1817 treaty between the British and the Asante.

While Osei Bonsu was Asantehene (1801—1824), the Muslims in Kumasi seem to have been not only tolerated but given preferential treatment. Imam Muhammad al-Ghamba is reported to have said, "The King's heart is towards me and I am a favourite servant." And he added, "The monarch would sometimes give ear to the law (the Shari'a) and never opposed the believers (Muslims) of Gonja; but on the contrary was a friend on whom they could always rely for protection."[40]

Visitors to the palace of the Asantehene in Kumasi in the 19th century observed that Muslims were members of the king's inner circle. One observer who visited the palace in 1820 wrote, "We entered the circle (of the King) a few minutes after 4 o'clock. Here a great spectacle presented itself: at least 20,000 warriors with bright muskets and long Danish guns now appeared in view and a hundred bands of music began to play at the same moment. The king and the captains were all dressed in cloth of the richest manufacture and decorated with ornaments of purest gold . . . a short distance before we came to the king we observed the Moorish chief Ali Baba to the left of his majesty dressed in the usual style of his nation with a large white turban in the centre of which was a small looking-glass; his cloak, shirt and trousers were of white silk . . . there were also two other superior Moors dressed in the same style . . .".[41]

It was not only on account of the fact that the Muslims in Kumasi were literate in Arabic and therefore useful as diplomats or in the chancery, or simply because they were important and influential traders that they were valued by the rulers and ordinary people of Asante. It is clear from many 19th-century records that they were also valued for their prayers and for the amulets they provided. Soldiers in particular seem to have had faith in their amulets. In the words of one observer "a few lines written by Baba (the Imam) is believed to possess the power of turning aside the balls of the enemy in battle and is purchased at an enormous price".[42] This, of course, made writing paper very valuable, and the same was true in Borno where it was the most sought after commodity of all.[43] The British in 1874, when they invaded

Kumasi, came across a prayer written in Arabic and translated by a Hausa soldier in Wolseley's army. It read: "This is a prayer to God and a wish that the white men would fight among themselves and return to their own country. May pestilence and disease seize them. The writer of this is the Great High Priest who invokes God to do these things . . .".[44]

Faith in the prayers of Muslims and in the Qur'an was widespread among the Asante. According to Depuis the Asante regarded the Qur'an as a divinely created book containing "ordinances and prohibitions most congenial to the happiness of mankind in general".[45] Osei Bonsu is quoted as saying that "the Qur'an is strong and I like it because it is the work of the great God; it does good for me and therefore I love all the people that read it."[46]

The majority of Muslims in Kumasi welcomed the fact that the king had confidence in them and was sympathetic towards Islam. They preferred to be in Kumasi than in Dahomey, where in their opinion the king was "the infidel of infidels".[47] Nevertheless, they were not satisfied with the state of affairs in Kumasi and made an attempt to eradicate certain un-Islamic practices for the most part by peaceful persuasion, and even on occasion refused to obey the king when they believed it was against their principles. In 1818, for example, Imam Muhammad al-Ghamba defied Osei Bonsu by withdrawing his Muslim followers from the expeditionary force fighting in Gyaman, possibly because it was engaged in fighting Muslims. Some Muslims, moreover, although they attended non-Muslim religious rituals at court, tried to persuade the king to abandon the custom of human sacrifice and substitute for it the sacrifice of an animal. Others went even further in their protest. Sharif Ibrahim, for example, from Bussa "rejected fetishes and absented himself from human sacrifices and other abominations".[48]

The approach adopted by Sharif Ibrahim was the one favoured by some of the Muslims in Kumasi who had been influenced by the Islamic reform movements in Hausaland and the upper and middle Niger regions. These Muslims argued that the Kumasi Muslims should withdraw, make hijra, from what was dar al-harb, the abode of war, a non-Muslim land under a non-Muslim king. They maintained, moreover, that it was unlawful to trade with unbelievers or fight in their armies.

In a sense the Muslims in Kumasi did live apart from the rest of society. They refused to sprinkle dust on their heads when greeting the king, a custom performed by the non-Muslims, and in their own quarter of the town justice was dispensed by a Muslim judge. They wore Muslim dress, and greeted the king or visitors not with the traditional greeting but in Arabic, reciting in a low voice the Fatihat al-Kitab, the opening chapter of the Qur'an which begins "In the name of Allah, the Gracious, the Merciful . . .".[49] Muslims, moreover, had their own schools, and refused to allow drums or other musical instruments to be played in their mosques.

Muslims in Kumasi, nevertheless, had to tread warily for it did not require a great deal of opposition to make their position insecure. Asantehene Kwaku Dua I, who ruled from 1834 – 1867, as part of his decision to nationalise the kola trade, prohibited Muslim traders from the north as well as traders from the coastal areas from travelling to Kumasi. Wilks suggests that part of the reason for this restriction on Muslims from the north may have been that

Kwaku Dua I was apprehensive about the growth of Muslim influence. No doubt this fear was heightened when in 1839 a leader of the Muslims in Kumasi was placed under arrest for allegedly taking part in a conspiracy to overthrow the Asantehene.[50]

The end result of this restriction on "stranger" Muslims which barred them from entering Kumasi was that for some 30 years, until Kumasi fell to the British in 1874, no new Muslim communities were established in Kumasi by Muslim traders from Hausaland, Nupe, Mossi and the northern states of the Asante empire. Given that Muslim traders played an important role in the development and spread of Islam this prohibition must have restricted the growth of Islam in Metropolitan Asante. However, Bouna to the north of Kumasi was an important centre of Islamic learning and continued to be a source of support and strength to the Muslim community in Kumasi, supplying it with learned Imams and scholars such as Usuman Kamatagay.

In the second half of the 19th century, therefore, despite the restriction on Muslim traders from the north, Muslims continued to play an important role in the political and economic life of Metropolitan Asante. And when condemned for not following the example set in Masina, Hausaland and elsewhere and launching a militant reform movement, they retorted that militant reform of the Sokoto type was impossible in their situation. Among the reasons they gave for this was that the Muslim reformers to the north who benefited from the economic influence of the Kumasi Muslims, had failed to provide the necessary inspiration and military assistance.[51] The Kumasi Muslims did, however, attempt to convert people to Islam. They acted on the belief, for example, that it was a meritorious act if one housed and instructed non-Muslims in the beliefs and practices of Islam. Moreover, they believed that through their influence in political and administrative circles they were slowly but surely leading the rulers towards Islam. Like the Muslims in Ibadan, they were of the opinion that they had to hasten slowly otherwise they might lose all their influence for good.

Therefore, although in the 19th century Islam in Metropolitan Asante was syncretistic and in need of reform, it nevertheless presented a strong challenge to the indigenous religion. As one observer commented in 1885 the priests of the indigenous religion "are beginning to lose their prestige, due to the spread of Islam which already counts many adepts in Asante".[52]

Islam in other regions of the forest zone in the 19th century.

The southern regions of the Ivory Coast.
In the late 19th and the early years of the 20th century Muslim communities were established in the southern region of what today forms part of the Ivory Coast Republic. Muslims from Futa Toro and Futa Jallon in the Senegambia, from Masina, from Hausaland and even from Syria came to settle for a time in the urban centres of the coastal region, and were involved mainly in commerce and administration.[53]

West African soldiers also helped the development of Islam in the Ivory Coast. Islam was spread in the interior north of Abidjan to places such as

Tiassale and Toumodi by Senegalese and Malian soldiers who took part in the French military expeditions in 1893 and 1896 which aimed at "opening up" the interior of the country. According to some accounts it was Lieutenant Moriba Keita who brought Islam to Toumodi.[54] Along the line of French penetration from Grand Lahou on the coast to Bouake in the interior, Senegalese and other West African soldiers established small Muslim communities after demobilisation from the army. Among these pioneers of Islam in the southern region of the Ivory Coast was Mamadu Diallo from Futa Toro who took part in the 1893 and 1896 expeditions before leaving the army and settling in the Ivory Coast as a trader. Mamadu Sakho from Segu in present-day Mali was another who soldiered in the Ivory Coast and then went into the rubber trade in the west of the country.[55] It was not, however, until the 20th century that Islam began to make any significant progress in the southern region of the Ivory Coast.

Sierra Leone and Liberia.
The Muslim community in the coastal region of Sierra Leone in the 19th century consisted in the main of Fulani and Mandinka from Futa Jallon and other parts of the upper Niger region. There were also, as we have seen, Muslims of Yoruba descent, known as Aku, the recaptives who were resettled in Sierra Leone.

The word Aku is today used only for Muslims of Yoruba descent, but in the past it referred to all Yoruba recaptives. In Sierra Leone the Aku started companies and benevolent societies, while others turned to street trading. The Hausa recaptive Emmanual Cline, for example, began as a street trader in Freetown and eventually made enough money to buy an estate at Fourah Bay which is today called Cline Town. Then there was John Ezzidio from Nupe in Nigeria who by the 1850s was importing to Sierra Leone about 3,000 pounds sterling worth of goods every year.[56]

Some of the Muslim recaptives settled in Freetown, Fourah Bay, Murray Town, Aberdeen and Hastings, while others joined the Fulani and Mandinka Muslims at Fula Town. In the 1840s, as I have already mentioned, some of the Muslims returned home to Nigeria and Benin (Dahomey) while others remained in East Freetown in Sierra Leone.

A number of trade routes linked the port of Freetown in Sierra Leone with Futa Jallon in Central Guinea (Conakry) and the upper and middle Niger regions. Muslims from these areas passed along the routes and established settlements in Sierra Leone. In the very first years of the 19th century a Muslim settlement known as Dallamodiya was established on the outskirts of Freetown and by the 1830s there were probably several thousand Muslims, some Soso, some Fulani, some Mandinka, some Temne, some freed slaves from Nigeria, Benin (Dahomey) and elsewhere residing in Freetown and the surrounding area.

While many of these Muslims were craftsmen or small time traders, others who arrived in Sierra Leone as warriors came to control large tracts of land and to have authority over a number of towns and villages. This was the case with Sattan Lahai Yansanneh, a warrior chief, who married a Temne and whose family carved out a small kingdom, Rowula, in northern Sierra Leone in the first half of the 19th century.[57]

Other Muslims became advisers to the local rulers, while others appointed themselves as chiefs or almamies (in this case rulers) of indigenous or "stranger" communities. The Muslim Sankoh family of Mellicouri, for example, proclaimed themselves Almamies of Port Loko. In some cases they built mosques and Muslim schools and established centres of Islamic studies like Medina in Bullom, and Gbileh on the Kolente river. Blyden, who visited Gbileh in 1872, spoke of it as being the "Oxford University of the region, where are collected over 500 men studying Arabic and Koranic literature . . . the President of this institution is Fode Tarawaly, celebrated throughout the country for his learning . . . (he) is of the Soosoo (Soso) tribe . ."[58] Burton observed that the Mandinka in Sierra Leone were as advanced educationally as any other group in Freetown.[59]

The Muslim community in Sierra Leone, finally, although they mixed un-Islamic beliefs and practices with their own religion, nevertheless through their schools and in other ways such as dress and ceremonies preserved to a degree their own Muslim identity. They also became "a positive reference point".[60] Many of them were successful in business, associating with the ruling élite, they were literate and skilled, and thereby stood out as people to be admired and if possible imitated. Moreover, both the local rulers and the British colonial administration in Sierra Leone enhanced the status of the Muslim community by employing leading members of it such as Binneh Sankoh, sub-chief of Port Loko from 1871 to 1896, as ambassadors.

The history of Liberia in the 19th century in some respects resembles that of Sierra Leone. Situated to the south-east of Sierra Leone, it also became a settlement for black immigrants. The American Colonisation Society, founded in 1816 to settle American blacks in Africa, took over land at Cape Mesurado in 1822 and the new settlement was named Liberia, and the capital Monrovia after the then American President, Monroe. Only about 20,000 of the free black population in America, which numbered about 200,000 at the time, decided to settle in Liberia, and these were joined by several thousand recaptives.

Islam made little progress in the 19th century among these settlers, many of whom were Christians. It did not make much headway either among the Grebo, the Kru and Bussa in the forest and coastal regions of Liberia. Among the Vai, however, and especially among their chiefs, influenced by Mandinka and other Muslims from the upper Niger region as early as the 17th century, Islam continued to gain ground. The Vai, moreover, possibly in response to the combined influences of Islamic and western education invented their own alphabet which was taught in their schools. This was not, incidentally, the only "indigenous" alphabet in West Africa. The south-eastern Igbo and Ibibio people and their neighbours had their own system of writing known as "nsibidi".[61] And in Kankan in Guinea in the 20th century the Mandinka scholar, Fode Suleiman, developed and spread the system of writing known as Nko.[62]

Islam in Liberia in the 19th century, then, was confined mainly to the Vai, the Mandinka, and to a small number of the Mande and Kpelle and other members of the Mande-speaking family.

Conclusions.

Many Muslims, then, in 19th century West Africa, some as a matter of principle and some out of necessity, chose the pacific as opposed to the militant approach to the spread of Islam. Al-Kanemi was an example of one who on principle chose this line of action, while Muslims in Kumasi, most of Yorubaland and elsewhere claimed that circumstances demanded a careful, gradualist, pacific approach to the spread and reform of Islam.

Notes.

Islam in the south-western Sahara.

1 H.T. Norris, editor and translator, *The Pilgrimage of Ahmad* (Warminster, England, 1977), p. x.
2 C. Stewart, *Islam and Social Order in Mauretania* (Oxford, 1973), p. 10.
3 *Ibid.*, p. 11.
4 *Ibid.*, p. 109 *ff.*
5 *Ibid.*, p. 43.
6 *Ibid.*, p. 11.
7 See Abun Nasr, *The Tijaniyya, op. cit.*, pp. 101 *ff.*
8 See D.M. Last, *The Sokoto Caliphate, op. cit.*

Islam in Borno, Bagirmi and Wadai.

1 T. Hodgkin, ed, *Nigerian Perspectives, op. cit.*, "Muhammad al-Kanemi: the case against the jihad", pp. 261 *ff.*
2 L. Brenner, *The Shehus of Kukawa* (Oxford, 1973), p. 39.
3 H.A.S. Johnson and D.J.M. Muffet, *Denham in Borno, an Account of the Exploration in Borno between 1823 and 1825* (Pittsburgh, 1973), pp. 177 − 8.
4 G. Nachtigal, *The Sahara and Sudan*, Vol. 2, edited with introduction and notes by A.G.B. and H.J. Fisher *op. cit.*, p. 242.
5 *Ibid.*, p. 161.
6 Last, *The Sokoto Caliphate, op. cit.*, p. 54, n. 44.
7 Adeleye, *Power and Diplomacy, op. cit.*, p. 10.
8 H.J. Fisher, "The Western and Central Sudan . . . " in Holt *et al*, *The Cambridge History of Islam, op. cit.*, p. 372.
9 *Ibid.*, p. 373.
10 G. Nachtigal, *op. cit.*, Vol. 4, p. 172.
11 *Ibid.*, p. 189.
12 *Ibid.*, p. 163.
13 *Ibid.*, p. 399.
14 Trimingham, *op. cit.*, p. 216.

Islam in the Volta Basin.

1 E.P. Skinner, "Islam in Mossi Society" in I.M. Lewis, ed, *Islam in Tropical Africa*, (London, 1980, 2nd edition), p. 179.
2 J. Audouin and R. Deniel, *L'Islam en Haute Volta* (Paris/Abidjan, 1978), pp. 34 *ff.*

3   M.O. Abdul, "Literacy in an 'Illiterate' Society" R.B.C.A.D. Ibadan, II (1975/6), pp. 13 *ff.*
4   I. Wilks, "The Transmission of Islamic Learning . . . " in Goody, *Literacy in Traditional Societies, op. cit.,* p. 167.
5   R. Bravmann, *op. cit.*
6   *Ibid.,* p. 69.
7   *Ibid.,* p. 16.
8   *Ibid.,* p. 21.
9   G. Nachtigal, *op. cit.,* Vol. 2, pp. 127–129.
10 *Ibid.*
11 Bravmann, *op. cit.,* pp. 99 *ff.*
12 *Ibid.,* pp. 147 *ff.*
13 For another, opposing, view see E. Elisofon and W.B. Fagg, *The Sculpture of Africa* (New York, 1958), p. 27 *et passim.*

Islam in the forest and coastal zones.

1   Samuel Ajayi Crowther quoted in P.J. Ryan, *Imale . . ., op. cit.,* p. 112.
2   J.O. Awolalu, *Yoruba Beliefs and Sacrificial Rights* (London, 1979).
3   Gbadamosi, *op. cit.,* p. 3.
4   *Ibid.,* pp. 10 *ff.*
5   *Ibid.,* p. 10.
6   J.F. Ade Ajayi, *The Christian Missions in Nigeria* (London, 1965), p. 20, n. 1.
7   E.A. Ayandele, "Chieftaincy in Ijebuland 1892–1948: the Interaction of Religion and Politics", paper presented at Makerere University, Uganda, Dec/Jan 1969, p. 2.
8   M.O. Abdul, "Islam in Ijebu-Ode", M.A. thesis, McGill University, 1967.
9   P. Amaurey Talbot, *The Peoples of Southern Nigeria,* (London, 1926), Vol IV, p. 104.
10 G.O. Gbadamosi, "The Imamate Question among Yoruba Muslims", *J.H.S.N.* VI (1972), p. 234.
11 H.A.K. Bidmus, "A Literary Appraisal of the Arabic Writings of the Yoruba 'Ulama", M.A. thesis, University of Ibadan, 1972, p. 71.
12 P.B. Clarke, "Islam and Change in Nigeria, c. 1918–1960", in R. Willis and A.Ross, eds, *Religion and Change in African Societies* (Edinburgh, 1979), pp. 97 *ff.*
13 Gbadamosi, *The Growth of Islam, op. cit.,* p. 3.
14 A. Hinderer, *Seventeen Years in the Yoruba Country,* (London, 1872), p. 167.
15 Gbadamosi, *The Growth of Islam, op. cit.,* especially Chapter 3 and 4, and Bidmus, *op. cit.*
16 Gbadamosi, *op. cit.,* p. 98.
17 *Ibid.,* p. 98 *et passim,* and Ryan, *op. cit.,* pp 177 *ff.*
18 A.J. Raboteau, *Slave Religion* (Oxford, 1980) p. 34.
19 *Ibid.,* pp. 46–7.
20 R.F. Burton, *Wanderings in West Africa from Liverpool to Fernando Po* (London, 1863), Vol. II, p. 225.
21 *Ibid.,* p. 225.
22 *Ibid.,* p. 226.
23 R.F. Burton and V.L. Cameron, *To the Gold Coast and Back* (London, 1883), p. 54.
24 Interview held by the author with Mr Daramola, Ijebu-Ode, March 1978.

25 I.A. Akinjogbin, *Dahomey and Its Neighbours 1708–1818* (London, 1967).
26 P. Marty, *Etudes sur l'Islam au Dahomey* (Paris, 1926), p. 162.
27 *Ibid.*, p. 160.
28 *Ibid.*, p. 169.
29 *Ibid.*, p. 108.
30 *Ibid.*, p. 89.
31 *Ibid.*, p. 18.
32 *Ibid.*, p. 34.
33 Levtzion, *Muslims and Chiefs, op. cit.*, pp. 78 *ff.*
34 *Ibid.*, p. 179
35 I. Wilks, "The Position of Muslims in Metropolitan Ashanti" in I.M. Lewis, *Islam in Tropical Africa, op. cit.*, p. 145.
36 Wilks, *Asante in the 19th century, op. cit.*, p. 254.
37 *Ibid.*, p. 253.
38 *Ibid.*, p. 254.
39 J. Dupuis, *Journal of Residence in Ashantee* (London, 1824), pp. 94–5.
40 *Ibid.*, p. 97.
41 W. Hutton, *A Voyage to Africa in the Year 1820* (London, 1821), pp. 209–217.
42 *Ibid.*, p. 323.
43 Johnson and Muffet, *Denham in Borno, op. cit.*
44 Wilks, *Asante in the 19th century, op. cit.*, p. 241.
45 Dupuis, *op. cit.*, p. 247.
46 *Ibid.*, p. 161.
47 Wilks, *Asante in the 19th century, op. cit.*, p. 259.
48 *Ibid.*, pp. 268 *ff*, on doubts entertained by the government about the loyalty of the Muslims in Kumasi.
49 Dupuis, *op. cit.*, p. 78.
50 Wilks, *op. cit.*, p. 268.
51 Wilks, "The Position of Muslims . . .", *op. cit.*, pp. 148 *ff.*
52 Wilks, *Asante in the 19th century, op. cit.*, p. 318, n. 39.
53 P. Marty, *Etudes sur l'Islam en Côte d'Ivoire* (Paris, 1922) and J.L. Triaud, "La Question Musulmane en Côte d'Ivoire (1893–1939)", Revue Française d'Histoire d'Outre-Mer, 61 (1974).
54 Triaud, *op. cit.*, p. 549.
55 *Ibid.*, p 549.
56 C. Fyfe, *A Short History of Sierra Leone* (new edition, London, 1979), p. 51.
57 D.E. Skinner, "The Role of the Mandinka and Susu in the Islamisation of Sierra Leone", Conference on Manding Studies, School of Oriental and African Studies, University of London, 1972.
58 Quotation cited by D.E. Skinner, *op. cit.*, p. 11.
59 Burton, *Wanderings . . ., op. cit.*, p. 255.
60 Skinner, *op. cit.*
61 E. Isichei, *History of West Africa since 1800* (London, 1978), p. 112 and p. 136.
62 L. Kaba, *The Wahhabiyya: Islamic Reform and Politics in French West Africa* (Illinois, 1974), p. 164.

7

c. 1900 – 1960: colonial rule, an era of rapid expansion and development.

The available statistical data, which must be handled with caution, and a great deal of óther evidence points to a very rapid expansion and development of Islam in West Africa during the colonial era (c. 1900 – 1960). Indeed, in terms of time scale the rapidity and extent of this expansion and development were without precedent in the previous eleven hundred and fifty years of Islam's history in West Africa. By the 1880s, which mark the beginning of the period of high or formal European imperialism in West Africa, while some parts of the region had only been very superficially influenced by Islam, others remained almost entirely non-Muslim. For example, in Senegal among the Serer in Sine-Saloum there were very few Muslims in the 1880s. The same holds for the southern region of the Ivory Coast, for Upper Volta and for many parts of Nigeria such as the Jos Plateau and the Middle Belt. And in the west and south-west of Nigeria, in towns such as Lagos, Ibadan, Benin and others Islam was the religion of only a small minority of the population.

In this chapter, given among other things the limitations of space, I have not attempted to examine the growth of Islam, a complex process, in West Africa as a whole during the colonial era, but instead I have decided to confine myself to considering at some length Islam's progress in Senegal, Upper Volta and the Ivory Coast, former French colonies, and in Nigeria, a former British colony. These case studies, along with some general comments on the development of Islam throughout West Africa, will provide an indication of the ways in which Islam developed and the rapidity and extent of its progress during the colonial era. I should point out, of course, that it was not always a case of expansion and growth. Islam in some areas made no progress whatsoever, and in others even declined. Before examining these issues of expansion and decline, however, I want to consider somewhat briefly the European occupation of West Africa, colonial "policy" towards Islam in West Africa and the "Islamic response" to colonialism.

The European occupation of West Africa.

Although European intrusion into West Africa dates back to the 15th century, the era of high European imperialism as far as most of West Africa's coastal region and hinterland are concerned began in the 1880s. Prior to the Berlin Conference of 1884 – 5, France, Britain and Portugal already had a foothold in West Africa. France possessed a relatively large colony in Senegal, and had other settlements along the West African coast. The British were established in Freetown and the surrounding peninsula, in the island and colony of Lagos, in the southern states of the Gold Coast (Ghana) and in Bathurst (Banjul) on St Mary's Island at the mouth of the Gambia. The Portuguese were in Cacheu and Bissau, part of modern-day Guinea Bissau, and in the islands of Sao Tomé and Cape Verde. Elsewhere these European powers frequently interfered in the internal affairs of West African states, a case in point being the British interference in the Niger Delta region. Germany, one of the European powers at the Berlin Conference, did not have colonial possessiohs in West Africa at the time the Conference was called but before the delegates had dispersed from the Conference she had laid claim to Togo and the Cameroons.[1]

The Berlin Conference did not directly initiate the European "scramble" for Africa in the 1880s but rather laid down the rules to be followed by a European power if its occupation of a part of Africa was to be considered valid by the rest of Europe. No consideration at all was given to African opinion. The Conference decided that effective occupation of an African territory was necessary before a European power could claim it as a colony. In some cases plans had already been drawn up with a view to expansion in West Africa. Faidherbe, for example, during his second term as Governor of Senegal (1863 — 5), had presented a plan of expansion in West Africa to the French government in 1863. The objective was to turn Senegal "into a compact and homogeneous territory bound by its natural frontiers".[2] This meant that France, using Senegal as a base, would advance as far south as the Gambia, a British sphere of influence at the time, and east as far as Timbuktu on the Niger. This accomplished, Faidherbe explained, "all the sources from which the trade of these coasts is drawn would be in our hands".[3]

This plan had to be shelved for a time for economic and political reasons, but what the Berlin Conference did was to stimulate and re-activate the interest where it was lacking in European colonial expansion in Africa. Of course, some Europeans, in particular the commercial and military groups, did not need any stimulating or re-activating. French soldiers like General Archinard, and British firms like the Royal Niger Company, were ready and willing to advance their own and French and British interests in West Africa.

Supplied, therefore, with the most advanced military equipment available, and benefitting from a relatively high level of industrialisation, the European powers began the full-scale colonization of West Africa in the late 19th century. France acquired the largest amount of territory and began with the intention of administering it as a single unit and as an extension of France. West Africa, according to this policy known as the policy of Assimilation, was simply an extension of France and was referred to in Paris as part of "Overseas France", "la France d'Outre-Mer". According to one of the many versions of Assimilation, France's African colonial subjects were to be given the same rights and treatment as Frenchmen.[4] There were, the Assimilationists agreed, no differences between the two that education could not eliminate. In addition, there was to be political, administrative and economic identity between France and her West African colonies.

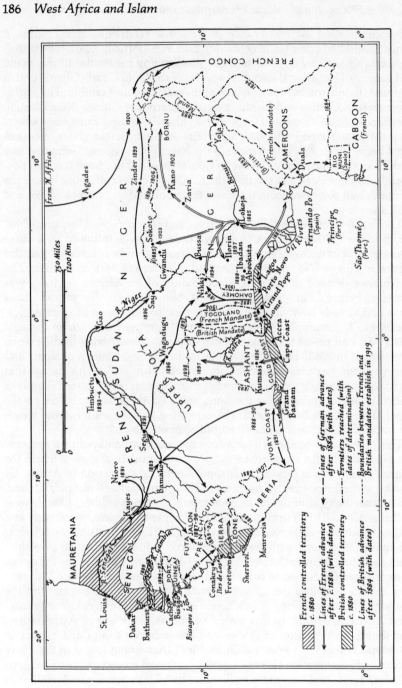

VIII European advance into West Africa

In practice, however, things turned out very differently. Only a very small minority of West Africans obtained French citizenship and therefore the same rights as Frenchmen. Moreover, very soon, as early as the first decade of the 20th century in fact, the policy of Assimilation had been abandoned for a system of Association. This involved the attempt by France to govern and administer her West African colonies through reorganised West African institutions rather than rely exclusively on French institutions. Because of a shortage of French personnel African chiefs, for example, stripped of many of their powers, were to act as "go-betweens". As one Governor-General of former French West Africa explained, they were to "serve our purposes among the people".[5] What obtained, therefore, in practice in the French colonial territories was a form of "indirect rule" similar to that operated by the British in their colonies. Before turning to the British occupation of West Africa I want to simply list the present-day West African states which were once colonised by France. They are Mauretania, Senegal, Mali, Niger, Upper Volta, Guinea (Conakry), the Ivory Coast and the Peoples Republic of Benin (Dahomey). Togo, occupied by Germany in 1884, was divided vertically between France and Britain after World War I, and placed under French and British mandate by the League of Nations in 1922.

Although France occupied almost three times as much of West African territory as the British, the British colonies contained a combined population twice the size of that found throughout former French West Africa. Britain like France, using military force and gunboat diplomacy, had by c. 1900 taken control of what are today, with some territorial adjustments, the republics of Nigeria, Sierra Leone, Ghana and the Gambia. The administrative policy applied by Britain throughout most of her former West African colonies was that of "indirect rule", a policy which in different areas took on different forms and meant different things to both the colonial administration and the colonised. In theory and sometimes in practice this policy gave the local traditional ruler a say, sometimes too big a say in terms of the indigenous constitution and political systems, in local government. It led, for example, to the creation of powerful chiefs where they did not previously exist, and in certain instances it made for fundamental constitutional changes. Prior to colonial rule in many parts of West Africa the kings or chiefs were ultimately responsible in some form or other to those over whom they ruled, but with colonialism responsibility to the people was replaced by responsibility to the colonial administration.

Although neither the theory nor the practice of "indirect rule" originated with Lugard, he did become one of the main exponents and practitioners of this method of ruling when he was High Commissioner of northern Nigeria (1900—1906), and from 1912 to 1918 when he had overall responsibility for the whole country. Lugard's successors continued the practice of "indirect rule" without giving much consideration to its limitations and impracticability in many areas of the country. What worked well in the north-east of the territory, Borno, or in parts of the Gambia, where there was a long tradition of strong central administration, did not and could not be made to operate effectively in the eastern or western regions of Nigeria where the traditional

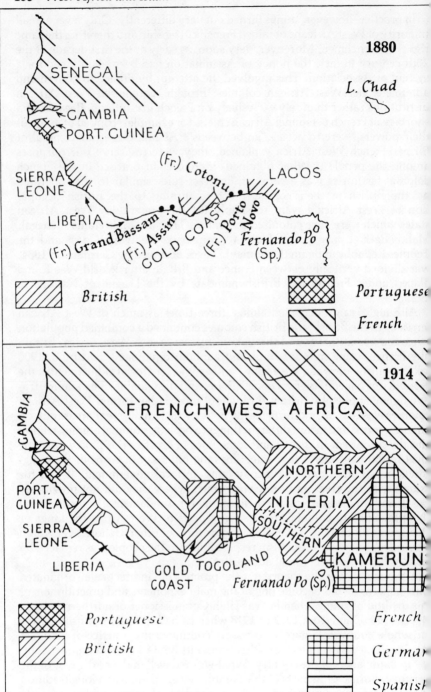

IX Pattern of alien rule in Africa

system of government was different.

Britain, then, came out of the "scramble" with four colonies: Nigeria, the Gold Coast (Ghana), Sierra Leone and the Gambia. She also administered part of Togo after World War I. Portugal held on to her possessions in Guinea Bissau and Cape Verde, and the small islands of Sao Tomé and Principé, while Germany lost her colonies of Togo and the Cameroons after World War I.

Colonial "policy" towards Islam in West Africa.

Much of what I have to say on colonial "policy" towards Islam in West Africa is stated for the most part implicitly in the section below on the Growth of Islam in West Africa during the colonial era (see p. 202). Here I simply want to make some rather general comments on what is a complex and much debated issue.

If what is meant by a "colonial policy towards Islam" is a well thought out, clearly defined strategy or approach applied with a measure of consistency by the colonial regimes to Muslims throughout West Africa, then there was very little of this in the French approach to Islam. According to Gouilly, French "policy" towards Islam was "often hostile, sometimes favourable . . . made up of contradictions . . . of sharp twists and turns".[6] The British approach, as we shall see, initially somewhat uncertain, was with the full implementation of "indirect rule" more consistent in what had come to be regarded as Muslim areas such as northern Nigeria.

Although many scholars would agree in broad terms with Gouilly's description of French colonial "policy" towards Islam in West Africa, nevertheless, as O'Brien has shown, certain aspects of this policy remained for a considerable length of time "fairly stable".[7] O'Brien is concerned mainly with the period 1854 — 1914, and during this period there is a good deal of evidence that suggests that not only were some of the practical measures adopted to deal with Islam but also that French colonial thinking about Islam's place in the hierarchy of civilisation and culture remained relatively unchanged. First I will consider in very summary fashion French colonial thinking about Islam, and much of what is stated here can also be applied to the British colonial perspective on Islam in the West African setting.

Although the European demand for cheap raw materials for industry led to the period of all out European colonialism in West Africa, there was also a cultural dimension to colonialism. To a limited extent at least, it was the product of what was at the time considered to be "scientific" thinking about the laws governing intellectual, social and generally speaking cultural development. The available evidence certainly points to a certain element of 'positivism" in the thinking of French and British colonial officials as far as the development of human thought and civilisation are concerned.

By positivism I mean here the philosophy propounded by men like Auguste Comte (1798 — 1857), regarded as the founding father of sociology as an academic discipline.[8] According to Comte the subject matter of sociology was the history of the human race regarded as a whole. However, Comte tended to see the history of Europe as synonymous with the history of the human race and believed that all civilisations would necessarily develop along the same lines as Western civilisation. Moreover, he maintained in his "Law of the Three Stages of Intellectual Development", that human thought gradually evolves, passing from the lowest stage, the theological stage, to an intermediate stage, the metaphysical, to the most advanced stage, the scientific or positivist stage. And in the religious sphere also there were stages of evolution. Comte maintained that religion originated in fetishism, that is the worship of animals and inanimate objects, and developed through a stage of polytheism until it reached its highest form in monotheism.

Combined with the influence of Darwinian evolutionary theory, and a general tendency to connect developments in religion to developments in the rest of the political, social and cultural system of society, Comtean "positivism" exercised considerable influence over the thought and outlook of many people during his own lifetime and throughout the 19th and early decades of the 20th century. Finally, before leaving Comte I should add that he, like the well-known sociologist Emile Durkheim, believed that religion was an important element in society. Among other things it "cemented" societies together and provided legitimations or justifications essential for the maintenance and stability of the social and political order.[9]

Whether they had read Comte or not many French and British colonial officials and students of Islam in West Africa thought along similar lines. In this context O'Brien quotes from a doctoral thesis on French policy towards Islam in West Africa presented to the Sorbonne University in Paris in 1910 by the French scholar Quellien. The quotation reads: "Muslim propaganda is a step towards civilisation in West Africa, and it is universally recognised that the Muslim peoples of these regions are superior to those who had remained fetishist, in social organisation, intellectual culture, commerce, industry, well being, style of life and education."[10] Moreover, Governor Faidherbe believed that Islam could be used both as a vehicle for the diffusion of a higher degree of civilisation among Africans and as an instrument for the unification of French-occupied West Africa.[11] This attitude explains his initial support for Ma Ba Diakhou Ba (see Chapter 5, p. 142). However, where Islam appeared to be too strong and a possible threat to French interests, steps were taken to undermine it. This is what happened in the case of the Tokolor empire and in innumerable other instances (see Chapter 5 and below).

What the French colonial administration sought was a controlled, a malleable, a pliable Islam that they could twist and bend to serve their purposes. In order to achieve this Muslims were on occasion given special privileges, donations were given towards the construction of mosques, and passages were paid to Mecca. But where there was any hint of opposition Muslims were harassed, imprisoned or deported. The French colonial administration was suspicious above all of the marabouts, those Muslim some of whom had been to Mecca and who had acquired some formal training in the Islamic sciences and enjoyed a certain reputation among the people. A number of administrative decrees were issued with the aim of suppressing these marabouts whom Governor-General William Ponty (1908–1915) among highly placed French colonial officials, believed disseminated anti-French propaganda and exploited the people.[12] Marabouts were, as we shall see, to come under attack from on the one hand Muslims dedicated to the reform of Islam and on the other those dedicated to the establishment of socialism.

The Dyula Muslim traders, on the other hand, were regarded as harmless and of positive benefit to the commercial and economic life of France's West African colonies. This view as it turned out was in some instances mistaken since some Dyula became in the 1940s fundamentalists and opponents of the regime. The French also attempted to reach a working understanding with the leaders of the Muslim brotherhoods. Moreover, by the establishment of Médersas, Franco-Arabic colleges, where the French language and culture were taught in combination with Arabic and the Islamic sciences, the French intended to create an Islamic élite both loyal to the regime and equipped with the requisite skills to serve in the administration. Muslims were preferred to Western educated Africans who were in some respects, as was the case in Sierra Leone and Nigeria, disliked and regarded as troublemakers and upstarts by the regime. All progress, the French and British colonial administrations believed, had to be gradual. In northern Nigeria Lugard told a group of missionaries in 1904 not to preach the equality of Europeans and natives at "this stage" because "however true from a doctrinal point of view it is apt to be misapplied by people in a low state of development and interpreted as the abolition of class distinction." On the other hand "habits of industry, of truthfulness and of social service and disciplined co-operation are virtues to be instilled".[13]

British colonial "policy" towards Islam, while less given to "sharp twists and turns" than French policy, appears nevertheless, as I have already indicated, to have been grounded in similar notions concerning social, cultural and intellectual development. It was also a "policy" dictated by circumstances and designed to secure the maximum co-operation from Muslims in the task of administering large territories where European personnel was lacking and financial resources were inadequate. In Kano Emirate, for example, in the first decade of the 20th century the ratio was one British official to about 200,000 people. In this situation the existing system of government in northern Nigeria, headed by the Emirs, was well-suited to form the basis of a policy of indirect rule.

The emirate system of government was modified by the British, and in theory it was to be "improved" as time went on. The main early adjustment to the emirate system of government consisted in altering the tax system, and in depriving the emir of certain judicial powers such as the power to impose the death penalty. The emir, however, was, under British supervision of course, the chief executive of his emirate and providing he administered his emirate "well" the British did not as a general rule interfere. Moreover, the colonial authority promised not to interfere with the Islamic faith and gave the emirs the authority to decide whether or not Christian missionaries should be allowed to operate in their territory. Consequently missionary activity, with a few notable exceptions, was confined to the non-Muslim areas until after World War II.

The British policy towards Islam in northern Nigeria, and a similar policy pursued in northern Ghana, is regarded by some as having been very

VIII Qur'anic school in Senegal

tolerant, sympathetic and even "protectionist". But it did not appear that way to all the Muslims in northern Nigeria. Some saw it as a real defeat for Islam. The Hausa trader in Kano, for instance, who in 1941 expressed his disapproval in a book he wrote called "Evidences of the Mahdi", was only one of a number who believed that the Indirect Rule system undermined the authority of the emirs. He wrote, "Emirs have no power, but they go to Kaduna (the headquarters of the colonial government in northern Nigeria), some in cars, some on horseback. . .".[14] Others, as self-government and then independence came in sight and as the pace of industrialisation quickened, were to attack the Indirect Rule system on the grounds that it was paternalist and was designed ultimately not to preserve or protect Islam but to dominate and control it and then subject Muslims eventually to overall rule by non-Muslims in a Federal Republic.[15]

That the British policy towards Islam was, like the French policy, shot through with pragmatism seems clear. It is also the case that it was designed at least up to the outbreak of World War II to curtail the growth of a potentially "recalcitrant" Western-educated Nigerian élite. Hanns Vischer, one-time Director of Education in northern Nigeria, totally opposed the introduction of English as the medium of instruction in schools, and so too did many of the emirs, but for different reasons. For the emirs, English was the language of the Christian; for Vischer, knowledge of English would create a type of Africa he did not much care for, and would lead to a "cultural schism". One of the consequences of the "ban" on English was that in places like Bauchi Emirate there were by 1952 only 18,000 people literate in English out of a population of over one million, and in Kano the figure was 23,000 out of a population of almost three and a half million.[16]

The British, although fairly satisfied with the Islamic education system in the north of Nigeria, wanted, nevertheless, better trained administrators and clerks and therefore established a number of educational institutions in which Arabic, Hausa and the Islamic sciences formed the core of the curriculum. They also took measures to improve the working of the Islamic legal system, as we shall see.

Outside northern Nigeria and northern Ghana, British policies did nothing to promote Islam. In fact in some areas such as Ijebu-Ode in western Nigeria it was difficult for Muslims to even obtain financial assistance for a Muslim school. Muslim schools had to be run on Western lines and a report drawn up in August 1931 on one such school in Ijebu-Ode indicates the criteria used to establish its viability. An extract from the report reads: "The organisation is quite satisfactory . . . the staff appear to be working in harmony . . . children are neat and well disciplined . . . all the necessary books and records are well kept . . . writing could be improved, especially in Standard IV where it is very poor . . . (and) there is a great necessity for teaching a uniform style. . . . Arithmetic: accuracy fair but not very neat."[17] There is no concern shown here for Islamic culture, yet at the time almost half the population of Ijebu-Ode was Muslim, and this was a Muslim school.

Colonial "policy" towards Islam, therefore, to the extent that one can talk about such a policy, was based on various positivist, evolutionary notions of human, cultural, social and religious development. It was infused with pragmatism. Rather than being formally and rationally thought out beforehand, it was often no more than an ideological justification for a policy dictated by circumstances.

Islamic responses to colonial rule.

Some general considerations.

Just as there was no co-ordinated, systematic colonial policy towards Islam likewise there was no co-ordinated Islamic response to colonial rule in West Africa. Islam, of course, does not demand that Muslims adopt a single, uniform strategy towards colonialism. Muslims may respond to the imposition of non-Muslim alien rule by having recourse to jihad of the sword or by *hijra*, withdrawal from the territory occupied by the alien, non-Muslim ruler. These responses, grounded in Islamic teaching, were among the many and varied Islamic responses to colonialism in West Africa in the 19th and 20th centuries.

Some Muslims offered what might be termed an introversionist, "oppositional" response to colonialism, seeing it as a form of evil which they must at all costs avoid. They refused insofar as this was possible to have any direct contact with it. And while they did not literally emigrate or withdraw from the territory ruled by non-Muslims, they did withdraw mentally, spiritually and culturally from all contact with European culture. This response is echoed in the chants of the Bamidele movement in Ibadan, western Nigeria. A verse from one of the chants goes: "My child will not travel to a European country . . . as for Mecca, he, his wife and child will go."[1]

Many movements of the Bamidele type emerged during the colonial era, in which Muslims stoutly defended their Islamic identity, refusing to wear anything but Islamic dress, speaking only in Arabic or their local language, and believing that the reform and purification of Islam was a necessary first step on the way to overthrowing colonialism. The Subbanu movement established in Mali in the 1940s is a case in point. The Muridiyya until 1910 at least, and the Hamalliyya brotherhoods also fall into the category of "oppositional" Islam which emerged as a reaction to colonialism. They were not simply a reaction to colonialism but were also a response to developments within Islam itself.

Other types of Islamic response to colonialism consisted not so much in avoiding contact with the colonial regime and all that it symbolised of Western, European values, but in working within the colonial system with the aim of limiting what they considered to be some of its more baneful influences. While not rejecting all the goals and values of the Europeans, they rejected many of the ideas and the methods used by the Europeans to achieve those objectives they considered worthwhile. This response, to an extent a "manipulationist" response, aimed at providing Muslims with the facilities and means to operate as Muslims within the framework of colonialism until such time as this framework was removed. And for the most part they expected that it would eventually be removed by a combined effort of human and supernatural means.

Islamic responses to colonialism should not be seen in isolation from that of the rest of society. Muslims were part of society and were influenced and affected by decisions taken by whole communities. Furthermore, many Muslims in West Africa must have been very confused about the whole question of the appropriate Muslim response to colonial rule. For example, while in November 1914 the Ottoman Sultan Mehmet V was calling on all Muslims in Africa to join Muslims in the rest of the world in a jihad against France, Britain and Russia, Muslim leaders in West Africa, like Shaikh Sidiya Baba in Mauretania and Ahmadu Bamba in Senegal, were encouraging people to support France, Britain and Russia against Germany and her allies which included the Ottoman Turks.

Moreover, the colonial authorities, who in many parts of West Africa had complete control over the media and the press, used these to shape and influence public opinion in general and on occasion Muslim opinion in particular.

During World War II, for example, the British colonial regime in Nigeria obtained a copy of a speech made in Mecca on 14 December 1942 by Abdul Aziz b. Sa'id. One of the extracts from the speech read: "We express our gratitude to the British Government for all the generous help and support they have given this country . . . had it not been for God's grace and after that the help of the British Government the Muslims would not have found this present plenty. . . . If we compare the state of this country with that which it was in in the last war (1914—18) we see a vast difference and that is due to God's grace and after that to the help the British Government has given us".[2] Circulating a copy of this speech to the Residents of the Western Province of Nigeria, the Secretary to the Government of these provinces commented: "In it (the speech) his majesty (Abdul Aziz b. Sa'id) expresses strong pro-British sentiments and it is thought that if the address was brought to the notice of leading Muslims they might like to quote part of it on the occasion of Id al-Kabir."[3] In addition to circulating this type of favourable publicity, Britain and France depicted themselves not only as the friend of Islam but also as the protector and defender of small nations threatened by communism and that other "anti-Christ" Hitler.

The fact that there were Muslims in West Africa, as there were non-Muslims, who were prepared to establish a working relationship with the colonial authorities does not necessarily mean that they did not oppose colonialism. To suggest that only those people who resorted to militant action or displayed openly, though in a pacific manner, their hostility to the colonial regime, were the sole opponents of colonialism is an oversimplification. Opposition to colonialism in West Africa was a much more complex phenomenon than that. As I have indicated, it was not to be found only in stable, organised militant or pacific on-going anti-colonial movements. This was something the colonial authorities realised. They were never sure of what they termed "the loyalty" of the Muslim population, not even of those they tried to buy off with privileges and trips to Mecca. The type of Muslims they feared most of all were not the leaders of the jihads like al-Hajj 'Umar but those often fragile, harmless looking Muslim religious teachers, the marabouts or mallams, who, as Governor-General William Ponty claimed, stirred up the people against the French.[4]

Case studies of the Islamic responses to colonialism in the late 19th and 20th centuries: Mauretania.

The French occupation and colonisation of Mauretania began in earnest in the early years of the 20th century. At first they decided to use diplomacy and negotiation rather than force. In 1902 a French officer, Coppolani, crossed into Mauretania on the orders of Roume, Governor General of what was then French West Africa. The aim of Coppolani's mission was to bring about a settlement to the dispute between the rival emirs in the Trarza emirate in southern Mauretania, just north of the Senegal river. This Coppolani managed to achieve and at the same time was able to turn much of southern and central Mauretania into a French Protectorate. In October 1904 Coppolani was made the Commissioner of a new civil territory of Mauretania with its headquarters at St Louis in Senegal. Coppolani had also reached an understanding with the important and respected Muslim leader and scholar Shaikh Sidiyya Baba, grandson of Shaikh Sidiyya al-Kabir. We shall return to Shaikh Sidiyya Baba later in this section.

Meanwhile there were other Muslims who were totally opposed to French rule. Among these was Shaikh Ma al-'Aynayn (1835–1910), a well-known scholar and mystic from northern Mauretania. Ma 'al-Aynayn was involved in the attack on the French fort at Tidjikja in central Mauretania in May 1905 in which Coppolani was killed.

Between 1905 and 1910 Ma al-'Aynayn, along with the emirs of Adrar and Tagant, struggled desperately to prevent the French from occupying these provinces. He also received political and military assistance for a time from Morocco. In 1906, however, the French took Tagant and in 1909 Adrar, bringing most of what today constitutes the Islamic Republic of Mauretania under French rule.

Ma al-'Aynayn regarded his struggle against the French as a *jihàd* of the sword against non-Muslims who were attempting to dominate a Muslim society, and after his death in 1910 the militant struggle continued. In 1923 a Muslim cleric, popularly known as Wadjaha, and a relative of Ma 'al-Aynayn organised, with the help of a Muslim religious leader Mokhri Ould Bukhari, a guerilla war against the French in Adrar in northern Mauretania. Moreover, in the 1920s and 1930s several serious assaults were made on French strongholds in Mauretania. In 1924, for example, Nouadhibou (Port Etienne) was attacked by the great camel-breeding group, the Reguebat, who claim descent from Prophet Muhammad's family. In 1932 the people belonging to the Awlad Dalim group, spurred on by the Muslim religious leader Muhammad al-Mamun, a brother of Wadjaha, and linked with the son of Ma al-'Aynayn, inflicted a heavy defeat on the French columns in Trarza.

However, from the middle years of the 1930s resistance to the French in the form of holy war began to crumble in Adrar and elsewhere in Mauretania. One of the reasons for this was the decision taken by some Muslim leaders in the north-west of the country to reach a working understanding with Spain who occupied what was then known as the Spanish Sahara (Rio de Oro), the territory fought over today by Morocco and the Polisario Liberation Front. Furthermore, in the centre and south of the country an increasing number of Muslim leaders came to terms with the French, including in 1936 the successors of Ma al-'Aynayn.

Long before the 1930s a number of Muslim leaders in Mauretania had taken the decision not to offer any form of active resistance, militant or otherwise, to the French regime. A case in point was Shaikh Sidiyya Baba (1862–1924), grandson of Shaikh Sidiyya al-Kabir, whose career and achievements were discussed in Chapter 6. Shaikh Sidiyya Baba, who taught at Boutilimit, not only enjoyed a reputation as an eminent scholar, a mystic and a visionary, but also exercised considerable religious, political and economic influence in Trarza, Brakna, Adrar and Tagant, and in the Senegambia. He was leader of the Sidiyya branch of the Qadiriyya brotherhood.

Shaikh Sidiyya Baba's main concern seems to have been with the reform and spread of Islam through teaching and preaching. However, being such a prominent figure in Mauretania he almost inevitably became involved in the politics of colonialism. Coppolani and other French officials and missionaries reasoned with him about the benefits that French protection would bring to Mauretania. Moreover, in the early years of the 20th century when France took the decision to impose colonial rule on Mauretania, Shaikh Sidiyya

Baba and his people, the Awlad Ibiri, were under repeated attack from other groups in Mauretania. There was also tension and disagreement among Shaikh Sidiyya Baba's followers, one group eventually aligning itself with Ma al-'Aynayn's successors.

It was over against this background that Shaikh Sidiyya Baba decided not to oppose the French occupation of Mauretania. He also at times, and in particular during the First World War, provided strong backing for colonial policies. In a letter, for example, to the French Roman Catholic Bishop in Senegal, Bishop Jalabert, Shaikh Sidiyya Baba stated that he asked God "to give a prompt and glorious victory to your generous, just and beneficent fatherland and also to her generous and noble allies."[5]

Muslim leaders in Senegal such as Sa'idu Nuru Tall, grandson of al-Hajj 'Umar, and Malik Sy, leaders of the Tijaniyya brotherhood, adopted virtually the same approach as Shaikh Sidiyya Baba towards French colonial rule. Others, however, like Shaikh Hamallah, the Mahdi of Wani, and the leaders of the Subbanu movement in Mali adopted a more aloof and oppositional stance towards colonialism.

Niger.

The French occupation of Niger, begun in 1897, took over 20 years to complete. The stiffest resistance to the French colonisation of Niger came from the Tuareg. At the outset the French entered into negotiations with the Tuareg in an effort to obtain their submission to French rule. One of the Tuareg leaders they negotiated with was al-Mekka, head of a branch of the Kel-es-Suq, a group of Tuareg devoted to learning and opposed to jihad of the sword. The French also opened negotiations with Fihrun, Amenukal (chief) of the Iwillimiden, a large confederation of western Tuaregs who constituted part of the ruling class.

Initially Fihrun showed a willingness to co-operate with the French, partly in the hope of obtaining arms and assistance against the Kunta. Relations between some Tuareg groups and the Kunta had been hostile and tense for a long time. The Kunta scholar and mystic, Shaikh Sidi al-Mukhtar al-Kunti al-Kabir, whose career and achievements were discussed in Chapter 4, had little but contempt for the Iwillimiden and the Tuaregs generally. He preferred the Moroccans as rulers to the Iwillimiden. The latter, according to this Kunta scholar, had no idea how to govern or administer a kingdom according to the principles enshrined in the Shari'a.

Shaikh Sidi may have been thinking along the same lines as Muhammad al-Jaylani who, as we saw, believed that Islam could not flourish among nomads and pastoralists living in rural or desert conditions (see Chapter 5, p. 125). Lending some support to this view a contemporary scholar writing about the Moors of Mauretania states: "In practice among the Moors, the more remote the community and the more nomadic it is, the more likely it is that the 'urf (the orally transmitted customary law of the Saharan nomads) will predominate in the actual running of the tribe's affairs. Where the Moors are settled in oasis towns, or where there are zawaya in large numbers, the

Shari'a will be followed. At least this will be so in theory. . .".[6]

In the conflict between the Tuareg and the Kunta the French supported the latter, supplying them with arms when armed conflict broke out between the two groups in 1905. French support for the Kunta led to strained relations between themselves and the Tuareg, and after escaping from exile in Timbuktu, Fihrun declared a jihad against the French in 1916.

The supporters of the jihad to the south of Air were quickly overcome by the better organised and better armed French troops. Further north the jihad was more organised under the inspiring leadership of Muhammad Kwasen, and received the support of the Sanusiyya brotherhood and that of Sultan Tegama of Agades. In December 1916 the jihadists, led by a nephew of Muhammad Kwasen, beseiged Agades. The French, however, aided by the British and troops from other parts of Africa, managed to relieve Agades by March 1917. Muhammad Kwasen, however, continued his resistance until his death in 1919. Sultan Tegama was captured in 1920 and taken to Agades where, according to official sources, he committed suicide.

The Muslim assault on Agades frightened the French who reacted by resettling almost all the Tuareg population of Air, at least all those who had not already fled to Nigeria. This in the short term weakened considerably the Islamic society, established over several centuries, in Air. Muslim scholars, however, such as Shaikh Bay al-Kunti who, like Shaikh Sidiyya Baba, advised people not to get involved in direct confrontation with the French, did a great deal to restore the Islamic way of life in Air.[7]

Despite Shaikh Bay al-Kunti's advice militant resistance to French rule in Niger continued. Mahdists, for example, attacked the French garrison at Tahsua in 1927, and revolts broke out in other parts of the colony. The resistance, however, was for the most part on a smaller scale.[8] The Islamic response to French rule in Niger as in Mauretania took at least two forms. There was the militant resistance inspired to an extent by the doctrine of jihad of the sword and also by internal political considerations, and the decision, taken in the main by scholars, not to engage in direct confrontation or active resistance to the French. It should be mentioned, however, that in general the Tuareg Muslim scholar, Ineslemen, displayed in his attitude and behaviour intense hostility towards the French, something that made the French colonial authorities believe that in the event of full-scale war they would side with the opposition.[9]

Nigeria.

The Islamic reaction to the colonial occupation in Nigeria was extremely complex and varied. There was the response based on the Islamic notion of hijra, withdrawal, from a territory occupied and ruled by non-Muslims. Attahiru, Sultan of Sokoto, eventually adopted this response. Then there was also the militant response manifested in Kano and Sokoto and in other emirates and at the battle of Burmi in 1903. Mahdism also played an important part in the response to colonial rule in Nigeria as elsewhere in West Africa.

There were those who, taking a less doctrinaire and hostile view of colonialism than this and, after receiving certain promises that the Islamic religion would not be interfered with, decided to refrain from showing any outward form of hostility towards the colonial regime.

Response by hijra (planned withdrawal).

In 1900 the British began their advance on the Sokoto Caliphate. In that year Frederick Lugard was appointed High Commissioner of the Protectorate of Northern Nigeria which consisted at the time of Ilorin and Bida emirates. Equipped with heavy artillery and some of the latest guns such as the Maxim and Gatling guns, Lugard's forces took control of Kontagora in 1900, Yola in 1901 and Bauchi and Zaria in 1902. Sokoto and Kano, the capital and the largest emirate of the Caliphate respectively, remained independent at this stage.

The Sultan of Sokoto, Abdurahman (1891–1902), had no intention of submitting to Lugard and wrote to him informing him that between the Sokoto Caliphate and the British there could only be war.[10] The Sultan's overriding concern was the protection and defence of Islam. The British reacted by first attacking and conquering Kano and then Sokoto in March 1903. At the time of this attack the Emir and a number of Kano notables were absent, and scholars have debated and continue to debate the reasons for this absence and the effect it had on Kano resistance to the British.[11] According to one account the majority of the people of Kano carried on their normal activities after the British conquest, but nevertheless retained their resentment which was simply driven underground.[12]

After Kano had been conquered the British then moved against Sokoto where in 1902 Attahiru I had succeeded Abdurahman as Sultan. Aware of the British victories in Kano and elsewhere and of the superior fire power at their disposal, some people in Sokoto counselled the Emir to submit to Lugard; others suggested that they should withdraw, perform hijra, from the territory about to be invaded by non-Muslims. Attahiru, like Aliyu, Emir of Kano, favoured hijra but the British preparations to attack Sokoto were well under way and left little time for a planned emigration. Attahiru, therefore, decided upon armed resistance, but the resistance was quickly overcome on 15 March 1903. Attahiru then resorted to his preferred strategy of hijra or withdrawal.

Attahiru with his followers left Sokoto for the east en route to Mecca. On his journey through Northern Nigeria many people, particularly those living in the rural areas, joined him, interpreting his withdrawal as a religious flight. The British Resident of Kano described what happened in the south-west of Kano: "The ex-Sultan Muslimi (Attahiru) arrived in Belli in the extreme south-west of Kano territory on the 20th instant (20 March 1903). . . . During these two days he must have quadrupled his following. Each time he passed through the people were told to follow him to Mecca otherwise they would become Kaffiri (pagan) and as a result half the population of every town tied up their bundles and joined in his train."[13] The same Resident wrote in May 1903 that he was obliged to send out a force to capture Attahiru for "to allow Attahiru to sit down even for a week unmolested in Kano territory would practically mean the population joining him en masse."[14]

In June 1903 Attahiru was joined in Bauchi province by other Muslims, some of whom were Mahdists while others belonged to the Tijaniyya brotherhood. Attahiru, as we shall see, was killed while fighting the British at the battle of Burmi in 1903. Before turning to the Mahdist response I want to look briefly at the general reaction of the emirs in Northern Nigeria after the British conquest.

One response was that given by the ulama of Sokoto who remained after the British conquest. They recommended, following the instructions of Usuman dan Fodio, that Muslims could work out some agreement with the non-Muslim party when it was obvious that they did not have the means to oust them from power. The agreement was to be verbal indicating outward acceptance only of the status quo. Inwardly or in the mind and heart there was to be no acceptance or submission, and when the moment was opportune Muslims were to reassert their opposition and re-gain their independence.[15]

The Battles of Burmi and the Mahdist response.

Burmi was, as we have seen, the headquarters of Mallam Jibril Gaini and a strong centre of Mahdism (see Chapter 5, p. 121). Jibril's army, I have already pointed out, was defeated in March 1902 by a British force under the command of Colonel T. Morland at the battle of Tongo. After this defeat Jibril's followers re-grouped and in 1903 put up stiff resistance against the British at the battles of Burmi. In May 1903, led by their Mahdist chief Mallam Musa, at one time an officer in Jibril's army, the people of Burmi drove away a British expedition under the command of Captain Sword. This was the first major defeat of a British expedition in northern Nigeria and had repercussions all over the country and beyond its boundaries.

The British, however, with a much larger and better equipped force, returned to launch another attack on Burmi in July 1903. Once again the British faced dogged opposition and in the conflict Attahiru and almost all his Sokoto followers who had performed the hijra with him were killed, along with some 600 other defenders of Burmi. British officers later attributed their victory to superior military equipment and ammunition.[16]

The British victory, however, did not undermine Mahdism. Many of those who survived the battles of Burmi migrated east to the Sudan to settle there in and around Mahdist villages, such as those established in the Blue Nile region by Mai Wurno, Attahiru's son, and by the one-time Emir of Misau, Mai Ahmadu. In the Sudan these people were the recipients of and helped to spread Mahdist propaganda, and in this way kept the Mahdist ideology alive.

The hajj or pilgrimage was perhaps one of the most effective means of spreading Mahdist propaganda. Through the hajj Mahdists from many African countries were interlinked. According to one colonial source in the 1920s about 20,000 Nigerians were to be found in the Sudan at any one time, many of whom were pilgrims and while en route to Mecca they worked on the cotton plantations at Gezira along with the more permanent residents or on the railways.[17] Some of these pilgrims stayed in Mahdist villages or moved in Mahdist circles, taking part in Mahdist dialogue.

In their conversations and literature these Mahdists made frequent attacks on the deplorable state of Islam and put forward the view that in order to defeat imperialism Islam would first have to be reformed. Mahdist tracts on these themes were in circulation as far south as the south-west of Nigeria. A copy of the "Dreams of Shaikh Ahmad", for instance, a Mahdist document widely circulated in the Sudan, was found on a Muslim trader travelling from Ilorin to Jedda, and there is evidence that a certain al-Hajj Fahmy from Lagos moved in Mahdist circles. In northern Nigeria in the 1920s one Mahdist poem in wide circulation was the "Song of the End of the World", which contains a violent tirade against the present rulers, modern ways and illiterate youth, that is youth illiterate in Arabic, and declares that all will be put right by violent revolution.[18]

In addition to spreading propaganda Mahdists also took part in revolts aimed at overthrowing the colonial regime and those who supported it, regardless of whether their support was simply a form of "external" compliance or not. There was, for example, the Satiru rebellion in 1906. In 1904 the chief of Satiru, a short distance to the north of Sokoto, proclaimed himself to be the Mahdi and was almost immediately arrested by the Sultan of Sokoto and died soon after in prison. His son, Isa, then took up the Mahdist cause and received support from Dan Makafo (Shuaibu) who came from Niger.[19]

The British, alarmed by the prospects of another Mahdist uprising, tried straight away to arrest the growth of the movement by sending troops to the area in February 1906. The British contingent, however, was routed at Satiru by the Mahdists and their supporters. Lacking the support of most of the emirs, for the reasons given and perhaps, as one historian puts it, because "they lacked the will and the leadership to turn the Satiru rebellion into a general revolt which Lugard, with the forces at his disposal, would have been unable to suppress"[20], the rebellion was crushed by the British in March 1906. This was the last serious militant Mahdist uprising in the Sokoto Caliphate during the colonial era, but it was not the end of Mahdism. As late as 1923 Mahdism in Nigeria was considered to be "a political problem of the first importance".[21]

In the 1920s Mahdist manifestos were found in several mosques in northern Nigeria, and Nigerian Mahdists were believed to have had links with the Hammallist movement (see p. 205) based at Nioro in present-day Mali. Kano later became the headquarters of Nigerian Mahdism and one of the foremost leaders was Sa'id b. Hayatu, who as we have seen was the son of the founder of the Mahdist state in Adamawa, Hayatu b. Sa'id (see Chapter 5, p. 120). Sa'id b. Hayatu was exiled by the British to Buea in the Cameroon in 1923. Meanwhile, many of his followers settled in Kano and when he was allowed to return to Nigeria in 1946 he joined his followers there.

Sa'id b. Hayatu never abandoned his Mahdist beliefs and even found some sympathy for them among the Kano mallams and was well treated by the then emir, Abdullahi Bayero. Moreover, the son of Muhammad Ahmad, the Mahdi of the Sudan, Sidi Abdurrahman, appointed Sa'id b. Hayatu as Caliph of the Western Sudan. In 1957 Sa'id published a book in which he spoke of, among other things, the acceptance of the idea of the Mahdi by the leaders of the Sokoto *jihad*, and of his belief that the Mahdi had already come in the person of Muhammad Ahmad of the Sudan who proclaimed himself Mahdi in June 1881.[22]

I have not attempted in the foregoing to provide a comprehensive account of the Islamic response to colonialism in West Africa, but simply to indicate the complex nature of this response, which took many different forms and was shaped by doctrinal, political, social and other considerations.

The development of Islam in West Africa during the colonial era, c. 1900 – 1960: some case studies.

Senegal.

Although a majority of the Wolof, Tokolor, Fulani and Mandinka speaking people of Senegal were Muslims by the beginning of the 20th century, there remained nonetheless a number of what can be described as "non-Muslim" areas in the country. While the Roman Catholic missionaries were hoping that they would evangelise these areas before the Muslims, others like Quellien were predicting that Islam would triumph both in the non-Muslim areas in Senegal and in West Africa as a whole. Quellien wrote that "the progressive and continuous expansion of Islam in West Africa is a fact that no-one who knows anything about the subject will deny". He stated that Christianity was remarkable alongside Islam "for its almost total failure in the same areas".[1] It is generally accepted, in fact, that Islam made much faster progress than Christianity in West Africa during the colonial era.

Among the "non-Muslim" areas of Senegal at the beginning of the 20th century were the Serer states of Sine and Saloum. Western Saloum did have a substantial minority of Muslims, but the majority of the Serer, the second largest ethnic group in Senegal today, were not only non-Muslim but had resisted attempts made by Ma Ba Diakhou Ba and others to convert them to Islam.

By the outbreak of World War I, however, Islam had gained according to Klein "a striking victory" in Sine-Saloum.[2] The Serer began turning to Islam in the 1890s and by c. 1900 many of the Serer chiefs in Saloum were Muslims. By c. 1913 an estimated 43 per cent of the Serer in western Saloum were Muslims. By the same year lower Saloum was 80 per cent Muslim, and Sine with the largest number of inhabitants was 15 per cent Muslim. And by the end of the colonial era some 50 per cent of all the Serer were Muslims.[3]

Although there were no doubt religious and ideological factors at work in the Islamisation of the Serer, this development of Islam in Sine-Saloum has also been attributed in part to "material" factors. The French occupation of Sine-Saloum in the 1890s brought about the "decline of the traditional state in Sine-Saloum".[4] The French introduced a number of administrative changes and took over the right to appoint chiefs and broke the power of the tyeddo, warriors who served and controlled to an extent the Burs (kings) and who were hostile to Islam. The French also introduced Muslim courts which operated alongside the traditional courts.

Other changes comprised the building of roads and the development of the groundnut industry. Both of these measures opened up Sine-Saloum to outside influences. Moreover, in 1898 Kaolack, a predominantly Muslim town, was made the capital of Sine-Saloum and attracted increasing numbers of Muslim merchants and *marabouts*. The Roman Catholic Bishop, Jalabert, when he visited Kaolack in March 1910, was struck by the number of Muslims there who from a position outside the Church "assisted religiously at the service".[5] Many of these Muslims moved on and settled in villages and towns, mixing with and teaching the peasants and becoming the unofficial leaders of the local community. Foundiougne-Niombato to the south-west of Kaolack, for example, was "swamped by Muslim immigrants" and was "heavily Muslim" by 1914.[6]

The Muslim brotherhoods, such as the Tijaniyya and the Muridiyya, also contributed to the growth of Islam among the Serer. It is not specifically the role of these two brotherhoods among the Serer that interests me here, however, but rather their impact on the development of Islam in Senegal, and, in the case of the Tijaniyya, beyond Senegal as well. The Muridiyya and the Tijaniyya, or to be more precise that branch of the Tijaniyya led by Ibrahim Niass, although they shared on some matters similar views and performed similar functions, illustrate two of the many different sides of Islam's development in Senegal in the colonial era. The founder of the Muridiyya, Ahmadu Bamba, a mystic and scholar, was in essence the "local" holy man who devoted himself mainly to the Wolof of Senegal, while Ibrahim Niass, though he had his roots and headquarters in Senegal and did a great deal to spread the Tijaniyya among the ordinary people, appeared all over the West African landscape and further afield in a bid to strengthen his following.

The Muridiyya.

Ahmadu Bamba (1850 – 1927) founded the Murid brotherhood in 1886. At first it was simply a branch of the Qadiriyya order and attracted in the main those who were displaced and uprooted by the French occupation of Senegal and whose way of life was being altered by the development and expansion of the groundnut economy. Defeated and displaced rulers as well as warriors and peasants joined the brotherhood.[7]

Although it resembled in many respects the other brotherhoods such as the Qadiriyya and the Tijaniyya, the Muridiyya *wird* (litany) for example being a compound of Qadiri and Tijani prayers and litanies, certain emphases in Ahmadu Bamba's teaching, together with a number of organisational developments, gave the Muridiyya an identity of its own. Ahmadu Bamba strongly emphasised, for instance, the spiritual importance of hard work and discipline in a way that seemed if not to devalue the importance of salat (the five daily prayers), at least made it appear to be of less importance. He would tell his disciples that they must work as if they were never going to die and pray as if they were about to die the next day. Disciples (*murids*) were to work hard and follow without questioning the advice of their shaikh or religious guide.

Obedience to a shaikh was of fundamental importance for the spiritual well-being of a disciple, according to Bamba. He wrote: "Truth is in the love one has for one's Shaikh, and . . . in obedience at all times and everywhere to his orders without offering him the least resistance . . . it is also necessary to remove one's free will for the opinions of the Shaikh are unassailable". And again, "Anyone who has not received over a period of time his training from a Shaikh will encounter difficulties. For whoever has not had a Shaikh for a guide will have Satan for a Shaikh wherever he goes."[8] According to a number of scholars these statements of Ahmadu Bamba's were designed to educate his followers to live an active, useful, moral and upright life in society while at the same time providing them with the basics of an Islamic education.[9] Concerning the emphasis on work as the principal means of achieving holiness and Paradise — Bamba also told his disciples "To work is to pray. Work for me and I will pray for you".[10] The explanation for such an emphasis, it has been suggested, lies in the specific historical circumstances in which Bamba's brotherhood emerged.[11] What then were these circumstances?

The first of the disciples to join Ahmadu Bamba's brotherhood did so at a time when, as O'Brien points out, the crisis within the Wolof states had reached "its most dramatic proportions".[12] This crisis, set in motion by the slave trade and the jihads of the 18th and 19th centuries, was brought to a climax as the French embarked upon their conquest of the western Sudan. The Senegalese resistance leader, Lat Dior, who as we have seen received assistance from Ahmadu Bamba's father during his campaign to turn Cayor into a Muslim state and who respected the learning and piety of Ahmadu Bamba himself, was defeated by the French at Dekkilé in 1886 (see Chapter 5). Dekkilé was, as O'Brien comments, "a moment of national defeat and humiliation".[13] After Dekkilé Lat Dior's followers were disarmed and dispersed. The same thing happened to the followers of Mamadu Lamine and on many other occasions during the French occupation of the Senegambia and the western Sudan as a whole.

The report of the chaplain who accompanied the French column sent out in 1881 by the then Governor of Senegal, Brière de l'Isle, to protect the construction of a telegraph line being erected between the two French posts of Saldé and Matam along the Senegal river in Futa Toro, gives but a glimpse of the upheaval and dislocation brought about by the French occupation.

The French column was operating in "fertile land . . . where people cultivated every sort of millet, and every sort of vegetable . . . it was not unusual to find cultivation on a large scale of between eight and ten kilometres. And the herds were of a great value to the country." However, when a chief, Abdul Bubakar, allegedly very hostile to the French, cut off communications between the upper Senegal and St Louis in protest against the construction of the telegraph line, Brière de l'Isle sent out French-led troops, villages were set on fire, people were killed and others were so badly injured that they had to have limbs amputated. The report states: "On returning one could see the spectacle of the village in flames, the one we had set on fire on leaving."[14]

The French colonial administration did make some provision for those displaced and uprooted by the military occupation of the Senegambia and the western Sudan as a whole. They established what were termed "villages of liberty" where the displaced could settle. However, it has been shown that these were in effect little better than camps where supplies of cheap labour were easily obtainable.[15]

Ahmadu Bamba, regarded as an opponent of colonialism, emerged to provide some of the uprooted with leadership, a community and work. Within a relatively short space of time, between 1886 and 1912, his brotherhood grew from being a mere handful of disciples into an organisation with an estimated 70,000 members, most of whom had little knowledge of Islam and had been displaced as a result of the political, social and economic developments outlined above.[16] Bamba's brotherhood was for many of these people a substitute for the society and world they had lost. The Muridiyya, however, was not simply an inward looking, introversionist, utopian sect whose members believed that the old order would through a combination of divine intervention and human effort be restored. Rather it played a role similar in some respects to the Pentecostalist churches among the Black community in North America and Britain, and the Independent churches in Africa during the late 19th and 20th centuries. Like these churches it not only upheld values and traditions of the old order, but also developed institutions such as the *dara* (collective farm) which enabled the members of the brotherhood to meet the demands of the new socio-economic order, an order which placed great emphasis on the cultivation of groundnuts as a commercial crop, and led to the break-up of the traditional family structure. There were also educational *daras* where Murids were taught the recitation of the Qur'an and some Islamic law and Arabic.

The Muridiyya, moreover, offered those who opposed colonialism a society, a community and an authority structure which, at least at the more immediate, local level, were Islamic and indigenous rather than non-Muslim and alien. One contemporary account speaks of the belief among Ahmadu Bamba's disciples that their leader would one day by a simple gesture strike down the Europeans and massacre them.[17]

For most of his life as a religious leader Ahmadu Bamba was suspected by the colonial authorities, often on the basis of reports submitted to them by jealous rivals, of plotting and scheming to overthrow the colonial regime. This led to Bamba's exile to Gabon in 1895, and to Mauretania in 1902. Shaikh Hamallah, leader of the Hamalliyya, a reform movement within the Tijaniyya, experienced a similar fate, being exiled on several occasions (see p. 213). In the case of both these men exile, rather than diminishing their prestige and status among their followers, increased it. Ahmadu Bamba returned to Senegal from exile in Mauretania, where he had been placed under the tutelage of Shaikh Sidiyya Baba, in 1907. Not allowed to settle in the village of Touba where he had been commanded in a vision to establish his order, Ahmadu Bamba decided to open a school further north in Louga. In 1910 this school was closed by the colonial authorities who continued to keep a close watch on Ahmadu Bamba's activities.

From about 1910, however, a gradual change began to take place in the attitude of the colonial regime towards Bamba. Moreover, the latter seems to have decided that there was no point in presenting an overtly hostile front towards the French who were now well in control of Senegal. In 1912 Ahmadu Bamba was allowed to settle in Diourbel in Baol and from this time his brotherhood, at times assisted by the French colonial authorities, began to expand even more rapidly throughout Senegal.

The colonial administration had begun to see more clearly that the Muridiyya, like the Tijaniyya and Qadiriyya, could play an important political and economic role on its behalf. With the policy of Assimilation abandoned throughout her West African colonies, except in the four communes of Dakar, St Louis, Rufisque and Gorée, the administration needed strong and respected leaders in order to operate its version of the policy of Indirect Rule, and Ahmadu Bamba and his associates fell into this category. In addition it became increasingly obvious that the dara, or collective farming system operated by the Muridiyya, was a valuable instrument for the expansion of the groundnut economy.

By 1915 favourable reports on Bamba were being submitted to the French headquarters in Dakar by colonial officials once hostile to the founder of the Muridiyya. Ahmadu Bamba for his part had begun to demonstrate his goodwill towards the regime by helping to recruit troops for the First World War and by instructing his followers not to oppose the French. In return for these and other co-operative measures he was appointed to the Consultative Committee on Muslim Affairs in 1916, and in 1919, in recognition of his services during World War I, he was named a Chevalier of the Légion d'Honneur. He was presented with the medal, shaped in the form of a cross, which, however, he refused to wear on the grounds that it was a Christian symbol. Ahmadu Bamba's support for the war effort, however, did not mean, and the French understood this, that he had become a firm and loyal supporter of the colonial regime. A report on him written by the Governor-General in 1927, the year of his death, concluded with the words: "His loyalty remained uncertain".[18]

Ahmadu Bamba probably never had any intention of using military means to overthrow the French administration. He was of the opinion that the French were too powerful to be toppled by force, and discounted the use of jihad of the sword. Although he opposed French rule, since it was Christian rule over Muslims, he advised his followers to treat the French in the same way as the Prophet commanded Muslims to treat Christians. Bamba's response to colonialism was complex. He regarded certain European ways as corrupting and believed that although he could not change the situation by the use of force he could shield his followers to an extent from its corrupting influences.

After Ahmadu Bamba's death in 1927 the Muridiyya continued to expand although rent by leadership disputes in 1927 and again in 1945, and by independence in 1960 had close to half a million members.[19]

The Tijaniyya.

The Tijaniyya brotherhood, as we have seen, entered Senegal from Mauretania in the early 19th century and was firmly established there mainly by al-Hajj 'Umar Tall in the 1840s and 1850s. In contrast to al-Hajj 'Umar, a number of Senegalese Tijani leaders, including his grandson Sa'idu Nuru Tall and Malik Sy, head of the large, mainly Wolof branch of the Tijaniyya, decided not to oppose the colonial regime but instead reached a working understanding with it. My main concern in this section, however, is not so much with the attitude of the Tijaniyya to the colonial regime but rather with the missionary and other activities of one Tijaniyya leader, Ibrahim Niass.

and his branch of the order referred to by one authority, perhaps somewhat mistakenly, as the "Reformed" Tijaniyya.[20]

Ibrahim Niass (1900—1975), a Wolof-speaking Senegalese born in the village of Taiba-Niassène near Kaolack, came from a family of ironworkers. His father, Abdullahi, was a scholar and a leader in the Tijaniyya brotherhood. He had contacts with the Tijaniyya in North Africa, made the pilgrimage to Mecca, and after spending some time in the Gambia and in Fez in Morocco settled in Kaolack in 1910. By 1922, the year of his death, Abdullahi had made the Niass family the leading Tijaniyya family in Sine-Saloum and the Gambia. He had also increased Tijaniyya involvement in the groundnut economy.

Abdullahi Niass was succeeded by his eldest son, Muhammad. Ibrahim, another of his sons and a respected scholar and mystic, decided in the late 1920s to separate from his brother Muhammad and establish his own independent branch of the Tijaniyya with its headquarters at Medina-Kaolack, close to Kaolack town. Ibrahim Niass soon attracted student-disciples (talibs), and in his teaching he laid great emphasis on Sufi doctrines and on the importance of modelling one's life on that of Prophet Muhammad. He also excluded the use of military jihad, emphasising the necessity instead of jihad of the heart.[21]

Several years after establishing this branch of the Tijaniyya Ibrahim Niass claimed to be the recipient of special divine gifts and powers. He maintained, for instance, that he was chosen to enjoy an unusually close relationship with God, and in 1930 proclaimed publicly that he was "The Saviour of the Age". He was also, he believed, endowed with "divine grace" which he could share with others who followed his teaching.

In 1937 Ibrahim Niass made the pilgrimage to Mecca and there met the Emir of Kano, Abdullahi Bayero. The latter is said to have accepted Shaikh Ibrahim as the Saviour of the Age. Moreover, on his return from Mecca Niass visited Fez and was given some indication there by the Caliph (leader) of the Tijaniyya, Shaikh Sukayraj, that he should take over the leadership of the Tijaniyya. And as Caliph of the Tijaniyya Ibrahim Niass began sending his representatives all over West Africa to encourage people to join the Tijaniyya and recognise him as the Saviour of the Age. This brought him a large following in Nigeria, particularly in Kano and the northern region, but people from Jos, Lafia, Makurdi, Lokoja, Ibadan, Lagos, Enugu, Onitsha, Afikpo, Nsukka and Benin also accepted his leadership. He also attracted supporters in many other West African states, including Ghana, Guinea (Conakry), the Gambia, Ivory Coast, Mauretania, Togo, Upper Volta and Mali. Followers or disciples from all of these countries went to Medina-Kaolack where they were initiated into the brotherhood before returning home as muqqaddam or local leaders of the Tijaniyya.

Ibrahim Niass travelled widely himself. In 1945 he visited Kano, and in 1952 he went to Ghana. Some of those who accepted his claim to be the Saviour of the Age saw in him a black person who was uniquely favoured and endowed by God in the contemporary situation.[22] Some of the followers of Muhammad Jumat Imam, who proclaimed himself the Mahdi in Ijebu-Ode in Western Nigeria in 1942, were also disposed to accept this leader's claims on account of the fact that he was a black prophet and an African.[23] To an extent, therefore, the widespread support given to Ibrahim Niass must be seen in the context of cultural nationalism. It was not an assertion that black people were better because they were black but rather an assertion in terms of religion, and by extension of politics, that there can be no colour bar.

Ibrahim Niass regarded it as his duty to complete the work of reviving and spreading Islam begun by al-Hajj 'Umar and the 19th-century reformers and interrupted by the European colonisation of West Africa. He emphasised, however, that Islam was to spread by peaceful and not militant means. Part of his philosophy was that "whatever is in aid of Islam must be considered good in the light of the Qur'an". Radios, tape recorders, and anything that assisted him in putting his message across was used. When asked in the 1950s about whether it was fitting to have Qur'anic recitations on the radio, he replied simply that certain innovations were good and that this was one of them.[24] In addition to the use of radios, tape recorders and similar techniques for the dissemination of his message, Ibrahim Niass encouraged active participation by women and children in the religious services. Purdah or wife seclusion is not practiced by the Niass branch of the Tijaniyya.

The Niass branch of the Tijaniyya, like the Muridiyya, probably attracted many people who were either alienated by the colonial system or who suffered from the changes in family life brought about by urbanisation and socio-economic change. Certainly in Kano and in other centres in Nigeria at the time when Niass was welcomed and accepted as a "Saviour", the pace of industrialisation had begun to increase rapidly and many of those who joined his branch of the Tijaniyya were economically deprived.

Economic deprivation, however, is not the only reason or even the main reason why people join salvationist or millenarian movements such as that founded by Ibrahim Niass.[25] As Hiskett points out, support for Niass's branch of the Tijaniyya is not limited to the disadvantaged but includes wealthy merchants, businessmen and professionals. Hiskett maintains that in addition to facilitating trade and business among its members the religious teachings of the order are also compelling.[26] It is of course often very difficult to make a clear distinction between spiritual and material interests. Niass's teaching does in fact provide a doctrine which vindicates or justifies good fortune by making it clear that material success is a gift of God. Moreover, there is the belief that special prayers said by Ibrahim Niass could bring success in terms of material prosperity as well as eternal salvation. By the same token there is a doctrine or vindication of misfortune which makes it clear to the disciple that God is the dispenser of all fortune whether good or bad. In addition the "special" prayers of Ibrahim Niass can bring both failure in this world and suffering in the next. Niass was generally presented, however, as a healer and protector against economic, political, social and religious misfortune. Many people believed that through his prayers and intercession on their behalf they would arrive safely in Paradise, without even having to undergo judgment on the Last Day.

Other Muslims, particularly those with Wahhabi tendencies, criticise Niass's teaching on several accounts. They object, for example, to what they regard as the excessive veneration given to Prophet Muhammad. The Niass branch of the Tijaniyya celebrate with great enthusiasm and devotion both the naming day and the birthday of the Prophet. The teaching that holy men can mediate between believers and God is also criticised. This teaching is regarded simply as a device used to extract money from the incredulous and the poor.

Despite the criticisms, Ibrahim Niass attracted millions of followers and perhaps did more than anyone else to popularise the teaching of the Tijaniyya in West Africa. He also, through the emphasis he laid on the necessity to acquire a sound education in Arabic and the Islamic sciences, did much to promote Islamic education, which suffered considerable neglect in many parts of West Africa during colonial rule. His disciples, however, were not encouraged to acquire a Western education. He told his followers in Kano: "We must confine ourselves to knowledge concerning Islam, for all civilisation can be found in the knowledge of Islam. . . . Western education is doing more harm than good and might destroy our spiritual beliefs in the very near future".[27]

Ibrahim Niass established zawaya, communities or cells of the "Reformed" Tijaniyya, in most West African countries. These communities were places of worship and in addition offered followers education or if they were travelling a place to stay, and this made them an obvious attraction to traders and pilgrims. Moreover, in addition to providing his followers with these multi-purpose local communities, Ibrahim Niass, through his international links and activities, connected his followers with Muslims in the rest of the world. He was Vice-President of the World Muslim Congress, the aim of which was to unite Muslims throughout the world. He was also involved with the World Muslim Congress centred in Egypt, with the Muslim World League centred in Mecca and with the Arab League.

Like Ahmadu Bamba then, Ibrahim Niass did much to popularise Islam. By way of contrast with Ahmadu Bamba, however, Ibrahim Niass moved much more frequently between the world of Islam in Senegal and that of international Islam, strengthening the ties between the two. While the former is said to have "Wolofised" Islam in Senegal, the latter, at a time when the colonial regime was striving to keep them apart, brought Islam in Senegal and West Africa into closer contact with world Islam.

Ibrahim Niass was not alone among Senegalese Muslim leaders in his attempts to unite Muslims in Senegal and West Africa with the rest of the Muslim world during the colonial era. There was also, for example, Shaikh Touré and his associates who established the Muslim Cultural Union (U.C.M.) in 1953 which had the aim of uniting Muslims, of spreading literacy in Arabic and of undermining the three enemies of Islam, colonialism, capitalism and maraboutism. Maraboutism was the practice whereby Muslim teachers or guides, known as marabouts, were alleged to be exploiting the credulity of the masses by taking their money in return for amulets and charms. The reformers and the colonial authorities were in agreement in condemning this practice. The marabouts were the "venal" Muslim teachers that al-Maghili, Usuman dan Fodio and, among other West African leaders Sekou Touré of Guinea (Conakry) attacked for peddling a corrupt version of Islam in return for a livelihood. The influence of the marabouts over the people, however, proved stronger than that of the U.C.M. and by the late

1950s the U.C.M. had toned down its criticism and were beginning to talk in terms of the vital role played by the marabouts in the spread of Islam.

In addition to the U.C.M. a Senegalese Muslim, Ly Cire, established the Muslim Association of African Students (A.M.E.A.) in 1954, and here again emphasis was placed on spreading literacy in Arabic and on undermining maraboutism, colonialism and capitalism. The movement, inspired by reformist trends in Egypt, resembled in many respects the Subbanu movement established in Bamako (Mali) in 1945.

Although these movements were more radical in terms of their economic philosophy than Ibrahim Niass, to the extent that they had as one of their main aims the dismantling of the capitalist system, they shared with the "Reformed" Tijaniyya the aim of developing and expanding the Islamic educational system and in particular improving people's knowledge of Arabic. This concern with the spread of Arabic can be attributed in part to the fact that Arabic is the language of the Qur'an, of prayer and of Islamic culture and civilisation.

Widespread literacy in Arabic, moreover, would enable Muslims to read for themselves the Qur'an and thereby lessen their reliance on the marabouts while at the same time breaking down the social barriers between the "literate" and "non-literate" and, by extension, between the different socio-economic groups within society. Furthermore, Arabic would help to preserve the Islamic identity of Muslims living in contact with Western ideas and attitudes, and often obliged to use a foreign language, French.

This was the thinking of Ibrahim Niass and of the followers of the U.C.M., the A.M.E.A., the Subbanu movement, and of a movement I have not so far mentioned, the "Movement for the Teaching of Arabic in Senegal" (M.E.A.S.) established in 1957. This last mentioned organisation soon broadened its scope and, in addition to the teaching and the dissemination of Arabic, it united with other Muslim associations to establish in 1962 the National Federation of Muslim Cultural Associations in Senegal.

These movements made for an improvement in the quality of Islamic education in Senegal, increased the numbers of Muslims literate in Arabic, and gave greater cohesion and unity to the Muslim community. Moreover, they represented an organised form of "oppositional" Islam, an Islam in which Muslims consciously decided and willed to be Muslims and sought their identity in Islamic culture over against either European or traditional non-Muslim culture. Of course these movements were not the principal agencies of Islamic development in either the urban or rural areas of Senegal during the colonial era. Jakhanke clerics continued to sponsor Qur'anic schools which non-Muslims were invited to attend, and established villages in, among other places, the non-Muslim Diola area of the Casamance in southern Senegal. These Qur'anic schools were highly effective particularly in those areas where there were no government or mission schools. In Diamal in Sine-Saloum, for example, there was neither government nor mission school so all the parents, whether Muslim or not, sent their children to the local Qur'anic school.[28]

Therefore, by 1960 Senegal was a predominantly Muslim country. There were, of course, a variety of different strands to Islam in Senegal as was the

IX The study of the Qur'an: the master and the student

case elsewhere in West Africa. There was, for example, the "oppositional" reformist strand alongside the more accommodationist, tolerant strand. While some Muslims, then, moved between the world of traditional religion and Islam and some were purists, others were attempting to integrate Islamic with Western perspectives. Then there were those who, like al-Hajj Badara Dia, had begun to build bridges between Islam and Christianity. Through the Ecumenical Mutual Aid Society, established in 1955 at Bopp, Muslims and Christians began to work together at the philanthropic and humanitarian level, having agreed not to discuss for the time being doctrinal issues.

However, although predominantly Muslim by 1960 there was no broadly-based Muslim community in Senegal that wanted to turn the country into an Islamic state and provide it with an Islamic constitution. Indeed, even when Lamine Gueye, in an effort to gain the support of the Muslim religious leaders, presented himself as the "Muslim candidate" in opposition to the Catholic candidate, Leopold Senghor, in the 1952 elections for the Territorial

Assembly, the election went in favour of Senghor in a country that was at the time over 80 per cent Muslim.

Upper Volta.

Islam made considerable progress in terms of organisation and expansion in Upper Volta during the colonial era, and in particular from the 1930s. There were relatively few Muslims, as we have seen, in Upper Volta in 1900. The highest number of about 30,000 out of a population of c. 400,000 lived in the province of Ouahigouya. There were also an estimated 7,000 Muslims out of a total of 300,000 inhabitants in Wagadugu province. By 1941 in the town of Wagadugu itself there were 27 Muslim schools, and in the rest of the province some 259 such schools. The total Muslim population of the province had risen to around 30,000. By the same year the Muslim population in Ouahigouya province was put at 80,000.[1]

The decade 1950—60 appears to have been a time of very rapid growth. Muslims made up 32 per cent of the population of Wagadugu town by 1956. The growth rate was not as rapid, however, in the rural areas of the province where two-thirds of the population were at this time non-Muslim. By 1959 it was estimated that there were c. 800,000 Muslims in Upper Volta, that is about 20 per cent of the total population.[2]

The Muslim traders, the Yarsé (known elsewhere as Dyula or Marka or Wangara) were responsible for much of this development.

Clozel, the Lieutenant-Governor of the colony of Upper-Senegal-Niger to which Upper Volta was attached for a time, commented in 1908 that whereas the Mossi tended to resist militant Islam seeing it as a threat to their way of life and culture, they entertained no such fear of the Yarse. The latter simply brought salt or kola to the village, said his prayers, talked to the people and moved on. Eventually he might return and was allowed to open a school or build a mosque, and the inhabitants of a village knew that his presence among them would bring the benefits of trade and commerce. As Clozel stated, each time a Yarse visited a village and then went away he left behind a little more of his religion.[3]

In addition to the Yarse the Muslim brotherhoods, in particular the Qadiriyya and the Tijaniyya orders, were active in Upper Volta during the colonial period. Both of these brotherhoods established branches in Wagadugu in the 1920s. There were also an estimated 68,000 followers of Shaikh Hamallah in Upper Volta, and this seems an appropriate place given the size of its following in Upper Volta to discuss the response of the Hamalliyya to colonial rule.

Shaikh Hamallah was the leader of the Hamalliyya from 1909. He was exiled on several occasions by the colonial administration and died in exile in France in 1942. The banishment of Shaikh Hamallah does not necessarily mean that he himself was striving to engineer the downfall of the colonial regime. In fact the decision to exile Shaikh Hamallah probably tells one more about the elements of irrational fear, suspicion and intuition in French policy towards Islam than about Shaikh Hamallah's attitude towards the colonial regime. It may also indicate something about how doctrinal issues and competition between Muslim brotherhoods played a part in preventing the emergence of a unified Muslim response to colonialism. It seems clear, for example, that Shaikh Hamallah was on occasion accused by Muslim opponents of hostility towards the colonial regime.[4]

Shaikh Hamallah and his followers were members of a branch of the Tijaniyya known as the Tijaniyya of the "Eleven Beads". The Tijani rosary has one hundred beads divided into groups of 12,18,20,20,18 and 12. Many Tijanis end their prayers by reciting twelve times the Prayer of Perfection (Jawharat al-Kamal). Shaikh Hamallah and his followers insisted that the founder of the Tijaniyya, Ahmad al-Tijani, instructed that this prayer be recited eleven and not twelve times, hence the name the Tijani of the" Eleven Beads".

The Tijani of the "Eleven Beads" attracted disciples not only in Upper Volta but also in Mauretania, Senegal, Mali, Niger, Guinea (Conakry) and the Ivory Coast. By the 1930s there were an estimated 68,000 Hamallists in Upper Volta alone, as I have already mentioned. These disciples were on several occasions involved in military confrontations with other Muslims, but whether the causes of such confrontation were always religious or whether they were directed against colonialism it is difficult to say. Moreover, it is not clear whether the Hamallists were entirely to blame for the conflicts, such as that which occurred in the province of Assaba, part of the former French Sudan, in August 1940. In this violent clash an estimated 400 people were killed and Shaikh Hamallah was held responsible by the colonial authorities and deported. According to one assessment, however, there is no conclusive evidence to show that this confrontation was directed against or intended to undermine French authority.[5]

Shaikh Hamallah was obviously regarded by the French as a threat to their authority. He was also seen by some Muslims as a destructive force and a heretic. In addition to accepting teaching concerning the Prayer of Perfection, something he learnt from the Mauretanian shaikh, Sharif al-Akhdar, founder of the Tijaniyya of the " Eleven Beads", Shaikh Hamallah while in exile in the Ivory Coast also abridged the Muslim prayer ritual. The reason for doing this is interesting. Shaikh Hamallah regarded himself while in exile in the Ivory Coast as being in a "pagan" land, and to indicate that he had no intention, if it was left to him, of staying there, he chose to adopt the abridged prayer ritual used normally by Muslims while on a journey.

Other ritual and doctrinal innovations were introduced too, many of them after the Shaikh's death. The Shahada, or confession of faith, was changed by some of his disciples to include "And our Shaikh Hamallah". One devout follower of Shaikh Hamallah was Musa Aminu, known as the Mahdi of Wani, who was initiated into the Tijaniyya of the "Eleven Beads" in 1940. Musa Aminu regarded Shaikh Hamallah as the precursor of the Mahdi and saw himself as the Mahdi. Claiming to be commanded in a vision by Prophet Muhammad to rout the "infidels", Musa Aminu settled in Bourem above Gao on the Niger and launched his holy war in March 1949. Nine people were killed in the course of the fighting including a French official, and Musa Aminu, disfigured in the encounter, himself died on 27 March 1949.

Neither Shaikh Hamallah himself nor all of his followers were aggressively or militantly anti-colonial. Moreover, some showed great tolerance towards other religions. Tierno Bokar, for example, from the family of al-Hajj 'Umar Tall, emphasised the necessity for charity, tolerance and equality above all else. On the question of equality he stressed that everyone had the same rights since all had a common divine origin.

The Hamalliyya movement was not, therefore, a militant resistance movement. Its aim at first was the reform of the Tijaniyya, and later it combined with this aim the tendency to repudiate any form of alliance with colonialism. Moreover, the movement rejected European values, in particular European social values which were regarded as profane. As one Hamallist put it, "These were a foul smelling swamp which one must pass over quickly".[6] The Hamallist retreat into mysticism may have been part of the effort to pass over this "swamp".

In addition to the brotherhoods and the charismatic leaders, the diviner also played an important role in bringing about conversions to Islam in Upper Volta and elsewhere in West Africa. One of the things many women in Upper Volta were most anxious about was whether or not they would be able to conceive. This, moreover, was an anxiety widespread among early converts to the Aladura Church in Nigeria after World War I. In order to find out the reasons why they were experiencing difficulties with regard to conception or why their children died soon after birth, women in Upper Volta went along to the diviner, just as women in Nigeria went along to the "prophet" of the Aladura Churches.[7] In some instances where there was difficulty in conceiving the diviner would recommend that the women consult a marabout. In cases where children died soon after birth the diviner explained that the reason this happened was that the child had been given a local rather than a Muslim name. To avoid this happening in the future women were advised to give their children Muslim names and to ask their husbands to build a Muslim prayer circle outside the home. One scholar comments that although he could never discover why non-Muslim diviners advised women to adopt Islam in this way, "nevertheless so effective was this technique for gaining converts to Islam that even members of the family of the chief animist priest of the village of Nobéré were not immune from it. This old man viewed the birth of Muslim grandchildren with resignation."[8]

A similar development took place in western Nigeria in the 19th century as Gbadamosi has shown. This historian writes with reference to the growth of Islam in Yorubaland in the period 1841–1908 that "some of the notables became Muslims because they heeded Ifa divinations which prescribed Islam for them as their "divine" religion.[9]

Islam also attracted converts in Upper Volta as it came to be regarded as a religion of prestige and status. Some of the Muslims in Upper Volta, like the scholar Sulayman Kafandé, became well known and attracted Muslim students from other countries. Sulayman Kafandé was considered to be "a brilliant Arabist".[10] A well educated and devout Muslim, he was highly thought of in parts of Upper Volta and became for some a reference point and a model. By 1960, then, Muslims formed between 20 and 25 per cent of the total population of Upper Volta and one of the key figures in providing

Muslims with a greater degree of unity and organisation was the marabout, Iya Haidara, from Kankan in Guinea (Conakry). He encouraged the marabouts in Wagadugu to join together and erect a central mosque and to recognise one imam or leader in prayer. This was not an easy task. The Yarse Muslim community disagreed on certain points with the Mossi Muslims, and the brotherhoods also had their differences. Moreover, the Mogho Naha was not a Muslim and, along with the colonial administration, did nothing to encourage the unity or organisational development of Islam.

Eventually all the Muslims in Wagadugu agreed to pray behind one Imam and in 1953 the colonial authorities gave permission for the building of a Grand Mosque. In 1958 a branch of the Muslim Cultural Union (U.C.M.) was established in Bobo-Dioulasso. This Union aimed at both strengthening the ties between the Muslim community at the local and national level. Moreover, in 1958 a Mauretanian marabout, Mawlay Hassan, laid the foundations of the Muslim Community of Wagadugu. This was a missionary organisation that sought to encourage and train Muslims to make use of the mass media for the propagation of Islam, and to contribute towards the building of schools, libraries and mosques. The efforts made towards integrating and organising the Muslims in Upper Volta more effectively continued on after independence, and in 1962 the Muslim Community of Wagadugu became the Muslim Community of Upper Volta with branches throughout the country.

Ivory Coast.

The Ivory Coast taken as a whole was regarded by the French colonial administration at the outset of colonial rule as a non-Muslim territory. While there were long established Muslim communities in the north of the country, there were, as we have seen, only very few, relatively small Muslim settlements in the south. However, by the beginning of World War II the colonial authorities had to change its opinion for by then, as one historian points out with a certain amount of exaggeration, "an Islamic Ivory Coast was a reality".[1]

By the outbreak of World War II Islam had certainly made remarkable progress in the southern region of the Ivory Coast, and by 1960 Muslims accounted for an estimated 22 per cent of the country's total population, as opposed to around 7 per cent in 1921.[2]

In the early period of colonial rule the French occupation and administration assisted the development of Islam in the Ivory Coast. Among other things it made the interior more accessible and also provided financial contributions towards the construction of mosques. In 1904, for example, 200 francs were given towards the construction of a mosque at Toumodi, and in the same year another 250 francs were donated to the building of a mosque at Tiassalé.[3] The administration's approach, however, changed over time and by 1910 attempts were being made to limit Islam's influence over the non-Muslim population. Moreover, Muslims were carefully watched and classified on the basis of their alleged activities as either "good" or "bad". The marabouts were placed among the "bad" or "subversive elements" and their movements on occasion were restricted, while the Dyula, so essential to the smooth running of the commercial network in the interior of the country, were allowed to travel freely.

In practice it proved impossible to destroy the influence of the marabouts. Indeed, it was the marabouts along with the Dyula who made the most significant contribution to the development of Islam in the southern region of the Ivory Coast during colonial rule. It was, for example, a marabout from Kong in the north of the country who brought about the conversion to Islam of the southern village of Ahua just before World War I.[4] According to one account of this conversion two brothers from Ahua, So Yao and So Komenan, traders who travelled between Grand Lahou and Tiassale, met the marabout from Kong and stayed with him when they were in Grand Lahou. Under his influence they eventually became Muslims and one day on returning home from Grand Lahou told their families to convert to Islam. Another account suggests that while visiting Ahua a marabout used his influence to have one of the brothers, So Yao, the chief of the village, released from prison. So Yao was freed, and he and his brother, So Komenan, and their families, impressed by the marabout's goodwill and the influence he could wield, became Muslims, and many others in the village followed their example. A similar mass conversion occurred, as we have seen, in Ijebu-Ode in western Nigeria in 1902 (see Chapter 6).

By the 1920s the Dyula were in all the important commercial centres and at the strategic points on the trade routes which crossed the region, and had established Muslim communities wherever they settled. The colonial authorities reacted to this forward march of Islam by refusing at least on two occasions in 1926 to grant Muslims permission to open Qur'anic schools. The reason given for this refusal was that the granting of permission might be seen by the non-Muslim population as an attempt by the colonial regime to favour the development of Islam at their expense.[5]

In addition to limiting the number of Qur'anic schools the authorities also attempted to control the inflow of Arabic books, journals and newspapers. Nevertheless, Qur'ans, books on Islamic history, on Arabic grammar and on other subjects arrived in the Ivory Coast from North Africa and the Middle East. Furthermore, an increasing number of Muslims in the Ivory Coast, many of them Dyula, began to adopt a more hostile approach to both the administration and to what they saw as the lax, corrupt form of Islam practiced by many Muslims in the Ivory Coast and elsewhere in West Africa.

From the 1930s to the 1950s Bouaké in the Ivory Coast was one of the most important centres of Wahhabism in West Africa. The Wahhabiyya movement, which I mentioned previously in connection with the 19th-century jihads and in relation to Ibrahim Niass's teaching, spread to towns in the Ivory Coast, Mali, Guinea, Senegal, Niger and Upper Volta. The movement is named after Shaikh Muhammad b. Abd al-Wahhab, who was born in the Najd Province of Central Arabia in 1703. Shaikh Muhammad entered into an alliance with Muhammad b. Saud, emir of Dariya in Saudia Arabia, and this alliance resulted in the establishment of the House of Saud. A campaign was launched against religious and moral laxity, against the veneration of holy men and their tombs, which they regarded as shirk, against Sufism and maraboutism. Sufism they considered to be a wrong innovation (*bid'a*) which did not exist or was not practiced in the Golden Age of Islam. Maraboutism was seen as *sihr*, or a form of magic which involved the use of the occult to change the original nature or form of an event or thing.

The Wahhabiyya was a revivalist movement which aimed at restoring Islam to its original pure form, and, as we have seen, had a limited influence on the thinking of West African Muslims in the 19th century. The movement suffered a setback in 1818 when its forces were defeated by the Egyptians, led by Muhammad Ali. Wahhabi ideas, however, continued to influence the thinking of Muslims in the Middle East and North Africa. In the 1930s a number of teachers and students at the University of al-Azhar in Egypt, a university attended by West African students, were inspired by Wahhabi doctrines. The pilgrimage to Mecca also brought Muslims from West Africa into contact with Wahhabi ideas.

Al-Hajj Abdullahi Ag Mahmud from Gao in Niger and al-Hajj Tiekodo from the Ivory Coast were but two of those influenced by Wahhabi ideas as a result of their pilgrimage to Mecca. The former attempted without much success to win over Muslims to the Wahhabi movement in Timbuktu and the surrounding areas. Al-Hajj Tiekodo, a petty trader from a Dyula clan, made the pilgrimage in the late 1930s. While in Mecca he learnt Arabic and improved his knowledge of Islamic law and philosophy, returning to the Ivory Coast in 1944. Back in the Ivory Coast he set about reforming the Islamic education system and began spreading Wahhabi ideas during his evening lectures. People apparently "crowded to these lectures". According to one report on Islam in the Ivory Coast, written in the 1950s by Governor Beyries al-Hajj, Tiekodo was "one of the most striking figures among the Ivory Coast Muslims . . . (and) the first person to have imported Ibn Wahhabi's ideas from the Hijaz (western Arabia)." The report continues, "He gave battle against the traditional clerics living in the Bouake region, then went and propagandised in Bobo-Dioulasso from where he was expelled . . . he made his own the reproaches made by the Wahhabi against the Sufi, the adoration of saints, the marabouts; he wants an Islam faithful to the Qur'an. . ."[6]

Although opposed by many Muslims, al-Hajj Tiekodo, who was arrested in 1947 and condemned to confinement in 1948, appealed to a substantial number of urban dwellers, particularly the young. They accepted his view that there was a need to emphasise the sovereignty and uniqueness of God and the establishment of a state run according to the principles of the Shari'a. At the same time these supporters of al-Hajj Tiekodo saw no conflict in supporting non-Muslim opponents of the colonial regime, such as Houphouet-Boigny and other members of the radical political party, the R.D.A.(Rassemblement Democratique Africaine). They justified their support of a non-Muslim leader by claiming that a person born a non-Muslim was not expected to embrace Islam but had simply to adhere to an ideology compatible with the stand of Muslims on secular matters. This is, of course, a very broad interpretation of Wahhabi doctrine. Many Wahhabis and Wahhabi sympathisers in the Ivory Coast joined the R.D.A. and backed the policies of the Christian, Houphouet-Boigny, who became President of the Ivory Coast in 1960.[7]

Islam, then, spread very rapidly in the southern region of the Ivory Coast during the colonial era. The much criticised marabout and the Muslim trader, at times assisted and at times hindered by the colonial authorities, were the two principal agents of this diffusion of Islam. In attempting, however, to meet the religious and material needs of the people, and to provide them selves with a livelihood, the marabouts and Dyula traders showed a great deal of tolerance for, and even mixed the practice of Islam with, unacceptible non-Islamic rituals and beliefs. This, along with colonialism which provoked a spiritual and cultural clash between colonizer and colonised, gave rise to a small but effective reformist, fundamentalist Islamic movement, based on Wahhabi principles, in the Ivory Coast. This movement, however, although one of its aims was to use Islam as a force for unity and as an instrument for creating an egalitarian society, had the effect of dividing the Muslim community, and was even denounced by the influential Sufi and scholar, the Sharif of Kankan, Shaikh Fanta Mahdi Kaba, as heretical. The Wahhabis still exist in the Ivory Coast but since independence they have been much less hostile to the traditional Muslim leadership and the marabouts.

Nigeria.

Northern Nigeria.

In this section, although the main concern is with the development of Islam in Nigeria during the colonial era, some further consideration will be given to the question of the Islamic response to colonialism in Nigeria. In assessing the growth of Islam in Nigeria in the period 1900−1960 I make use of a certain amount of statistical data which I would like to emphasise from the outset is not altogether reliable. C.E. Meek stated with reference to the Religious Statistics for Northern Nigeria gathered in the 1921 Census, "They are rather estimates rendered by the enumerators after − in many cases − somewhat haphazard inquiry. Nevertheless they are of great value as giving an approximate idea of the relative strength of the three main forms of religion (Islam, Christianity and Traditional Religion) practised".[1] Meek's comment applies with certain qualifications to most of the statistical data on religious development collected during the colonial era and since.

The jihad and the establishment of the Sokoto Caliphate in the early 19th century did not lead to the wholesale conversion to Islam of the population of northern Nigeria. Indeed by 1900 there were still substantial non-Muslim minorities in all the emirates of Northern Nigeria. Although Bauchi Town, for example, the capital of the Bauchi Emirate, was predominantly Muslim, the people of Dass, some 40 kilometres to the west of Bauchi Town, were almost entirely non-Muslim. Moreover, regions such as the Jos Plateau were once again almost 100 per cent non-Muslim. To this day in certain areas of northern Nigeria, such as Birnin Gwari in Kaduna State, the majority of the population of the rural areas are non-Muslim. As Murray Last has pointed out for Hausaland, the main non-Muslim areas in northern Nigeria are to be found "on the boundaries between the major emirates, between Sokoto and Katsina, Katsina and Kano, Kano and Zaria". These non-Muslims in

Hausaland are referred to by the Muslims as Maguzawa, "people whom it was justifiable to have living alongside Muslims in peace". The same scholar then makes the interesting point that the Maguzawa "were not really the targets for jihad even in the early 19th century . . . the jihad of 1804 was primarily a reform movement, reforming lax Muslims, not converting pagans. It was ideologically probably less concerned with the Kufr (unbelief) of pagans than with the Kufr of those Muslims who opposed the jihad."[2]

The attitude of the Muslim rulers to the Maguzawa, as outlined by Last, deserves a brief mention. The Maguzawa were liable to be more heavily taxed than Muslims and to have more demands made upon them but were also seen as an asset. They were hard workers and bold fighters and the emirs were careful not to alienate them or drive them out of their territory. The emirs disapproved of their "unbelief", the fact that they did not perform salat to Allah, but nevertheless considered them to be good citizens who evidently feared Allah and made up for their unbelief by being very generous when it came to acts of charity such as almsgiving. This attitude towards non-Muslims did not differ a great deal from that of some of the Muslim Dyula who did not take any steps to convert non-Muslims, believing that any non-Muslim who led a good life would after death become Muslims before entering Paradise and would thereby be saved. Of course I am not suggesting that non-Muslims were never the targets of jihad, or that they were never captured and enslaved. They were, and some of the resistance to Islam and the opposition to learning Arabic found today among non-Muslims in northern Nigeria is in part attributable to the fact that Muslims have in the past conquered and enslaved their people. The point, however, needs to be made that Islam did not set out to force all non-Muslims to become Muslims at the point of the sword, nor did it enslave or despise all non-Muslims in northern Nigeria.

In northern Nigeria, as was the case in southern Nigeria and in many other places in West Africa during the colonial era, Islam made considerable headway. In the Bauchi Emirate of northern Nigeria Muslims constituted about 50 per cent of the population in 1920 and by 1952 they formed about 75 per cent. In Adamawa province during the same period there was an actual decrease in the Muslim population of about 0.7 per cent. In Borno Emirate in north-eastern Nigeria between 1931 and 1952 the Muslim population rose from 74.9 per cent to 83.5 per cent.[3] The table below sets out the average percentage increase or decline in the Muslim population in northern Nigeria according to province between 1931 and 1952.

The system of indirect rule which the British colonial administration operated in northern Nigeria and the improvements in communications appear to have facilitated the growth and expansion of Islam. Muslims took advantage of the construction of roads and railways and the establishment of new towns such as Jos, in Plateau State, to expand their commercial and "religious" interests. Literate in Hausa and Arabic, and with a developed trading network, many Muslims travelled along the new roads and railways into non-Muslim areas such as the Jos Plateau, and even into the south and east of Nigeria, to commercial centres such as Ijebu-Ode, Ibadan, Lagos, Onitsha, Benin and Port Harcourt.

PROVINCE	PERCENTAGE OF MUSLIM POPULATION		INCREASE	DECLINE
	1931	1952		
Adamawa	30.8	30.1		0.7%
Bauchi	65.8	74.1	8.3%	
Benue	6.1	10.6	4.5%	
Borno	74.9	83.5	8.6%	
Ilorin	43.5	62.6	19.1%	
Kabba	7.5	22.4	14.9%	
Kaṇo	97.5	98.0	0.5%	
Katsina	-	95.2	-	
Niger	44.6	44.1		0.5%
Plateau	10.1	24.1	14.0%	
Sokoto	92.1	94.0	1.9%	
Zaria	-	64.4	-	

TABLE I:　*Percentage of Muslim population in northern Nigeria according to province, 1931—1952.*

Furthermore, with a system of law not confined to a particular locality and not bound by ethnic ties, Muslims saw in the expanding economy and commercial system the opportunity to display their talents for trade and commerce. And in trade and commerce lay wealth, which for the vast majority of Nigerians was a symbol of status and upward social mobility. In addition Muslims had a secure hold over much of the "traditional" commercial and trading activity, and over many of the still important arts and crafts. They were also, through long experience, skilled in the organisation and administration of large markets and were extremely literate in terms of market language and values.

I will give two examples of how Islam took root among non-Muslims in northern Nigeria in this way during the colonial era. The first example concerns the Dadiya people of the Tangale-Waja region of the Bauchi Emirate and the second the Pyem people of the Jos Plateau.

The Dadiya district of the Tangale-Waja region was entirely non-Muslim prior to 1907.[5] In that year Hausa traders, trading in ivory, came to Dadiya from Kano. These traders took the ivory to the Muslim market near Kano. While in Dadiya "these Hausa pray five times a day, slaughter any animal before eating it, fast every year . . . the Dadiya people observed all this and some began to practise it. . . . And when the Dadiyans began to want to cooperate more with the Hausa people they were told there is not any other religion leading to Paradise apart from Islam". Here one can see in operation in the conversion process what has been termed the "genius of ritual". But what is even more interesting and relevant is the fact that the Hausa "refused to share food with the Dadiyans because they said they could not eat with non-Muslims". Further, the Muslims could not allow the Dadiyans to be "full" trading partners until they became Muslims. "Many Dadiyans, informants say, "became Muslims in order to share in the meal and to be able to co-operate with the Hausa . . . some went off to Borno to study Islam under Mallam Adamu . . . and on returning home opened a Qur'anic school, others became traders . . . the Hausa, a number of whom were mallams, left the area eventually, moving on to Yola on the river Benue".

The Pyem live on the south-east escarpment of the Jos Plateau, and although composed of a number of immigrant groups they have a common language and at the onset of colonial rule acknowledged the ritual authority and leadership of the Bwalbon or head priest. The Pyem's first contacts with Islam were made in the 19th century through their links with the Bauchi Emirate, established by Emir Yakubu in 1805. The Pyem were the middle men in the trade between the Bauchi Emirate and the non-Muslim, unconquered peoples in the south of the Jos-Bauchi Plateau. Moreover, Muslim Fulani pastoralists stayed in Pyem territory while purchasing slaves in return for cattle, and in the 1830s built a mosque in the Pyem settlement of Dutsen Langai. Very few of the Pyem, however, became Muslims in the 19th century. Yet by 1960 an estimated 60 per cent of them were Muslims.[6]

A number of measures taken by the colonial administration facilitated the growth of Islam among the Pyem in the 20th century. First of all the Pyem district was incorporated into the Bauchi Emirate in 1907 and administered by Ajiya of Bauchi. Then the colonial administration appointed chiefs, known as "European" chiefs, who took their place alongside the priest-chiefs as their assistants, in whom formerly political and religious authority resided and who wielded considerable economic power.[7] However, when there was a disagreement between the priest-chiefs and the European-appointed chiefs, the administration tended to throw its weight behind the latter, thereby further undermining the authority of the former.

Furthermore, colonial rule made it easier for the Muslim trader to move freely and unmolested in Pyem territory and on the Jos Plateau generally, whereas in the 19th century occasional wars between the Plateau and the Emirates of Zaria and Bauchi had made such freedom of movement more difficult.[8] By the 1920s Muslims had established markets in Pyem towns such as Gindiri, and Muslim craftsmen and mallams joined the Muslim traders to swell the ranks of the Muslim community. A new system of administration, therefore, combined with a new authority structure and Muslim control of the markets — the most frequented and important place in any African town or village — assisted the growth of Islam among the Pyem, an estimated 60 per cent of whom were Muslims by 1960.[9] I do not, of course, wish to suggest that conversion to Islam among the Pyem or any other group or in the case of individuals for that matter was simply the consequence of "material" developments and interests, but simply that these appear to have assisted the spread of Islam. As Max Weber suggests, people are motivated by ideal as well as material interests.[10]

Other factors also assisted the development of Islam in northern Nigeria during the colonial era. I have mentioned the role of the Muslim traders in Dadiya, and one must also bear in mind the activities of such influential Muslim leaders as the Sardauna of Sokoto, Ahmadu Bello, around the time of and shortly after independence. The Sardauna, partly to counterbalance the success of Ibrahim Niass "Reformed" Tijaniyya movement, increased the strength of the Qadiriyya brotherhood, the oldest brotherhood in northern

Nigeria, and engaged in conversion tours throughout northern Nigeria. The numbers converted according to some estimates run into hundreds of thousands. It was recorded that during the 1964 conversion tour some 100,000 people in Zaria and Niger provinces converted to Islam.[11] I shall return to the Sardauna in the next chapter, but before leaving him at this point it is worth mentioning that like Ibrahim Niass he was concerned with strengthening the ties between Muslims in Nigeria and the rest of the Muslim world. He was also like Niass an active campaigner for the spread of literacy in Arabic.

Meanwhile, increasingly from the 1940s other Muslims in northern Nigeria, in contrast to the Sardauna and Niass, were emphasising that although the Islamic education system should not only be preserved but also developed and expanded, it was also necessary to provide far more people, both men and women, with the skills and qualifications gained in the Western education system. Persuaded of the necessity to provide all his people with the advantages offered by both the Islamic and Western education systems, the Emir of Katsina opened a school for Muslim girls. This was of course in line with the teachings of Usuman dan Fodio who in his book 'Nur al-Alhab' strongly condemned as an "impious practice" the fact that most of the 'ulama left their wives and daughters uneducated. Usuman, although he was referring here primarily to the religious education of women, also in the same work and in his other writings speaks of the need to educate women in, for example, commercial subjects. He wrote, "It is as binding upon her to endeavour to know these (commercial subjects) as it is . . . to know about other matters pertaining to her religion like ablutions, fasting and praying".[12]

In addition to their understanding of the Qur'an, which encourage Muslims to seek knowledge wherever it is to be found, some Muslim leader in northern Nigeria were also encouraged to demand a more broadly based education for their people as a result of economic and political developments. During World War II the process of industrialisation gained momentum in northern Nigeria, particularly in Kano, and an ever increasing number of Muslims began to seek employment in factories, on the railways and in the administration. But although there was a "northernisation" policy which gave preference to people born in the north, the northerner was considered to have one major disadvantage, namely that he or she lacked the skills provided by a Western education, in particular literacy in English. Out of an estimated 12 million people in northern Nigeria in 1952, only about a quarter of a million had a basic competence in English, while in Kano, as I have already mentioned, only about 23,000 out of 3 million people were literate in English, and of these 50 per cent were from other parts of Nigeria.

This situation created fear and tension and led to frequent attacks on the inadequacy and pragmatic nature of British colonial policy. Aminu Kano who from the 1940s campaigned against illiteracy among all sections of the population and in particular among girls, condemned the indirect rule system as "a political belief fashioned solely for the purpose of maintaining law and order . . . a system . . . (that) makes the progress towards independence infinitely slow".[13] Other voices, such as that of Isa Wali, were raised against "ignorance" and the oppression of women. Wali wrote in 1956: "As for public life there is nothing in Islam which prevents a woman from any pursuit she desires . . . modern history in fact is full of the accounts of Muslim women . . . who had been glorious rulers, counsellors, jurists and great public servants."[14]

The industrialisation and independence processes, therefore, prompted a number of prominent Muslims in northern Nigeria to attack the indirect rule system and to demand the modernisation of the educational and political institutions of the north. Governor Bourdillon had realised the consequences of preserving the "status quo" in the north in 1940. In a memorandum to the Secretary of the Northern Provinces he stated: "Surely the question we have to ask ourselves is "Can the inhabitants of the Northern Provinces play their full part in the political, economic and social life of their country without a greatly extended use of the English language?" There can be only one answer — No!"[15]

A number of literacy schemes were implemented and more schools were built. These changes, however, some northern Nigerians argue, came too late. Haroun Adamu argues that the "backwardness" of northern Nigeria is due to the reluctance of the colonial government and the emirs to introduce English from the beginning of colonial rule. Northerners as a result were not equipped to deal with the challenges of industrialisation and modernisation. The idea that the colonial government intended Nigeria to be dominated by the south is also present. Sa'adu Zungur's fictitious interview between the "North" and the colonial master has been quoted more than once by disillusioned northerners: "I have now discovered that it is your intention to release the Southern forces to come and march on me. I feel that you have reneged on your promise. Why did you fail to wake me up much earlier?"[16] A Permanent Secretary in the Federal Government, a northern Nigerian, commenting on Lugard's educational policy in Nigeria from 1900 to 1906 and from 1912 to 1918 wrote, "We can only deduce from the evidence of contemporary records that the educational policy in Northern Nigeria was a carefully designed muddle calculated to retard the progress of a naturally intelligent people and to isolate the North from the South."

The educational policy of the colonial administration was no doubt "pragmatic". There is evidence that it implicitly at least was designed to preserve the *status quo* in the north and thereby secure a firm foundation for the colonial regime. It is, however, a fact that there was little demand for Western education in northern Nigeria until the Second World War. Colonialism encountered an Islam concerned like itself, but for different reasons, to preserve the Islamic politico-religious system established by the Sokoto jihadists in the first half of the 19th century.

However, with the emergence of organised independence parties and the developments in industrialisation from the 1940s, some northern Nigerians began to see the indirect rule system and the limitation of Western education in the North to a chosen few as "paternalism" and an attempt to maintain European mastery. This perspective, however, has somewhat altered in the age of nation-building since independence when the emphasis is on the preservation of Nigerian culture, now being undermined by neo-colonialism. Analysing the unsuitability of Western models — educational, political and economic — for Nigeria, some Nigerians claim that indirect rule, by not completely destroying Nigerian culture, left a foundation on which Nigeria can now build her own political and educational systems. These people suggest, moreover, that Hausa, never replaced by English as the main vehicle of communication in northern Nigeria, could be used as the *lingua franca* for the whole country.

Southern Nigeria.
Statistics vary as to the extent of the Islamisation of southern Nigeria during the colonial era (c. 1900−1960). In 1926 Amaurey Talbot wrote, "By far the greater part of the population of the Southern Provinces (of Nigeria) is heathen and devoted to animism and ancestor worship."[17] Muslims, according to Amaurey Talbot's statistics, constituted 5 per cent of the total population of the Southern Provinces, and the Christians 9 per cent. (See Table II below.) By 1963, according to one group of statistics, Muslims made up 43.4 per cent of the population in western Nigeria and 44.3 per cent of the population in Lagos.[18]

Although there are many possible explanations for the advance of Islam in western and southern Nigeria during the colonial era, it seems to me that one of the most important reasons is to be found in the sphere of education. As we saw in the last chapter, Muslims felt with some justification that Western education was simply an instrument to be used for the purpose of converting them and the rest of the non-Christian population to Christianity. Sensitive to the Muslim feeling on this issue the colonial government reacted by creating government-aided Muslim schools with an integrated curriculum. This system, however, was poorly financed and proved inadequate. Muslims, nevertheless, still anxious to preserve and defend their faith developed their own methods of dealing with Western education. Encouraged by African nationalists like Edward Blyden, by the British-born Muslim solicitor, Abdullah Quillam, who visited Lagos in 1894, by the Sultan of Turkey and by the colonial administration, and anxious to participate in the modern sector of the economy, Muslim organisations emerged with the aim of providing Muslims with a Western education while at the same time giving them a firm grounding in the Islamic sciences. These societies removed, as far as Muslims were concerned, the need or the fear of having to convert to Christianity in order to acquire the skills necessary for full participation in the new administrative and economic order.

TABLE II:	*Percentage proportion of adherents of each religion in southern Nigeria to the total population, 1921.*	
RELIGION		% of total population
Protestants		7
R. Catholics		2
Total Christians		9
Muslims		5
Traditional Religionists		86

The movement to modernise Islam and integrate Western and Islamic education began, as I have already mentioned, in the 1890s. Societies like the Egbe Killa were established in Lagos then, with the aim of introducing to Muslims all those ideas and developments including Western education not in conflict with Islamic principles. Soon the society had branches in many towns in western Nigeria. The Ahmadiyya movement, which emerged in India in the 1880s and established a branch in Lagos in 1911, had similar aims to .the Egbe Killa as far as education was concerned. Regarded by Sunni Muslims as heretical because, among other things, of its teaching about its founder, Ghulam Ahmad, the Promised Messiah, which is said to go against orthodox Muslim teaching, the Ahmadiyya movement was less influential than other organisations such as the Ansar-Ud-Deen Society founded in 1923. This society's constitution laid down that Muslims were to be given a full and complete training in the Islamic sciences and that the society was to enter into the broader field of education on the model of the Christian missions. By 1960 the society had about 50,000 members and ran several teachers training colleges, secondary schools and over 200 primary schools. Other movements with the same objectives emerged in southern Nigeria: the Muslim Association of Nigeria, the Nawair Ud-Deen Society, the Ijebu Muslim Friendly Society and the Isabatudeen Society.[20]

The Ijebu-Ode Muslim Friendly Society established in 1927 opened a Muslim school in January 1930. The purpose of the society was, according to its constitution, to "prevent the conversion of Muslims to Christianity and to rescue our fellow Muslims from backwardness". In addition to the school, the society started a tennis club and a football club "to play matches against the Europeans". A drama society was also started where "only plays with practical lessons on the shortcomings of our people are to be presented".[21] Tea parties were held for Muslims returning from Mecca and the qualifications for membership of the society were an unswerving commitment to Islam, good character and "at least Standard IV English".

In Ibadan a woman, Alhaja Humana Alaga, founded the Isabatudeen (Band of religious enthusiasts) Society in the 1950s to provide Muslim girls with a sound Muslim and Western education.[22] Alhaja Humana cites the Qur'an, for example, Suras 2 v269, 20 vv114, 29 v20, 39 v9, 58 v11 and 96 vv1-5, to prove that there is no incompatibility between the two systems. At Isabatudeen Girls Grammar School, Ibadan, Islamic Knowledge, Arabic, English Language and Literature, History, Geography, Domestic Science and Mathematics are taught. Outlining her reasons for establishing this school, Alhaja Humana stated that she found it difficult to get her daughters into mission schools, that girls in mission schools changed their names and religion and that "Muslims did not have confidence in themselves and that their brothers of other religions did not have confidence in them either . . . also the society wants to raise the status of Islamic women".[23]

The Muslim decision to accept Western education is not solely explicable in terms of its being a response to the challenge of Christianity and the need to acquire skills to participate in the political and economic order. The emergence of nationalist parties, such as the Nigerian Youth Movement, put considerable pressure on Muslims to acquire a Western education. So, too, did developments in local politics where it was becoming apparent to Muslims that the Western-educated, who also for the most part happened to be Christians, were dominating affairs. The Nigerian Youth Movement (N.Y.M.) in its newspaper, the *Daily Service*, carried on a campaign throughout the 1930s and 1940s to encourage Muslims to see in Western education a revolutionary force which they could use to improve their standard of living, and put an end to Western exploitation and domination. The N.Y.M. dissociated Western from Christian education, criticising the latter on the grounds that it alienated Africans by its exaggerated emphasis on the "other worldly" dimension of life. "Africa," the *Daily Service* stated in one of its editorials, "is no longer the Dark Continent where the ignorant Native can be carried away with obsolete theories of a heaven in some geographical region to which he may proceed after impoverishing himself below by selling all he has."[24]

Muslims were encouraged to embrace Western education in order to be able to participate in the government and administration of the "New Africa". "The welfare of Nigeria as a whole," the *Daily Service* argued, "is dependent on the education of the Muslim masses." Christians were asked to help the Ansar-Ud-Deen Society, "that progressive band of renascent Muslim youth", to build schools. This did actually happen in Ondo and elsewhere.[25]

I do not want to give the impression that the Muslim associations that advocated the integration of Islamic and Western education and attempted to "modernise" Islam so to speak, appealed to all Muslims. There were Muslim scholars in western Nigeria whose main concern was not to adapt Western education to Islam but rather to construct an Islam with its own separate, distinct identity. In their writings and preaching these scholars launched frequent and vigorous attacks on the indigenous religion, and put forward a variety of arguments to prove the "oneness" and "uniqueness" of God. It was argued that, for example, the uniformity of creation proved that there could only be one creator. This uniformity was evidenced by the fact that all creatures have the same features.[26] A number of writings were devoted to Sufism. The Tijani scholar, Alfa Oke-Koto, wrote about the qualities imparted by Sufism, one of which was the quality to love and hate the right people, another was the quality to order people to do good and avoid evil and another to serve God loyally. Muslims were warned against taking part in politics because they would be obliged to compromise their beliefs by associating with non-Muslim rulers. Given the whole history of the alliance between mallams and chiefs in western Nigeria this was a particularly radical demand. Traditional practices, further, such as scarification and prostration when greeting an Oba (chief) or elder were condemned as un-Islamic. The Muslim, it was argued (and al-Maghili, Usuman dan Fodio and many other Muslim scholars who had observed this custom made the same point) should use his body only to show homage and respect to God. To prostrate before a superior was to equate him with God. The practice, nevertheless, of women "genuflecting" to their husbands was considered lawful.[27]

The increase in the pilgrim traffic from southern Nigeria to Mecca, the establishment of Muslim printing-presses and the growth in volume of Tijani, Mahdist and Wahhabi literature in the region also contributed to the emergence of this reformist tradition. Prior to 1918 very few southern Nigerians

are on record as having made the pilgrimage to Mecca. In 1918, 34 left for
Mecca from Abeokuta and a number from Lagos and Ilorin.[28] By the 1920s
pilgrims were leaving from Ijebu-Ode, Ibadan, Iwo, Ondo, Oyo, Ogbomoso
and other towns in southern Nigeria. The hajj took, in some cases, up to 10
years and some of the pilgrims stayed in Mahdist villages, such as that of Mai
Wurno in the Sudan. Others worked on the cotton plantations at Gezira.
They were exposed to a considerable amount of pan-Islamic and anti-
Western propaganda.[29] Some of the pilgrims attended lectures at al-Ahzar,
others became agents for publishing houses in Egypt and the Middle East.

Not all pilgrims, however, returned from Mecca full of reforming zeal and
orthodox views. An informant who made the pilgrimage in 1947 stated: "All
human beings are complete. Some things you can change, some you cannot.
In Mecca they smoke big pipe, long one, longer than yours . . . you cannot
practice that one here in Nigeria."[30] Others read what they wanted into what
they saw and observed. If Muslims in the Sudan and Hijaz, some argued, visit
the tombs of their prophets and saints, why should we not visit the tombs of
Nigerian prophets?" Some did conclude that it was lawful to visit the shrine
of Birikisu in the forest at the village of Oke-Eri near Ijebu-Ode.[31] On
balance, however, the evidence suggests that pilgrims were inclined to be
more fundamentalist and orthodox as a result of such an experience as the
hajj: "You can see everything there (in Mecca) . . . the place where Adam was
buried, the mountain where Muhammad hid himself," one pilgrim stated. He
added, "The religion was very good . . . not like here in Nigeria."[32]

The establishment of Muslim printing-presses in southern Nigeria in the
1930s assisted those Muslims intent on reforming Islam. The first Muslim
printing-press was set up in Abeokuta in 1933. The Sebbiotimo Press in Ijebu-
Ode, the Barika Printing Works in Ibadan and the Ugunbanwo Printing
Works in Oyo followed. By 1952 there were 16 printing-presses in Abeokuta,
publishing works in Arabic and Yoruba such as "A Guide to Prayer" which
sold 5,000 copies on the first edition and ran to four editions. Other books, on
"Intention", Sufism, Arabic grammar and the life of Prophet Muhammad
were also published.[33] The printing-presses, like the pilgrimage, contributed
to the creation of a more thorough-going Muslim culture. Islam came to be
seen more as a blueprint of the social order than as a private, personal belief
system. Further evidence of this can be seen in the demands, more frequent
from the 1920s, for the implementation of the Shari'a and the establishment
of Shari'a Courts. The colonial system of justice began to be regarded as a
form of "Christian" law which militated against Muslim interests. When a
mallam, preaching in Lagos, was assassinated and the assassin, on grounds of
insufficient evidence it was alleged, was not convicted, Muslims argued that
the assassin had hidden behind the Christian law.[34]

The Bamidele movement, founded in Ibadan in the 1930s, although not
typical of the reform movement as a whole, imposed what it regarded as the
observance of Islam on its members. Purdah and seclusion were imposed on
women, and men were obliged to wear the turban and *riga* (gown), and shave
their heads and grow beards, in imitation of Prophet Muhammad. The movement also imposed its own version of the Shari'a: for adultery between 40 and
80 lashes are administered. The students, for pedagogic reasons, administer

the punishment. Scarification, tatooing and such like practices are forbidden under pain of hell fire.[35]

The Bamidele and similar organisations tended to attract those people who were left hanging between two worlds, in particular the semi-literate, whose standard of education tended to take them a step away from the old pattern of living but was not sufficient to enable them to succeed in the "new order".[36] As one person expressed it in Ibadan in 1929 in a letter to the *Yoruba News*: "Western education . . . has come to naught . . . it has been an increasing source of prolific affliction and poverty. Many formerly employed are now unemployed. A man who formerly ate from a table now eats from a leaf. . . . Our fathers were not Europeanised and could carry out their responsibilities."[37]

The Qur'anic school, on the other hand, had the advantage of not raising pupils' hopes too high in terms of employment prospects in the civil service and similar institutions. Moreover, while the Ansar-Ud-Deen schools catered for many, they could not cater for all. Many, many people had neither the time nor the money to pursue a secondary education. The educational needs of these people were met by the Qur'anic school, which enjoyed enormous success during the colonial era. In Ijebu-Ode alone between 1894 and 1960 some 57 Qur'anic schools were established, and through them, with fees being paid in kind, the tenets and practices of Islam, along with a basic knowledge of Islamic history and of Arabic, were imparted to many who either wanted little or expected little from the new order.[38]

Other parts of Nigeria.
Islam made significant progress in the old "Middle Belt" zone of Nigeria which during the colonial era formed part of the Northern region. In 1931 an estimated 6 per cent of the people of the Middle Belt were Muslim and by 1952 Muslims formed an estimated 10 per cent of the population, which means that there were about 100,000 Muslims in the region, which of course incorporated part of Ilorin and Lafia. Many of these Muslims were traders from cities further north such as Kano and Jos. As early as the first decade of the 20th century the Catholic missionaries in eastern Nigeria were alarmed by the number of Muslim traders moving from the north to the south.[39]

It has also been pointed out that the emergence of a dynamic and expanding Islam in the Middle Belt was assisted by the involvement in the region of the Northern People' Congress (N.P.C.) prior to and during the 1959 Federal election. It is not clear that, according to one scholar, the N.P.C. consciously made use of this obvious appeal (Islam) during the 1959 election.[40] The N.P.C. did, however, put a great deal of money into the Middle Belt, and did in certain areas, where the Muslim population was small, adopt non-Muslim candidates.[41]

The growth of Islam in the mid-western region during the colonial era was largely the result of the establishment of Muslim communities there by Muslim traders from northern and western Nigeria. Moreover, the Ahmadiyya movement, and more recently the Ansar-Ud-Deen Society, have been active in the mid-western region, the area covered roughly today by

Bendel State. Furthermore, in the old eastern region of Nigeria a number of Muslim communities were established during the colonial era, and others have been established since then. There are Muslim centres, for instance, in Enugu, Onitsha, Owerri, Umuahia, Nsukka and Awka among other places.

Throughout the colonial period there were Muslims in eastern Nigeria, that is from about 1903, but they were mainly traders and simply passed through. Some did settle and sent their children to Christian mission run schools. It was not, however, until the 1930s that an organised, "indigenous", Muslim Community began to emerge in the former eastern region of Nigeria. Two of the first and most influential and active leaders of this community were Alhaji Sufiyan Agwasim, a Roman Catholic who converted to Islam in 1935, and Yesufu Awah who also became a Muslim in 1935.[42] The former established a Consultative Islamic Society, the Jama'atu Muharrar ul-Musulumi, and the latter became the muezzin of the Owerri Central Mosque. Other relatively old centres of Islam in the east of Nigeria are Ibagwa-Nkwo and Nsukka.

Conclusions.

For Islam, then, the colonial era was one of rapid expansion. According to one estimate, 34 per cent of the total population of West Africa was Muslim by the 1950s.[43] We have seen that in the southern region of the Ivory Coast, in western Nigeria, and in Upper Volta, among other places, Islam made considerable headway during the period c. 1900 — 1960. By 1960, moreover, Mauretania was almost 100 per cent Muslim, and Muslims formed the majority of the population of Senegal, the Gambia, Guinea (Conakry) and Mali by the same date. There was also a very substantial Muslim population in Liberia and Sierra Leone by independence.

In the colonial period the administrations adopted different policies towards Islamic as circumstances dictated and the Islamic responses to colonialism were highly complex and varied. Moreover, adherents of the traditional religions reacted in a variety of different ways to Islamic penetration, while Muslims adopted different approaches towards indigenous religions. While in western Nigeria and the Ivory Coast, for example, there were what amounted to "mass conversions to Islam" from the indigenous religions, attempts were made elsewhere to revive the indigenous religion and turn it into a barrier against Islamic penetration. Such a revival was led by M'Penni Dembelé in Walo, in the district of San in Mali. M'Penni Dembelé, the "Man of Walo", is said to have been the recipient of revelations in 1945, and inspired and guided by these revelations he attempted to unify local rituals and reinforce the traditional moral basis of rural society.

The relations between Muslims and Christians were at the official level in certain areas characterised by mutual suspicion and competition. At the grass roots, in the towns and villages, these relations were generally speaking characterised by mutual tolerance and respect, although at this level also there was debate and competition, and on occasion attitudes of superiority were adopted by both sides.

As was the case during other periods, there were during the colonial era a variety of strands to Islam in West Africa, some of which were to an extent the product of the rather bizarre situation created by colonialism. There were, for example, revivalists who emphasised the uniqueness and all-embracing, eternal relevance of Qur'anic teaching and who opposed any form of change or innovation, which meant that among other things they opposed all "Western" ways and ideas. Then there were others who, while believing that they were being just as faithful to the Qur'an, looked for ways and means of reconciling Islamic teaching with ideas and practices that they claimed were in appearance only foreign to Islam, whether they were "Western" or part of the indigenous culture and heritage. Then, without much debate or reference to the Qur'an or Hadith, there were those Muslims who were prepared to absorb into Islam a variety of different influences, ideas and practices regardless of whether or not there was "doctrinal" justification for doing so.

Finally, we saw that as colonialism approached its "sudden death" Islam in many parts of West Africa was becoming more organised and began increasingly once again as had been the case in the pre-colonial period to strengthen its links with the rest of the Muslim world. These two trends are among the most striking aspects of Islam's development in West Africa in the post-colonial period.

Notes.

Colonial "policy" towards Islam.

1   M. Crowder, *West Africa Under Colonial Rule* (London, 1968), pp. 62 *ff.*
2   Hargreaves, ed, *France and West Africa, op. cit.*, p. 147.
3   *Ibid.*, p. 147.
4   M. Crowder, *Senegal: A Study of French Assimilation Policy* (Oxford, 1962).
5   Hargreaves, *op. cit.*, p. 212.
6   A. Gouilly, *L'Islam dans l'Afrique Occidental Française* (Paris, 1952), p. 261.
7   D. Cruise O'Brien, "Towards an Islamic Policy in French West Africa", *J.A.H.* VIII (1967), p. 303.
8   R. Aron, *Main Currents in Sociological Thought* (Middlesex, England, 1977), Vol. 1, pp. 63–111.
9   E. Durkheim, *Elementary Forms of Religious Life*, translated by J. Ward Swain (London, 1971), p. 209 *et passim.*
10   Cruise O'Brien, *op. cit.*, p. 305.
11   Hargreaves, *op. cit.*, p. 148.
12   A. Quellien, "La Politique Musulmane dans l'Afrique Occidentale Française", Thèse de Doctorat, Sorbonne, Paris, 1910, p. 178.
13   P.B. Clarke, "The Methods and Ideology of the Holy Ghost Fathers in Eastern Nigeria 1885–1905" in O.U. Kalu, ed, *Christianity in West Africa* (London, 1980), p. 45.
14   J. Paden, *Religion and Political Culture in Kano* (California, 1973), p. 172.
15   See for example the poems of Sa'adu Zungur in *The Poetry, Life and Opinions of Sa'adu Zungur*, edited with an introduction by Dandatti Abdulkadir (Zaria, 1974).
16   J. Paden, *op. cit.*, pp. 319–320.
17   Nigerian National Archives (N.A.I.) IJE-PROF 4J819, Supt of Education's report on the Muslim school, Ijebu-Ode, 11/8/1931.

Islamic responses to colonial rule.

1 W.O.A. Nasiru, "Islamic Learning among the Yoruba 1896 — 1963", Ph.D. thesis, University of Ibadan 1977, p. 147.
2 N.A.I. IJE-PROF 1/2061 Letter from the Secretary of the Western Provinces to Resident Ijebu Province, 17/12/1942.
3 *Ibid.*
4 Quellien, *op. cit.*, pp. 178 *ff.*
5 C.S. Sp Archives, Paris, Boîte 164, Doss B, Lettres Divers, 1911 — 1919.
6 Norris, *Shinqiti Folk Literature and Song*, *op. cit.*, p. 18.
7 Norris, *The Tuaregs*, *op. cit.*, pp. 168 — 171 *et passim.*
8 P.B. Clarke, "Mahdism: The History of a Revolutionary Ideology in West Africa with special reference to Nigeria 1900 — 1950", University of Ibadan Staff and Post-Graduate seminar paper, 1978. Also "Islamic Millenarianism in West Africa: A Revolutionary Ideology?" in *Religious Studies* 16, (1980), pp. 317 — 339.
9 Norris, *The Tuaregs*, *op. cit.*, p. 172.
10 Adeleye, *Power and Diplomacy*, *op. cit.*, p. 343.
11 *Ibid.*, pp. 261 *ff.*
12 *Ibid.*, p. 274.
13 Quoted in Paden, *op. cit.*, p. 54.
14 *Ibid.*, p. 55.
15 Adeleye, *op. cit.*, p. 284.
16 *Ibid.*, p. 309
17 N.A.I. C.S.O. 26/1/0937 Vols 1 and 2, Files on Islamic political movements compiled by G.J.F. Tomlinson and G.J. Lethem.
18 Clarke, "Mahdism . . .", *op. cit.*, pp. 6 *ff.*
19 Adeleye, *op. cit.*, pp. 323 *ff.*
20 *Ibid.*, pp. 325 — 6.
21 Tomlinson and Lethem, *op. cit.*
22 Paden, *op. cit.*, p. 178.

Development of Islam during the colonial era:

Senegal.
1 Quellien, *op. cit.*, p. 70
2 M. Klein, *Islam and Imperialism in Senegal* (Edinburgh, 1968), p. 218.
3 *Ibid.*, pp. 219 *ff.*
4 *Ibid.*, p. 219.
5 C.S. Sp Archives, Paris, Boîte 164, Doss B, Lettres Divers, 1900 — 1910.
6 Klein, *op. cit.*, p. 220.
7 D. Cruise O'Brien, *The Mourides of Senegal* (Oxford, 1971). And for a critique of studies on the Murids see J. Copans, *Les Marabouts de l'Arachide* (Paris, 1980), especially Chapters 1 and 2.
8 Copans, *op. cit.*, p. 170.
9 *Ibid.*, p. 169.
10 *Ibid.*, p. 169.
11 *Ibid.*, p. 169.
12 Cruise O'Brien, *The Mourides of Senegal*, *op. cit.*, p. 13.
13 *Ibid.*, p. 11.
14 C.S. Sp Archives, Paris, Boîte 159, Senegambia 1880 — 1890, Rapport sur la colonne de Fouta, St Louis, 2/1/1882.
15 D. Bouche, *Les Villages de Liberté en Afrique Noire Française 1887 — 1910* (Paris, 1968).

16 Cruise O'Brien, *The Mourides, op. cit.*, p. 77.

17 C.S. Sp Archives., Paris, Boîte 164, Doss B, Lettres Diverses 1911–1919, Voyages des Séminaristes à Rufisque, 25–27/1/1913.

18 L. Behrman, "French Muslim Policy and Senegalese Brotherhoods", *Boston University Papers on Africa* V, 1971, p. 194.

19 Cruise O'Brien, *The Mourides, op. cit.*, p. 216.

20 Paden, *op. cit.*, p. 69 *et passim* on the emergence of the Reformed Tijaniyya. And M. Hiskett, "The Community of Grace and Its Opponents, The 'Rejectors': A Debate about Theology and Mysticism in Muslim West Africa with special reference to its Hausa expression" in *African Language Studies (A.L.S.)* XVII(1980), p. 102, n. 4. Here Hiskett suggests that in Shaikh Ibrahim Niass's Tijani movement the element" of popularisation is more salient than that of reform because . . . this extends only to the concept of jihad and the method of prayer in which the Jama's differs from the "Umarian tradition. ."

21 Hiskett, "The Community of Grace. . .", *op. cit.*, p. 102.

22 *Ibid.*, p. 109.

23 Clarke, "Islam and Change in Nigeria, c. 1918–1960", *op. cit.*, pp. 108 *ff.*

24 Paden, *op. cit.*, pp. 133–134.

25 On the subject of deprivation and millenarian and/or salvationist religious movements see M. Douglas, *Natural Symbols* (Penguin, 1973).

26 Hiskett, "The Community of Grace . . .", *op. cit.*, pp. 109 *ff.*

27 Paden, *op. cit.*, p. 140.

28 Cheikh Amalla Diallo, "Contribution à une Etude de l'Enseignement Privé Coranique au Sénégal", in *Le Mois en Afrique*, 73–78, No 76, April 1972.

Upper Volta.

1 Audouin and Deniel, *op. cit.*, p. 59.

2 *Ibid.*, p. 65.

3 *Ibid.*, p. 37.

4 See A. Gouilly, *op. cit.*

5 *Ibid.*

6 *Ibid.*

7 My information on the Aladura is based on interviews in Ijebu-Ode during the period 1976–8. I was also allowed to read the *Book of Records and Faith* kept by Pastor Sadare at the Faith Tabernacle Church in Ijebu-Ode. There were also documents in his library such as "An Account of the Work at Iwo", and "Cures through Prayer in Ibadan District". In the entries in the latter document under the heading "Illness" for September 1930, "Pregnancy" was the most frequently recorded, followed by witchcraft, bellyache, and so on.

8 Skinner, *Islam in Mossi Society, op. cit.*, pp. 183 *ff.*

9 Gbadamosi, *The Growth of Islam. . . op. cit.*, p. 68 *et passim.*

10 Skinner, *op. cit.*, p. 187.

Ivory Coast.

1 Triaud, *La Question Musulmane . . ., op. cit.*, p. 546.

2 *Ibid.*, p. 546, n. 14.

3 *Ibid.*, p. 550.

4 J.L. Triaud, "Un Cas de passage collectif à l'Islam en basse Côte d'Ivoire au début du siècle: le village d'Ahua", *Cahiers d'Etudes Africaines* XVI (1974) pp. 317–337.

5 Triaud, *La Question Musulmane, op. cit.*, p. 559.

6 L. Kaba, *The Wahhabiyya, op. cit.*, p. 60.

7 *Ibid.*, especially Chapter 8.

Nigeria.
1   C.K. Meek, *Northern Nigeria* (London, 1925), Vol.II, p. 246.
2   D.M. Last, "Some Economic Aspects of Conversion in Hausaland" in Levtzion, ed, *Conversion to Islam* (New York, 1979).
3   L.J. Cantori, "The Political Implications of Islam in the Middle Belt of Nigeria", Ph.D. thesis, Chicago, Illinois, 1962, p. 16.
4   Cantori, *op. cit.*, p. 16.
5   The account of the conversion of the Dadiya to Islam is based on field work by the author and Sa'idu Musa, 1974—5. The following quotations are from my field notes.
6   R. Bruce, "Conversion among the Pyem", Seminar Paper, Ahmadu Bello University, Zaria, 1975.
7   J. Morrison, "Jos Plateau Societies . . . 1800—1935", Ph.D. thesis, University of Ibadan, 1975.
8   *Ibid.*
9   Bruce, *op. cit.*
10 R. Bendix, *Max Weber: An Intellectual Portrait, op. cit.*, pp. 46—7.
11 Paden, *op. cit.*, pp. 187—8.
12 See Usuman dan Fodio in Hodgkin, *Nigerian Perspectives, op. cit.* pp. 254—5.
13 For a discussion of Aminu Kano's views on indirect rule see Paden, *op. cit.*, pp. 285—288, *et passim.*
14 *Ibid.*, p. 290.
15 A. Adeniran, "Personalities and Policies in the establishment of English in Northern Nigeria during the British colonial administration", Seminar Paper, University of Ibadan, 1976, p. 13.
16 Sa'adu Zungur, "The North — Republic or Monarchy?" in *Poetry, Life . . . op. cit.*, p. 89.
17 Amaurey Talbot, *op. cit.*, p. 103.
18 J. Cuoq, *Les Musulmanes en Afrique* (Paris, 1975), pp. 244—5.
19 Amaurey Talbot, *op. cit.*, p. 103.
20 Clarke, "Islam and Change in Nigeria . . .", *op. cit.*, p. 100.
21 *Ibid.*, p. 100.
22 A.M. Ayeni, "Isabatudeen Society in Ibadan", Long essay, University of Ibadan, May/June 1973.
23 *Ibid.*
24 Clarke, "Islam and Change in Nigeria . . .", *op. cit.*, p. 101.
25 *Ibid.*, p. 101.
26 Bidmus, "A Literary Appraisal . . .", *op. cit.*, p. 71.
27 *Ibid.*, pp. 72—77 *et passim.*
28 N.A.I. C.S.O. 26/1/06790/60
29 Clarke, "Mahdism: The History of . . .", *op. cit.*
30 P.B. Clarke, Interviews, Ibadan, June 1977.
31 *Ibid.*, Oke-Eri, April 1978.
32 *Ibid.*, Ijebu-Ode, June 1978.
33 B.L. Koledola, "The Arabic Printing Press in Abeokuta" Long Essay, University of Ibadan, 1977.
34 Clarke, Interviews, Ijebu-Ode, 1977—8.
35 *Ibid.*, Ibadan, June 1978.
36 T. Asuni, "Socio-Medical Problems of Religious Converts", *Psychopathologie Africaine* IX (1973), pp. 223—236.
37 *Yoruba News*, 29/10/1929.

38 Abdul, "Islam in Ijebu-Ode", *op. cit.*, and Nasiru "Islamic Learning among the Yoruba" *op. cit.*
39 Clarke, "The Methods and Ideology . . .", *op. cit.*, p. 45.
40 Cantori, *op. cit.*
41 *Ibid.*
42 A.R.I. Doi, "Islam in Nigeria: changes since independence" in Fasholé Luke, R. Gray, A. Hastings and G. Tasie, eds, *Christianity in Independent Africa* (London, 1978), pp. 334–357.
43 Crowder, *West Africa under Colonial Rule, op. cit.*, p. 356.

8

c. 1960 — 1980: Islam since independence. Case studies.

The growing strength of nationalist movements and the impact of events such as World War II in which West Africans played an important part, brought about the "sudden death" of European rule in West Africa. Beginning with Ghana in 1957 and ending with Guinea Bissau's successful armed struggle against Portugal in 1975, one West African country after another regained its independence. For many West African countries the independence period to date has been one of rapid political, economic and social change. The pace of this change, the colonial economic, political and cultural legacy, the irrational behaviour of the international economic order, internal strife and natural disasters such as the Sahel drought of 1972—4, have made the independence period in many cases a problem ridden era. However, whatever the problems, West Africa taken as a whole has moved forward in many areas since independence, although there are those who believe that the process of full, real liberation, as understood by writers like Franz Fanon, has hardly begun.

It is against this background and with an eye on the theoretical and concrete proposals advanced in the search for the ideal post-colonial society that I provide this analysis of Islam's post-independence development in three West African states, Senegal, Upper Volta and Nigeria. Although there is some discussion here of the actual expansion of Islam, I do not intend to leave matters at the level of a blow by blow account of gains here and losses there. I want also to consider such related issues as the organisational development of Islam, the growth and impact of the pilgrimage, the relations between Islam in West Africa and the Muslim world as a whole, Islam's position vis-a-vis secularism and constitutional development, and Muslim-Christian relations in West Africa since independence.

Senegal.

Relating the history of a society or movement to the activities and personality of a leader or group of leaders is always somewhat misleading in that, among other things, it produces an over-simplified account of what generates change in a society or movement. Nevertheless, at the risk of over-simplification, it is clear that, to a considerable extent, the history of Islam in Senegal since

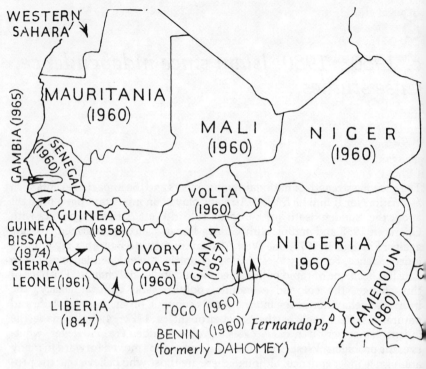

X Independent West Africa

independence has been fashioned by the perspectives and the activities of men like Abdul Aziz Sy, Sa'idu Nuru Tall, Ibrahim Niass, Abdou Lahatte M'Backé and other leaders from the Tijani and Murid brotherhoods.

Today, of the estimated five million inhabitants of Senegal, perhaps as many as two million are members of the Tijaniyya, while an estimated one and a half million belong to the Muridiyya. Urbanisation, Western education and the diversification of the economy do not seem to have lessened the direct and immediate influence of the Tijani and Murid leaders over their followers. If anything, according to some Senegalese scholars, this influence has increased.[1] Moreover, as Behrman has shown in her study of Muslim politics and development in Senegal, all political parties in Senegal, whatever their ideology, have had to use the leaders of the brotherhoods and the marabouts as intermediaries in their search for support. Behrman also maintains that the spread of (Western) education "has not yet led to a move away from loyalty to the marabouts by the rural peasants".[2] The influence of the leaders of the Muslim brotherhoods has also been evident among workers in the urban areas. In 1968, for example, when a call was made for a general strike, the then leader of the Murids, Falilou M'Backé, advised his followers to go to work and the majority acted on this advice.[3]

Although predominantly a Muslim country at the time of independence in 1960, there still remained some three-quarters of a million non-Muslims in

Senegal at that time. Some of those, however, have been turning to Islam in increasing numbers in recent times. The Diola, of whom there are some 260,000 in Senegal, are, I understand from recent interviews, a case in point. This has been attributed to the declining influence of Western and indirectly Christian influence since the withdrawal of the French, and the activities in the Casamance region of such charismatic figures as Shaikh Sounta Badji.[4]

Moreover, as Western influence has tended to decline, cultural, religious and economic contacts with the Islamic countries like Saudi Arabia, Egypt and Iraq have increased. Between 1975, when the Arabic Bank for Economic Development in Africa (BADEA) began providing loans containing a grant element, and 1978 Senegal was on two occasions the recipient of a loan. Other West African countries to receive financial aid twice in the same period were the Gambia, Benin (Dahomey), Guinea-Bissau, Cape Verde, Guinea (Conakry) and Liberia; Ghana, Mali, Niger and Upper Volta received loans on three occasions in the period; and the Ivory Coast, São Tome, Principe, Sierra Leone and Togo each received only one loan. Nigeria by 1978 had received nothing from BADEA.[5]

In addition to the strengthening of economic links between Senegal and the Muslim world of North Africa and the Middle East, educational and cultural links have also been strengthened. More Senegalese students are going to Saudi Arabia and other Muslim countries for study and research and this has tended to enlarge the circle of those dedicated to the revival of pure, "orthodox" Islam, of those who regard War Dyabe's Takrur as the model for present-day Senegal.

Opinions, however, differ a great deal in Senegal on the question of the necessity and feasibility of turning Senegal into an Islamic state. Some prominent Muslims like Shaikh Anta Diop, a scientist and leader of the Rassemblement National Démocratique (R.N.D.), are opposed to the idea of turning Senegal into an Islamic state. Others like Shaikh Touré, editor of the journal *Etudes Islamiques* and a Muslim reformer of long standing, would like to see Senegal become an Islamic state eventually, that is at a time when a majority of Senegalese are sufficiently well educated to accept it with enthusiasm and commitment. Shaikh Touré emphasises, however, that the constitution of such a state, while being truly Islamic, would have to take into consideration the Senegalese situation where there are a minority of Christians and Traditional Religionists. According to Shaikh Touré, an Islamic constitution for Senegal would have to guarantee equal political and other rights to all Senegalese, irrespective of creed.[6]

The majority of Muslims in Senegal, including the leaders of the brotherhoods, do not appear to want any wholesale change in the constitution. Some, however, want certain laws altered, laws which they believe are contrary to certain basic Islamic precepts. They are, for example, opposed to certain provisions of the Family Code of 1972. Among other things this code permits three options with regard to rules governing marriage. One of these options, and one which Muslims criticise and would like to see changed, permits the husband to choose among three types of marriage: a) polygamy, in which case the number of wives is limited to a maximum of four; b) limited polygamy, where the husband is permitted to have fewer than four wives simultaneously; and c) monogamy. If the husband chooses monogamy his choice is definitive. If he chooses limited polygamy he can further limit but he cannot increase his number of wives.[7] Some Muslims see these provisions as being contrary to the Islamic law relating to marriage, according to which a man can have up to four wives simultaneously if he so desires and has the necessary means.

Many Muslims also want religious education to be made a compulsory subject in public (i.e. government) schools. During colonial rule and since independence public schools have been regarded as lay or secular institutions in which religious instruction was forbidden. However, in January 1981 at a General Assembly or *Etats Généraux* called to discuss and find solutions to the problems besetting teachers and the education system in general in Senegal, a request was made that religious instruction should form part of the curriculum in all schools. This request, to the satisfaction of many Muslims, was accepted in principle by the Government. And many Muslims are now hopeful that, through the public schools as well as by means of such institutions as the Islamic Institute in Dakar opened in 1974, they will be able to deepen the knowledge, faith and commitment to Islam of young Muslims in Senegal. Improving the quality of Islamic education so that the young in particular will come to regard it in the same way as they regard "Western" education, that is as "modern" and relevant, is a major preoccupation of many Muslims in contemporary Senegal. The women's branch of the Muslim Cultural Union (U.C.M.), for example, at its national conference held in Kaolack in April 1981, adopted resolutions in favour of the establishment of more Franco-Arab colleges and the introduction of religious instruction in public schools. They also demanded the amendment of the laws relating to marriage which were contrary to the practice of Islam.[8] And in Kaolack, Abdoulaye Niass, successor of Ibrahim Niass, has almost completed the construction of an Islamic Educational Institution in which Arabic, French and eventually English will be offered in addition to the Islamic sciences. Unlike his father, Abdoulaye Niass is not opposed to the teaching of French, maintaining that his father's refusal to allow the teaching of French was born of his opposition to colonialism.[9]

Apart from the doctrinal reasons which they put forward, it is worthwhile mentioning some of the other arguments Muslims use in support of their demands for the creation of more and better quality Islamic schools and for the recognition and implementation of Islamic law in whole or in part. These demands often grow in situations where there are mounting social problems as a result of the break-up of the traditional social or family structure. The Muslim women at their conference in Kaolack mentioned above stressed that respect for Islamic law and the improvement and expansion of Islamic education was the only way to put an end to the "excessive numbers of divorce cases and the evil psychological and social effects which this entails".[1] Again, where the existing legal system and law enforcement agencies seem incapable of dealing with crime, in particular robbery and theft, some people see an answer to this problem in Islamic law. I quote in this context the Mauretanian Government spokesman who, in February, 1980, announced that a new Islamic Court was being set up because "Modern law has no proved capable of curbing criminals".[11]

Islam also appeals to some as an appropriate ideology for Senegal and other West African states on the grounds that it is "socialist". Muslims, however, make the point that Islamic socialism is in some ways a distinct brand of socialism. There is, for example, in addition to Islamic socialism, African socialism, Marxist socialism and what is referred to as Democratic Socialism. African socialism was the official ideology in Ghana until the overthrow of President Nkrumah in 1966, and it is still the official ideology of Tanzania, Guinea (Conakry), Gambia and Mali, although Mali decided in March 1981 to dismantle the state sector of the economy by 1985. This involves, among other things, the handing over of the important cereal trade to the private sector. Islamic socialism was the state ideology in Egypt during the Nasser era, and since 1969 has become the state ideology in Libya. In Algeria under Boumedienne a form of Marxist socialism co-existed alongside Islamic socialism.

There are similarities between these various types of socialism. There is, for instance, the emphasis on a classless society in all of these socialist ideologies. Moreover, Muslims and Communists have co-operated in the African context, and elsewhere, for example in Indonesia, particularly during the struggle to end colonialism. In West Africa Muslims in the Ivory Coast, Mali and elsewhere in former French West African colonies joined the political party, the R.D.A., which had strong links with the French Communist Party. Islam, however, opposes any form of socialism that espouses a purely materialistic philosophy of life and change. This is something that, it would appear, the Soviet Union is well aware of, since in its English radio broadcasts to Africa it points out that religious beliefs and practices are not ideologically unacceptable there. In one such broadcast, for example, an account was given of a French journalist's visit to a number of churches and a theological college in Odessa on the Black Sea. The broadcast went on to say that in Odessa there are six Orthodox churches, a Catholic church, a synagogue, an "Old Believers" church, a cathedral and communities of Seventh Day Adventists and Pentacostalists. In conclusion the broadcaster states that "what I said about Odessa applies to the whole of the Soviet Union. There are more than 20,000 Orthodox Churches, mosques, Catholic, Lutheran. . .".[12]

Although there are many other points one could make concerning the similarities and differences between Islamic and other forms of socialism, Islamic socialism, at least as it is understood by some Muslim political scientists, in seeking equality and social justice, sees the individual as the basis of the social structure and has "no place for the concept that the state as a whole is greater than the parts".[13]

Another issue that is and has been of some importance in Senegal and Nigeria and elsewhere in West Africa since independence is that of Muslim-Christian relations. In Senegal, as in Upper Volta and Nigeria, for example, there was a tendency during the colonial era for each side to see itself as being discriminated against by the authorities. In the early 20th century the Roman Catholic missionaries in Senegal were convinced that the colonial administration with its secularist outlook was determined, by taking over the Church schools, to undermine their missionary work.[14] On the other hand Muslims felt that the harassment, detention and exiling of Muslim leaders like Ahmadu Bamba was an all too obvious indication of the administration's hostility to Islam.

Tolerance has been the chief characteristic of Muslim-Christian relations in Senegal. Since independence there has been considerable dialogue between the two faiths. Muslim and Christian youth in Dakar, despite the hostile attack on Islam by Bishop Léfèbvre, former Roman Catholic Bishop of Dakar, have worked together to establish socialism. In 1963 the African Society for Culture (SAC), composed of Muslims and Christians, requested the Catholic Church, the largest Christian church in Senegal, to consider ways and means of initiating dialogue between Muslims and Christians in Africa. The bishops were later to recommend, among other things, that the Society study the Vatican Council II declaration on "Non-Christian Religions" of October 1965, and the 1969 "Guide for a Dialogue between Muslims and Christians".

With regard to Islam in Senegal, therefore, continuity persists amid change and development. The leaders of the brotherhoods are still very influential and receive loyal support from their disciples. The marabouts, like Shaikh Badji, continue to expand the frontiers of Islam in Senegal, while its links with the rest of the Muslim world have been strengthened through the pilgrimage, economic aid and scholarship. There are among Senegalese Muslims some reformers, like Muhammad b. Sa'id Bá of Medina-Gonasse near Tambacounda, who want to see a pure Islamic society without any Western accretions.[15] There are other reformers who seek a fusion of the best elements in the Islamic and Western traditions. There are, finally, those who, like Shaikh Badji, are prepared to absorb aspects of all cultures and traditions.

Islam in Senegal, therefore, has since independence continued to spread, gaining ground among the Diola in particular. The reaction of some of the Diola converts to Islam is worth mentioning here for it resembles in certain respects that of, for example, the first converts to Islam from among the rulers of the Mossi in Upper Volta in the 18th century. Like the Mossi rulers of that period many Diola family heads today who become Muslims do not oblige either their wives or sons to follow their path. Moreover, with regard to their sons they encourage them to wait until they have attained a mature age before making a decision as to whether or not they should become Muslims. Consequently, there are Diola villages in the Casamance region of Senegal, and in the Gambia, where although the adult male population is almost entirely Muslim the women and the children have remained Traditional Religionists.[16]

Muslims in Senegal have not only continued to spread Islam during the independence era but have become more and better organised and are beginning to provide for young Muslims an Islamic education of high quality on a much wider scale than in the past. Finally, since independence the increasing numbers of Senegalese students studying in Muslim countries, the twinning of Senegalese towns with towns in other Muslim countries (for example St Louis in northern Senegal is twinned with Fez in Morocco) the growing number of Senegalese Muslims who make the pilgrimage to Mecca, and the economic aid given by the oil-producing Muslim world to Senegal have contributed towards the fostering of stronger ties between Muslims in Senegal and the wider Muslim world, something the colonial administration strove to prevent.

Upper Volta.

Muslims in Upper Volta believe, and some of their Christian compatriots agree with them, that for most of the colonial era Islam was shackled. According to Deniel, Christians in Upper Volta recognise that during the colonial era "Muslims were not free" and that if in a village "you were to say that you were a Muslim, a chief would not listen to you". The Muslim opinion is that "before (during the colonial era), we were captives, we practised our religion in secret".[17]

From the 1950s when the colonial regime became somewhat more liberal, and even more so since independence, Muslims in Upper Volta have felt freer to organise themselves into a community. I mentioned previously the establishment of the Muslim Community of Wagadugu in 1958—60, and that by 1962 this organisation had grown to become the Muslim Community of Upper Volta. The inspiration behind the formation of this Community was, according to its leaders, "fidelity to the Qur'an, and the necessity to assemble for Friday prayer and to proclaim Muslim unity and brotherhood". There was also the desire to organise and unite Muslims to enable them to contribute to national unity and development.[18]

Since 1962 the Community has been involved in intense activity to spread Islam and build up the Muslim Community. In 1964, at the General Assembly, 500 delegates represented some 55,000 members, 83 regional branch committees and 176 sub-committees. In addition there were 771 mosques and 11 Qur'anic schools associated with the Community, and in two years it had been responsible for almost 11,000 converts to Islam.[19]

In an attempt to involve the young more in the service of Islam the first Cultural Committee of Muslim Youth was held in Wagadugu in 1972. The youth were requested to participate in the dissemination of Arabic, with the aim of making it the language of culture in Upper Volta. The Community also has a programme to instruct Muslims about Islamic regulations and ritual for, among other things, marriage and funeral ceremonies. Moreover, there have been campaigns to promote "worthy and authentic" radio programmes, to prevent Muslims using the pilgrimage to Mecca for material gain, against the exploitation of the people by the marabouts, and to raise the standard of education in the Qur'anic schools, which is generally regarded as being very low.[20]

Some Muslims, however, feel that the Muslim Community of Upper Volta is too introspective and that its activities are of little value in terms of the country's overall economic and social development. What are regarded as the Community's limited and essentially other worldly concerns have in fact created a reaction among some Muslims who have now set out to demonstrate to non-Muslims that Islam is concerned with the development of the country's economy, with improving the health of the community and with the raising of the standard of living in general. [21]

Despite the difficulties and problems, Muslims in Upper Volta since independence have become a much more united and better organised community. In the opinion of some the organisational progress made by Islam in Upper Volta since independence may well be considered exceptional when compared with Islam's organisational development in the rest of West Africa. [22]

Nigeria.

Islam in Nigeria since independence, as in Senegal and Upper Volta, has been able to assume a much more trans-ethnic, national and trans-national character and dimension. A variety of factors have contributed to this development including the independence political process itself, the greater influence in Nigeria of the Muslim brotherhoods, such as the Niass branch of the Tijaniyya, the forging of stronger ties with the Muslim world of North Africa and the Middle East, and the political process involving the drafting of a new constitution for the return to civilian rule in October 1979.

That aspect of the independence political process which involved the implementation of a political system based on the Westminster model made for a deeper involvement of the Muslims in northern Nigeria in the rest of Nigeria, and of Muslims from the south in the north of the country. To obtain a majority of seats in the first Federal Parliament the predominantly Muslim Northern Peoples' Congress Party (N.P.C.) had to campaign vigorously in the less Islamised and non-Islamised areas of Nigeria, such as the Middle Belt. This region, which was about 21 per cent Muslim in 1959, was crucial to the N.P.C's overall electoral success in 1959. And, in addition to winning other seats, the N.P.C. won five entirely non-Muslim constituencies, supporting in these and in other instances non-Muslim associations and standing non-Muslim candidates. [1]

More important perhaps than the independence political process itself in developing closer links between Muslims throughout the Federation and in some areas leading to an expansion of Islam was the establishment in 1973 of the Islamic Council for Nigeria. One of the purposes of this Council is to act as a bridge between the different Muslim communities in Nigeria and also to enable Muslims to speak to the government of the day with one voice on matters concerning Islam. Representatives from each state of the Federation are appointed to the Council's governing body which is presided over by the Sultan of Sokoto. Since 1973, therefore, it has been possible for Muslims at the Federal level to debate, discuss and state their point of view on such matters as education and the law. According to Alhaji Saka Fagbo, the establishment of the Islamic Council for Nigeria was "the culmination of many years of tireless efforts to get Muslims in this country under one central organisation". [2] One of the first actions taken by this Council which demonstrated its "national" character was to make a representation to the government of

X Friday prayer in front of a modern mosque

what was then the Western State over the issue of withdrawing the Higher
School Certificate courses from the Ijebu-Muslim College.[3]

Another Muslim organisation that has played a prominent part in the expansion and development of Islam in Nigeria since independence is the Jama'atu
Nasril Islam (Society for the Victory of Islam), established in January 1961.
One of the aims of this society, which has its headquarters in Kaduna, is to
transcend any divisions among Muslims created by allegiance to the different
brotherhoods. In the early years of its history the Jama'atu Nasril Islam
debated issues such as the pilgrimage, the franchise of women, and the
correct position for the arms while at prayer. Some Tijani, for example the
followers of Ibrahim Niass, pray with their arms crossed (*Kablu*), while other
Muslims pray with their arms by their sides (*Sadlu*), and in one of several
decisions on this issue the Jama'atu advised that the latter (Sadlu) was the
more correct position.

The Jama'atu Nasril Islam is both an educational and missionary organisation. It trains and sends out missionaries to all parts of Nigeria and also
runs a number of schools and colleges. The national character of the movement, however, has only really been in evidence since the end of the civil war.
From 1970 the Jama'atu began to establish branches outside the old northern
region in Lagos, Benin, Port Harcourt, Enugu and Calabar, and this has led to

the conversion to Islam of considerable numbers in these areas, including by 1973 an estimated 500 Ibo-speaking people.[4]

These national organisations have not eliminated all the differences between Muslims in the various parts of the Federation, differences which exist in part on account of the different historical circumstances in which Islam has developed. Muslims in the south of Nigeria, exposed more and longer to Western influence, have different needs and anxieties and have a different perspective on such matters as Western education and Islamic law from Muslims elsewhere in the Federation. While the franchise of women, the education of girls beyond the age of puberty, purdah and seclusion have not been central issues for the majority of Muslims in southern Nigeria (the Bamidele and Sangliti sects being among the exceptions) they have been very important concerns for Muslims in northern Nigeria. Again, in practice at least, the question of Muslim-Christian relations is more central in the southern situation than in most of the northern states. One of the areas where Muslims in southern Nigeria would like to see more "equality" is in the educational system, which they believe does not cater adequately in terms of religious instruction for the Muslim population.[5]

In northern Nigeria the Muslim reaction to the introduction of Universal Primary Education (U.P.E.) in 1976 varied from rural to urban area, and from one socio-economic group to another. Many mallams, who were not opposed to Western education in itself, felt that U.P.E. would spell the ruin of the Qur'anic school, the basis of the Islamic education system. Farmers believed it would lead to a "work avoidance syndrome", to the young not wanting to do any "real" work but preferring to "live off" someone else. Other ordinary people suggested it would lead to a lowering of moral standards and the corruption of Islam, since Muslims would be bound to mix regularly with non-Muslims. Some believed it would destroy the traditional criteria for establishing whether an individual had the capacity, temperament and character necessary for leadership. Western education was seen by others as irrelevant, leading to the neglect of local arts and crafts and the rural way of life, while others maintained there was no moral, "spiritual" content to Western education. There was strong protest against the use of English as the medium of instruction and against girls attending school beyond the age of twelve. Western-educated women, in the view of some, would take over roles traditionally performed by men.[6]

Some Muslim leaders, however, both during the colonial era, as we have seen, and since independence, have advised and encouraged girls to pursue their education beyond the primary school level. In recent times many of the Emirs of northern Nigeria have been encouraging parents to send their daughters to school and to allow them to pursue their education beyond the primary school level. Whereas the tendency in the past was to encourage girls to limit their interests to domestic subjects, today they are being advised to broaden their horizons and qualify themselves for entry into the teaching and nursing professions in particular. It is often pointed out in support of this stand on the education of women that Usuman dan Fodio did not limit the education of women to domestic subjects and that his daughters, Khadija and Asma, were highly educated women.

XI Muslim ablutions before prayer

A Western education does not by any means lead all Muslim women to abandon Islamic domestic and religious norms and values. It has been shown, for instance, that some Muslim women in Sokoto in northern Nigeria who had received a Western education, willingly accepted such traditions as purdah, and did not object to their husband having more than one wife.[7] Although, therefore, some Muslims in northern Nigeria oppose the education of girls beyond the age of twelve and want women to be confined to such professions as nursing, others are of the opinion that girls and women should have the same opportunities as men. "In present-day Nigeria," one Muslim wrote in 1971, "we are under a moral and religious obligation to ensure that an equal opportunity in education is given to Muslim girls in all our schools and higher institutions of learning".[8] Until the introduction of U.P.E. very few Muslim girls in northern Nigeria had received any education apart from the religious and moral education provided by the Qur'anic school. By way of contrast, by 1938 there were an estimated 53,143 girls at school in southern Nigeria, and by the 1940s women had begun to enter the legal, medical, teaching and other professions.[9] It is not certain how many of the 53,143 were Muslim girls but it seems that a substantial minority of them were Muslims.

The preparation for the return to civilian rule in Nigeria, which began formally in 1976 and was completed in October 1979, also gave rise to discussions on the role, status and rights of Muslim women. It gave rise to the demand for unconditional franchise for all women from Muslim women like Hajiya Gambo Sawaba from Zaria. The latter began campaigning for women's rights in 1947 after reading in the Hausa newspaper, *Gaskiya Tafi Kwobo*, about the activities on behalf of women of Mrs Funmilayo Anikulapo-Kuti. She later became President of the women's wing of the old political party, the Northern Elements Progressive Union (N.E.P.U.). Often persecuted for her views, Hajiya Gambo was only partially satisfied when the franchise was granted to women in northern Nigeria in 1976, because in her view it was not unconditional. The Draft Constitution recommended that every Nigerian, including women, should have equal rights, obligations and opportunities before the law, providing the right to equality did not invalidate any rule of Islamic or customary law. It was this qualification that Hajiya Gambo and others, like Mrs A. Ehiemua, objected to on the grounds that it could justify the continuing inequality between men and women.[10]

In the local government elections held in November 1976 Muslim women in northern Nigeria exercised the franchise, and five of the women who stood for election in Kano and Kaduna states won comfortably; Hajiya Gambo won unopposed in a ward in Zaria. Again in the 1979 state and Federal elections Muslim women throughout Nigeria exercised their right to vote.

Much of the protest against U.P.E., to return to this subject, was not, it seems, intended to prevent the introduction of the scheme but was rather a form of "protest of corrective censure". It was designed to alert those responsible for the scheme to the needs and aspirations of the ordinary people. The decision to allow Hausa to be used as the medium of instruction and the more generous provisions made for the teaching of religion in primary schools satisfied a great number of people, and it has been predicted by Muslims in, for example, Yauri in Sokoto state that the U.P.E. scheme will eventually bring about the Islamisation of the non-Muslim areas in that part of the emirate.[11]

Since independence Islam in Nigeria has become much more international in character. Although never completely isolated from the rest of the Muslim world during the colonial era, contacts with the Muslim world were limited and often supervised. For example, enquiries were made and a watch kept by the colonial administration into the activities of Nigerian Muslims in the Sudan, and Nigerian Muslim students at al-Azhar.[12]

In the period immediately preceding independence and during the post-independence period far more Nigerian Muslims than ever before have been making the pilgrimage to Mecca. Whereas in 1956 the figure was only 2,483, in 1973 an estimated 49,000 Nigerian pilgrims went to Mecca, and in 1977 about 106,000 Nigerians performed the hajj, making the number of pilgrims from Nigeria the second highest in the world. In 1978, in order to "minimise the sufferings of our people", as one local government official in Lagos State put it, measures were introduced to limit the number of Nigerian pilgrims to 50,000.[13] In some states applicants were obliged to undergo an examination which consisted in answering questions on salat, the five daily prayers, and some of the "tenets and rudimentary norms of Islam". Some people apparently "failed all the questions put to them."[14] Women with advanced pregnancy, old people unaccompanied and children under 15 years were also barred from the pilgrimage. Nevertheless, the total of 50,000 pilgrims far exceeds the numbers who went to Mecca in the pre-independence period, and obviously one of the reasons for this is the relatively high level of economic prosperity achieved in Nigeria since 1970, and the improvement in the transport and communications system. Despite these developments, however, many pilgrims have experienced great hardship and difficulties. In 1974 the then Head of State, Yakubu Gowon, felt it necessary to make a profound apology to pilgrims for the delays and hardships they experienced in attempting to reach Mecca.[15]

The increase in the number of pilgrims going to Mecca during the post-independence period has not been confined to Nigeria alone. In Mali, the Ivory Coast, Upper Volta and elsewhere there has been a similar upward trend. The view has been put forward that the pilgrimage tends to radicalise those who make it, so that when they return they begin to seek for ways and means of reviving "pure" Islam in their own country. Lansine Kaba's study of the Subbanu movement and the spread of Wahhabi reformist ideas in Mali and the Ivory Coast, lends a good deal of support to this view. Kaba writes: "The pilgrimage influenced some leading marabouts who contributed to the diffusion of the Wahhabiyya in many areas . . . the impact of Mecca was not negligible in terms of religious reassessment."[16] In Ijebu-Ode in western Nigeria, pilgrims returning from Mecca in the late 1920s were very active in the movement to reform Islam there. And we have seen something of the effect of the pilgrimage on al-Hajj'Umar Tall and Mamadu Lamine in the 19th century. The pilgrimage affects different people in different ways. Not all return home as reformers and revivalists. I have already quoted one person who told me that he liked very much what he saw in Mecca, it was a wonderful experience, "but one cannot do all those things here (Ibadan); it's a different people, with different customs".

The impact of the pilgrimage seen from the point of view of the non-Muslim population could be profound. In Ibadan, for instance, when an estimated 150 people died in the floods in April 1978, the adherents of the indigenous religion who worshipped Iyemoja, goddess of waters, attributed the disaster to the fact that the one-time priestess of Iyemoja had been to Mecca and become an alhaja and could, therefore, no longer evoke the spirit of Iyemoja.[17]

The pilgrimage is above all a religious duty and a profound religious experience for very many. It makes a great difference if one sees it as a spiritual journey. To Charles Doughty, author of *Arabia Deserta*, the Hijaz was "a dead land where if he dies not a man shall bring home nothing but weariness in his bones".[18] The Muslim mystic, Ibn Farid, however, wrote of the same land, "when the anguish of pain settles in my soul the aroma of the fresh herbs of the Hijaz is my balm . . . my very life is in its sandhills and its dwellings are my desire. Its earth is my fragrant spire, and its waters a full well for my thirst. In its soil are my riches."[19]

In addition to this type of experience, the pilgrimage gives Muslims a sense of solidarity, of equality, an appreciation of the universalism of Islam. Some, however, like the Mahdi of Ijebu-Ode, react differently, for, while remaining profoundly attached to Mecca, they nevertheless seek to establish an African Mecca in their own region and end up by proclaiming themselves God's chosen prophet for Africa.[20] Generally speaking, however, the pilgrimage does tend to reinforce the feeling of oneness among Muslims and to strengthen the solidarity of the Muslim community, and of mankind. The catechism of the Ansar-Ud-Deen Society in Nigeria states with reference to the hajj that "it teaches that everybody on earth is equal before the Lord".[21] The international dimension of Islam in Nigeria has also been fostered by the increasing number of Muslim missionaries, teachers and doctors in Nigeria from Pakistan, Bangladesh, India, Saudi Arabia and Egypt. Egyptian graduates from al-Azhar teach in a number of colleges and schools, such as the Madrassa al-Azhariyya in Ilorin, which is affiliated to the university of al-Azhar. There are others teaching in Lagos, Ibadan, Kaduna and other Nigerian towns. Saudi Arabia runs the Islamic Institute in Ibadan, and, like Libya, supplies text books and other equipment. The text books for geography and history, I was told by one student at the Islamic Institute in Ibadan, are very heavily slanted towards the history and geography of the Muslim world.[22]

There are Muslims, however, who, while deeply interested in the history and geography of the Islamic world, are also engaged in the study and preservation of Nigerian history and culture. Some Muslims, for instance, defend participation in traditional festivals and masquerades on the grounds that they are "our culture".[23] At the same time there are those who are opposed to any form of participation in un-Islamic practices, whether or not they are part of Nigeria's history and culture. In a lecture on "The Stand of Islam on the Current Cultural Revival in Nigeria" given in 1975 in Kano, Shehu 'Umar Abdullahi was quoted as saying that "Islam frowns at any attempt to revive the pagan culture" and he is said to have cited the unnecessary mixing of the opposite sexes in public as one of the consequences of this revival. Other aspects of what was termed "the current cultural revival in the country" were condemned as immoral, indecent and absolutely opposed to Islamic doctrines, and all Muslims in Nigeria were called upon to disassociate themselves from whatever tended to recall pagan times.[24] Thus, amid great changes, great dilemmas persist.

One change that has occurred in Nigeria, and one which marks a contrast with Senegal, concerns the Muslim leaders. Whereas in Senegal there is no evidence of a decline in the overall influence, political and otherwise, of the Grand Marabout, the role and influence of the emirs in Nigeria has altered in recent times. For example, the 1968 Local Government Reforms, as applied in Kano, meant that the emir lost his formal judicial powers and was limited to a single vote on legislative matters at the Emirate level. Some mallams reacted to this by refusing to pray for the government since it was undermining the authority of the emirs. This was a reaction I came across in Bauchi Emirate from chiefs and mallams in 1974−5. Consequently, and many people in Bauchi and Yauri expressed this opinion, emirs have come to be seen much more as religious leaders and as occupants of a religious office and as playing only a very limited role in the modern administration. This, of course, could very well increase their influence, status and prestige among the people since they are now less likely to be held responsible for maladministration or ineffective government. The scope and force of the reforms of 1968 should not, however, be exaggerated. Among other things, the emir retained the power to appoint district heads, the executive arm of territorial administration.

There are finally two other issues that have been widely discussed and debated by Muslims in Nigeria in recent times, and these are "secularism" and the Shari'a.

Islam and "secularism" in Nigeria.

"Secularism" was a live issue in Nigeria during the colonial era, especially in the 1940s and 1950s when serious debate got under way concerning the future post-colonial constitutional arrangements. The poems of Sa'idu Zungur reflect to an extent the preoccupation with secularism and republicanism. Here I want simply to give some idea of the Islamic response to "secularism" in the period 1975—9. During this period "secularism" and Islamic law became lively issues in the context of the drafting, debating and endorsement of a new Nigerian constitution, the constitution of the Second Republic, which became effective from 1 October 1979.

The Constitution Drafting Committee began work in 1975 and at one stage in the proposed section of the constitution on the State and its Fundamental Objectives, it was suggested that Nigeria be described in the following way: "Nigeria is one and indivisible sovereign Republic, *secular*, democratic and social." Later the term "secular" was dropped.[25]

Against the background of these discussions and proposals many Muslims and Christians, debated on television, radio, in the press and in universities and colleges whether it was fitting and appropriate to describe Nigeria as a "secular" state. Some Muslims, using the *Shorter Oxford Dictionary* definition of "secularism", which defines this concept as the doctrine that morality should be based solely on regard to the well-being of mankind in this present life to the exclusion of all considerations drawn from belief in God or in a future state, opposed the inclusion of the term in the constitution.[26]

The Constitution Drafting Committee, however, seem to have used the term "secular" to imply state neutrality in matters of religion, the sense in which it is used, for example, in the Indian Constitution. Of course many Muslims may well have believed that even if this was the case, the term "secular" is open to a variety of interpretations, including the one cited above, and was therefore unacceptable. In certain circumstances, they maintained, a ruler hostile to religion could make use of the provision "secular state" to impose restrictions on religion. Furthermore, they may well have had in mind what happened in Turkey when Ataturk imposed his model of "secularism" in 1922.

Moreover, in support of their opposition to "secularism" Muslims quoted, among other verses of the Qur'an, Sura — an Nisa — v. 59: "Let there arise out of you a nation uniting all that is good, enjoining what is right and forbidding what is wrong." "Secularism," they affirmed, "has no place in Islam since Islam is a religion as well as a system of life and government. You cannot separate religion and politics in Islam for religion must exert the correct influence on politics . . . this is the justification for Islam insisting that politics must be clean politics."[27] For these and other reasons, such as the importance attached by law to taking religious oaths and the fact that Nigerians do not want an "irreligious" state, Muslims wanted the Draft Constitution changed with the phrase "secular state" omitted, and a description inserted characterising Nigeria as a "multi-religious state".[28]

Some non-Muslims saw this anti-secular state stance of the Muslims as simply another ploy to advance the cause of Islam. To agree, they argued, to describing Nigeria as a "secular" state would imply abandoning Muslim designs to establish an Islamic state. This, it was argued, the Muslims were not prepared to do and consequently their ultimate objective was seen by some to be to turn Nigeria into an Islamic republic.[29] In reply, Muslims emphasise that they are enjoined by the Qur'an to uphold the principles of popular representation and free discussion "since sovereignty rests with the people". Therefore, aspects of the constitution of which they disapprove, Muslims argue, must be changed democratically; for example, the section which encourages intermarriage among persons of different religions, and the one which permits those born out of wedlock to inherit.[30]

In the present situation of religious pluralism in Nigeria Muslims state that they are obliged to observe "pacts with hypocrites . . . and are duty bound to observe strictly every term of agreement entered into with those of the revealed religions such as Christians and Jews who are close relations of the Muslims".[31]

The Shari'a debate.

Also during the period when the new Draft Constitution was being drawn up and at the time when it was being debated for approval by the Constituent Assembly (1977 – 8), the Shari'a even more than "secularism" became in the words of the Nigerian press "the hot issue".

In essence the Shari'a debate concerned whether or not constitutional provision should be made for the establishment of a Federal Shari'a Court of Appeal, and for Shari'a courts at the state level where they did not already exist. It became, however, a much wider issue involving such questions as religious freedom, the nature and ethos of the Nigerian judicial and legal systems as a whole, the question of the structure of the working week, and of the nature of Nigerian federalism. The Constitution Drafting Committee did in fact make provisions — which had to be endorsed by the Constituent Assembly — for the establishment of Shari'a courts at state level throughout the Federation and for the establishment of a Federal Shari'a Court of Appeal.

Muslims, and some non-Muslims, advanced a number of arguments in favour of such provisions. One argument put forward was that since half of the population of Nigeria was subject to Islamic personal law, it was necessary − if the Federal system was to be sound − to recognise the diversity arising from this fact.[32] Further, it was maintained that a Federal Shari'a Court of Appeal would enable the development of a coherent and consistent body of Islamic law to operate throughout the Federation. Others maintained that the incorporation of the Shari'a Court into the constitution would help the Nigerian state to regain its moral consciousness and responsibility, generate the necessary collective spirit and help to solve Nigeria's social problems.[33] Nigerian Muslims, it was suggested, were backward because of the overthrow of the Shari'a by the British at the beginning of the century.[34] In addition, the overthrow of the Shari'a by the British impeded Islamic progress. Furthermore, the present legal system in operation in Nigeria did not satisfy Muslims in terms of "the general need for social justice among Muslims". The high rate of street begging was attributable "to the neglect by the British colonial administration of the traditional relief (provided by) the Muslim religious system".[35]

Arguing that Nigerian federalism was "a co-operative federalism" and that the unity of Nigeria should be made manifest in its diversity and not in uniformity, a Muslim graduate approved of the C.D.C. proposal for a Federal Shari'a Court of Appeal. A different line was taken by an editorial in the *New Nigerian* newspaper of 12 October 1976, which pointed out that, as far as Muslims were concerned, there had been a miscarriage of justice in Nigeria: "Cases were being decided at Appellate Courts where Islamic law was hardly given any recognition due to the ignorant jurists steeped in Western law and nothing else". The Shari'a Court, it was maintained, would go a long way towards correcting this anomaly.

The C.D.C. proposals for a Federal Shari'a Court of Appeal gave rise almost inevitably to a demand for an "equal deal for all religious groups". If there were to be special courts for Muslims, why not make the same provisions for Christians and Traditional Religionists? A Christian pastor wrote of the problems that would be created for Nigerian unity if the provision for a Federal Shari'a Court were to be endorsed by the Constituent Assembly. He referred to the role of religion in the Nigerian Civil War, the minorities issue, the issue of Church-State relations and the advisability of the separation of church and State. The creation of more Shari'a Courts in Nigeria and the establishment of a Federal Shari'a Court of Appeal, the clergyman maintained, would make the separation of church and state impossible and lead to discrimination in principle against Christians. In Islam, he pointed out, there can be no separation of mosque and court, no *locus standi* for a civil law not based on the Shari'a, no distinction between sacred and profane.[36]

Others saw it as a conspiracy aimed at turning Nigeria into an Islamic state, while some saw it as an instrument which outsiders could and were in fact using to divide Nigerians. As one group put it, the Shari'a debate was being used "to sow the seeds of division and confusion among us in order to divert attention from seeing the way they (the neo-colonialists) exploit us and carry away our resources".[37] Imperialists were using religion to divide and rule Nigeria. Other opponents of the Shari'a Federal Court of Appeal were of the opinion that Islamic law could not deal with the pressing problems of contemporary Nigeria, offering outmoded solutions to present problems.

The objection that Islamic law was "barbarous", antiquated and irrelevant was countered by many arguments. It was claimed, for example, that Islamic law provides a powerful and effective deterrent against the lowering of moral standards and against crime. Moreover, in a development situation where there is dislocation, disorientation and anomy, Muslims saw the Shari'a as providing firm guidelines, security and certainty. They argued, further, that the penalties imposed by the Shari'a are no more "barbarous" than for example those imposed in America or France, such as electrocution or the guillotine. Muslims pointed out that the "imported" legal and judicial systems have failed in Nigeria, just as the Westminister constitutional system failed. Crime rates, they maintained, had risen dramatically and the present system of justice — laborious, inefficient and corrupt — was inadequate to deal effectively with the increasing amount of violent crime.[38]

After a prolonged and heated debate in the Constituent Assembly, the Draft Constitution proposals concerning the establishment of a Federal Shari'a Court of Appeal were not endorsed. After Chief Simon Adebo's sub-committee reported that the decision was to delete the relevant section of the Draft Constitution, the Chairman of the Assembly, Chief Justice Udoma, declared the debate on the Shari'a closed. Eighty-eight members of the Assembly, all Muslims, withdrew from the Constituent Assembly. Five more members followed them later. These events took place between 7 and 10 April 1978. Explaining their reasons for withdrawing from the Assembly, the members declared that they represented at least 50 per cent of the national population and more than 50 per cent of the registered voters of the country.[39] In their absence the Chairman of the Assembly took the decision to wind up the discussion on Chapter VII of the Draft Constitution Bill.

The Shari'a debate and the debate on "secularism" may have had political dimensions but they were also about religious faith and practice and about the whole question of ensuring that Nigeria had a fitting and workable constitution. These debates were also extended to include law and order in general, and issues such as cultural identity, imperialism, the colonial legacy, mental and legal de-colonisation. These debates were also in part an attempt to deal with some of the social effects of rapid industrialisation. Many Nigerians, as a consequence of such things as traffic congestion in towns such as Lagos, were having to live much more private, less community and family centred lives. They were becoming more isolated in their apartments or houses, less able to travel with any degree of ease and comfort to meet family and friends. In this situation, more people were being reduced simply to role performers and moral beliefs and values were tending to become somewhat more arbitrary and privately contrived and constructed.

In this era of rapid industrialisation and modernisation, among the few institutions which provide a coherent view of life at the intellectual, emotional and work-a-day world level are the religious institutions. And for those Nigerians whose religion is Islam — and no doubt Christians and Traditional Religionists feel the same way — they find that it offers a clear, explicit, intelligible view of life, applicable to the contemporary situation. Some Muslims are convinced that in order to communicate this message effectively Islamic institutions such as the Shari'a are vitally important. At the same time, however, it seems to be the case that Muslims who take this view are not prepared to pursue their objectives regardless of the rest of society. As one prominent Muslim expressed it, "once two or more communities are united by political bonds sanctified by the Constitution which is a Fundamental Treaty of permanent brotherhood, common action and destiny, it would not only be criminal but a grievous sin in Islam for the terms of the treaty to be violated by acts of discrimination and intolerance. The Holy Qur'an provides a veritable precedent for us on this matter."[40]

After the decision reached in the Constituent Assembly in 1978 the Shari'a debate died down. There are those, however, who believe the debate assisted in speeding up the decision to develop a Nigerian code of law acceptable to all Nigerians whatever their religious persuasion. Meanwhile, Muslims for their part have been assisting the Nigerian Law Review Commission, set up to work out the new Nigerian code of law. Muslims believe, for example, that aspects of Islamic commercial law, of Islamic law on theft, properly understood, might well find a place in the Nigerian code of law and be of benefit to the country as a whole.[41]

Meanwhile, as some debated and discussed relevant and important issues such as "secularism" and the Shari'a, and used the mass media to explain and elucidate Islamic beliefs and practices, others have continued to spread Islam by the traditional methods. The "unattached" mallam still makes his way from village to village, from town to town and from state to state, offering his advice and assistance to people in all walks of life, and converting some of them to Islam in the process. In Akwanga Local Government Area in Plateau State, for example, in September 1976, a mallam was instrumental in converting a number of people, some of them Christians, to Islam. Many people, including representatives of the Emirs of Lafia, Keffi and Nassarawa, and several chiefs, turned out to witness the ceremony held to mark this "group conversion" to Islam.[42]

Mallams still exercise great influence and their help is sought by people from all walks of life. Businessmen, deeply involved in their business concerns and with little leisure time, seek out the mallams and give them donations in return for prayers for the success of their businesses, much in the same way as lay Christians in some Christian denominations ask their religious leaders to pray on their behalf. Other people go to the mallam with family problems, and many others find that the mallams have a good deal to say of interest and value on life's problems and difficulties in general.

The advice given by many mallams has not changed much over the years. There is no evidence of mallams having become more radical as the disparities in wealth, housing and other areas have become more obvious with increasing economic development and prosperity. The mallam does not analyse such inequality in socio-economic terms. Here I will cite a few extracts from a *khutbah* (sermon) given in a small town which indicates the type of advice given to those who might think that they are "deprived". "Anyone", the mallam stated, "who fails to rejoice or to appreciate the little things or the good things done for him . . . he should leave the sky, he is committing sin and should go and die. . . . Anyone who wakes up early in the

254 West Africa and Islam

morning and gets annoyed with all the things in this world, regarding himself
as poor and abandoned, is like someone who holds a spear looking for
the wisdom of God to destroy it . . . one should not get annoyed with the
world."[43]

Some people do, of course, get annoyed with the world. In Kano in
December 1980, for example, a certain Muhammad Marua Maitatsiné, of
Cameroonian origin and who had lived in Kano for many years, preached to
his followers, mainly poor people, that it was "Their time". At a primary
school, which he had apparently taken over, and at open air meetings he told
his supporters that they should not accept as inevitable the fact that "the rich
were rich and the poor, poor". Then in mid-December, 1980, this self-pro-
claimed prophet made a bid to take over the Kano Central Mosque, and in the
disturbances that followed an estimated 1,000 people were killed, including
Muhammad Marua Maitatsiné.[44]

In Nigeria, then, as in Senegal and Upper Volta, the Islamic community has
become much more organised at the national level since independence. It has
also strengthened its ties with the wider world of Islam. These two developments, however, and the greater force and assurance with which some
Muslims in Nigeria put the Islamic case against "secularism" and for Islamic
law, do not mean that the Muslim community exists as a state within a state in
the Nigerian context. In fact the evidence suggests that Muslims in Nigeria
now more than in the past see themselves as part of one nation. The old
division of the country between a Muslim north and a non-Muslim south, so
marked in the colonial era and reflected for example in some of the poetry of
Sa'adu Zungur, is no longer evident in contemporary Nigeria to anything like
the same extent as in the past. The level of co-operation and interaction
between Muslims and non-Muslims is much higher today, and this may be
due to the fact that in the colonial era, when the initiative lay with others,
both Muslims and non-Muslims in Nigeria could do little more than react to
policies and decisions, whereas in the present situation both hold the initiative and hence have the responsibility for the country's future.

Conclusions.

We have seen in this chapter that, while much of Islam's history in West
Africa in recent years has been simply a continuation of its past history, there
have also been significant developments, some of which have been discussed
above. To what extent the drive to unify and organise Islam, to oppose
"secularism", to give greater force and scope to the Shari'a, is part of what is
widely referred to in contemporary society as "the resurgence of Islam", it is
difficult to say. Certainly there is evidence that the Islamic revolution in Iran
under the leadership of Ayatollah Khomeini, has influenced the attitudes and
thinking of Muslims in West Africa. He was voted "Man of the Year" for 1979
in a poll held in one heavily islamised region of West Africa, but it was not
clear whether his popularity was due to the fact that he opposed what was
seen as United States' interference and exploitation in Iran or to the fact that

he had brought about an Islamic revolution in that country.[45] Some Muslims undoubtedly did support the Ayatollah's attempts to turn Iran into a "genuine Islamic state", and while others saw it as an attack on neo-colonialism, there were those who regarded it as an unwitting invitation to outsiders to control and dominate a developing country.[46]

The "resurgence of Islam" is a complex phenomenon. It incorporates a reaffirmation of Islamic identity and may arise primarily from religious belief. It includes a demand for a return to a pure, orthodox form of Islam, the type of Islamic society which, for example, Usuman dan Fodio sought to establish. In some cases it may be no more than an attachment to Islam as a "cultural" community. It could also be part of a well financed movement in the Islamic world which challenges the global concept of modernity which is based on Western, industrial, "Christian" civilisation. In West Africa all these various aspects of "Islamic resurgency" have been manifest at one time or another. "Islamic resurgency", however, should be seen in perspective. In a sense there is little that is entirely new in the demands and perspectives of Muslims who, for instance, advocate that the Shari'a should be allowed greater force and scope, and who demand a return to the "Golden Age" of Islamic orthodoxy.

Muslims in West Africa today, although better organised, more self-confident and more in touch with the rest of the Muslim world, do not form a community characterised by rigid uniformity. As in the past, so too in the

II Mallams/Qur'anic school teachers

contemporary situation, there are a variety of strands to Islam in the West African setting, and a variety of responses to the wider world. The majority of Muslims would not wish to assert the all-embracing, self-sufficiency of Islam and exclude any consideration of other values and ideas. In practice there is considerable tolerance and even "mixing".

Generally speaking, then, the variety of perspectives and responses to the wider society apart, what does seem clear is that in the comtemporary situation in West Africa many Muslims, whether one labels them conservatives, modernists, fundamentalists or whatever, while not necessarily wanting to see an Islamic state established, are as convinced now as ever they were of the relevance of certain Islamic ideas and principles to the social, intellectual and cultural well-being of West Africa. This no doubt poses a problem for those secularisation theorists who tend to link a decline in commitment to religious values and practices to industrialisation and "modernisation".[47] There is little evidence of such a decline insofar as Islam in West Africa is concerned.

Notes.

Senegal and Upper Volta.

1   Interviews with Senegalese Muslims, January 1981.
2   L. Behrman, "Muslim Politics and Development in Senegal", *Journal of Modern African Studies* XV (1972), p. 276 *et passim.*
3   C. Coulon, "Pouvoir Politique et Pouvoir Maraboutique au Sénégal", *Année Africaine* (1971), p. 158.
4   Interview with Senegalese Muslim, 8/3/1981.
5   BADEA, *Quarterly Review*, first issue, June 1979.
6   Interview with Shaikh Touré, Dakar, 13/4/1981.
7   Francis G. Snyder and M.A. Savane, *Law and Population in Senegal: a Survey of Legislation*, Afrika Studiencentrum (Leiden), 1977, pp. 126 ff.
8   *Le Soleil*, 23/4/1981: *Report on the U.C.M. Conference*, 21−23 April, 1981.
9   Interview with Abdoulaye Niass, Kaolack, 17/4/1981.
10 *Le Soleil*, 24/4/1981, Report on the U.C.M. Conference, *op. cit.*
11 Statement reported in *Le Monde*, 24/2/1980.
12 Moscow Radio (England, Africa), September 1979: Review of Listeners' Letters in *Summary of World Broadcasts* (S.W.B.), BBC, Sept. 1979.
13 Abbas Kelidar of the School of Oriental and African Studies, London University, "Islam and Socialism−Are They Compatible?", typescript in the author's possession.
14 See note 10.
15 Yahaya Wane "Cerno Muhamadu Sayid Baa . . ." in *Cahiers d'Etudes Africaines* 56, XIV−4, pp 671−698, 1974.
16 One such village exists near Bwiam in the Gambia, and I was informed in interviews in April 1981 that others exist in the Casamance.
17 Deniel, "Croyances Religieuses et Vie Quotidienne Islam et Christianisme à Ouagadougou", *Recherches Voltaiques* 14 (1970), p. 115 *et passim.*
18 Audouin and Deniel, *op. cit.*, p. 71 *et passim.*

19   *Ibid.*, pp. 71−2.
20   *Ibid.*, p. 72.
21   Deniel, "Croyances Religieuses . . .", *op. cit.*, pp. 305 *et passim.*
22   Audouin and Deniel, *op. cit.*, p. 73.

Nigeria.

1   Cantori, *op. cit.*, p. 119 *et passim.*
2   Doi, *op. cit.*, p. 349.
3   *Ibid.*, p. 350.
4   *Ibid.*, pp. 348 *ff.*
5   Interview with Alhaji D.O.S. Noibi, Ibadan, 1980.
6   P.B. Clarke, "The Religious Factor in the Developmental Process in Nigeria: A Socio-historical Analysis", *Genève-Afrique* XVII (1979), pp. 45 *ff.*
7   J. Trevor, "Western Education and Muslim Fulani/Hausa Women in Sokoto, Northern Nigeria" in G.N. Brown and M. Hiskett, eds, *Conflict and Harmony in Education in Tropical Africa*, (London, 1975), pp. 247 *ff.*
8   S.A. Galadanci, "Education of Nigerian Women in Islam with reference to Nigeria", *Nigerian Journal of Islam*, I (1971), p. 10.
9   G.A. Williams, "Education and the Status of Nigerian Women", paper presented at University of Lagos, 1976.
10 (Nigerian) *Sunday Times*, 12/12/1976, interview with Hajiya Gambo Sawaba. See also *The Great Debate: Nigerian Viewpoints on the Draft Constitution 1976/77*, ed by W.I. Ofonagoro (Lagos, 1978), pp. 501−2.
11 Interviews, Yauri (Yelwa), 1980.
12 Tomlinson and Lethem, *op. cit.*
13 *Daily Times*, 21/7/1978.
14 *Ibid.*
15 *New Nigerian*, 10/2/1975.
16 Kaba, *op. cit.*, pp. 59−60.
17 *Daily Sketch*, 24/4/1978.
18 Quotation from K. Cragg: *Islam and The Muslim*, Open University Press, 1978, p. 56.
19 *Ibid.*
20 Clarke, "Islam and Change in Nigeria", *op. cit.*, p. 108.
21 Quoted in Ryan, *Imale, op. cit.*, p. 287; see also M.O. Abdul, *Islam as a Religion* (Lagos, 1971), p. 85.
22 Interviews, Ibadan, 1978.
23 Ryan, *Imale, op. cit.*, p. 210.
24 *New Nigerian*, 30/5/1975.
25 See Reports of the Constitution Drafting Committee, Vol.II, Federal Ministry of Information, Lagos, 1976, p. 36.
26 L. Adegbite, "The Role of Muslim Leaders in the Government of Nigeria", paper presented at the Religious Studies Conference, Ibadan, 1978, p. 3.
27 *Ibid.*
28 *Ibid.*
29 Ofonagoro, *The Great Debate, op. cit.*, pp. 356 *ff.*
30 Adegbite, *op. cit.*, and interviews with Alhaji D.O.S. Noibi, 1977−8, 1980.
31 Adegbite, *op. cit.*
32 Ofonagoro, *op. cit.*, p. 371.
33 *Ibid.*, p. 373.
34 *Ibid.*, p. 372.

35   *Ibid.*, p. 372.
36   E.A.A. Adegbola, "Equal Deal for All Religious Groups", in Ofonagoro, ed, *The Great Debate, op. cit.*, pp. 374 *ff.*
37   "The Shari'a Court and You", document circulated by the Nigerian Workers Students and Peasants Alliance for a Just, Equal and Democratic Society (N.W.O.S.U.P.A.) in association with the Anti-Poverty Movement of Nigeria (APMON), the All Nigerian Patriotic Denominational Council (ANAPADECO) and the Muslim Committee for a Progressive Nigeria (MCPN).
38   Interviews, Ibadan, 1977—8.
39   See reports on these events in *New Nigerian*, 11/4/1978.
40   Adegbite, *op. cit.*, p. 5.
41   Interview, Ibadan, 1980. Alhaji D.O.S. Noibi was very helpful on many of the issues discussed in this chapter. The interpretation, however, is entirely my own.
42   *New Nigerian*, 10/9/1976.
43   Clarke, "Islamic Millenarianism in West Africa" *op. cit.*, p. 338.
44   Information based on interview held in Kano, Jan. 1981.
45   BBC Hausa Service, Man of the Year Contest, 1979. Assessment based on reasons provided by those who wrote to the BBC during the Man of the Year Contest, 1979.
46   *Ibid.*, and see "The Shari'a Debate and You", *op. cit.*
47   P.L. Berger, *The Social Reality of Religion* (Penguin, 1973), pp. 157 *ff.*

Conclusion: African conversion to Islam — some general comments.

In the late 19th century and early years of the 20th century when Islam was rapidly gaining ground in West Africa, many observers of the situation looked upon this advance as if it were inevitable. I have already quoted the French scholar Quellien, who wrote in 1910 that "the progressive and continuous expansion of Islam in West Africa is a fact that no-one who knows anything about the subject will deny". Alongside Islam, Quellien continued, Christianity was remarkable "for its almost total failure in the same areas".[1] To the historian and social scientist, however, events and developments are simply possibilities before they happen and only certainties afterwards. What then lies behind Islam's success in West Africa? Why did so many West Africans convert to Islam over the period of twelve hundred years covered in this book?

These are not easy questions to answer. Moreover, the historian and social scientist is at best capable of providing only a partial explanation. For many people conversion is a religious, spiritual experience which the historian and social scientist have neither the method or techniques for analysing or comprehending. Granted this fact, it is nonetheless the case that conversion does not take place in a social vacuum, so to speak. If one allows for its ultimately spiritual nature, it is nevertheless the case that the process of conversion can and often is triggered off or facilitated by ordinary, concrete human events and in turn affects the ordinary, everyday world.

We have seen that from the 8th century North African Muslim traders accompanied by Muslim missionaries were attracted to the commercial centres of the Sahara and Sudan by the prospects of obtaining plentiful supplies of gold and slaves among other things. They came into contact with the Sanhaja and Tuareg who acted as their protectors and guides along the trade routes and also mixed with, and eventually settled and established Muslim quarters in, the capital cities of West African states, such as Koumbi-Saleh in Ancient Ghana. This was the beginning of Islam in West Africa and throughout the period of twelve hundred years covered in this book trade has been important in terms of introducing and even attracting many people to Islam. Not all the conversions, of course, which began in this way were lasting and permanent. Samory's ancestors, for example, once Muslim traders, returned to their traditional religion.[2]

However, to regard the whole expansion and development of Islam in West Africa as simply a by-product of trade and commerce would, it seems to me, be a gross oversimplification and distortion of what in fact actually seems to have happened. While it is the case that it was in the pursuit of trading interests that Islam was first established in certain areas of West Africa, and the same is true of Christianity, it is also the case that many West Africans became Muslims, not as a result of encountering Muslim traders and out of a desire to participate in the Muslim trading network, but for a variety of other reasons as well. In the local accounts of early conversion to Islam, for example, in parts of what is today the West African Republic of Ghana there is very little reference to the role of Muslim traders as carriers or vehicles of Islam to those regions.[3]

Islam, for some of those who embraced it, was seen as a highly prestigious religion. Muslims were literate, they had wide-ranging diplomatic contacts, a formal system of education and a simple but effective legal system. They were a modernising force with the skills essential for the efficient administration of expanding, developing states or empires.[4]

The fact that Islam offered something new in terms of its vision of life, of the world, of man and his destiny, and skills and techniques that were considered to be essential for progress and development undoubtedly contributed to its growth in West Africa. It is also possible that conversion to Islam was facilitated by the fact that in many instances there was a close affinity or "significant equivalence" between Islamic and African ideas on certain issues of importance concerning the world, society, ethical and moral questions, and scientific approaches to explaining and interpreting natural and supernatural events. In some respects the Islamic and African views or orientations on certain issues were sufficiently similar as to make possible a correlation between them.[5]

The notion of a Supreme Being, for instance, was widespread in African religions, although the emphasis on the worship of the Supreme Being alone, without having recourse to intermediaries, was not apparently very widespread. Again Fisher has shown that in the interpretation of dreams and visions there was a possible point of contact between Islam and African traditional religion. Fisher states that "the very dream . . . may be an avenue for the acceptance of new ideas or objects, or even of religious beliefs, being thus in itself a channel of conversion".[6] To cite but one example of dreams as a channel of conversion: a recent convert explained that he was searching for the "right path" when he came across a "Muslim book" which said that "if you want to find something, you wake up at night and put it (what you want to find) in a prayer, and you may be lucky. And after once, twice or thrice you will dream . . . about the thing you want to do. So I did this and was getting convinced that I should go to Islam."[7]

While there are no doubt certain affinities between Islamic and African world views and orientations to life which make possible a correlation between them and facilitate conversion to Islam, I feel that there has been a tendency to over-emphasise the similarities. Richard Burton and Mary Kingsley, among others, referred to the "Africanness" of Islam when compared with Christianity. But Mojola Agbebi, the Nigerian Christian pastor, was probably reflecting the situation more accurately when he suggested that Islam, though not necessarily more African in essence than Christianity, *adapted* itself better than some Christian denominations to the African condition.[8] The Islamic vision of man, of God, and of the world claims to be, and has been shown to be, unique and original in certain respects.[9] Moreover, it is not embraced by West Africans simply because it is a soft option. It can be a very demanding religion ethically, morally, intellectually and in other ways.

In addition to trade, dreams and visions, literacy, valued for its utilitarian as well as its supposedly religious qualities, and the modernising aspects of Islam which facilitated conversion, Islam also had an international dimension and integrative qualities which made it attractive to rulers governing large empires where there was considerable cultural and religio-political pluralism and diversity.

Jihad of the sword as we have seen was also instrumental in bringing parts of West Africa within dar al-Islam, the land of Islam. But even more important than jihad of the sword was the work of the Sufi brotherhoods and the "unattached" wandering mallams, about whom so much has been said in this book and elsewhere. Then there were, and are today, the charismatic individuals, from 'Abdullah b. Yasin to Ibrahim Niass, who broke through barriers, geographical and cultural, and whose claims met with a positive response from a wide range of people. Moreover, the ease with which Muslims, relying on the local materials available, can set up a school or a mosque or a praying ground facilitates the expansion of Islam. Furthermore, and related to the points just made, the educative effects upon individuals and whole communities of Islamic ritual has been important in the spread of Islam. This was something the great Muslim philosopher and theologian, al-Ghazali (1058–1111 A.D.), appreciated. Muslims are often identifiable by their dress, by what they eat or do not eat. Moreover, they pray anywhere and in the open and thus make Islam a highly visible, public religion. Islamic ritual has been termed the "genius" of Islam,[10] and has counted for a great deal in the diffusion of Islam in West Africa. As we have seen, the Christian missionary Hinderer, working in Ibadan in the 19th century, realised this and so too did one contemporary Nigerian pastor who explained recently that the Christian concentration on building stone edifices and the tendency to confine prayer and worship to church premises may well be a mistake.[11]

History is made in the present and understood by looking backwards, and it is clear that many different, sometimes interrelated, factors have over the centuries from c. 750 A.D. onwards assisted the development of Islam in the West African setting.

Notes.

1 Quellien, *La Politique Musulmane, op. cit.,* p. 178.
2 Y. Person, "Les Ancêtres de Samori", *Cahiers d'Etudes Africaines* VIII (1963), pp. 133–4.
3 Levtzion, *Muslims and Chiefs, op. cit.,* p. 144.
4 B. Davidson, *Africa, History of a Continent,* (London, 1966), pp. 98 ff.
5 M. Dia, *Islam et Civilisations Négro-Africaines,* Dakar, 1980.
6 H.J. Fisher, "Dreams and Conversion in Black Africa" in Levtzion, *Conversion to Islam, op. cit.,* pp. 217 ff.

7   Interviews, Ibadan, May 1978.
8   M. Echeruo, *Victorian Lagos* (London, 1977), pp. 91–3.
9   W. Montgomery Watt, *What is Islam?* (London, 1979, 2nd edn), pp. 15–18 *et passim*.
10   Al-Ghazali, *Ihya 'Ulum al-Din, Worship in Islam*, translated by E.E. Calverley (London, 1957), and "Bidayat al Hidayah, The Beginning of Guidance" in Montgomery Watt, *The Faith and Practice of al-Ghazali* (London, 1953).
11   Interviews, Ibadan, April 1978.

Glossary.

Allah	the name used by Muslims for God/Supreme Being.
'Alim (pl.'ulama)	a scholar in Islamic religious science.
Amir	one who commands in battle especially in jihad or a governor of a Muslim-ruled territory.
Amir al-mu'minin	commander of the Muslim Faithful and leader in spiritual and temporal matters.
Baraka	a spiritual blessing.
Caliph (Khalifa)	a successor to Prophet Muhammad as spiritual and temporal leader of the Muslim community.
Dar al-harb	non-Muslim territory.
Dar al-Islam	territory ruled by Muslims.
Dhikr	a mentioning, saying, remembering or for mystics (Sufis) a litany.
Dhimmi	a protected person: a Jew or Christian under Muslim rule has the right to practise his/her religion in return for recognising Muslim law and Muslim authority.
Hadith	the authentic sayings of Prophet Muhammad.
Hajj	pilgrimage to Mecca.
Hijra	emigration for doctrinal reasons.
'Id	a Muslim religious festival.
Jama'a	a Muslim community under a religious leader.
Jihad	exertion or struggling for the purpose of doing God's Will.
Jizya	tax paid by dhimmis in recognition of Muslim authority and rule.
Kufr	unbelief.
Mahdi	the God-guided one whom some Muslims believe will, at the end of the world, ensure the final triumph of Islam.
Mujaddid	a restorer, renewer of Islam.
Muqaddam	a member of a religious, Sufi, brotherhood charged with the spiritual welfare of its members and with inducting recruits into the order.
Qadi	Muslim judge or arbitrator.
Ramadan	the annual Muslim fast of one lunar month.
Shahada	confession of faith in the unity and oneness of God and in Muhammad's prophethood.

Shaikh	a leader of his people or of a group.
Shari'a	Islamic sacred or revealed law.
Shirk	the association of something or someone human with Allah. Polytheism.
Sunna	the example and way of life of Prophet Muhammad.
Sufi	an ascetic or mystic. Normally a member of a religious brotherhood.
Talaba (sing. talib)	the followers of a Sufi guide or shaikh.
Tariqa (pl.turuq)	a Sufi brotherhood.
Tasawwuf	mysticism.
Umma	the Muslim community taken as a whole.
Wird	the litany of a Sufi brotherhood.
Zakat	obligatory almsgiving.
Zawiya (pl. zawaya)	the residence of a Sufi Shaikh and his followers.

Essay questions/Topics for discussion.

1. 'It is essential for an understanding of the development of Islam in West Africa to have some knowledge of the early history of the Islamic community in Mecca and Medina and of its founder Prophet Muhammad.' Discuss. (See Chapters 1 and 5 in particular.)
2. Assess the aims of the Almoravid Movement and its impact on the development of Islam in West Africa. (See Chapters 2 and 3.)
3. 'Almoravid relations with Ancient Ghana and other West African states were characterised by interdependence rather than by rivalry and hostility.' Discuss. (See Chapters 2 and 3.)
4. Describe the development of Islam in West Africa between c.800 and c.1600, and assess its impact on the political systems of Ancient Ghana, Kanem-Borno, Mali and Songhay. (See Chapter 3.)
5. What effect did Arab and Kunta migrations in the 15th century have on the development of Islam in West Africa prior to the 18th century? (See Chapters 3 and 4.)
6. Compare and contrast the development of Islam in the Senegambia and Hausaland up to 1600. (See Chapter 3.)
7. Describe the role played by al-Maghili and al-Suyuti in the development of Islam in West Africa. (See Chapter 3 in particular.)
8. How would you account for the rejection of Islam by the Mossi rulers and the persecution of the 'ulama of Timbuktu by Sunni Ali of Songhay? (See Chapter 3.)
9. Explain some of the reasons why rulers like Mansa Musa of Mali, Askiya Muhammad Ture I of Songhay and Idris Alooma of Borno saw in Islam a religion of 'progress'. (See Chapter 3.)
10. With regard to the development of Islam in West Africa, the 17th and 18th centuries have been described as an era of 'Islamic Stagnation and Pagan Reaction'. Do you agree? (See Chapter 4.)
11. Outline the causes and trace the possible links between the jihads in the Senegambia in the 17th and 18th centuries. (See Chapter 4.)
12. Why in your opinion did some Muslim scholars, dedicated to the pursuit of learning, begin to abandon the pen for the sword in the 17th and 18th centuries? Explain your answer with reference to Air and Hausaland. (See Chapter 4.)
13. Describe the origins and growth of Islam in the Volta Basin and the forest

and coastal zones of West Africa up to 1800. (See Chapter 3 and in particular Chapter 4.)

14. From what you know of the history of the development of Islam in West Africa, is there any evidence of a convincing nature that suggests that the urban setting is more favourable to the growth of Islam than the rural setting? (See Chapter 5 *passim*.)

15. Examine the causes and aims of the jihads of Usuman dan Fodio and al-Hajj 'Umar. (See Chapter 5.)

16. Assess the extent to which the jihads of the 19th century contributed towards the development of Islam in West Africa. (See Chapter 5.)

17. Borno was attacked by Sokoto, Masina by al-Hajj 'Umar and Kong by Samory. In your opinion were these attacks justified and, if so, on what grounds? (See Chapter 5.)

18. Examine the strategy adopted by the French to defeat militant Muslim reformers and nationalists in the Senegambia and elsewhere in West Africa in the second half of the 19th century. (See Chapter 5.)

19. Trace the growth of Islam in Asante and Yorubaland in the 19th century. (See Chapter 6.)

20. Account for the continued reluctance of the Mossi rulers in the 19th century to become thoroughgoing Muslims. (See Chapter 6.)

21. Examine the role of the Muslim brotherhoods in the spread of Islam in West Africa in the 19th century. (See Chapter 6 in particular and Chapters 5 and 7.)

22. Describe the attitude of Muslims in West Africa, in particular those west of the Black Volta River, to African representational art. (See Chapter 6.)

23. Discuss the part played by freed slaves and recaptives in the development of Islam in West Africa in the 19th century. (See Chapter 6.)

24. Assess the reasons for the rapid advance of Islam in West Africa during the colonial era. (See Chapter 7.)

25. Examine and account for the variety of ways in which Muslims responded to the imposition of colonial rule in West Africa. (See Chapter 7.)

26. Did the colonial authorities in your view have any coherent policy towards Islam? (See Chapter 7.)

27. Why were the French colonial authorities so opposed both to marabouts and Mahdists? (See Chapter 7.)

28. Compare and contrast the role of Ahmadu Bamba and Ibrahim Niass in the development of Islam in West Africa. (See Chapter 7.)

29. Account for the origins and rapid growth of such organisations as the Ansar-Ud-Deen Society during the colonial era. (See Chapters 7 and 8.)

30. How would you characterise Islam's development in Senegal, Upper Volta and Nigeria since independence? (See Chapter 8.)

31. Discuss the Muslim reaction in the independence period to Western institutions with special reference to education and law. (See Chapter 8.)

32. Analyse the ways in which the Muslim community in West Africa has, since independence, strengthened its ties with the rest of the Muslim world. (See Chapter 8.)

33. Both literacy in Arabic and the pilgrimage (hajj) can have a conservative

as well as a revoluntionary impact. How is this so? (See in particular Chapter 8, and Chapters 4 and 5 *passim*.)

34. 'To see the development of Islam in West Africa as due almost entirely to trade and commerce is to misunderstand the complex nature of that development.' Discuss.

Select bibilography*

Abun Nasr, J.M., The Tijaniyya: A Sufi Order in the Modern World, Oxford, 1965.
Adeleye, R.A., Power and Diplomacy in Northern Nigeria, 1804–1906, London, 1971.
Abdul, M.O.A., The Historical Origins of Islam, Lagos, 1973.
Ajayi, J.F.A. and Crowder, M. (eds), History of West Africa, Vols I and II, London 1972 and 1974 respectively.
Audouin J. and Deniel, R., L'Islam en Haute Volta, Abidjan/Paris, 1978.
Ba, A.H., and Daget, J., L'Empire Peul du Macina, Dakar, 1959.
Boahen, A., Topics in West African History, London, 1966.
Behrman, L., Muslim Brotherhoods and Politics in Senegal, Cambridge, Mass., 1970.
Bovill, E.W., The Golden Trade of the Moors, London, 1958.
Bravmann, R.A., Islam and Tribal Art in West Africa, Cambridge, 1974.
Brenner, L., The Shehus of Kukawa, Oxford, 1973.
Brown, G.N. and Hiskett, M. (eds), Conflict and Harmony in Education in Tropical Africa, London, 1975.
Cissoko, S.M, Timbouctou et L'Empire Songhay, Abidjan-Dakar, 1975.
Copans, J., Les Marabouts de l'Arachide, Paris, 1980.
Crowder, M., West Africa under Colonial Rule, London, 1968.
Crowder, M. (ed), West African Resistance, London, 1971.
Cuoq, J., Les Musulmanes en Afrique, Paris, 1975.
Dia, M., Islam et les Civilisations Negro-Africaines, Dakar, 1980.
Esposito, J.L. (ed), Islam and Development, New York, 1980.
Fafunwa, A.B., History of Education in Nigeria, London, 1974.
Fage, J. (ed), Cambridge History of Africa, Vol.2, Cambridge, 1978.
Fika, A.M., The Kano Civil War and British Over-Rule, Oxford, 1978.
Fisher, H.J., Ahmadiyyah: A Study in contemporary Islam on the West African Coast, London, 1963.
Flint, J. (ed), Cambridge History of Africa, Vol. 5, Cambridge, 1976.
Gbadamosi, T.G.O., The Growth of Islam among the Yoruba, 1841–1908, London, 1978.
Goody, J. (ed), Literacy in Traditional Societies, Cambridge, 1968.
Hamdun, S. and King, N., Ibn Battuta in Black Africa, London, 1975.
Hargreaves, J.D. (ed), France and West Africa, London, 1969.

* For a more detailed bibliography see footnotes after each chapter.

Hiskett, M., *The Sword of Truth: The Life and Times of Shehu Usuman dan Fodio*, New York, 1973.
Hodgkin, T. (ed), *Nigerian Perspectives*, Oxford, 1960.
Hogben, S.J. and Kirk-Greene, A.H.M., *The Emirates of Northern Nigeria*, London, 1966.
Holt, P.M. *et al*, (eds) *Cambridge History of Islam*, Vol 2A, Cambridge, 1970.
Holt, P.M., *The Mahdist State in the Sudan*, Oxford, 1958.
Kaba, L, The Wahhabiyya: *Islamic Reform and Politics in French West Africa*, Evanston, 1974.
Klein, M., *Islam and Imperialism in Senegal*, Edinburgh, 1968.
Kritzeck, J. and Lewis, W.H. (eds), *Islam in Africa*, New York, 1969.
Last, D.M., *The Sokoto Caliphate*, London, 1967.
Levtzion, N., *Muslims and Chiefs in West Africa*, Oxford, 1968.
Levtzion, N., *Ancient Ghana and Mali*, London, 1973, reprinted 1980.
Levtzion, N. (ed), *Conversion to Islam*, New York, 1979.
Levtzion, N. and Hopkins, J.F.P. (eds), *Corpus of Early Arabic Sources for West African History*, Cambridge, 1981.
Lewicki, T., *Arabic External Sources for the History of Africa to the South of the Sahara*, Lagos, 1974.
Lewis, I.M. (ed), *Islam in Tropical Africa*, London, 1980 (2nd edition)
Martin, B.G., *Muslim Brotherhoods in 19th-Century Africa*, Cambridge, 1976.
Monteil, V., *L'Islam Noire*, Paris, 1971.
Nachtigal, G., *Sahara und Sudan*, Berlin 1879−1889, translated with introduction and notes by A.G.B. and H.J. Fisher, Vol.4, London, 1971; Vol.1, London, 1974; Vol.2, London, 1980.
El-Nagar, U., *The Pilgrimage Tradition in West Africa*, Khartoum, 1972.
Niane, D.T., *Sundiata: an Epic of Old Mali*, translated by G.D. Pickett, London, 1965.
Norris, H.T., *Shinqiti Folk Literature and Song*, Oxford, 1968.
Norris, H.T., *Saharan Myth and Saga*, Oxford, 1972.
Norris, H.T., *The Tuaregs, Their Islamic Legacy and Its Diffusion in the Sahel*, Wiltshire, 1975.
O'Brien, D.B.C., *The Mourides of Senegal*, Oxford, 1971.
Ofonagoro, W., *The Great Debate*, Lagos, 1978.
Oliver, R. (ed), *Cambridge History of Africa*, Vol.3, Cambridge, 1977.
Oloruntimehin, O., *The Segu-Tokolor Empire*, London, 1972.
Paden, J., *Religion and Political Culture in Kano*, London, 1973.
Palmer, H.A.R., *Sudanese Memoirs*, 3 vols, Lagos, 1928. (Contains the "Kano Chronicle")
Palmer, H.A.R., *Borno, the Sahara and Sudan*, London, 1936.
Peters, R., *Islam and Colonialism*, The Hague, 1979.
Quinn, C., *Mandingo Kingdoms of the Senegambia*, Evanston, 1972.
Ryan, P.J., *Imale: Yoruba Participation in the Muslim Tradition*, Ann Arbor, Michigan, 1978.
Sanneh, L., *The Jakhanke*, London, 1979.
Stewart, C., *Islam and Social Order in Mauretania*, Oxford, 1973.

Suret-Canale, J., *Afrique Noire*, 2 vols, Paris, 1961.
Suret-Canale, J, *French Colonialism in Tropical Africa*, London, 1971.
Sy, C. Tidjane, *La Confrérie Sénégalaise des Mourides*, Paris, 1969.
Tibawi, A.L, *Islamic Education*, London, 1979.
Triaud, J.L., *Islam et Sociétés Soudanaises au Moyen-Age*, Paris-Ouagadougou, 1973.
Trimingham, J.S., *Islam in West Africa*, London, 1959.
Trimingham, J.S., *A History of Islam in West Africa*, London, 1962.
Watt, W.M., *Islam and the Integration of Society*, London, 1966.
Wilks, I., *Asante in the 19th century*, Cambridge, 1975.
Willis, J.R., (ed), *Studies in West African Islamic History*, Vol.1, London, 1979.

Index

Trimingham, J.S., 17, 108, 110
Tsoede, 102
Tuareg, 36, 48, 53−8, 66, 91−3, 103, 123−6, 197−8
Tyeddo, 144−5

'Umar, Caliph (634−644), 5−6
'Umar, son of al-Kanemi, 159, 164
Umar b. Idris, Mai, 69
Umar b. Muhammad Naddi Koi, 53
al-Umari, 39, 43−4
'Umar Tall, al-Hajj, 81, 114, 114, 119, 131−7, 141, 146−8, 165, 206, 208
Umayyad, 6−10, 67−8
Universal Primary Education (U.P.E.), 244−5
'Uqba b. Nafi, 8, 30, 67
Uro Djobo II and III, 174
Usuman dan Fodio, 3, 32, 34, 50, 56, 96, 99−102, 113−23, 155, 165, 222
Uthman, Caliph (644−656), 5−6

Wa, 96
Wadjaha, 196
Wagadugu, 59, 93−4, 162, 212−5, 241
Wathiqat al-Sudan, 113−4
Wahhabiyya, 208, 216−7, 247
Wajjaj b. Zalwi, 14−5, 23
Waladaidi, 104
Walata, 24, 31, 38, 43, 48

wali, 89−90
Walo, 33, 80, 145
Wangara, 24, 34, 58, 60, 64, 96
War Dyabe, 32−3, 35, 237
Weber, Max, 23, 89
Wilks, I., 75, 109, 183
Willis, J.R., 148, 150
Wolof, 33, 78, 145

Yahya b. Ibrahim, 13−4
Yahya b. 'Umar, 15−6
al-Yaqut, 22
al-Ya'qubi, 40
Yarse, 34, 58−9, 212−15
Yatenga, 59, 93
Yoruba, 106, 166−72
Yums, Shaikh, 160
Yusuf b. Tashfin, 17, 24

Za al-Ayaman, 47
Zafunu, 22
Zakariya b. 'Abdullah, Shaikh, 54
zakat, 87
Zaki, Mallam, 104
Za-Kossoi, 47
Zamfara, 60, 99, 115−20
Zaria, 65−6, 99, 119
zawaya, 29−31, 78, 153−7, 209
Zawila, 67
al-Zuhri, 10, 18−9, 37